NEW ZEALAND'S
WILDERNESS HERITAGE

TEXT BY LES MOLLOY
PHOTOGRAPHY BY CRAIG POTTON

craig potton publishing

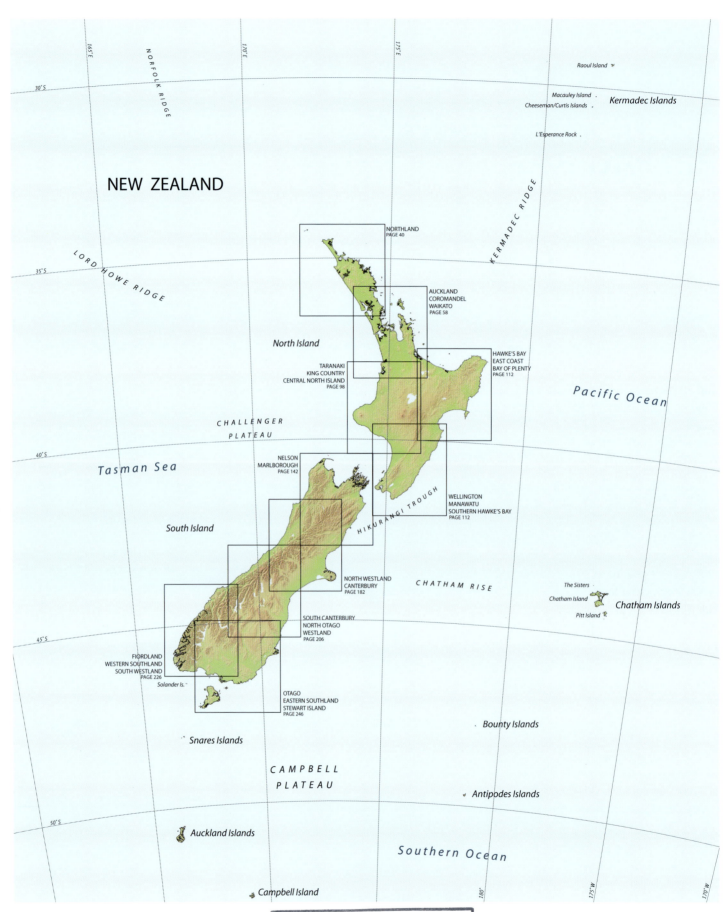

NEW ZEALAND

Raoul Island

Macauley Island .
Cheeseman/Curtis Islands . Kermadec Islands

L'Esperance Rock .

NORFOLK RIDGE

KERMADEC RIDGE

LORD HOWE RIDGE

NORTHLAND
PAGE 40

AUCKLAND
COROMANDEL
WAIKATO
PAGE 58

North Island

HAWKE'S BAY
EAST COAST
BAY OF PLENTY
PAGE 112

Pacific Ocean

TARANAKI
KING COUNTRY
CENTRAL NORTH ISLAND
PAGE 98

CHALLENGER
PLATEAU

Tasman Sea

NELSON
MARLBOROUGH
PAGE 142

WELLINGTON
MANAWATU
SOUTHERN HAWKE'S BAY
PAGE 112

HIKURANGI TROUGH

South Island

CHATHAM RISE

The Sisters

Chatham Island

NORTH WESTLAND
CANTERBURY
PAGE 182

Chatham Islands

Pitt Island

SOUTH CANTERBURY
NORTH OTAGO
WESTLAND
PAGE 206

FIORDLAND
WESTERN SOUTHLAND
SOUTH WESTLAND
PAGE 226

Solander Is.

OTAGO
EASTERN SOUTHLAND
STEWART ISLAND
PAGE 246

Bounty Islands

Snares Islands

CAMPBELL
PLATEAU

Antipodes Islands

Auckland Islands

Southern Ocean

Campbell Island

PREFACE

*Wilderness is the raw material out of which man has hammered
the artifact called civilization.*
— Aldo Leopold, *A Sand County Almanac*

In 1988 Weldon Publishing, in association with the Australian Conservation Foundation, produced an impressive two-volume publication, *Australia's Wilderness Heritage,* covering Australia's world heritage sites (Vol.1) and flora and fauna (Vol.2). Craig was intrigued with the quality and breadth of the publication, and began thinking how New Zealand's very different wilderness heritage could be given the benefit of a similarly comprehensive treatment in a single volume. He approached me with the idea in the early 1990s. But the time was not right; we were both consumed with other conservation (and publication) projects and another decade passed, but Craig never let the vision of such an ambitious book fade. We reconsidered the book project again in 2004 and with Robbie Burton, Managing Director and Publisher of Craig Potton Publishing, made a commitment to do it.

On a personal level, Craig and I have both benefitted incalculably from growing up in New Zealand at a time when free access to our wilderness was considered everybody's birthright. Craig, a born and bred South Islander, grew up and played on the coastline when young and still seeks out surf as a solace to urban existence. By adolescence, he was tramping and climbing in the Southern Alps and was soon involved in the conservation battles to protect the remains of our untouched lowland habitats. He is still deeply involved in all these activities 35 years on.

In my case I grew up in the shadow of the Tararuas, at Silverstream in Upper Hutt, where the forested hills and the clear waters of the Hutt River were always the natural landscape backdrop of daily life. Learning bushcraft through scouting and progressing to tramping club trips in the Tararuas were natural steps in my outdoor apprenticeship. But the life-changing wilderness experience for me came shortly before my 18th birthday, with my first club trip to the untracked 'Olivine Country' of what was soon to become Mount Aspiring National Park. The view of Mt Earnslaw and the Cosmos Peaks at the head of Lake Wakatipu from the decks of the S.S. *Earnslaw* on a perfect summer day was simply overwhelming – love at first sight! There was no going back. I felt a freedom in my spirit and the enticing romance of setting out to explore unknown valleys and peaks; the challenge for me and my other young companions was to get the measure of this wilderness in front of our eyes, yet respect its hazards and, over time, come to feel at ease in its solitude.

This book touches on more than 50 wilderness places known to us both, and discusses at least 40 major threats and natural heritage conservation priority actions which we would like addressed. The text is opinionated and often takes a historical approach, sometimes outlining a series of past events at a level of detail that may seem of limited relevance to some readers. I make no apology for looking at the lessons of history however. As the philosopher Santayana concluded, 'Those who do not remember the past are condemned to relive it.' And New Zealand is certainly a textbook of costly ecological mistakes in the past, which are relived every day. Fortunately, as a country we are now investing enormous energy and capital in trying to move towards becoming a 'conserver society', but sometimes we still need to look back and evaluate if, and how well, we can avoid repeating the mistakes of the past. Our remaining wilderness heritage is a priceless taonga gifted to us. We both hope that our efforts to explore it in words and photos in *New Zealand's Wilderness Heritage* will challenge our present generation to pass it on to the next, intact and restored where possible.

Les Molloy, August 2007

CONTENTS

CHAPTER ONE

NEW ZEALAND'S WILDERNESS HERITAGE

WHAT IS WILDERNESS?

The word 'wilderness' must be one of the most misunderstood in the English language. Most dictionaries define it in historically negative and anthropocentric terms – a fearful desert or barren place, uncultivated and uninhabited, a wasteland, or a garden grown wild. Positive concepts of wilderness as a place to experience spiritual, emotional and physical re-creation really only began to be expressed in the early 19th century. The romantic poets William Wordsworth and Samuel Taylor Coleridge were inspired by the wild beauty of the Lake District, and called for a return to natural environments as the Industrial Revolution laid waste to much of the English countryside. But it was mainly New World explorers, writers, poets and philosophers who popularised the term, especially those voicing their concern as America's primeval forests, prairies, and mountains were explored and opened up for settlement. Henry David Thoreau felt that 'In wildness is the preservation of the world', while Ralph Emerson believed that 'In the woods we return to reason and faith.' The preservation of America's diminishing wilderness heritage became an all-consuming quest for generations of its visionary leaders – like President Theodore Roosevelt; John Muir, the founder of the Sierra Club; Aldo Leopold, Robert Marshall, and Gifford Pinchot, foresters of both preservationist and conservationist persuasion; and historians and educators like Roderick Nash.

Just as the young American nation gave the world the notion of national parks, the idea of legally protecting large areas of wilderness also had its origin in North America and culminated in the passing of its Wilderness Act in 1964. New Zealand's concept of an individual wilderness experience and places called 'wilderness areas' (see p.29) largely stems from this American model. Indeed, it was exposure to the writings of Aldo Leopold and other wilderness advocates during a 1939 visit that stimulated Lance McCaskill to bring the idea of wilderness areas back to New Zealand national park circles. As a result, New Zealand's vision of wilderness experience is similar to that of America's – that wilderness is primarily a natural resource capable of being experienced first hand only through wilderness recreation. Of course, wilderness has intrinsic values which need no justification by way of human utility; likewise, it has enormous biodiversity and ecosystem values which defy being quantified in economic terms. But ultimately wilderness has to be experienced on its own terms, not locked away from humans as some type of scientific preserve. As Aldo Leopold concluded, 'Wilderness areas are first of all a series of sanctuaries for the primitive arts of wilderness travel.'[1]

There is a wonderfully rich wilderness literature recording the feelings and experiences of those who have felt the urge to seek out wilderness. Their reasons vary, but most seem to involve personal growth through experiencing:

- Solitude: that precious commodity so difficult to find in our frenetic urban society where we are constantly bombarded with noise and consumerism. Occasionally mankind needs 'to be confronted with an alien, untamed world to be reminded that he is caretaker, not creator, of his universe.'[2]
- Freedom: by travelling at will, simply, on nature's terms, and having the freedom to make mistakes – and pay the price. Again, this sentiment has been eloquently expressed by Aldo Leopold: 'Wilderness can give rewards and penalties for wise and foolish acts... against which civilization has built a thousand buffers.'[3]

Ferns are a highly distinctive element of New Zealand's flora, with nearly 200 species, mainly distributed in rainforest in all manner of growth forms – from tiny filmy ferns, to tufted, climbing and perching ferns, and tree ferns.

- Romance: by standing on the threshold of unknown land, or venturing in the footsteps of pioneer explorers who left graphic diaries of their wilderness journeys – like William Colenso in the Ruahine Ranges, Charles Heaphy and Thomas Brunner in the Buller/West Coast region, Alphonse Barrington in the Olivine Country, and many others.

- Challenge: by testing that deep human urge to gamble and probe the limits of our endurance. Admittedly, challenge is not unique to wilderness recreation, but wilderness survival does require the ability to handle major uncertainties such as unpredictable weather, route-finding, and difficult terrain. Overcoming the challenge of travelling through a hazardous natural environment can

The wilderness experience can encompass the romance of standing on the threshold of an unknown land; or venturing in the footsteps of those who pioneered the exploration of wild places like Lake Norwest, above Lake Manapouri in Fiordland National Park.

develop self-reliance and powerful bonds of friendship through shared skills and teamwork. In the words of Sir Edmund Hillary:

Nature needs time for growing and sleeping, free from automobile fumes and massive tractors, away from the cacophony of snowmobiles and trail bikes. There are plenty of tamed wonders for all to goggle at through vehicle windows – we must also retain our wilderness areas where nature can develop in its own calm way and where only those humans who are prepared to walk and sweat a little qualify to go.[4]

The rest of this chapter briefly summarises what is distinctive about the physical and biological character of the wild, uninhabited archipelago that came to be known as New Zealand, and outlines historically what we have done to conserve (or destroy) this natural heritage.

NEW ZEALAND'S DISTINCTIVE GEODIVERSITY

What forces over geological time gave us the diverse landforms and biodiversity that confronted the first humans to reach our shores? Geologists tell us that over 80 million years ago the mini-continent that is sometimes called 'Zealandia' broke away from the Australia-Antarctica residue (often termed 'Australis') of the ancient super-continent of Gondwana; Zealandia then headed off on a turbulent journey over time into isolation in the Southern Ocean. The geographical extent of Zealandia would have encompassed an area well beyond New Zealand's present day continental shelf. This continental block extended east to include the Chatham Rise, south to the Campbell Plateau, north-west to the Challenger Plateau and the Lord Howe and Norfolk ridges beyond, and north-east along the Kermadec Ridge towards Tonga – an area about 10 times New Zealand's current size of 27 million hectares. At the other extreme, during the so-called 'Oligocene drowning' (about 25 million years ago) Zealandia slowly sank and was greatly reduced in size to a number of smaller islands. Subsequently, the development of a tectonic plate boundary forming a rupture line in the thin crust of Zealandia led to the onset of mountain-building during the late Miocene (around 5–10 million years ago) which has continued to the present day.

The dynamic nature of our land is largely a consequence of straddling this boundary between the Pacific Plate to the east and the Australian Plate in the west. On land, the rupture line can most easily be seen as the trace of the Alpine Fault, which runs almost in a straight line for more than 600 km from the mouth of Milford Sound to Cloudy Bay and Cook Strait; here, the plates are grinding past each other laterally with enough friction to push up the Southern Alps/Ka Tiritiri o te Moana. North of Cook Strait, the rupture continues off the east coast of the North Island as the deep Hikurangi Trough; here, the plates are colliding head on, and the denser oceanic Pacific Plate is pushing under the Australian Plate (in a process known as subduc-

tion). Again, the result is mountainous landforms on the lighter continental plate (the axial ranges of the North Island), but in addition, the subducting plate melts as it is pushed down into the mantle, allowing magma to stream to the surface – resulting in the volcanic landforms we know as cone volcanoes and calderas. The volcanic rift valley we know today as the Taupo Volcanic Zone extends northeast from Mt Ruapehu to White Island, and beyond to the underwater Kermadec Ridge and other volcanoes of the Pacific 'Ring of Fire'. Overall, 60 per cent of the country is higher than 300 m and 70 per cent is either hilly or steep.

New Zealand's climate is another very dynamic component of our environmental character, both historically and in our day-to-day weather changes. During the Oligocene drowning the climate was distinctly tropical; at the other extreme, during the Ice Ages of the Pleistocene, vast ice sheets covered large areas of the South Island, and West Coast glaciers extended far beyond present-day shorelines. Essentially, today the country is a wall of mountains and hill country standing in the path of the moisture-laden westerly winds that circle the globe constantly in the southern temperate latitudes. As this maritime air is forced up over the mountains it cools rapidly, and the moisture condenses as cloud and rain. This is particularly so along the westernmost mountains of the South Island – a barrier 750 km long and over 1500 m high which runs from Fiordland, through the Southern Alps/Ka Tiritiri o te Moana and the Paparoa Range to the Tasman Mountains. This unbroken mountain wall gives the West Coast its super-humid climate, the life-source of its rainforests, wetlands and glaciers. At sea level in Milford Sound the average annual rainfall is high enough at over 6000 mm; yet on the western flanks of the Alps further north precipitation is much higher – as high as a phenomenal 18,440 mm measured in one year (to October 1998) in the Cropp River, a high altitude tributary of the Whitcombe River. At the other extreme, the eastern basins in the rain-shadow of the Alps are the driest places in the country; in Central Otago, the annual rainfall can be as low as 350 mm, with hot summers, frosty winters and a semi-arid landscape.

Indeed it is no understatement to say that the landform diversity of an entire continent has been squeezed into the New Zealand archipelago. Certainly there are no deserts or currently active shield volcanoes but consider the following range of iconic landforms:

- Over 700 islands and a very long and intricate coastline of more than 15,000 km;
- Fiords, some reaching more than 30 km from the Tasman

Sea into the remote mountainous interior of Fiordland;

- Flights of uplifted marine terraces, boldly expressed in the coastal landscapes around Charleston, Tirakirae Head or Mahia Peninsula; at Waitutu in southern Fiordland, 11 ancient uplifted beaches can be recognised, from sea level up to 1000 m altitude;

- The trace of the Alpine Fault through the West Coast, one of only four places in the world where the collision of the Earth's tectonic plates can be seen on the land;

- Franz Josef Glacier/Ka Roimata o Hine Hukatere and Fox Glacier/Te Moenga o Tuawe, descending into West Coast rainforest;

- The 'basin and range' topography of Central Otago; block mountains like the Dunstan, Rock and Pillar, and Old Man ranges with superb examples of periglacial landforms on their summits (schist tors, solifluction lobes, soil stripes and stone nets);

- Aoraki/Mt Cook (the highest peak at 3754 m), the Tasman Glacier, and the hundreds of peaks and glaciers of the Southern Alps/Ka Tiritiri o te Moana;

- The huge outwash fan of the Canterbury Plains, with the spectacular braided beds of the Waimakariri, Rakaia and Rangitata rivers; the braided river landforms are unique to the high country and shared with only a few other mountainous regions of the world, like the Himalaya, the Tibetan Plateau, Alaska and Andean Patagonia;

- The ancient, extinct shield volcanoes of Banks Peninsula, Otago Peninsula and Chatham Island, now deeply eroded by the sea;

- Kaikoura Canyon, where depths of 1000 m are reached only 3 km offshore;

- Farewell Spit, a 30 km long arc of sand sweeping out from the north-western tip of the South Island;

- The karst landforms of Paparoa, Oparara and Canaan, containing some of the longest and deepest caves in the Southern Hemisphere;

- Cook Strait, possibly the largest erosional feature on New Zealand's continental shelf; both the strait and the nearby Marlborough Sounds are huge 'sags' in the Earth's crust;

- The cone volcanoes, Ruapehu, Ngauruhoe and White Island/Whakaari, among the most frequently active volcanoes in the world;

New Zealand's geodiversity includes a wide variety of iconic landforms, such as the Franz Josef Glacier/Ka Roimata o Hine Hukatere (pictured here) and the Fox Glacier/Te Moenga o Tuawe which descend from the Southern Alps/Ka Tiritiri o te Moana into the temperate rainforest of the West Coast.

- Lake Taupo, the lake-filled caldera of the Taupo super-volcano, site of the world's most recent super-eruption (the Oruanui Eruption 26,500 years ago) and the largest known eruption (Taupo Eruption, c.1826 years ago) in the last 7000 years;
- The caldera volcanoes of Taupo and Okataina (Rotorua) are some of the most 'productive' in the world (in the sense of volume of tephras produced over time);
- Rotorua's high-temperature geothermal phenomena (especially geysers like Pohutu), found on this scale in only a few other places in the world.

In summary then, over geological time the changes wrought on the landforms of proto-New Zealand by earth-

Looking north into the mountainous wilderness of Te Wahipounamu (South West New Zealand) World Heritage Area, from above the Wick Mountains of Fiordland towards the Southern Alps/Ka Tiritiri o te Moana – a vast area of 2.6 million ha, or 10 per cent of New Zealand's land area.

quake and tectonic uplift, volcanic eruption and ice-age glaciation, river down-cutting and rises in sea level have been enormous. In addition, the insidious agents of erosion have both worn away and rejuvenated the soil through the regular cycles of freeze and thaw, rain and wind. In so many ways the dynamic character and youthfulness of the New Zealand landscape stands in sharp contrast to that of our nearest continental neighbour – the old, dry, red and worn flat land of Australia.

NEW ZEALAND'S DISTINCTIVE BIODIVERSITY

As the last (Otiran) glaciation began to wane around 14,000 years ago, forests began to reclaim the extensive periglacial grasslands and shrublands, so that by 2000 years ago forests had expanded to their maximum extent (about 78 per cent of the land area). So, prior to the arrival of humans, dense, evergreen forests would have dominated the landscapes of the archipelago. However, the alpine zone of permanent ice and snow, fellfield, herbfield and snow tussock grassland covered 14 per cent of the total land and was a major feature of the South Island (much as it is today). South Island 'drylands', treeless areas with less than 650 mm of rainfall per year, would have made up another 4 per cent; and the remaining 4 per cent consisted of lakes, swamps, open riverbeds, dunelands and the eruption-induced tussock grassland/shrublands of the central North Island. The colonisation of the post-glacial landscape by forests and shrubs would have been greatly aided by birds distributing seeds, especially those of the large podocarp trees – matai, totara, kahikatea, rimu and miro. The podocarps (sometimes called 'southern conifers') are members of a predominantly Southern Hemisphere plant family (the Podocarpaceae) with strong Gondwanan biogeographical links. Along with kauri (also with an ancient southern lineage) and beech they are arguably the trees that impart a distinctive character to New Zealand's forests. Although podocarps occur in forest associations with other conifers like kauri and cedar, they are mostly found with broadleaved trees like tawa, rewarewa, rata or beech. This podocarp/broadleaf forest became the most widespread and complex of our forest associations, eventually extending from Northland to Stewart Island/Rakiura.

In contrast to the deciduous and coniferous forests of Northern Hemisphere temperate latitudes, the podocarp/broadleaf forests are more stratified and have a strong resemblance to the montane rainforests of the tropics. This feature was noted nearly a century ago by the eminent New Zealand botanist Leonard Cockayne: 'The general appearance and structure of the New Zealand forest is quite different from that of Europe, temperate Asia, and North America. On the contrary, it bears the unmistakable stamp of a mountain forest in a moist tropical country such as Java, and thus comes into the plant geographical class of rainforest.'[5]

In this type of forest climbing ferns and lianes drape the branches, and trunks are entwined with root climbers like the climbing ratas and kiekie. Another distinctive feature is the profusion of epiphytes, uninvited passengers (such as ferns, orchids, and the *Collospermum* and *Astelia* 'nest lilies') which can manufacture or scavenge their own organic soils so that they can survive perched high in the forest canopy. A profusion of epiphytes and lianes is generally associated with tropical rainforests but the temperate rainforests of New Zealand are their rivals. An apparent world record of 28 different liane and epiphyte species (as well as numerous mosses, liverworts and lichens) have been found on one old kahikatea tree in South Westland.[6]

Compared with the podocarps, kauri was slower to exert its influence as post-glacial warming allowed forests to once more clothe the landscape. Kauri was unable to compete south of a line between Kawhia and Tauranga because temperatures were not high enough; so, kauri forest became locally dominant in Northland, and on the Coromandel Peninsula and Great Barrier Island, often forming an intimate mixture with podocarp/broadleaf forest. The warming climate in early post-glacial times initially gave podocarp and broadleaf trees a competitive advantage over beech but the return of drier, frostier conditions about 7000 years ago suited the expansion of beech forest. Beech began to move out of its montane refuges and steadily invaded the podocarp/broadleaf forests of the wetter hill country and the podocarp woodlands of the intermontane basins along the eastern side of the Southern Alps.

The beech species show a remarkable ability to capitalise on local small-scale catastrophes like landslips, floods and the windthrow of older forest trees. Beech is also adept at spreading downstream from an upstream source, forming a riverine beech ribbon and then infiltrating sideways into the surrounding podocarp/broadleaf forest. The visual character of beech and podocarp/broadleaf forest is very different: beech forests are much simpler in structure, lacking the diversity of sub-canopy species, and usually have a tight canopy and form a very sharp treeline. Overall, New Zealand's beech forests do not warrant the epithet of 'rainforest', for they have very few similarities to tropical rainforests. Rather they are the southern equivalent of the Northern Hemisphere's temperate deciduous and cold-temperate coniferous forests.

A very distinctive feature of many of New Zealand's forest and shrubland plants is their divaricating habit. A divaricating plant is usually a woody shrub up to 3 m high, with a tight, interlocking network of branches with tough wiry stems and small leaves. Although there are similar plant forms in deserts elsewhere in the world, only in New Zealand's vegetation is the phenomenon so prevalent – in more than 50 species ranging across 17 different plant

families. Divaricating plants became widespread, but mostly on forest margins and in open habitats: matagouri (*Discaria toumatou*) choking the river flats of the high country, or clumps of springy *Coprosma propinqua* dotting the windswept Wellington coastline, or dwarf kowhai (*Sophora prostrata*) clinging to the sunny faces of the montane dry grassland valleys of Canterbury and Marlborough. Also, some large trees, like matai, are divaricating as juveniles. It is a puzzling fact that many species of *Coprosma*, *Olearia* and *Pittosporum* are divaricating, yet other members of each genus are not. The reason for the divarication enigma in New Zealand's flora has provoked vigorous scientific debate, the probable cause being either an evolutionary adaptation to withstand browsing by moa, or the response of tropical elements in the flora to the extremely arid, windy and frosty climate of the Pleistocene ice ages – or both.

On most mountain slopes where beech came to form

LEFT Silver beech (*Nothofagus menziesii*), its branches draped in mosses, lichens and perching ferns, is the dominant tree in the wet forests close to the treeline on most of New Zealand's mountain ranges. ABOVE An attractive mosaic of one of the umbrella mosses (*Hypnodendron* sp.) and a mat-forming *Nertera* (with the red berries) on the forest floor.

the treeline there was a sharp transition to alpine snow tussock herbfields. However, in beech-free localities and in some valley heads, a tangled mass of mountain shrublands developed instead. In places this has developed into an almost impenetrable 3–7 m high wall of shrubby species of *Olearia*, *Dracophyllum*, *Hoheria* and *Pseudopanax*, often extending for 300 m upslope. This subalpine shrubland (often termed 'leatherwood') covered the southern Rua-hine Range, and was also well developed on Mt Taranaki, the western Tararua Range, central Westland and Stewart Island/Rakiura.

TOP Divaricating shrubs, like these matagouri (*Discaria toumatou*) on river flats of the high country, are a distinctive feature of New Zealand's plant biodiversity. The term 'divaricating' refers to their tight, interlocking network of branches with tough wiry stems and small leaves. Although there are similar plant forms in deserts elsewhere in the world, only in New Zealand's vegetation is the phenomenon so prevalent – in more than 50 species ranging across 17 different plant families.

RIGHT New Zealand's alpine vegetation is often considered to be its botanical glory, both aesthetically and scientifically. About 30% of New Zealand's total native plant species are found above the treeline, and perhaps as many as 500 of these species are restricted to the alpine zone. Diverse ecological niches – scree slopes, splash zones beside snowfield rivulets, boggy margins of alpine tarns, exposed rock outcrops, or sheltered crevices among moraine boulders – allow a wide range of alpine plant communities to thrive, like this *Aciphylla* speargrass among snow tussocks.

But it is New Zealand's alpine vegetation which is its botanical glory, both aesthetically and scientifically. Diverse ecological niches – whether mobile scree slopes; splash zones beside rivulets of snowfield meltwater; boggy, peaty margins of alpine tarns; exposed rock outcrops; or sheltered, shady crevices among moraine boulders – allowed a wide range of alpine plant communities to evolve. Indeed, about 30 per cent of New Zealand's total native plant species are found above the treeline, and perhaps as many as 500 of these species are restricted to the alpine zone. Furthermore, 93 per cent of the alpine plant species are endemic (compared with around 80 per cent for the rest of the higher plants). The snow tussock herbfields are the most distinctive element of this alpine landscape, because of the sheer size of the *Chionochloa* snow tussocks (1–2 m tall) and their tawny colour. They are remarkably long-living perennial grasses, larger specimens being several centuries old. Like beech trees they seed infrequently but profusely, probably as a result of a warm summer the previous year.

New Zealand's higher plants have a high level of endemism at the species level (around 85 per cent) and this gives the natural landscape its own distinctive character. Nevertheless, there are no examples of endemism at plant family or order level. As George Gibbs has commented, 'New Zealand's flora conforms fairly closely to that in other parts of the Southern Hemisphere. All New Zealand plants… are part of a wider southern flora.'[7] In contrast, however, a number of orders and families of higher animals (such as tuatara, moa, and kiwi) are found only in New Zealand, reinforcing the argument for their ancient Gondwanan origins because such a level of endemism would have required a very long period of isolation.

Of particular significance is the tuatara, its two species (*Sphenodon punctatus* and *S. guntheri*) being the sole surviving members of the Sphenodontia order. Sphenodontia is one of the four orders of reptiles (the others being turtles; crocodiles; lizards and snakes), which was represented by many species 200 million years ago. As all the other members of the order died out around 65 million years ago, the tuatara is of outstanding international interest to biologists. It can be considered an ancient reptile which has adapted well to a cold environment, using a very low breeding rate (adults can live to 70 years) and varying the incubation temperature of its eggs to determine the sex of its offspring. New Zealand's other reptiles are a very rich and diverse fauna of endemic skinks and geckos, most of which give birth to live young (suggested as an adaptation to the cold climate) in contrast to most of the world's lizards which

instead lay eggs. Geckos are considered to be quite ancient lizards whose centre of origin was in this southern continent. New Zealand's four species of native frog all belong to the very primitive, endemic Leiopelmatidae family, whose lineage also reaches back to Gondwana. They are secretive and silent, small and long-lived, and unlike most frogs they do not have a free-living tadpole stage.

Moa, which were eventually hunted to extinction by Maori (see p.21), and New Zealand's other giant ratite group, kiwi, share a very ancient lineage. Kiwi are flightless, nocturnal birds with many attributes more typical of mammals. Like a cat, kiwis have sensory whiskers and, like most mammals (and unlike birds), an acute sense of smell. They burrow in the ground like moles, exude an earthy musty smell and may use their strongly smelling burrows to mark out their territory. Kiwi are the most unbirdlike of birds. Certainly they are distinctive – worthy of their status as a national symbol for modern New Zealand. Another highly distinctive member of our avian biodiversity is the kakapo, the world's rarest and largest parrot. With its large eye-discs it looks somewhat like an owl; like an owl it is also nocturnal. It is a solitary bird, and has a strong, musk-like smell, like many mammals. The male is the only member of the parrot family known to perform nightly lek displays during the breeding season (along with using an intricate 'track and bowl' system for courtship), with a distinctive, eerie call known as booming.

The invertebrate fauna is also of great interest to scientists because of its antiquity, long isolation and very high level of endemism (about 95 per cent). Many spiders, bristletails, moths and dragonflies have features that elsewhere in the world can be found only in fossils. Caddisflies, stoneflies and mayflies – all insects that frequent cold running water – comprise another group with strong links to Gondwana. A feature of the beetles and other insects is their flightlessness and large size, attributes of invertebrates living in cold, windy climates where there are no mammalian predators. Some of the most spectacular are the large, flightless weevils, such as the giant giraffe weevils. Other endemic and often primitive lower-animal groups are the flatworms, giant earthworms, giant land snails and *Peripatus*. The land snail fauna of New Zealand is one of the richest in the world, reflecting the primeval wet-forest environment – and, probably, the lack of mammalian consumers. A feature of the land snails is their restricted geographical distribution, often reflecting land connections that existed earlier during the evolution of the country's shape through uplift, glaciation and erosion.

Weta, members of the large insect order Orthoptera (which also includes grasshoppers, locusts and crickets) stand out for their rather striking – indeed, frightening – appearance and for their antiquity. There are more than 70 species, all endemic. New Zealand's giant wetas may be among the most ancient and unchanged members of Orthoptera, dating back nearly 200 million years in the Gondwana fossil record. In an evolutionary response to the lack of mammalian foragers and predators, these dinosaurs of the insect world have developed heavy bodies weighing up to 70 g, and resemble small rodents like mice and rats in their diet and strictly nocturnal activity.

Biologists describe the New Zealand biota as being depauperate (i.e., lacking in major groups of plants and animals) but very rich in life forms that have developed from the limited parent stock or have been eliminated elsewhere. In essence, then, while there is great diversity in some biota – such as seabirds and alpine plants – the attraction of most of New Zealand's biodiversity stems from its antiquity and

The attraction of most of New Zealand's biodiversity stems from its antiquity and its many curiosities – like the kakapo (*Strigops habroptilus*), the world's largest and rarest parrot. Kakapo are nocturnal, looking more like owls, and the male makes an eerie 'booming' call during the breeding season.

its many curiosities. Ancient species include tuatara, wrens (rock wren and rifleman, our 'non-singing' songbirds, last survivors of the ancestral type of passerine bird), *Peripatus* (a zoological oddity which is neither worm, centipede, nor caterpillar but with an affinity to all three), and the plant 'living fossil' *Tmesipteris* (one of the few surviving members of the primitive order Psilotales which thrived during the Devonian 400 million years ago). Among the curiosities are not only kakapo, weta and kiwi, but also alpine geckos and parrots, 'vegetable sheep' (*Raoulia* and *Haastia*), and a preponderance of inconspicuous flowers which are generally de-colourised (mostly white) and de-specialised.

HUMAN IMPACT ON THE WILDERNESS

The densely-forested and mountainous temperate wilderness may have seemed strange, even alien, to the Polynesian voyagers who reached this new land, which they called Aotearoa, about 1100 years ago. To these first Maori settlers all natural things possessed mauri, a universal life-essence which was recognised and protected through tapu, a notion of sacredness. Their unity with the land and desire for its well-being was emphasised in their name for themselves – tangata whenua (people of the land). And through their whakapapa they traced their relationship to their ancestors, their tribal canoe, mountain and river, and ultimately their relationship with other living things. They were the first explorers of the wilderness and the shadows of their tipuna (ancestors) spread across all the land, their exploits commemorated in place-names – names that today still confer historical meaning and character on most of the geographical features of modern New Zealand.

However, Maori had only limited technology at their disposal for survival in this new temperate and dynamic living environment. Their most powerful tool was fire, and it was used to devastating effect. During the ensuing centuries fires swept away the forests of the drier eastern parts of Aotearoa. By the time Pakeha settlers arrived in the early 19th century, they had reduced forest cover from about 78 per cent to 53 per cent of the land area. In particular, pre-European fires devastated the lowland matai/totara and kahikatea forests that then covered the more fertile alluvial and organic soils of modern-day lowland Canterbury, Otago, Marlborough and central Hawke's Bay. As a consequence of the fires and hunting, moa became extinct. In addition, their introduction of the Pacific rat, the kiore, had a very significant impact on an extensive range of indigenous fauna – small birds, bats, lizards, tuatara, large flightless insects and land snails.

In the much shorter period of Pakeha settlement – from 1840 until the present day – the area of native forest was halved again, to only about 26 per cent of the land. Ten native birds, including the huia, the piopio and the Stephens Island wren, became extinct during this period. While the clearing of lowland forest, wetland and coastal habitats by Pakeha settlers had a massive impact on the indigenous fauna, pests introduced by the settlers decimated wildlife and irreversibly modified vegetation communities. Some, like rats and mice, were introduced unwittingly; others, like the rabbit and brush-tailed possum, were introduced for food or fur. Many garden plants, like traveller's joy (which today we call old man's beard), soon escaped to the wild.

The huia (*Heteralocha acutirostris*) was one of the very few bird species in the world whose sexes had different bill shapes, allowing the bonded pair to complement each other in their foraging for insects. Their demise is the most graphic and best-documented of the many New Zealand birds driven to extinction through destruction of their habitat, predation by alien animals, and unsustainable hunting after the arrival of humans (ROD MORRIS).

Acclimatisation societies introduced deer, trout and game birds for sport but their main impact was on native plants and animals. The long isolation from mammalian predators that made New Zealand's wildlife so unique, especially in the characteristics of flightlessness and large size, was over. As Elsie Locke wryly observed in verse for children who would hopefully grow up into wiser adults:

> With the deer and the cat and the goat and the pig
> They chewed up the land to make themselves big,
> They all ran wild with the stoat and the rabbit
> Whose numbers were growing too much of a habit.[8]

And long before the main phase of Pakeha settlement, marine mammals, especially the New Zealand fur seal and several species of whales, had already been hunted almost to extinction; both are still recovering to the levels that our marine environment sustained prior to the late 18th century.

It is easy with 21st century hindsight to judge our forebears harshly for their zeal in so transforming, in little more than 1000 years, the landscape of what till then was arguably the last of Earth's major archipelagos to remain isolated and uninhabited by humans. To most of the early European colonists the wilderness was not only a place to be feared but also in need of salvation through axe, plough and the surveyor's theodolite. Some romantics, like the early paint-

The windswept Solander Islands, the eroded remnants of an andesitic volcano at the western end of Foveaux Strait, are a specially protected outlier of Fiordland National Park. Like many of New Zealand's offshore islands they are a haven for threatened biodiversity.

er and writer Augustus Earle, rejoiced at 'the countryside, wild, magnificent, fresh from the land of nature and inspiring thoughts of God'[9], but they were few. Most equated the subjugation of nature and the establishment of familiar pastoral countryside with virtue and godliness.

Gradually the wild landscapes and indigenous biodiversity of New Zealand retreated from the lowlands to the mountainous hinterland, to the offshore and outlying islands and to the South Island's wet West Coast. Most lowland regions – especially Manawatu, southern Hawke's Bay–Tararua district, East Coast, Waikato, Taranaki and the Southland Plains – were almost completely transformed to pasturelands of ryegrass and clover, cocksfoot and browntop. In the half-century from 1860 to 1910, New Zealand experienced possibly the most rapid virgin landscape transformation of any nation; over 6.5 million hectares of lowland indigenous forest was cleared. This is an extraordinary 25 per cent of our total land area – as much as had been destroyed during the preceding 900 years of Polynesian settlement.

WILDERNESS APPRECIATION AND CONSERVATION BEGINNINGS

There were, however, some far-sighted individuals who eloquently questioned the conventional exploitative ethic of those pioneering days, among them:

- Te Heuheu Tukino Horonuku of Ngati Tuwharetoa, who gifted the summits of Mts Ruapehu, Ngauruhoe and Tongariro as the core of Tongariro National Park;

- William Fox, explorer, artist and Prime Minister, who urged protection for the geothermal wonderland of the Volcanic Plateau;
- Thomas Mackenzie, explorer of Fiordland's wilderness and Prime Minister;
- Thomas Potts, naturalist and politician, an early advocate of 'national domains' as refuges for native birds;
- Harry Ell, politician and conservationist, who played a key role in raising public awareness of the need for scenery preservation and reserves;
- Rua Kenana, the Maori visionary who stressed the values of self-sufficiency and community to the Tuhoe people of Te Urewera;
- Leonard Cockayne, botanist and teacher, who wrote the first comprehensive ecological account of New Zealand's remarkable vegetation;
- A.P. Harper, mountaineer, wilderness explorer and companion of the legendary surveyor Charles 'Mr. Explorer' Douglas;
- W.H. Guthrie-Smith, farmer, naturalist and author.

By the 1870s, the inexorable loss of indigenous forests was widely decried, prompting Prime Minister Julius Vogel to introduce the Forests Bill of 1874 to parliament. During the debate on the bill even this arch-advocate of public works development lamented what was happening to New Zealand: 'New Zealand entirely unsettled – New Zealand in its old wild state – might be very much more valuable, clothed with forest, than New Zealand denuded of forest and covered with public works.'[10]

Gradually, influential scientific groups were able to convince the government of the need for offshore island 'flora and fauna reserves' as sanctuaries for our rapidly-disappearing wildlife. In quick succession, Resolution Island (1891), Secretary Island (1893), Little Barrier Island (1895) and Kapiti Island (1897) reserves were designated. Another legislative landmark was the passing of the Scenery Preservation Act 1903. This was the first law allowing the Crown to adopt a truly national approach to establishing reserves, although the imperative was more to do with the protection of scenery for tourism rather than any conservation of landforms and biodiversity for their intrinsic values.[11] Not until the formation of the NZ Forest Service in 1920, the Royal Forest and Bird Protection Society in 1923 and the Federated Mountain Clubs of New Zealand (FMC) in 1931 were there any coherent voices urging the conservation of our remaining wild lands. And even then the focus was generally on the soft option of

reserving more of the uninhabited back country unsuitable for farming or plantation forestry – the twin pillars of the Dominion's rural development.

The folly of the wide-scale deforestation of the highly-erodible Tertiary mudstones of the northern Hawke's Bay–Gisborne–East Cape hill country was dramatically exposed during the disastrous floods in the Esk and Waipaoa valleys in the 1930s. As a consequence of these and other widespread erosion calamities, a powerful movement towards soil and water conservation emerged during the 1940s and 1950s. Regional catchment boards were established throughout the country and the NZ Forest Service played a central role, especially when deer control eventually became its responsibility. Essentially the Forest Service became the Crown's principal back-country manager, marrying deer and possum control with re-afforestation and the wider conservation management (including wilderness recreation) of the steeplands – the so-called 'protection forests'.

ACCESS TO WILDERNESS PROTECTED IN PUBLIC LAND

Two parallel philosophical streams emerged in colonial New Zealand's early attempts to protect wild and scenic places – on the one hand for science, and on the other for the 'common man' to enjoy. The small but influential scientific community which led the drive for the flora and fauna reserves discussed above, were not interested by and large in encouraging the public to visit these priceless sanctuaries. However, many worker, farmer, and artisan settlers wanted to be free of the Old World class and tenure barriers which might prevent them from enjoying ready access to the wildest and most beautiful places in their new land. This was a New World phenomenon, an egalitarian ethic which stressed access to the public land 'commons' and became enshrined in our legislation through provisions like the Queen's Chain along the margins of sizeable rivers and lakes. Just as Maori expected the Treaty of Waitangi to guarantee them continued use of their forests and fisheries, so too was the Crown expected to acquire public lands where all New Zealanders could freely enjoy their natural and historic heritage.

The popularity of the 'scenic wonderlands' of New Zealand grew markedly during the 1880s and 1890s, and the increasing number of visitors highlighted the need to protect these places as parks or reserves.[12] The first significant step in this regard was not a government initiative, but a remarkable gift to the nation of the volcanic cones which in 1887 became the core of our first national park, Tongariro

(see p.79). Tongariro became the world's fourth national park only 15 years after the first, Yellowstone in the United States, had been protected by Congress 'for the benefit and enjoyment of the people'. Other prime tourist attractions were the Pink and White Terraces (until the 1886 Tarawera eruption) and other Rotorua geothermal areas. The Whanganui River was promoted as the 'Rhine of New Zealand' during the 1890s when steamers carried tourists up-river, some of them venturing on by coach to Tongariro National Park, Taupo and Rotorua. In the South Island the first Hermitage Hotel was opened at Mount Cook in 1884. By 1890 Quintin Mackinnon and Donald Sutherland had opened up the Milford Track and glacier guiding was available at Waiho (Franz Josef Glacier) by the turn of the century.

But the concept of national parks, and the prevention of commercial opportunities within them, still did not come easily to a colonial society beholden to agriculture for export incomes. Our second national park, Egmont, was formed in 1900, but only after a strenuous campaign for its protection. Even then, the park boundary was tightly drawn around the circumference of Mt Taranaki's circular ringplain, scribed along a mere 6 mile (9.65 km) radius from the summit. There was to be no buffer zone around this perimeter – the dairy farms began abruptly where the forest ended, typical of a 'fenced island' approach that New Zealand public reserve administrations would hold for the next 80 years. Fiordland became a national park in 1904 and Arthur's Pass in 1929 but the next decades of depression and war meant there was virtually no progress in national park designation apart from Abel Tasman in 1942. The issue of unhindered access to the high country of the South Island, and especially the attempts of a private company to commercialise the Mount Cook Reserve, were of concern to A.P. Harper and many mountaineers during the 1920s.[14] There was an obvious need for government to clean up the rather chaotic system of parks and reserves legislation and be proactive in facilitating free access for all New Zealanders to their wilderness heritage.[14]

Only with the passage of the far-sighted National Parks Act in 1952 was public frustration turned into action with the setting up of the National Parks Authority, park boards and a national parks section in the Department of Lands and Survey. Several parks were formed in quick succession:

Tane Mahuta, the largest remaining kauri (*Agathis australis*) in Waipoua Forest Sanctuary. The public demand during the 1940s for a kauri sanctuary in Waipoua was a forerunner of the major forest conservation controversies of the 1970s and 1980s.

Mount Cook in 1953, Urewera in 1954, Nelson Lakes in 1956 and Westland in 1960. When the alpine wilderness around Mt Aspiring was declared our tenth national park in 1964, political leaders stated that this was likely to be the last of New Zealand's national parks (see p.237); and for the next 20 years it seemed this was to be the case.

CHANGING TIMES: REPRESENTATIVE PROTECTED AREAS AND CONSERVATION CONTROVERSIES

One of New Zealand's greatest natural resource tragedies, largely lamented only in hindsight, was the failure of successive governments in the first half of the 20th century to rein in the wasteful exploitation of our State indigenous forests by the timber milling industry. If our once-vast podocarp, tawa, beech and kauri forests had benefited from careful sustained-yield management, they would have been capable of producing a small but perpetual yield of high quality indigenous timbers. Instead, the Crown allowed most of the merchantable forests to be 'mined', so much so that by 1960 the remaining resource was insufficient to sustain a viable long-term industry. Indeed, from the 1940s to the mid-1980s, the NZ Forest Service increasingly found itself in an impossible situation – doggedly adhering to its multiple-use philosophy while a large section of the New Zealand public cried 'enough' and demanded representative reserves of the wide range of forest ecosystems.

The first serious challenge to the multiple-use philosophy in State forests occurred during the 1940s, in opposition to the magnificent kauri forests of Waipoua being milled. Public pressure for a national park, led by a troika of Forest & Bird, the Auckland scientific community and a Waipoua Forest Preservation Committee, mounted over the decade as distrust of the NZ Forest Service increased. Ultimately, the service was able to retain management control, but only by grudgingly amending the Forests Act to establish the first strictly protected area in the State forest system – the Waipoua Forest Sanctuary. But it was a bitter battle, not helped by the patronising attitudes of many leading foresters towards what they considered were extreme preservationists who would 'lock up' the nation's dwindling timber resources. Prophetically, in 1946 the NZ Institute of Foresters editorialised: 'The existing state of public misinformation and distrust of forest service activities could be largely avoided if it kept the public better informed of its aims and methods.'[15] In this sense Waipoua was the forerunner of the many representative forest sanctuaries and ecological areas set aside after scientific surveys

during the South Island Beech Utilisation scheme and other indigenous forest multiple-use controversies that raged country-wide throughout the 1970s and 1980s.

The NZ Forest Service, however, did learn a lesson from the Waipoua controversy when it came to countering FMC's proposal for the Tararua Range to be declared Tararua National Park as an appropriate Wellington celebration of New Zealand's Centennial in 1940. Instead, the service convinced all recreational stakeholders to accept a multiple-use alternative – Tararua Forest Park – which still gave priority to soil and water conservation (and wild animal control) but was otherwise more sympathetic to back-

New Zealand's first truly national wilderness protection campaign was the concerted effort to save Lake Manapouri, in Fiordland National Park, from having its level raised to provide hydroelectricity for Comal co's aluminium smelter.

country recreation. The forest park concept was widely accepted by trampers and hunters and 18 parks were gazetted during the 1960s and 1970s, mainly in the State Forests of the axial ranges of the North Island.

Changing government attitudes and the rise of the conservation movement throughout the 1970s also led to major revisions of the national parks and reserves legislation administered by the Department of Lands and Survey. With the passing of the new National Parks Act 1980, the former park boards lost their executive powers but gained region-wide responsibility for the planning of reserves and other protected areas. The mood was for much less emphasis on scenic grandeur, the hallmark of the original parks; instead, there was a desire for New Zealand to urgently achieve a protected area network that would be truly representative of the country's landforms and biological diversity. This goal has been nowhere better expressed than in the wording of the 1977 Reserves Act: 'Ensuring as far as possible, the survival of all indigenous species of flora and fauna, both rare and commonplace, in their natural communities and habitats; and the preservation of representative samples of all classes of natural ecosystems and landscape which in the aggregate originally gave New Zealand its own recognizable character.'

Indeed, an authoritative 1980 DSIR publication, *Land Alone Endures* confirmed just how skewed New Zealand's complex system of protected areas had become: 'National-ly, a very high proportion of our total park and reserve area is mountain land unsuited to any reasonable "developed" use at all … In real terms this means that less than 0.5 per cent of New Zealand's area has been designated National Park or reserve in preference to a use forgone; there has been very little real sacrifice.'[16]

Protecting representative ecosystems for scientific rea-sons was given impetus in the mid-1980s when the NZ Bio-logical Resources Centre co-ordinated the subdivision of New Zealand into 268 ecological districts and the launch of a Protected Natural Areas Programme (PNAP). The goal of PNAP was to biologically map each ecological district and recommend new protected areas, to ultimately achieve an augmented protected area system which was truly repre-sentative of New Zealand's biodiversity and geodiversity.

However, the first truly national campaign on a wilder-ness conservation issue was not about forests, but concerned the destructive intrusion into our largest national park. The 'Save Manapouri' campaign began spontaneously by Southlanders under the leadership of Ron McLean in Oc-tober 1969, in an eleventh-hour effort to stop the govern-ment raising the levels of Lakes Manapouri and Te Anau in Fiordland National Park. The Electricity Department wanted to raise the level to supply cheap hydroelectricity to the Comalco aluminium smelter at Bluff. The protest spread across the country and contributed to the govern-ment losing the 1972 election. Emboldened by the victory (the level of Manapouri was subsequently controlled but

not raised), a new breed of younger conservation activists spawned a variety of environmental conservation groups, from Ecology Action to the Native Forest Action Council, from small specialist groups of lawyers and scientists like the Environmental Defence Society to umbrella coalitions like ECO – Environment and Conservation Organizations (of New Zealand).

Environmental concerns became big political issues throughout the 1970s and early 1980s: nuclear power, 'Think Big' energy developments and Maui gas, the Clyde Dam on the Clutha River, the Aramoana smelter propos-al, mining proposals on the Coromandel Peninsula, and many others. However, the main wilderness protection campaigns were for wild and scenic rivers, marine reserves, wilderness areas and, most controversially of all, to save our remaining lowland indigenous forests from logging. Initially, the public were not really aware that the Forest Service had largely given up any hope of sustaining cutover indigenous forest; instead, the service seemed to deem most podocarp/hardwood forests as too slow to grow the next rotation, and therefore too difficult and costly to man-age in the long term. Increasingly, cutover forest was being burnt and converted to faster growing pines and other North American conifers. In 1969, a highly respected DSIR scientist, Charles Fleming, took the brave step of calling the NZ Forest Service to account with a *Listener* article en-titled 'Mammon on the Mamaku'.[17] This perceptive and persuasive analysis exposed the short-sightedness of the service's multiple-use policy, especially the attendant loss of habitat for indigenous biodiversity – in the case of the Mamaku Plateau, for the iconic endangered kokako.

For the next 15 years, in a dozen or more forests, battles raged between conservationists, local sawmilling commu-nities and the Forest Service. The main forest conserva-tion objectives of the campaigners were expressed in the Maruia Declaration, presented to parliament in July 1977; it was the largest petition ever collected in New Zealand, with 341,160 signatures. Many of those indigenous timber communities, like Minginui and Tihoi, are now ghostly shadows of their former vitality. Some of the beautiful names of the forest battlefields – Mangatotara, Mamaku, Maruia, Warawara, Waihaha, Whirinaki, Erua, Rangataua, Pureora, Orikaka, Paparoa, Inangahua, Ahaura, Okarito, Waikukupa and Waitutu – have been forgotten, but all were ultimately saved, even if only in part, to be conserved and visited by future generations.

DIMINISHING WILDERNESS: CAMPAIGNS FOR WILDERNESS AREAS

The need for protected areas to preserve New Zealand's diminishing wilderness was given impetus by the 1949 visit of Olaus Murie (then President of the Wilderness Society who was in New Zealand for the NZ/USA Fiordland Expedition and to attend the Pacific Science Congress), who urged that wilderness areas be included in the forthcoming national park legislation. The idea was supported by the main architects of the bill, Lance McCaskill, A.P. Harper of FMC, and Ron Cooper of the Department of Lands and Survey. So, the 1952 National Parks Act made legal provision for wilderness areas in New Zealand for the first time (reinforced subsequently by the Forests Act amendment of 1976, the Reserves Act in 1977, and the Conservation Act in 1987).

But action in setting aside wilderness areas in New Zealand's back country was painfully slow initially. FMC

A wilderness of weather-sculpted granite outcrops, tangled low forest and moorland characterise the proposed Pegasus Wilderness Area in southernmost Stewart Island/Rakiura.

pressed for a number of large 'mountaineers' wilderness' areas, especially in the Olivines and Landsborough but these were outside national parks. Instead, the first *de jure* wilderness areas were rather small and fragile. Otehake Wilderness Area (12,000 ha) in Arthur's Pass National Park was gazetted in 1955 (with Lance McCaskill playing a major role in its designation), followed by Te Tatau Pounamu and Hauhangatahi (each less than 10,000 ha) in Tongariro National Park in the early 1960s. Otehake has since gone the same way as a later West Sabine Wilderness Area in Nelson Lakes National Park (see p.173) – revoked because it wasn't robust enough. It took more than 20 years for the

The idea of wilderness is very personal. It embodies remoteness and discovery, challenge, solitude, freedom and romance. It fosters self-reliance and empathy with wild nature. Wilderness is therefore principally a recreational and cultural concept which is compatible with nature conservation.

Wilderness recreation is available to everyone and is an important part of the wide range of recreational opportunities that exist and should remain in New Zealand. A wilderness experience can be gained in a variety of natural landscapes but …. To retain the widest opportunities for outdoor recreation, management of some large remote areas as wilderness is necessary.

The wild lands of the world are rapidly shrinking and will become rare in the near future. The opportunities New Zealand can offer for wilderness recreation are therefore of international significance.

WILDERNESS AREAS

Wilderness areas are wild lands designated for their protection and managed to perpetuate their natural condition and which appear to have been affected only by the forces of nature, with any imprint of human interference substantially unnoticeable. Wilderness areas should:

- Be large enough to take at least 2 days' foot travel to traverse;
- Have clearly defined topographic boundaries and be adequately buffered;
- Not have developments such as huts, tracks, bridges, signs, nor mechanised access.

A wilderness area system should have a wide geographic distribution, and contain diversity in landscape and recreational opportunity.

Abbreviated extract from the *New Zealand Wilderness Policy* (1985)

WILDERNESS AREAS

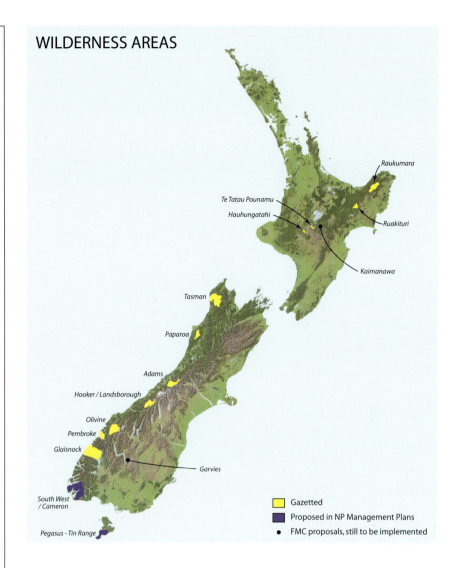

first significant wilderness areas (Pembroke and Glaisnock, both in Fiordland) to be set aside in the national park system in 1974. The need for a comprehensive 'New Zealand wilderness preservation system' was still urged by FMC, which celebrated its 50th jubilee in 1981 by organising New Zealand's first wilderness conference. Ten large *de facto* wilderness areas were proposed by FMC[18] – Raukumara, Kaimanawa–Kaweka, Tasman, Paparoa, Adams, Hooker, Olivine, Garvies, Preservation–Waitutu and Pegasus. Each wilderness area proposed was larger than 30,000 ha (and some as large as 80,000 ha) and in total covering 3 per cent of New Zealand's land area. The areas were evaluated at the conference and subsequently by a government-appointed Wilderness Advisory Group (WAG) which also developed a Wilderness Policy. The policy defining the character of

wilderness areas and how they are to be managed (see box above) has stood intact since 1985.[19]

The NZ Forest Service, embattled with the indigenous forest controversies discussed above, was keen to balance the forest management ledger in some way. It therefore gave priority to two of FMC's proposals within its forest park system. Both advanced slowly through public consultation procedures until in 1988 the first wilderness areas outside the national park system were designated – the 40,000 ha Raukumara, centred on the rugged Raukumara Range and the Motu River catchment (see p.127), and the 87,000 ha Tasman in the Tasman Mountains of North-west Nelson Forest Park (now Kahurangi National Park, see p.165). The National Parks and Reserves Authority, on the other hand, showed little interest and no further wilderness areas were formed in the national park system for another 15 years.

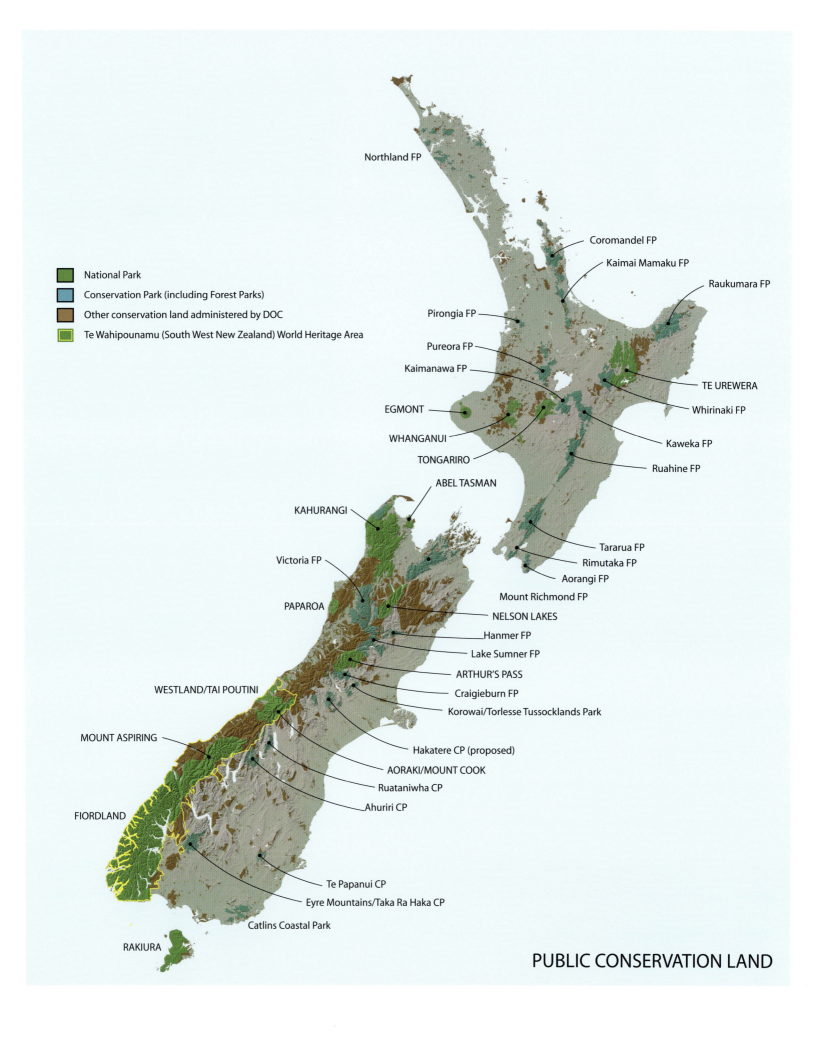

National Park

Conservation Park (including Forest Parks)

Other conservation land administered by DOC

Te Wahipounamu (South West New Zealand) World Heritage Area

Northland FP

Coromandel FP

Kaimai Mamaku FP

Raukumara FP

Pirongia FP

Pureora FP

Kaimanawa FP

TE UREWERA

EGMONT

Whirinaki FP

WHANGANUI

Kaweka FP

TONGARIRO

Ruahine FP

ABEL TASMAN

KAHURANGI

Tararua FP

Rimutaka FP

Victoria FP

Aorangi FP

Mount Richmond FP

PAPAROA

NELSON LAKES

Hanmer FP

Lake Sumner FP

ARTHUR'S PASS

WESTLAND/TAI POUTINI

Craigieburn FP

Korowai/Torlesse Tussocklands Park

MOUNT ASPIRING

Hakatere CP (proposed)

AORAKI/MOUNT COOK

Ruataniwha CP

Ahuriri CP

FIORDLAND

Te Papanui CP

Eyre Mountains/Taka Ra Haka CP

Catlins Coastal Park

RAKIURA

PUBLIC CONSERVATION LAND

PROTECTING WILDERNESS HERITAGE IN THE DEPARTMENT OF CONSERVATION'S FIRST 20 YEARS

Ultimately, government and public patience ran out with the conflicting missions, tunnel vision, and entrenched attitudes of the existing natural-resource agencies. The radical government environmental reorganisations of the mid-1980s were set in train; eventually, virtually all publicly-owned natural and historic heritage was made the responsibility of a new Department of Conservation (DOC) in 1987. The department inherited a very fragmented public estate, which now consists of more than 17,000 parcels of land legally protected for conservation purposes, distributed throughout the three main islands and outlying islands and covering more than 8.15 million hectares (or around 31 per cent of New Zealand's total land area). In its first 20 years of operation the department has established an international reputation as possibly the 'most effective biodiversity conservation agency in the world'. But perhaps the most impressive achievement has been to facilitate a sea change in public attitudes towards natural heritage conservation. It has gone from being a lonely conservation orphan in 1987, to a situation in 2007 where it has matured and forged many productive partnerships with community groups, industry, regional and local government, and iwi and emerged as the leader of an effective, diverse and influential movement committed to conserving our natural and historic heritage.

The very strategic approach to halting New Zealand's inexorable decline in indigenous biodiversity that DOC progressively developed is briefly outlined in Chapter 16. In the rest of this chapter, by way of setting the scene for the more detailed descriptions in the following regional chapters, the main events in the conservation of our five main wilderness heritage entities over the past 20 years are summarised. The five, spanning land, freshwater and marine environments, are: national parks, conservation parks and South Island high country, wilderness areas, wild and scenic rivers, and our marine environment.

National Parks

Internationally, national parks are prized as the Crown jewels of a nation's natural and historic heritage. By their very name they are of national – not regional or local – significance. Whereas some developed countries like Australia and the United Kingdom have debased the term by designating as national parks some which are clearly only of regional or state significance, New Zealand has kept its national park standards high, holding very much to the American national park ideal. The National Parks Act 1980 requires them to be 'preserved in perpetuity' for 'their intrinsic worth and the benefit, use, and enjoyment of the public', and for them to contain 'scenery of such distinctive quality, ecological systems, or natural features so beautiful, unique, or scientifically important that their preservation is in the national interest'.

Two major national park events in 1987 engaged the new Department of Conservation – the opening of Paparoa National Park and the National Parks Centennial celebrations at Tongariro. Paparoa was the most controversial of our modern national parks, a landmark victory for conservationists after more than a decade of debate and compromise with the NZ Forest Service. It was also the first of the new 'scientific' parks, its boundaries carefully drawn to protect sensitive karst landforms, including some impressive cave systems, and coastal forests. The National Park Centennial was widely celebrated, but DOC was at pains to highlight how the conservation mandate of the new department was much wider than national parks. In the next few years many traditionalists were critical of DOC for turning its back on national parks (particularly after the National Parks and Reserves Authority and park boards were replaced with a NZ Conservation Authority and conservation boards). Although national parks were still very important in the eyes of the public and overseas visitors, DOC's senior management seemed to view them as just one of many ways of acknowledging the value of our natural heritage – especially when most of this heritage was already protected as conservation land. Instead, most of DOC's conservation efforts were directed towards other priorities: endangered species, conservation through resource-management legislation, marine reserves, forging conservation partnerships with iwi, and planning visitor services for the burgeoning numbers of overseas tourists.

When the government finally decided in 1989, after decades of debate and evaluation, to deny the option of logging publicly-owned indigenous forests south of the Cook River on the West Coast, 311,000 ha of magnificent lowland podocarp forests became conservation land. Immediately, Forest & Bird and the National Parks and Reserves Authority recognised that these forests could be linked with the four national parks in the south-west corner of the South Island – Mount Cook, Westland, Mount Aspiring and Fiordland – to form a 'super-park' of global importance. In 1990, UNESCO listed this 'super-park' – Te Wahipounamu (South-West New Zealand) – as a World Heritage site on all four natural heritage criteria.

With a total area of 2.6 million hectares (or 10 per cent of New Zealand's total land area) Te Wahipounamu was recognised as one of the world's outstanding wilderness landscapes (see p.199).

Further north, Paparoa National Park was the setting for one of New Zealand's worst back-country calamities – the Cave Creek tragedy of 1995. A viewing platform built by DOC collapsed, killing 13 polytechnic students and a DOC ranger, and seriously injuring four others. The inquiry identified serious shortcomings in DOC's operational procedures and accountabilities. Against a backdrop of diminishing funding yet increasing public expectations for recreational opportunities and facilities, the department had developed a robust, but flawed, culture of 'do more with

Okarito Forest, a superb example of lowland podocarp forest (mainly rimu), was threatened with logging until it was incorporated into Westland/Tai Poutini National Park.

less'. After such an avoidable tragedy it was predictable that the pendulum would quickly swing to the other extreme: strict conservation management procedures enveloped all operations, the department was restructured into a more conventional modern bureaucracy, and a safety inventory of the extensive visitor facilities infrastructure on conservation lands was undertaken. Many of the latter, among the more than 12,000 km of tracks, 960 huts, and 13,000 boardwalks, bridges, staircases and viewing platforms, were found to be in need of upgrading, or removal.

The whole crucial issue of the future management of conservation land for recreation and tourism was then addressed by DOC in its 1996 Visitor Strategy.[20] The strategy took the sensible step of segmenting the visitor spectrum into seven groups based on their skills and experience, ranging from 'short-stop travellers' to 'remoteness seekers'; and it urged redirecting the effort of providing most facilities into the 'front country' or more accessible back-country areas. For the remoteness seeker the strategy belatedly committed DOC to make more effort in implementing the Olivine, Paparoa, Adams, Poteriteri–Waitutu and Pegasus wilderness areas. But back-country groups like FMC faced a dilemma with the strategy's proposal to cease maintaining many lesser-used back-country huts, tracks and bridges: although some were old or poorly-sited, they were often of practical and sentimental value to trampers and hunters (who had built many of them in earlier days when amateurs provided the labour and materials to develop the track and hut network in the parks); yet their removal would have the desirable effect of allowing much of the back country to revert to *de facto* wilderness without visitor facilities.

Initially, the irony of DOC's new self-imposed risk-averse culture was not lost on traditional wilderness visitors. At one extreme a number of costly, unnecessary, or over-built aesthetic monstrosities (mostly bridges) were erected for the 'day visitor' group; at the other, large numbers of existing structures of acceptable quality to most 'back-country adventurers' were removed. Because DOC was liable for the safety of visitors only when they used DOC-managed facilities, a bureaucratic maxim of 'if in doubt, pull it out' seemed to carry the safety decisions of the day. To its credit, in 2002 the government funded DOC's bid for a 10-year visitor facilities maintenance programme to the tune of around $350 million; then, in 2004, DOC began a broad consultation with back-country recreational groups and the wider public over just what facilities should be retained. By and large, the resulting Visitor Assets Management System (VAMS) is one of the most professional and successful approaches DOC has applied to the management of our back country. It has quietly established a network of facilities attuned to the needs of both the visitor and the park's natural environment, while attracting far less media hype and political spin than DOC's many recovery programmes dealing with our charismatic mega-fauna.

Since Paparoa was gazetted, only two more national parks have been recognised: Kahurangi (incorporating virtually all of the former North-west Nelson Forest Park) in 1996, and the most recent, Rakiura (covering most of Stewart Island/Rakiura), in 2002. So in summary, in the 120 years since 1887 New Zealand has designated 14 terrestrial national parks covering 3,085,764 hectares or 11.5 per cent of our total land area (see map p. 30). Four of these parks – Tongariro, Te Urewera, Egmont and Whanganui – are in the North Island. The South Island, with a much higher proportion of wild landscapes, has ten – Abel Tasman, Nelson Lakes, Kahurangi, Paparoa, Arthur's Pass, Aoraki/Mount Cook, Westland/Tai Poutini, Mount Aspiring, Fiordland and Rakiura with a combined area of 2.6 million hectares (about 17 per cent of the South Island's area). Our largest national park, Fiordland, at 1,261,310 ha is one of the world's great wilderness landscapes; the smallest, Abel Tasman, is 22,689 ha. There are still no marine national parks.

Conservation Parks (including Forest Parks)

Like the larger national parks, the conservation parks vary in size, generally from 50,000 ha to 150,000 ha. Most of them are the forest parks established by the NZ Forest Service more than 20 years ago in the wild hinterland of the axial ranges of the North Island (extending from the Raukumara Range in the East Cape to the Rimutaka and Tararua ranges near Wellington) and in the lower altitude ranges in the northern part of the South Island (Richmond, Victoria, and Lake Sumner forest parks). But from 2002 DOC initiated a new and welcome trend by establishing conservation parks in the tussocklands of the eastern South Island high country. These now include the Korowai/Torlesse Tussocklands Park around the Waimakariri River in Canterbury, Ahuriri Conservation Park, Eyre Mountains/Taka Ra Haka Conservation Park, and Te Papanui Conservation Park on the rolling tussock plateaux and patterned mires in the Lammerlaw and Lammermoor ranges of Otago. It is the stated intention of government and DOC to create a network of such high country conservation parks along the eastern side of the Alps, from Marlborough to Southland. In contrast to our national parks, most conservation parks have a lower profile with tourists; tracks are generally of tramping instead of walking standard, and huts more rudimentary in terms of their facilities.

Wilderness Areas

The legal designation of further wilderness areas was also a low priority for the fledgling DOC in 1987; it considered mountain wilderness to be secure, at least in the short term. However, in 1990, one substantial (if non-threatened) wilderness area recommended by FMC and

WAG slipped quietly through: the Hooker–Landsborough Wilderness Area, 41,000 ha of magnificent mountain country in South Westland. Finally, after nearly 50 years of advocacy, an 83,000 ha Olivine Wilderness Area in western Mount Aspiring National Park (centred on the Olivine Ice Plateau, Olivine Range and the Red Mountain ultramafic belt) was designated in early 1997. FMC's two West Coast wilderness area proposals, Paparoa (30,768 ha) and Adams (56,000 ha), became realities in 2002. Then, late in 2003, New Zealand's wilderness area system gained one more wild landscape, through the persistence of the East Coast Conservation Board – the Ruakituri Wilderness Area, 23,500 ha of montane beech forest on the south-eastern slopes of the Huiarau Range in Te Urewera National Park (see map p.29).

Wild and Scenic Rivers

The loss of many of our wild and scenic rivers, through damming for hydroelectricity development or by water abstraction for irrigation, emerged as a major conservation issue in the 1970s. The Manapouri power scheme markedly reduced the flow of the lower Waiau River and the Tongariro, Waitaki, and Clutha (with the Clyde Dam) power schemes significantly altered the characteristics of three of the largest wild rivers in the country. Legislation was passed in 1981 to allow for Water Conservation Orders, and the middle reaches of the Motu River, flowing along the edge of the Raukumara Wilderness Area in Raukumara Forest Park, became the first river so protected in 1984. The Motu was very much a test case, a river highly prized by rafters as the longest challenging wilderness river in the North Island; yet it was protected only at the eleventh hour because planning for its hydro development was already in an advanced stage. The Rakaia River received a conservation order in 1988 and since that time another 10 major rivers – Manganui-o-te-Ao, Ahuriri, Grey, Rangitikei, Kawarau, Buller, Mataura, Motueka, Mohaka, and Rangitata (or major sections of them) – have been protected.

Marine Reserves

New Zealand has a large, diverse, and biologically rich marine natural heritage, which covers 480 million hectares (or 18 times our land area). Like our terrestrial plants and animals, a high proportion of the 15,000 marine species in our seas are only found in our region.

The beautifully symmetrical male flowers of puawhananga, our best-known native clematis (*Clematis paniculata*).

The Buller River, the largest in the northern part of the West Coast, was under threat of damming until the 'Save the Buller' campaign began in earnest in 1986. It took another 15 years of legal process before the main Buller and most of its tributaries were protected by a Water Conservation Order – a resounding victory for a broad cross-section of New Zealand's conservationists, anglers, kayakers and rafters.

How best to conserve our marine resources has always provoked lively debate among marine stakeholders, not least over how much of our territorial sea, and which areas, should be off-limits to fishing. New Zealand's first marine reserve (Cape Rodney–Okakari Point) near Leigh north of Auckland was established in 1975 and was one of the world's first no-take marine reserves. Since then, another 28 marine reserves have been established. Over half of these marine reserves applications have been lodged by public interest groups or tangata whenua, rather than DOC, and most have involved protracted rounds of consultation and refinement – often with an outcome of little satisfaction to all parties. Progress in protecting marine ecosystems under existing legislation (the Marine Reserves Act 1971) has been excruciatingly and unacceptably slow. While New Zealand has an outstanding reputation internationally for terrestrial protected areas (31 per cent protected as types of conservation land), the picture is quite depressing for marine protected areas, with only 0.3 per cent of our total marine environment in marine reserves. As of 1st April 2007, the 28 marine reserves covered 1,269,382 ha (or 7.6 per cent) of New Zealand's territorial sea. However, 99 per

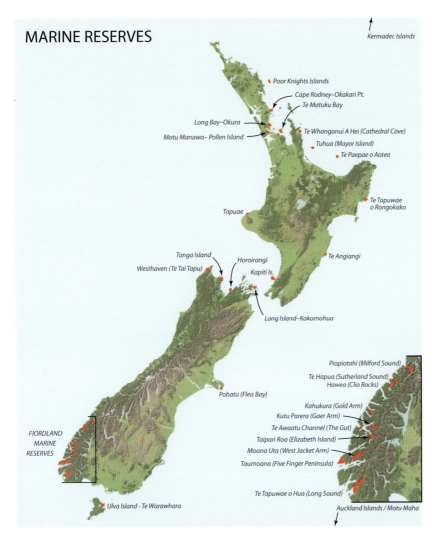

MARINE RESERVES

Kermadec Islands

Poor Knights Islands

Cape Rodney–Okakari Pt.
Te Matuku Bay

Long Bay–Okura

Motu Manawa– Pollen Island

Te Whanganui A Hei (Cathedral Cove)

Tuhua (Mayor Island)

Te Paepae o Aotea

Te Tapuwae
o Rongokako

Tapuae

Tonga Island

Horoirangi

Te Angiangi

Westhaven (Te Tai Tapu)

Kapiti Is.

Long Island–Kokomohua

Piopiotahi (Milford Sound)

Te Hapua (Sutherland Sound)
Hawea (Clio Rocks)

Pohatu (Flea Bay)

Kahukura (Gold Arm)

Kutu Parera (Gaer Arm)

Te Awaatu Channel (The Gut)

Taipari Roa (Elizabeth Island)

Moana Uta (West Jacket Arm)

FIORDLAND
MARINE
RESERVES

Taumoana (Five Finger Peninsula)

Te Tapuwae o Hua (Long Sound)

Ulva Island - Te Warawhara

Auckland Islands / Motu Maha

scientific study, including prohibition of any marine farming, mineral extraction from the seabed, or fishing; essentially a no-take philosophy. Furthermore, marine reserves can extend only out to 12 nautical miles from shore, so they cannot be used to protect the outer seas within New Zealand's Exclusive Economic Zone (EEZ).

Future Prospects

Future prospects for improvements in the conservation of New Zealand's wilderness heritage – especially in the control of pests, regulation of tourism, protection of marine ecosystems, and retention of remaining natural South Island high-country landscapes – are addressed in the concluding chapter. But first we need to travel the length and breadth of New Zealand, from the Kermadec Islands to the New Zealand subantarctic islands, and even the Ross Dependency of Antarctica, to explore our wilderness heritage in more detail. Each of the following 14 regional chapters takes an overview of the physical and biological character of the region, then focuses on 4-6 main wilderness landscapes, and concludes with an account of some of the main threats to the geodiversity and biodiversity of the region and the conservation priorities.

ENDNOTES

1 Aldo Leopold, *A Sand County Almanac,* Oxford University Press, London, 1949, p. 270.

2 R.J. Hay, 'On Remoteness', *New Zealand Alpine Journal* 27, 1974, pp. 99–100.

3 Aldo Leopold, *A Sand County Almanac,* p. 270.

4 Edmund Hillary, *Nothing Venture, Nothing Win,* Coronet, UK, 1977.

5 Leonard Cockayne, *New Zealand Plants and their Story,* (E. J. Godley Ed.), Government Printer, Wellington, 1967, p. 66.

6 See: K.J.M. Dickinson, A. F. Mark & B. Dawkins, 'Ecology of lianoid/epiphytic communities in coastal podocarp rain forest, Haast Ecological District', *J. Biogeography,* 1993, pp. 687–705.

7 George Gibbs, *Ghosts of Gondwana,* Craig Potton Publishing, Nelson, 2006, p. 19.

8 Elsie Locke, *Look Under the Leaves,* Pumpkin Press, Christchurch, 1975.

9 Augustus Earle, *Narrative of a Residence in New Zealand.* 1832 (Republished Oxford 1966), p. 174.

10 Julius Vogel, *NZ Parliamentary Debates 16,* 1874. p. 93.

11 For an account of the growth of the Scenery Preservation Movement see: T. Nightingale & P. Dingwall, *Our Picturesque Heritage: 100 Years of Scenery Preservation in New Zealand,* Department of Conservation, Wellington, 2003.

cent of this is made up of two enormous marine reserves around offshore island groups – the 748,000 ha Kermadec Islands Marine Reserve (see p.42 and p.53) and the Auckland Islands Marine Reserve (484,000 ha, see p.286). The other 26 marine reserves protect very little of our mainland coastline.

Why has this unsatisfactory situation developed? There are many reasons:

• New Zealand was slow to extend legal protection to its marine ecosystems;

• An initial lack of ecological information on which to base options for reservation;

• Government's lack of vision and fragmented approach to marine protection;

• Widespread opposition from commercial and recreational fishers, and tangata whenua.

A barrier to marine reserve acceptability in the current legislation is its rather narrow focus on preservation for

Mt Ruapehu in eruption, 1996. The volcano was part of the gift of Te Heuheu Tukino Horonuku, which formed the core of Tongariro National Park, New Zealand's first national park, established in 1887.

12 See accounts by David Thom in *Heritage: The Parks of the People*, Lansdowne, Auckland, 1987.

13 See accounts by Rod Syme in *Fifty Years of Mountain Federation*, (R.W. Burrell Ed.), Federated Mountain Clubs of NZ, Wellington, 1981, pp. 144–5.

14 Jane Thomson, *Origins of the 1952 National Parks Act*, Department of Lands & Survey, Wellington, 1976.

15 Editorial notes, 'Waipoua Kauri Forests', *New Zealand Journal of Forestry*, Vol. 5, No. 3, 1946, p. 175.

16 G.C. Kelly, in Ch 4, 'Landscape and Nature Conservation', *Land Alone Endures*, (Comp. L. F. Molloy et al.), DSIR, Wellington, 1980.

17 Charles A. Fleming, 'Mammon on the Mamaku', *NZ Listener*, 14 Nov. 1969, p. 5.

18 Les Molloy, 'Wilderness Recreation – the New Zealand Experience', in L. F. Molloy (Ed.), *Wilderness Recreation in New Zealand*, Federated Mountain Clubs of NZ, Wellington, 1983, pp. 4–19.

19 Les Molloy, 'Wilderness Preservation in New Zealand, 1981 – 2006', *FMC Bulletin* No. 163, March 2006, pp. 26–34. See also essays on wilderness in Gordon Cessford (Ed.), *The State of Wilderness in New Zealand*, Department of Conservation, Wellington, 2001.

20 Department of Conservation, *Visitor Strategy*, DOC, Wellington, 1996.

CHAPTER TWO

NORTHLAND AND THE KERMADEC ISLANDS

Northland is very different from the rest of mainland New Zealand. Its climate is warm temperate and humid, and its topography more subdued. There are no high mountains, with the highest point, Te Raupua in the Waima Range, only 781 m above sea level. Compared with other parts of the North Island, Northland escaped the direct impact of the Pleistocene ice age glaciations and the cataclysmic eruptions from the Taupo Volcanic Zone. Consequently, many of its landforms are of greater age, and its rocks and soils are therefore more weathered. The soils of Northland were the despair of pioneer farmers, and their diversity and subtle patterns in the landscape long fascinated soil scientists and ecologists. As a generalisation, the soils are clay-rich and have poor physical properties. The reasons are complex. In part, Northland's soils missed out on the beneficial rejuvenation provided to other parts of New Zealand by the regular addition of fresh minerals as a result of erosion caused by tectonic uplift and glaciation. In addition, although Northland has a number of young basaltic volcanoes in the Whangarei and Kerikeri districts, the contribution of their more nutrient-rich tephra to the region's soil fertility is only localised. The widespread occurrence of kauri in Northland's original forests was another soil-deterioration factor. Kauri is a long-lived tree which produces deep layers of highly acidic litter. Rainfall carries the powerful natural organic chemicals in the litter into the soil, where they leach away most nutrients over time.

Although not immediately obvious, the complex geology of Northland also underlies many of the interesting biodiversity features in the region. A number of isolated rugged uplands are notable within the landscape. These massifs – the Maungataniwha, Tauwhare, Tangihua and Tutamoe ranges – consist of ancient volcanic rocks (mostly sheet lava flows and flood basalts), and today carry most of Northland's remaining indigenous forests. They are wildlife habitat 'islands', set in lower sedimentary country which has mostly been converted to pasture or plantation forest. Over the last few million years there have also been times when the entire Northland Peninsula has been an island, or several islands, as sea levels have fluctuated. This is particularly true for the Far North, especially the Te Paki and Houhora localities on the Aupouri and Karikari peninsulas. As a consequence of long periods of isolation from the mainland, a number of endemic plants, land snails, stag beetles and possibly lizards have evolved on these islands in the past.

The other outstanding landscape features of Northland are its coastlines and offshore islands. The western coastline is a near-continuous 300 km long sweep of sand from Muriwai Beach (see Auckland's Wild West Coast, p.59) to Cape Maria van Diemen, interrupted only by the Tauroa Peninsula and the short rocky headlands of the Whangape coast. The best-known of these long sandy beaches is Ninety Mile Beach, an arc of yellow sand curving north from Ahipara. The beaches have been built up from longshore drift of sands swept northwards by the strong currents that scour the western coastline of the North Island. Here sea temperatures are considerably lower than on the eastern coastlines and the marine biota is dominated by cool-water species. In sharp contrast, the eastern coastline has been etched out of the ancient basement greywacke rocks of New Zealand, giving an intricate pattern of rocky headlands and drowned valleys. Cape Brett and the Whangamumu and Whangaruru peninsulas are highly scenic examples of

The Kermadec nikau palm (*Rhopalostylis baueri* var. *cheesmanii*) is a predominant feature of the forests of Raoul Island. The Kermadec nikau is one of 23 plants endemic to the Kermadec Islands.

KERMADEC
ISLANDS

Raoul Island

29°3'

Kermadec Island
Marine Reserve
(includes 12NM buffer around L'Esperance Rock,
a further 96km SSW of Curtis Island)

30°0'

• *Macauley Island*

178°W

Cheeseman Island
Curtis Island

30°3'

0   50km

Great Island

Three Kings Islands / Manawatawhi

*Kerr
Point*

*Torn
Bowling
Bay*   *Surville Cliffs*

Cape Reinga   ① *North Cape*

Columbia Bank   *Waikuku Beach*

Te Werahi Beach   *Spirits
Bay*

Cape Maria van Diemen   • Te Paki

Twilight Beach   *Parengarenga Harbour*

Scott Point   *Kokota Spit*

Te Paki Dunelands   *Te Paki Stream*

■ Houhora

Aupouri Peninsula

Rangaunu Bay   *Karikari Peninsula*

Ninety Mile Beach   *Doubtless Bay*

Whangaroa Harbour   *Cavalli Is.*

■ Mangonui

Awanui ■   ■ Whangaroa   *OMAHUTA FOREST*

Kaitaia   *PUKETI FOREST*

Takou Bay

Tauroa Peninsula   ■ Ahipara   *Purerua Peninsula*

②   *Bay of Islands*   *Cape Brett*

HEREKINO FOREST   ② *Waipoua R.* ■ Kerikeri

Whangamumu Peninsula

MAUNGATANIWHA RANGE   *Russell Peninsula*

L. Omapere   ■ Waikare

■ Tapuwae   Kawakawa ■   *Whangaruru Peninsula*

Whangape Harbour   ■ Rawene   ② *RUSSELL FOREST*

Tnuwhare   *Poor Knigh*

WARAWARA FOREST   Kaikohe ■   *Tawhiti Rahi Is.*

Omapere   *Aorangi Is.*

Hokianga Harbour ■ Te Raupua   *Poor Knights Islan*
                                             Marine Reserve

WAIMA FOREST   ②

MATARAUA FOREST   ③ Waipoua   ■ Tutukaka

WAIPOUA FOREST   *Ngunguru*

Waipoua River

TROUNSON FOREST

Maunganui Bluff   ■ Whangarei

TUTAMOE RANGE   *The Nook Peninsula*

                                             Whangarei Harbour

TANGIHUA RANGE   ②   *Bream Head*

                                             Hen and Chicke

■ Dargaville   *Tarar*

Wairoa River

■ Mangawhai Heads

Cape Ro
Okakari
Marine Re

Bryderwyn ■

■ Ruawai

Pouto Peninsula

■ Wellsford   *Leigh*

Kaipara Harbour   *Tapora Bank*

■ Warkworth

Papakanui Spit

N ↑

① North Cape Scientific Reserve
② Northland Forest Park
③ Waipoua Forest Sanctuary

NORTHLAND

0   25   50   75   100km

the former; and the Bay of Islands is the largest drowned valley system on the eastern coast of the North Island. The eastern marine environment contains many warm temperate and subtropical species because of the warm oceanic currents. Furthermore, the Northland Peninsula is deeply indented with the most impressive series of shallow estuaries in the country – the Parengarenga, Rangaunu, Hokianga, Whangarei and Kaipara harbours being the largest of a dozen or more. These estuaries are highly valued for their conservation importance, especially the millions of wading birds they support, many of them migratory visitors from the Arctic – godwits and knots, turnstones and curlews. The Northland estuaries are also notable as a stronghold of the New Zealand mangrove (*Avicennia marina* var. *resinifera*); along with Tauranga Harbour, they are probably the most distant from the equator of any of the world's mangrove habitats.

Three outstanding island groups – the Three Kings, Poor Knights, and Hen and Chickens Islands – are strictly protected as nature reserves and are free of introduced pos-

The grey ternlet (*Procelsterna cerulea*) is widely distributed throughout the Pacific but its New Zealand stronghold is the Kermadec Islands, particularly Macauley and Curtis Islands. There are now more than 10,000 breeding pairs on Macauley, with numbers probably increasing because of the eradication of goats.

sums, cats, mustelids and most rodents. The Three Kings group is nearly 60 km north-west of Cape Reinga and the Poor Knights group 25 km north-east of Tutukaka – both far enough (and surrounded by an ocean deep enough) to have remained distinct island groups during the low sea levels at the height of the Last Glaciation. The Hen and Chickens Islands are much closer to the Northland mainland, just 10–15 km off Bream Head at the entrance to Whangarei Harbour. They lie on the continental shelf, and were connected to eastern Northland when sea levels were 110–120 m lower than at present, so consequently lack the endemic biota of the other two island groups. Visually, the Hen and Chickens are an impressive sight, especially the stark profile of the largest island, Taranga, the remnant of an old andesitic volcano where forest now clings to the

Curtis Island, one of 15 islands in the Kermadec archipelago, is still volcanically active. It is the tip of just one of a series of volcanoes along the Kermadec Ridge, part of the Pacific 'Ring of Fire'.

sheer rock towers of its rocky summit. The Hen and Chickens Islands are important for the continued conservation of several threatened wildlife species, especially North Island saddleback, stitchbird, little spotted kiwi and tuatara.

THE KERMADEC ISLANDS

The Kermadec archipelago contains the northernmost land in New Zealand. Raoul Island, with an area of 2900 ha, is by far the largest of the 15 islands (total land area 3280 ha) which are linearly spread in four clusters over 250 km of ocean (see inset map, p.40). Although they lie some 1300 km north-east of the Northland coast, the Kermadecs have a geological affinity with the Taupo Volcanic Zone, for these small islands are just the tips of a chain of enormous deep-sea volcanoes (the Kermadec Ridge) rising to heights of as much as 10 km from the depths of the Kermadec Trench. They lie roughly midway between White Island and the Tongan Islands, and are part of the great Pacific 'Ring of Fire'. Two of the islands, Raoul and Curtis, are still volcanically active – Raoul erupting in 1964, and again, violently and without warning, in March 2006.

However, it is the pristine marine ecosystems surrounding these island specks that have given the Kermadec Islands their reputation for outstanding ecological values. The water temperatures (20–24˚ C) are about four degrees warmer than the waters of the east coast of Northland, and so, the Kermadecs occupy an intermediate position between the tropical islands of the Pacific (they have reef-forming coral species but lack coral reefs) and the temperate New Zealand mainland (they lack most of the large brown seaweeds found around the mainland). They have an interesting marine fauna which includes sea snakes, turtles, and giant limpets. The most notable marine inhabitant is the huge spotted black grouper. The waters around the Kermadec Islands sustain one of the last surviving populations of these fish which can grow up to a metre in length and possibly live for 100 years.

The land fauna and flora of the Kermadec Islands is also very interesting. Like the Hawaiian Islands and the New Zealand subantarctic islands (such as Campbell and the Auckland Islands), the Kermadecs are true oceanic islands. Such islands have never been joined to continents by land bridges and, consequently, they usually lack indigenous reptiles and mammals. Their floras are quite restricted in extent, most plants having arrived through their seeds being carried on the wind, floating across the ocean or being attached to the feathers of migrating birds. Like many of the volcanic islands of the Pacific, the warm temperate forest of Raoul Island is dominated by a species of the genus *Metrosideros*, here the Kermadec pohutukawa (*M. kermadecensis*). Nikau palms are widespread, conferring a distinctly subtropical look to the landscape; the common trees ngaio and mapou have evolved as endemic species. However, because the Kermadec Islands are still very young, insufficient time has elapsed for the evolution of a large number of truly indigenous plants. Nonetheless, the level of endemism is still high – 23 out of a total of about 115 indigenous plants – and the flora of the islands is considered to be of international importance because of the many examples of adaptive evolution of distinctive Kermadec species from mainland New Zealand genera that have somehow made their way to the islands.

TE PAKI: THE FAR NORTH

Te Paki is one of the most distinctive wilderness landscapes in New Zealand. It lies at the northernmost tip of the Aupouri Peninsula, a narrow stretch of sand (a tombolo) linking the headlands of Cape Reinga and North Cape with the rest of the North Island mainland around Kaitaia. Most of the rocky headlands and cliffs of Te Paki are the remnants of ancient lava flows – hard rock 'anchors' which have secured the ever-shifting sands to produce some of the finest and most isolated beaches and wetlands in the North Island. The best-known headlands are Cape Maria

CLOCKWISE FROM TOP LEFT Masked booby (*Sula dactylatra*) watching over young on Curtis Island (ROD MORRIS). The large spotted black grouper (*Epinephelus daemelii*), which can live for over 100 years, is the most notable marine species protected in the Kermadec Islands Marine Reserve (MALCOLM FRANCIS). The Kermadec petrel (*Pterodroma neglecta*) nested in numbers as high as 500,000 on Raoul Island at the beginning of the 20th century. They were virtually eliminated by 1970, primarily through predation by Norway rats and cats and harvesting by settlers, before the islands were declared a flora and fauna reserve. The graceful red-tailed tropicbird (*Phaethon rubricauda*) breeds on many islands in the Pacific and Indian oceans, and around 120 birds breed on the Kermadec Islands (ROD MORRIS).

Van Diemen and the popular tourist destination of Cape Reinga (more correctly known as Te Rere i nga Wairua, a place of great significance to Maori, where the spirits of the dead depart for Hawaiki-Nui and the spirit-land, Te Reinga). There is an overwhelming feeling of awe when standing beside the historic lighthouse at Cape Reinga – the wind, the dramatic coastal landscapes to east and west, the turbulent churning waters of the Colombia Bank where the currents of the Tasman Sea and the Pacific Ocean meet, and the indistinct but rugged outline of the Three Kings Islands/Manawatawhi far to the north-west.

Five Te Paki beaches – Twilight Beach, Te Werahi Beach, Spirits Bay, Tom Bowling Bay and Waikuku Beach – are of outstanding recreational and scenic value. They are also of national significance for the biodiversity of the native plant communities on their sand dunes; together with the dune ecosystems of Fiordland, they are the most botanically valuable dune systems in the country. The most accessible dunes, however, lie around Te Paki Stream south of Scott Point. These remarkable white sands are a popular tourist attraction, with some dunes as high as 150 m. In total, they cover 2000 ha and stretch inland in a 4 km wide band from Ninety Mile Beach. To the east lie the intricate waterways of beautiful Parengarenga Harbour, the northernmost estuary in New Zealand and probably the largest one remaining in a natural state. The gleaming white sands of Kokota Spit are a notable feature at the harbour entrance, and the salt-marsh, eelgrass and mangroves in the estuary are habitat for thousands of migratory wading birds. The wetlands around the margins of Parengarenga Harbour

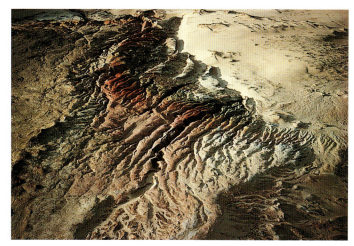

LEFT At the northern end of Ninety Mile Beach the Te Paki dunelands sweep inland in a 4 km wide band, an ever-changing landscape with ephemeral dune lakes and some dunes up to 150 m high; Cape Maria Van Diemen can be seen in the distance. ABOVE Wind and rain occasionally expose underlying sands weathered to warmer colours.

ABOVE An overwhelming feeling of awe when standing beside the historic lighthouse at Cape Reinga is created by the wind, the dramatic coastal landscapes to east and west, the turbulent churning waters of the Colombia Bank where the currents of the Tasman Sea and the Pacific Ocean meet, and the indistinct but rugged outline of the Three Kings Islands/Manawatawhi far to the north-west. RIGHT The nationally endangered Te Paki flax snail (*Placostylus ambagiosus*), or pupuharakeke, is one of 34 endemic land snails found only in this isolated locality (ROD MORRIS).

support many of New Zealand's rarer birds, such as spotless crake, New Zealand dabchick, fernbird, scaup and bittern.

Te Paki is one of the smallest but most distinctive ecological districts in New Zealand. Long ago the Te Paki locality was probably a group of islands of volcanic origin which became linked to the Northland mainland when sea levels dropped during the Pleistocene ice ages and longshore drift of sands allowed the Aupouri tombolo to form. This long isolation allowed the development of a high level of diversity and endemism in the Te Paki flora and fauna. Although centuries of fire and human habitation have destroyed most of the coastal forest, 80 per cent of the district is still covered in indigenous vegetation; much of this is manuka–kanuka shrubland and rushland, an important habitat for nine species of lizard and the many endemic species of insects and land snails, including *Placostylus* flax snails.

From a plant biodiversity perspective, the most interesting corner of Te Paki is the 'serpentine shrubland' protected in the 683 ha North Cape Scientific Reserve. The Surville Cliffs and the plateau between Kerr Point and North Cape are one of several localised areas of ultramafic rocks in the country, the other sizeable outcrops being in Marlborough–Nelson, northern Southland and South Westland. Ultramafic rocks (like the serpentinite found here) have a high content of iron- and magnesium-containing minerals and give rise to soils that have poor structures and are toxic to most plants. Such ultramafic landscapes are usually largely devoid of forest vegetation and instead support a tangled cover of hardy grasses and stunted, woody shrubs. The latter often adopt a sprawling, creeping growth habit (compared with the same or related species on adjacent non-ultramafic areas). Examples include tanekaha, mingimingi, tauhinu, and species of *Coprosma*, *Pomaderris* and *Pittosporum*. But what makes the ultramafic environment of North Cape so special compared with the no less visually dramatic South Island serpentine shrublands is its high level of floristic diversity and plant endemism. Over 330 different indigenous vascular plants are found in the North Cape–Waikuku locality, and around 20 of them are endemic (with most now described as distinct species). Why? Again, because of the relative warmth and landform stability of the Far North, isolated from the glaciations which most likely stripped the ultramafic mountains of the South Island back to bare rock. Consequently, serpentine species and varieties evolved over time at North Cape, whereas the southern ultramafic soils and flora have reestablished themselves only in post-glacial times. A quarry for serpentinite (often added to superphosphate fertiliser as a magnesium supplement) threatened the ecology of the North Cape ultramafic area from 1968 until its closure in 1984.

THE THREE KINGS AND POOR KNIGHTS ISLANDS

The Three Kings Islands/Manawatawhi are a group of 64 islands, islets and stacks strung out over a length of 15 km. Their total area is 685 ha, but one island, Great Island, is by far the largest (400 ha). They are the remnants of very old volcanic lavas, breccias and tuffs (both basaltic and andesitic), probably erupted more than 100 million years ago. These islands have been separated from the rest of Northland for at least 20 million years – long enough for a distinct terrestrial biota to evolve. The islands' flora contains 15 endemic plants, including two which are ranked among the rarest in the world – the Three Kings kaikomako (*Pennantia baylisiana*) and the Three Kings trumpet vine (*Tecomanthe speciosa*) – each occurring naturally as only one plant on Great Island (although the attractive *T. speciosa* is now widely available from plant nurseries because of its popularity as a garden ornamental). The islands are also notable for the absence of rats and their large numbers of breeding seabirds and endemic geckos and skinks (one of the latter, *Oligosoma fallai*, can grow up to 25 cm long, making it probably the largest skink in New Zealand). There is also a high level of endemism in the invertebrate fauna, especially the land snails (more than 30 species, virtually all endemic), weta, spiders and centipedes.

The seaweed 'forests', which are known to extend to depths of 50 m around the Three Kings Islands, are even more impressive. The combination of isolation from the mainland and a location where both cold and warm currents mix has given rise to a marine flora with many peculiarities, and affinities not only with the warm eastern Northland coastline but also with Australia and the colder waters of southern New Zealand. Many of these brightly coloured, luxuriant seaweeds are endemic to the Three Kings and are still undergoing exploration and description. They are quite different in their patterns from those of the Kermadec or Poor Knights Islands.

The Poor Knights Islands have an international reputation for the diversity of their marine fauna. As a result, 1890 ha of the waters surrounding the islands (with a land area of only 271 ha) were protected as New Zealand's second marine reserve in 1981. The islands are remnants of old rhyolitic volcanoes, their margins carved by the sea into sheer 200 m high cliffs (which also extend up to 100 m

below sea level). The cliffs are riddled with caves and archways, which add to the scenic diversity and the diving attractions of the Poor Knights. The islands lie in the warm East Auckland Current, allowing many species from tropical waters far to the north to thrive here. There are schools of trevally, blue maomao, wrasses and demoiselles, and a colourful array of anemones, sponges, bryozoans and spiny urchins clinging to the rocks.

A large Maori population lived on the Poor Knights until inter-tribal warfare in the early 1800s led to the islands becoming tapu and uninhabited. Since then, low coastal forest (kanuka, kohekohe, puriri, pohutukawa, karaka and tawapou) has established itself on the undulating summits of the two main islands, Tawhiti Rahi and Aorangi. The icon plant of the islands is *Xeronema callistemon*, the rare Poor Knights lily, which forms extensive carpets on the open ground and along the cliff edges. Because the islands have been separated from eastern Northland for at least 120,000 years – and remained free of rats and cats – the lizard and insect faunas, in particular, are notable for the

Blue maomao (*Scorpis violaceus*) congregate in large schools in archways and around headlands off the Poor Knights Islands and the Northland coastline, seeking planktonic food in the flowing current (ROSS ARMSTRONG).

number of endemic and rare species. There are large weta, such as the cave weta and Poor Knights giant weta. The islands are an important tuatara habitat, too, and there are two species of gecko (including Duvaucel's gecko, the largest in the country) and five skinks. The islands are also an important breeding ground for millions of seabirds, especially petrels and shearwaters.

THE KAURI FORESTS OF NORTHLAND FOREST PARK

Kauri (*Agathis australis*) is New Zealand's only member of the great Southern Hemisphere conifer family, the Araucariaceae (which also includes large ornamental trees like the Norfolk pine and monkey puzzle tree). When the first Polynesian settlers arrived, 80 per cent of Northland

CLOCKWISE FROM TOP LEFT Large snapper (*Pagrus auratus*) are once again a frequent sight around Goat Island. Since the designation of the Cape Rodney–Okakari Point Marine Reserve over 30 years ago, snapper numbers within the reserve have increased about 16-fold over those outside the protected area (IAIN ANDERSON). Falla's skink (*Oligosoma fallai*), or the Three Kings Islands skink, is one of New Zealand's largest skinks and is found only on these islands, where it inhabits rocky, shrubby areas (ROD MORRIS). The Australasian bittern (*Botaurus poiciloptilus*) is now rarely found in Northland's wetlands, its numbers having declined through habitat loss (swamp drainage) and damage (cattle grazing). Duvaucel's gecko (*Hoplodactylus duvaucelii*), New Zealand's largest gecko, is extinct on the mainland but found on islands off the North Island and is seen here on the striking flowers of the rare Poor Knights lily (*Xeronema callistemon*) (ROD MORRIS). The mangrove forests and saltmarshes of Northland and the northern islands are strongholds of the colourful banded rail (*Rallus philippensis*).

was covered with forest, 35 per cent of which was dominated by kauri. Kauri trees tended to prefer the ridges and spurs of rolling lowlands, often in association with other warm temperate broadleaved trees like taraire, puriri, tawhero, towai, karaka and kohekohe, as well as podocarps like rimu, kahikatea, tanekaha, miro and totara. The timber of kauri is so prized that it has been largely milled from the Northland Peninsula over the last 200 years. Whereas there were around 200,000 ha of kauri-dominated forest in 1800, only about 6000 ha remain today – mostly as strictly protected pockets in Waipoua, Trounson, Warawara, Herekino and Puketi–Omahuta forests, all components of Northland Forest Park.

Northland Forest Park consists of 19 far-flung forest remnants (with a total area of 77,686 ha) scattered across the breadth of the Northland Peninsula. Five of these forests make up the two largest wild forest landscapes in Northland. Puketi and Omahuta forests (with a combined area of 17,000 ha) lie between 200 m and 400 m altitude on the broken, sedimentary country around the scenic Waipapa River at the head of Hokianga Harbour. Although much of their kauri/podocarp/broadleaf component was logged, both forests are of outstanding value for their biodiversity and recreational opportunity. Many mature kauri remain, and the logged areas are regenerating vigorously. They are an important habitat for New Zealand pigeon/kukupa, kiwi, kaka, kakariki, bats, geckos, and another carnivorous land snail, the kauri snail. In 1980, Puketi was considered to have Northland's largest population of the endangered kokako (more than 100 birds). However, since then predation from introduced pests has reduced them to perhaps no more than two or three pairs; indeed, the Puketi kokako population may now be extinct – a rather inexplicable failure by DOC to intervene early enough.

The other contiguous wild area (23,000 ha) is made up of Waima, Mataraua and Waipoua forests on the old basaltic massifs lying to the south-east of the entrance to Hokianga Harbour. Waima and Mataraua forests are on much higher landforms (500–750 m), and both have a dominant podocarp and rata element, with little kauri. Waima contains at least 20 rare plants, including the endemic *Olearia waima* and *Coprosma waima*. Mataraua Forest

The kauri (*Agathis australis*) is New Zealand's only member of the great Southern Hemisphere conifer family, the Araucariaceae. This magnificent specimen is named Te Matua Ngahere (The Father of the Forest) and is found in Waipoua Forest Sanctuary. It is New Zealand's second-largest standing kauri and is probably more than 2000 years old, although age estimation is notoriously difficult.

has a distinctive wet plateau forest type, with rare swamp towai and swamp maire. The locality is also the northern limit for the endangered red mistletoe, *Peraxilla tetrapetala*, that grows on isolated pockets of hard beech. However, the best-known kauri forest is in the Waipoua Kauri Sanctuary, 12,817 ha of the Waipoua River catchment. The campaign to protect the kauri in Waipoua was eventually successful in 1952 but it was a long and bitter battle, the earliest of New Zealand's forest conservation controversies (see p.25). The drive along SH 12 through Waipoua Forest is an unforgettable experience. Huge kauri with magnificent crowns of widely spreading branches, as well as many rimu and rata, tower over a canopy of tawa, towai and pukatea. Short walks lead to some remarkable kauri trees like The Four Sisters, and two so large and impressive that tangata whenua long ago gave them their own names – Tane Mahuta and Te Matua Ngahere.

THREATS AND CONSERVATION PRIORITIES

Relative to much of New Zealand, the subdued topography, accessible estuaries (with plentiful mahinga kai) and benign climate of Northland has long made it one of the most attractive regions for human settlement. The human impact on the lowlands has been enormous, and the remaining islands of indigenous landscape are threatened by a myriad of animal pests and weeds. Fortunately, the impact has been far less severe on Northland's remarkably diverse and long coastline (at 1500 km, equivalent to the length of mainland New Zealand, from North Cape to South Cape at the southern tip of Stewart Island). Threats to this natural heritage and the potential for future conservation gains are discussed below for four key habitats.

Increased Marine and Coastal Ecosystem Protection

The Northland region contains possibly the most diverse range of coastal ecosystems in New Zealand – large estuaries, long sandy beaches with dunelands, rocky headlands, deep-water harbours and large peninsulas, as well as many offshore islands. Yet the level of protection for these coastal habitats is lamentable. The only marine reserve on the Northland mainland is at Cape Rodney–Okakari Point (547 ha) near Leigh (and this is arguably in the Auckland region). Admittedly there is a marine reserve – extremely important for both biodiversity conservation and recreation – around the Poor Knights Islands but not around the Three Kings Islands, despite their extraordinary diversity of marine biota (including more unique algae than in any

other part of New Zealand's waters). The Northland mainland has probably the largest area of relatively unmodified duneland in the country, most of it unprotected. Its estuaries contain large areas of highly productive mangrove, salt-marsh and tidal mudflats – priceless habitats for many of our rarer indigenous coastal birds like banded rail, brown teal, bittern, fernbird, New Zealand dotterel and even marsh crake. Inexorably, degradation of these coastal habitats continues: accelerated sedimentation from soil erosion, trampling by wandering stock and recreational off-road vehicles, reclamations for ports and marinas, and marine farm, residential and tourism development.

Leadership from DOC and Northland iwi is crucial to future coastal conservation in Northland. The Fisheries Act 1996 allows for 'iwi fishing caretakers' to be set up to establish conservation measures in mataitai reserves, or taiapure; however, while they enable iwi to manage their customary fishing resources more wisely, they are primarily aimed at tangata whenua better regulating *their* fishing, rather than achieving marine conservation per se. The serious deficiencies in the Marine Reserves legislation have

Mangrove forests are a key ecosystem in coastal Northland as wetland habitats for rarer indigenous coastal birds like banded rail, brown teal and bittern.

now been addressed in the government's December 2005 'Marine Protected Areas: Policy and Implementation Plan' (see Ch.16, p.309), but government itself needs to be far more proactive in the identification of a representative 10 per cent of Northland's coastline and marine ecosystems.

Some coastal conservation actions need to occur now, as matters of priority. These include DOC making greater effort to develop partnerships with landowners surrounding the wetlands and mangroves of Parengarenga, Rangaunu, Hokianga, Whangarei and Kaipara harbours, so that the areas may be fenced off and their fragile margins protected from wandering stock. Another priority is to attempt to purchase natural dunelands and wetlands on the Karikari Peninsula, a beautiful area which has long been the scene of conflict between conservation and inappropriate tourism development. Remaining coastal vegetation sequences at Waikare, Tapuwae, Ngunguru, Ahipara and Waipoua are another priority for acquisition. Finally, the use of the Conservation Act 1987 to create conservation parks on key coastal localities could bring recreational users into a more fruitful conservation partnership in managing a coastal landscape cherished by all parties. A case in point is the Kaipara Harbour, which supports around 30,000 wading birds, many migrating enormous distances from Siberia and Alaska. A Kaipara Harbour Conservation Park could assist in regulating off-road vehicles and dogs, which are causing problems for the breeding of Caspian terns, fairy terns, New Zealand dotterel and many other indigenous shorebirds, especially around the key habitats of Papakanui Spit, Tapora Bank and Pouto Peninsula.

A Kermadec Islands Marine Reserve World Heritage Site

The Kermadec Islands have had more than 800 years of human contact, and the Polynesian archaeological relics are of great importance because they illustrate another distinct phase of the adaptation of the Polynesian culture to the Aotearoa environment. Attempts at European settlement began nearly 200 years ago, after whalers realised that the islands lay within the seasonal migration route for sperm whales. The whalers unfortunately introduced goats to Raoul and Macauley islands to provide food for their whaling bases. Shipping contact also eventually brought the Norway rat and cats, whose disastrous impact on the wildlife added to that already caused by the Polynesian navigators' introduction of the Pacific rat/kiore. The introduced predators multiplied rapidly, and the ill-advised, if colourful and courageous, family settlements of Sunday Island (as Raoul was known) led to the further introduction of sheep and cattle – and their unwelcome companions, exotic weeds and fire. The New Zealand government annexed the islands in 1887 and eventually evacuated the last settler in 1937, having lost patience with the last of many ill-conceived attempts to farm subtropical produce for export to the New Zealand mainland. Fortunately, the islands were given strict protection as a nature reserve in 1934 and then, in 1990, the outstanding marine environment was protected as the 748,000 ha Kermadec Islands Marine Reserve – the second largest protected area in the country (after Fiordland National Park). Steady progress has been made in the removal of weeds and pests from the islands in the group. A landmark was achieved in 2004 with the eradication of rats and cats from Raoul Island.

The Kermadec marine environment and diversity of seabirds matches that of New Zealand's subantarctic islands as the most pristine in the country because of

Parengarenga Harbour is the northernmost estuary in New Zealand, and probably the largest one remaining in a natural state.

an historic lack of exploitation. With mammalian pests eradicated and the likelihood that the remaining weeds on Raoul Island will be eradicated within a couple of years, there is now a strong case for listing the Kermadec Islands, the surrounding Kermadec Islands Marine Reserve and some of the seamounts along the Kermadec Ridge as a World Heritage site. Their underwater volcanic landforms, marine ecosystems, and land flora exhibiting the adaptive evolution of distinctive Kermadec species are indeed of 'outstanding universal value'.

Mainland Islands in Northland

Close to Waipoua lies Trounson Kauri Park Scenic Reserve, a 586 ha remnant of superb mature kauri forest which is one of six mainland islands managed by DOC. Trounson, like Waipoua, is an important North Island brown kiwi habitat, and intensive control of possums, rodents, cats, stoats and hedgehogs within Trounson since 1996 has yielded impressive results. The kiwi chick survival rate has increased to 85 per cent, with more than 200 birds now estimated to thrive within the reserve; even more apparent are the large flocks of kukupa. The pest-control lessons learned at experimental sites like Trounson are of enormous value because they can be transferred to other forest habitats throughout Northland.

The topography of Northland is well suited to the mainland island concept. The volcanic upland plateaux are forested islands which, although large, are capable of being fenced. The long, narrow coastal peninsulas, such as Cape Brett, Whangaruru and Whangarei, are ideally suited to predator fencing at their narrowest points. Successful

The Four Sisters, a stately and graceful group of large kauri trees, are one of the more popular attractions in Waipoua Forest Sanctuary.

A public discussion paper was widely distributed, public submissions sought, and an investigation commissioned of 47 separate land units (all administered by DOC and totalling 105,249 ha). The Northland Conservancy of DOC eventually reported its favourable findings back to the NZ Conservation Authority in July 1992 – five years after the original proposal. The Northland Kauri National Park envisaged was indeed bold, for its 'cluster' concept (i.e. a collection of geographically separate but thematically related areas) was a first for New Zealand's internationally regarded national park system.

Public expectations for a national park were initially high, for the overwhelming majority of submissions supported its establishment. But for the past 15 years the proposal has become hopelessly bogged down in the tortuous political process of settling the claims and grievances lodged by Tai Tokerau iwi with the Waitangi Tribunal. Most tangata whenua have stated that their support for a national park is conditional on satisfactory resolution of their claims – which seem to progress through the tribunal with the pace of a kauri snail! The Northland Kauri National Park concept is a sound one and it is to be hoped that vision and energy can once again be found to progress it. The widely endorsed Ngai Tahu settlement (covering 90 per cent of the South Island) stands as a successful model for tangata whenua and the Crown to move forward in partnership and conserve our natural taonga. In Northland, however, there are dozens of disparate Tai Tokerau iwi claims still to be resolved, and it is hard not to be pessimistic about the eventual outcome for conservation.

examples of community-supported kiwi recovery zones have already been developed through intensive predator trapping (without the cost of fencing) at Bream Head and The Nook Peninsula near the entrance to Whangarei Harbour, and on the Russell Peninsula in the Bay of Islands. At North Cape, the unique serpentine shrubland in the scientific reserve (see above) was being degraded by fire, weeds and animal browsing. With the support of the landowners, the Muriwhenua Corporation, a 2.5 km long electric animal-exclusion fence was erected on private land across the neck of the North Cape isthmus. The fence not only excludes feral horses and cattle, it also increases the prospect of achieving real control of rabbits and possums. Now the only remaining significant threats are two introduced weeds – pampas grass and hakea – which unfortunately thrive on ultramafic soils.

A Northland Kauri National Park

The concept of a Northland Kauri National Park had been around since the establishment of Waipoua Kauri Sanctuary, but the first proposal to be based on discrete forests was advanced by Federated Mountain Clubs of NZ in July 1987 as a fitting way to celebrate the National Parks Centennial. The idea was quickly supported by Forest & Bird, the Northland National Parks and Reserves Board, and a large proportion of Auckland's urban population.

Known as kukupa by northern Maori (and as kereru further south), the New Zealand pigeon (*Hemiphaga novaeseelandiae*) is one of the more common forest birds in Northland. It plays a very important ecological role as a major disperser of seeds from fruits it has ingested, especially those which are too large to be eaten by smaller birds (e.g., miro, puriri, karaka, tawa and taraire).

CHAPTER THREE

AUCKLAND, COROMANDEL, WAIKATO

New Zealand's most populous city – Auckland – straddles a narrow volcanic isthmus which joins Northland to the rest of the North Island. To the east lie Waitemata Harbour and all the islands of the Hauraki Gulf. The deeply indented eastern Auckland coastline from Cape Rodney to the Firth of Thames is a delightful landscape of rocky headlands and peninsulas, small sandy beaches and mangrove-fringed estuaries, its waters sheltered by the out-thrust arm of the Coromandel Peninsula and Great Barrier Island and several degrees warmer than those of the wilder west coast. In sharp contrast, westerly winds sweep the Tasman Sea coastline in the west, pounding surf against the volcanic buttresses of the Waitakere Range and extending a smooth line of 'ironsand' duneland all the way from the Kawhia Harbour, past the mouth of the Waikato River, to the headlands enclosing the Kaipara Harbour.

Most remaining forested hill country lies along the eastern margin of the region, in a line from the Barrier Islands, through the Coromandel Range, to the Kaimai Range. There are no alpine environments, but the heights of Mt Hauturu (722 m), Mt Hobson/Hirakimata (621 m), Mt Moehau (892 m), Table Mountain (846 m) and Mt Te Aroha (953 m) attest to the rugged nature of this volcanic spine of andesitic and rhyolitic peaks and ranges. A number of extinct volcanoes, such as Karioi (756 m), Pirongia (959 m) and Maungatautari (797 m), are prominent landmarks in western and southern Waikato. However, they are younger and isolated cones (albeit deeply eroded), remaining as precious forested islands of indigenous biodiversity surrounded by the rolling pastoral loamlands of the lower Waipa and middle Waikato Rivers. The Waitakere Range is also of volcanic origin, the eroded remnant

of the huge andesitic 'Waitakere Volcano' which began to form on the floor of the Tasman Sea about 22 million years ago. In comparison, the basaltic lava flows, cratered scoria cones, tuff rings and ash deposits of the 50 or so volcanoes underlying Auckland City are very much younger – most erupted only 50,000 to 10,000 years ago. Although some of Auckland's volcanic cones have been quarried away, many remain as city landmarks – steep-sided scoria cones like Mt Wellington and Mt Eden, or gently sloping shield volcanoes like One Tree Hill/Maungakiekie, Rangitoto Island or Brown's Island/Motukorea which, with its scoria cones, tuff ring and lava flows extending undersea, is a whole Auckland volcanic system in miniature.

Estuaries and freshwater wetlands are very important natural landscapes in the Waikato. The Hauraki Plains and the Waikato Basin are dotted with shallow lakes and wetlands, while the Aotea and Kawhia harbours in the west, and the Firth of Thames, are very significant wildlife habitats. The Maniapoto karst country in the south-west is a landscape of outstanding ecological significance, adding another dimension to the geological and biological diversity of the region. In the south, a line roughly along latitude 38°S, from Kawhia to Whakatane in the Bay of Plenty, is an interesting botanical boundary – the southern boundary of a number of northern plants like kauri, mangrove and tawhero, and the northern boundary of kamahi and silver beech. Most kauri forest in the region occurred on the deeply weathered clay soils of the Waitakere, Hunua, Coromandel and Kaimai ranges and Great Barrier Island. The larger trees were logged long ago, but vigorous regeneration of young kauri is widespread throughout the remaining protected forests, especially on Great Barrier and

Rangitoto Island, a gently sloping shield volcano formed through basaltic lava eruptions around 600 years ago, is the best known natural feature in Auckland's Waitemata Harbour.

AUCKLAND, COROMANDEL, WAIKATO

0   25   50   75km

TANGIHUA RANGE

Dargaville

Ruawai

Bream Head

Hen and Chickens Is.

Mokohinau Is.

Taranga Is.

Whangapoua Estuary

Rakitu (Arid Is.)

Te Paparahi Conservation Area

Bryderwyn

Mangawhai Heads

Wairoa River

Kaipara Harbour

Papakanui Spit

Pouto Peninsula

Wellsford

Leigh

Cape Rodney -
Okakari Point
Marine Reserve

Cape Rodney

Mt Hauturu

Boulder
Beach

Kaikoura Is.

Hauturu
(Little Barrier Is.)

Mt Hobson / Hirakimata

Kaitoke Swamp

Great Barrier Island / Aotea

Warkworth

Kawau Is.

Motuora Is.

Fletcher Bay
Sugar Loaf, The Pinnacles

Cuvier Is.

Moehau

Coromandel Peninsula

Helensville

Tiritiri Matangi Is.

Long Bay - Okura
Marine Reserve

Waitemata
Harbour

Waiheke Is.

Waikawau Bay

MOEHAU RANGE

Mercury Islands

Red Mercury Is.

Motuto Pt

Middle Is.

Motu Manawa - Pollen Is.
Marine Reserve

Rangitoto Is.

Motutapu Is.

Coromandel

Castle Rock

Mercury Bay

Shakespeare Cliff
Cathedral Cove

Whitianga

Muriwai Beach
Moutara Is., Oaia Is.

O'Neill Bay
Te Henga Wetland
Te Henga / Bethells Beach

Whites Beach
Piha Beach
Lion Rock, Taitomo Cave, The Gap

Karekare Beach

Waitakere R.

AUCKLAND

WAITAKERE
RANGE

Piha

Motukorea
(Brown's Is.)

Te Matuku
Marine Reserve

Whanganui-a-Hei (Cathedral Cove)
Marine Reserve

CORMANDEL RANGE

Table Mountain
Tauranikau
The Pinnacles

Pauanui

Whatipu

Manukau Harbour

Mt Eden
One Tree Hill
Mt Wellington

HUNUA
RANGE

Firth of Thames

Kauaeranga R.

Hikuai

Broken Hills

Kaiaua

Thames

Miranda

Kopu

Pukekohe

Whangamarino
Wetland

Meremere

Piako R.

Waihou R.

Tuhua
Marine Reserve

Waikato River

Rangiriri

L. Whangape

L. Waikare

HAURAKI PLAINS

Paeroa

Waitekauri R.

Waihi

Karangahake
Gorge

Mayor Island / Tuhua

Huntly

Te Aroha

Te Aroha

Tauranga
Harbour

WAIKATO BASIN

Morrinsville

Ngaruawahia

KAIMAI RANGE

Tauranga

N

Raglan

Kariori

HAMILTON

HAMILTON
BASIN

Matamata

Mangatotara
Strm

Otawa

Cambridge

Hinuera Valley

Gannet Island
/ Karewa

Bridal Veil
Falls

Pokaka R.

Waipa R.

L. Ngaroto

Otanewainuku

Te Awamutu

Maungatautari

Mangorewa R.

Aotea Harbour

Pirongia

Putararu

Ngongotaha Strm

Kawhia

MAMAKU
PLATEAU

Kawhia Harbour

L. Arapuni

Lake
Rotorua

L. Okareka

Taharoa Dunelands

Ngongotaha

Rotorua

Whakarewarewa
Geysers

L. Tikitapu

MANIAPOTO
KARST

Otorohanga

KING COUNTRY

Waitomo
Caves

Tokoroa

1. Little Barrier Island Nature Reserve
2. Te Paparahi Conservation Area
3. Tiritiri Matangi Island Scientific Reserve
4. Northland Forest Park
5. Coromandel Forest Park
6. Goldie Bush Scenic Reserve
7. Te Henga Recreation Reserve
8. Kopuatai Wetland Management Reserve
9. Kaimai–Mamuku Forest Park
10. Pirongia Forest Park
11. Aotea Heads Scientific Reserve
12. Karewa / Gannet Island Wildlife Sanctuary
13. Te Kauri Park Scenic Reserve
14. Maungatautari Mountain Scenic Reserve

in the Coromandel/Kaimai ranges. Many kauri dams and other relics of the destructive water-powered 'kauri drives' remain, protected (and sometimes restored) as historical features but also reminding us of the highly exploitative nature of New Zealand's pioneer timber industry.

Although the Auckland–Coromandel–Waikato mainland is intensively farmed and is New Zealand's most populous region (with over 40 per cent of our total population), it nevertheless has an impressive network of regional parks, forest parks and other protected areas. There are no large national parks or wilderness areas, but the extensive marine ecosystems and the outer islands of the Hauraki Gulf – especially Hauturu/Little Barrier, Great Barrier/Aotea, Cuvier, and the Mokohinau Islands – contain some of the most important biodiversity in the country.

Waves breaking over a rocky inter-tidal shore platform north of Piha on Auckland's wild west coast.

AUCKLAND'S WILD WEST COAST: MURIWAI TO WHATIPU

The western slopes of the Waitakere Ranges have been carved by the pounding waves of the Tasman Sea into what is popularly called 'Auckland's wild west coast'. The 25 km of scenic coastline between Muriwai and Whatipu at the entrance to the Manukau Harbour features a number of dramatic headlands, stacks, sea arches and blowholes, all eroded in the weakly consolidated volcanic conglomerate and breccia. Lion Rock, The Gap and Taitomo Cave at Piha are some of the best known of these landmarks. Here a variety of inter-tidal rock platforms, pools and crevices, boulders and reefs shelter a wonderful diversity of marine life – mussels, whelks, anemones and swirling strands of

The critically endangered Maui's dolphin (*Cephalorhynchus hectori maui*) is found in the waters off Auckland's west coast. It is the world's smallest dolphin and its population is estimated at only about 150, making it New Zealand's rarest dolphin. To conserve this highly vulnerable subspecies of Hector's dolphin, set netting has been banned in North Island west coast waters from Maunganui Bluff near Waipoua Forest in Northland to Pariokariwa Point in northern Taranaki (STEVE DAWSON/NZ WHALE & DOLPHIN TRUST).

bull kelp up to 25 m in length. The rocky sections of coastline separate a string of black ironsand beaches – some, like Muriwai, Bethells/Te Henga, Piha and Karekare, accessible and popular for swimming and surfing; others, like O'Neill Bay and Whites Beach, small and remote, classic west coast beaches nestled into the arms of former volcanic craters and dykes. At Whatipu, so much sand has accumulated in the last 80 years that the beach has moved about a kilometre westwards, leaving an extensive sand flat dotted with freshwater ponds frequented by herons, shags and ducks. Small native herbs colonise the damp flats between the dunes, and the mobile fore-dunes carry the largest expanse of the native sand-binding grasses, spinifex and the golden pingao, remaining in the Auckland region.

Most of the Waitakere Ranges are protected within the 16,000 ha Waitakere Ranges Regional Park, and in the smaller Muriwai Regional Park and Te Henga/Goldies Bush reserves. The interior of the ranges still retains the original forest character – large rimu, rata, totara, miro, kahikatea and, in Cascade Kauri Park, the best mature kauri

forest remaining in the area. Closer to the coast, the forest contains more coastal trees, like puriri, karaka, kohekohe, whau, tree fern and nikau palm, with pohutukawa clinging to the cliff edges. Te Henga/Bethells Swamp covers 80 ha in the lower reaches of the Waitakere River, making it the largest coastal freshwater wetland near Auckland.

The Waitakere Ranges are notable for their diverse fauna of land snails, some (such as the kauri snail) rare or uncommon. The best-known wildlife attraction is the so-called Takapu Refuge, two headlands just south of Muriwai Beach which were fenced off by the local Forest & Bird branch to protect a breeding colony of Australasian gannets/takapu.

The stitchbird or hihi (*Notiomystis cincta*) is the rarest of New Zealand's three honeyeaters (the other two are the bellbird and tui). This bird on Hauturu/Little Barrier Island is a male in the 'alert' stance (ROD MORRIS).

The gannets spread to the Muriwai mainland in 1979 when their expanding numbers had exhausted the nesting sites on nearby Oaia and Motutara islands (also shared with nesting spotted shags, red-billed gulls and white-fronted terns). The gannet colony now includes more than 1000 birds during the peak of the breeding season, and it is easily the most accessible of the three mainland New Zealand colonies of this most attractive bird (the other two being Cape Kidnappers and Farewell Spit). Now each year more than a million people visit Muriwai Regional Park, a paradise for surfers and birdwatchers alike.

RANGITOTO AND THE BARRIER ISLANDS

Rangitoto is a forested emerald set in the turquoise Waitemata, lying only 4 km, but a world away, from the shops and cafes of St Heliers and Kohimarama. Its origin, age, shape and vegetation make it simply unique among New Zealand's islands. In its shape it is a miniature version of the great shield volcanoes of Mauna Loa and Mauna Kea on the island of Hawaii – except that Mauna Loa is still very active. Rangitoto is the largest and youngest of Auckland's basaltic volcanoes, roughly circular, and with a land area of 2333 ha protected by DOC as a scenic reserve. Its gentle slopes consist mostly of rough (aa-type) lava flows erupted about 600 years ago, while the 269 m summit consists of a steeper-sided scoria cone with a perfect 60 m deep crater.

The doyen of our pioneering plant ecologists, Leonard Cockayne, considered Rangitoto to carry 'one of the most remarkable plant associations in New Zealand'. Returning to the analogy with Hawaii, the inhospitable lava-fields of both Hawaii and Rangitoto are colonised by similar *Metrosideros* species – what we call 'pohutukawa' on Rangitoto (although most of the trees are hybrids with northern rata) and the Hawaiians call 'ohia'. Yet the flora of Rangitoto is unexpectedly rich and interesting for such a small and inhospitable island: nearly 230 indigenous vascular plants (including 50 families of flowering plants, and over 40 ferns and 20 orchids); mangroves that grow directly on the basalt lava; and a number of plants (like puka, northern rata, orchids and ferns) that usually grow as epiphytes on trees, here growing directly on the 'soil-less' lava.

Hauturu/Little Barrier Island, the deeply dissected 2,817 ha remnant of an andesitic volcano, is an imposing sight in the outer Hauraki Gulf because of its steep slopes and height (722 m). The island has the honour of being the first legally protected nature reserve in the country (in 1895), and for more than a century it has served as a key sanctuary for some of our most threatened wildlife, especially tuatara, wetapunga, stitchbird and bats. Indeed, the island is considered to be a haven for more endangered bird species than any other island in New Zealand. Three features contribute to its conservation significance: its isolation from the mainland (it lies 22 km ENE of Cape Rodney); an unbroken forest cover, most of which has never been logged or browsed; and the absence of Norway rats and ship rats. The forest is the best altitudinal sequence of indigenous vegetation in northern New Zealand, from gnarled pohutukawa at sea level, through unusual associations of kauri, tawa and hard beech, to a cloud forest where filmy ferns and mosses festoon the branches of tawhero and tawa trees. Little Barrier's plant diversity is one of the highest in the country for such a small island – over 370

ABOVE The wetapunga or Little Barrier giant weta (*Deinacrida heteracantha*) is one of the most impressive of New Zealand's insects, an ancient taxon which has evolved over the millennia into large, heavy and flightless forms because of the lack of large predators (ROD MORRIS). RIGHT The Boulder Beach is a well known landmark on the coast of Hauturu/Little Barrier Island. Beyond the fringing ferns and shrubs lies the island's remarkable unbroken sea-to-island crest sequence of forest – flowering pohutukawa at sea level rising to an unusual association of kauri, tawa and hard beech.

ABOVE Gnarled pohutukawa (*Metrosideros excelsa*) in bloom on the Hauturu/Little Barrier Island coastline. Along with our rata species, the pohutukawa is the best known New Zealand member of the myrtle family, its crimson flowers heralding the arrival of summer and Christmas. *Metrosideros* is very much a circum-Pacific genus, its 50 or so species spreading as far north as the Ogasawara (Bonin) Islands and Hawaii but also touching the southern continental tips of Africa and South America. RIGHT Mt Hobson/Hirakimata is the highest point (621 m) on Great Barrier Island/Aotea. The old volcanic rocks around the peak carry an unusual stunted montane conifer forest association of kauri, yellow-silver pine, and monoao.

higher plants, including 90 varieties of fern – yet it lacks common plants like putaputaweta, cabbage tree and most of the podocarp trees.

The island has served as an important site for the translocation of fauna threatened by habitat loss and predation on the mainland. The elimination of cats in 1980 was a major advance and allowed the reintroduction of saddleback, kokako and kakapo. Sadly kakapo did not breed, possibly because the rugged topography restricted their 'track and bowl' network, and the Pacific rat/kiore were able to prey on eggs and chicks. Consequently, in 1998, DOC spirited the Little Barrier kakapo off to the more easily managed sanctuary islands of Maud and Codfish/Whenua Hou. After a long and difficult dialogue with tangata whenua, in 2004 DOC commenced the poisoning of kiore, the last significant mammalian predator, and these rats are now considered to have been eliminated.

Great Barrier Island/Aotea is the largest island (28,500 ha) lying off the North Island. It too is primarily of volcanic origin, a mixture of andesite, rhyolite and ignimbrite from eruptions 5–15 million years ago. Essentially the island is an extension of the Coromandel Peninsula, separated only since sea levels rose at the end of the Last Glaciation. The western coastline is deeply indented, a spectacular landscape of cliffed headlands, islands and sheltered harbours. In contrast, the eastern side of the island is blessed with many fine sandy beaches. Of the 60 per cent of the island which is protected as conservation land (an area of 18,500 ha), most of it lies within two large forest blocks: Te Paparahi and the central area around Mt Hobson/Hirakimata (621 m). The Te Paparahi block (3300 ha) is a wilderness of unlogged forest (because it contains little kauri) with a canopy of taraire, tawa, kohekohe and occasional northern rata, rewarewa, puriri and rimu. This undisturbed forest is a habitat for kokako, black petrel, kaka, long-tailed bat, Hochstetter's frog and Great Barrier skink. Much of the central block was logged for its kauri (which is now regenerating profusely). The summit of Hirakimata is unmodified, however, and carries a unusual low-stature montane conifer forest of kauri, yellow-silver pine (*Lepidothamnus intermedius*) and monoao (*Halocarpus kirkii*). Two other wetland habitats of high natural character are Whangapoua Estuary (one of the least modified in New Zealand) and Kaitoke Swamp, a 266 ha refuge for rare birds like bittern, brown teal, spotless crake, banded rail and fernbird.

Great Barrier Island/Aotea is of outstanding significance for conservation because it is the largest area in the country that remains free of possums, mustelids and deer,

The North Island saddleback or tieke (*Philesturnus carunculatus rufusater*) was eliminated from the North Island mainland by 1910, mainly through the combined predation of rats, cats and mustelids. Since 1964, birds from the surviving population on Hen Island/Taranga have been successfully transferred to a number of island sanctuaries, including Hauturu/Little Barrier Island (ROD MORRIS).

except for the latter on Kaikoura Island (since this island was purchased as a public reserve in 2005 through the Nature Heritage Fund, the Motu Kaikoura Trust has been working to eradicate all pests and establish a sanctuary for endangered indigenous species). Great Barrier/Aotea has 50 threatened higher plants and one of the most diverse populations of lizards (13 species) in the country. The island is also the stronghold of the brown teal/pateke, one of the world's rarest ducks; around two-thirds of the estimated remaining population of 1200 is found in Whangapoua Estuary and other wetlands around the island.

The marine environment around the island has come under increasing pressure from fishing and, since 1991, DOC has been trying to get a substantial marine reserve established off the north-east coast. The original Arid Island/Rakitu proposal was small (4050 ha) and was withdrawn in 1994. In March 2003, a substantially larger proposal (52,772 ha), extending from the north-east coast out to the 12 nautical mile limit of the territorial sea, was proposed by DOC to encompass eight major marine ecological types (including the Whangapoua Estuary). In June 2005, the Minister of Conservation approved a slightly smaller reserve area (50,100 ha), with the Whangapoua Estuary and Beach excluded because of their importance to the local people. So, when the Minister of Fisheries eventually gives his concurrence to the Great Barrier Island/Aotea Marine Reserve, it will be far larger than any of the existing

The bellbird or korimako (*Anthornis melanura*), seen here on a yellow-flowered *Metrosideros*, is a common forest bird on the offshore islands of the Auckland and Coromandel region. The conservation vision of 'restoring the dawn chorus' refers to the famous chorus of impressive and melodious bell-like notes issuing from bellbirds at dawn and dusk in localities where they survive in high numbers (ROD MORRIS).

marine reserves around the New Zealand mainland, and even larger than the five existing small marine reserves in this region put together.

COROMANDEL PENINSULA AND MERCURY ISLANDS

In evaluating New Zealand's remaining wilderness heritage, the Coromandel Peninsula receives a very mixed report card. On the one hand, it is celebrated for the scenic quality and recreational attractions of its coastline, a seemingly endless succession of rocky headlands, sandy beaches and sheltered harbours. On the other hand, the peninsula contains some of the most degraded forests in the country, with less than 0.5 per cent of the original kauri forest remaining unlogged (mostly in the 482 ha Manaia Forest Sanctuary). In addition, most of the original coastal forest and dense podocarp forest of the peninsula have gone, and the indigenous dunelands and saline wetlands are severely depleted. The steepland and montane forests (associations of miro, Hall's totara, toatoa, kaikawaka, tanekaha, kamahi and quintinia), however, are well protected within the 71,897 ha Coromandel Forest Park which extends along most of the rugged spine of the Coromandel Range. The largest of the park's six ecological areas, Moehau (3634 ha), is a northern outlier, protecting the upper slopes of the Moehau Range which rises as a forested island sheer from the sea. The undulating, boggy crest of the Moehau Range carries the northernmost subalpine shrublands and herbfields in the country, with a large number of plants that are far more typical of the axial greywacke ranges far to the south-east. Because of Moehau's physical integrity and isolation from the rest of the Coromandel Peninsula, DOC has set up the Moehau Kiwi Sanctuary and volunteers have made considerable strides in protecting this population of the North Island brown kiwi. The forests of the park are also the habitat of the smallest of New Zealand's ancient and unusual amphibians, Archey's frog (*Leiopelma archeyi*). At lower altitudes, however, the protected-area network is quite inadequate to conserve what remains of indigenous coastal vegetation (including the dunelands and wetlands). There is only one small (840 ha) marine reserve, Te Whanganui-a-Hei, around Cathedral Cove in Mercury Bay.

Yet the geodiversity of the Coromandel is quite amazing. Its ancient volcanic rocks have made it a geomorphologist's and mineralogist's paradise – the latter exploited by a mining industry that still survives in Waihi, and which at various times laid waste to the landscapes and waterways of Broken Hills, the Waitekauri Valley, the Karangahake Gorge, and Mt Te Aroha in the northern part of the adjacent 39,648 ha Kaimai–Mamaku Forest Park. Geological phenomena account for many of the popular landmarks around the Coromandel coastline:

- remnants of old volcanoes, like Sugar Loaf and The Pinnacles east of Fletcher Bay;
- spectacular jointed columns, like the vertical basalt columns at Motuto Point, or the clusters of rhyolitic columns and 'stepping stones' south of Pauanui;
- many impressive wave-cut cliffs, caves and arches in the thick white ignimbrite deposits east of Whitianga (Shakespeare Cliff, Cathedral Cove and the Big Bay blowholes).

The crest of the Coromandel Range has also been eroded into no less impressive landforms over the millennia:

Sunrise in late summer touches Te Hoho Rock, one of the impressive ignimbrite stacks on the coastal margin of the Te Whanganui-a Hei (Cathedral Cove) Marine Reserve on the Coromandel Coast (HARLEY BETTS). The name Cathedral Cove was bestowed because of the striking landforms of caves and archways, reminiscent of a cathedral, eroded by the sea in the Hahei Dome, one of several rhyolite lava domes extruded long ago from a volcanic vent.

The Waikato freshwater wetlands are an important habitat of the native longfin eel (*Anguilla dieffenbachii*). The longfin eel is a top predator in freshwater ecosystems, preying on koura and indigenous fish like galaxiids, bullies and young eels (ROD MORRIS).

- the volcanic plugs now towering as monoliths near the Kopu–Hikuai Road;
- the sheer walls of Castle Rock;
- the spectacular landmarks around the head of the Kauaeranga Valley – the Kauaeranga Gorge itself, Tauranikau, The Pinnacles and the remarkably flat top of Table Mountain (probably the surface of an ancient lava lake).

Red Mercury Island, and the five small islands in the Mercury Islands group, are all volcanic in origin and strictly protected as nature reserves because of their high value for wildlife conservation. Marine birds have transferred vast amounts of nutrients to their topsoils, creating conditions ideal for the development of unusual milk tree and wharangi–mahoe forest associations, as well as a diverse and prolific fauna of invertebrates and lizards. One of the small islands, Middle Island, is only 13 ha in area but it is the habitat of some remarkable rare animals, such as the omnivorous and formidable-looking Mercury Island tusked giant weta, three species of gecko and seven species of skink (including the rare Whitaker's skink and the robust skink). Other notable Mercury Island fauna are tuatara and a large carnivorous centipede capable of feeding on small lizards.

THE FRESHWATER WETLANDS OF THE WAIKATO

Throughout its history the Waikato River has carried large quantities of tephra from the volcanic eruptions in the central North Island (see Ch.4, p.77) and deposited this material as alluvium in the Waikato lowlands. At times the river flowed to the Firth of Thames via the Hinuera Valley and the Hauraki Plains; at other times (especially for the last 19,000 years) it has flowed close to its present course through the Hamilton Basin. As the river wandered across these lowlands, it deposited alluvium which blocked off small local streams, ponding them to form small peat lakes (like the present-day Lake Ngaroto). In the lower Waikato Valley, larger lakes developed like Lake Waikare (the largest, at 3440 ha), along with extensive areas of raised bog and fen-type wetlands.

The larger Waikato bog and fen wetlands are of major conservation value. Although 70 per cent of Waikato's wetlands have been drained for agriculture during the past century, the 30 per cent remaining in a natural state is much better than the depressingly low national average of only 10 per cent. The unique feature of the Waikato wetlands is that they are mainly restiad bogs – so named for their dominant vegetation, two jointed rushes (wire rush and cane rush), members of the Restionaceae family. The Kopuatai Peat Dome, between the Piako and Waihou rivers on the lower Hauraki Plains, remains as the largest and most natural of the peat bogs in the region, and possibly the whole North Island. DOC protects most of this wetland as the Kopuatai Wetland Management Reserve (9180 ha) which, along with another 1000 ha of surrounding buffer wetland, is listed as a 'wetland of international importance' under the Ramsar Convention. The 7290 ha Whangamarino Wetland in the lower Waikato Valley near Meremere is another of New Zealand's small number of 'wetlands of international importance', but it is of the fen type – younger (about 1800 years old compared with around 15,000 years for Kopuatai), and with more nutrients and less acidity in its water source.

The tidal flats around the southern shores of the Firth of Thames between Miranda and Thames make up the third (7800 ha) 'wetland of international importance' in the Waikato region. This estuarine wetland supports up to 40,000 birds, many of them migratory wading birds, such as sandpipers, dotterels, knots, plovers, turnstones and godwits, as well as New Zealand's own oystercatchers, pied stilts and unique wrybill. The section of coastline northwards from Miranda to Kaiaua is a geomorphic enigma of international significance, where a series of stranded

TOP Bar-tailed godwits (*Limosa lapponica*), the commonest Arctic waders to migrate to New Zealand, flock on a shell bank. They congregate in flocks of up to 10,000 each summer in the Manukau Harbour and Firth of Thames (ROD MORRIS). LEFT An adult male New Zealand dotterel (*Charadrius obscurus*), an endemic shore bird which is very vulnerable to human disturbance of its breeding sites along the Northland, Auckland and Waikato coastlines (ROD MORRIS). ABOVE The terek sandpiper (*Tringa terek*), a migrant from the Baltic coasts and Siberia, is a rare visitor to the estuaries of Northland and Auckland, the Manawatu River, and Farewell Spit.

The Waitomo Caves are the best known of the many caves, shafts and natural bridges in the Maniapoto karst of the King Country in south-west Waikato.

beach ridges have formed on top of swamp deposits in a tectonically stable environment.

MANIAPOTO KARST COUNTRY AND TAINUI COAST

The Waitomo Caves and many of the landforms of the Maniapoto karst country in the south-west of the region are an international tourist attraction. But west of the Waipa and Mokau rivers there also lies one of the least-accessible and little-known areas of wild hill country and coastline in the North Island: Pirongia Forest Park, Aotea and Kawhia harbours, the Herangi Range, and the remote Marokopa to Awakino coastline.

The Maniapoto karst country consists of about 100,000 ha of hill country between Otorohanga and the lower Mokau River, where karst landforms have developed in limestone rocks. Because of the commercial reputation of Waitomo Glowworm Cave, Mangapu Cave, Ruakuri Cave and Natural Bridge for guided glowworm viewing and caving adventure, the heritage significance of the Maniapoto karst has often been overlooked. Yet this landscape contains:

- the highest density of polygonal karst yet recognised anywhere in the world;
- the longest cave in the North Island;
- the deepest tomos (shafts) and largest natural bridges in the North Island;
- several endemic plants and invertebrates.

In the past, the management of the Maniapoto karst landscape was fragmented, and some natural features suffered from human impacts, especially the reduction in water quality through forest clearance and farming. Research has shown that the glowworms seem to be quite resilient, even with the current large numbers of visitors (in strictly controlled groups and with a high level of built access structures). Other outstanding features, however, like the unique gypsum speleothems of the Puketiti Flower Cave, are very fragile, and access to this type of karst phenomenon has to be strictly controlled because of its vulnerability.

Pirongia Forest Park (16,773 ha) consists of the deeply eroded and heavily forested old cones of Pirongia (959 m) and Karioi (756 m), the largest of the so-called 'West Waikato Volcanoes'. The mid-altitude forests have a tawa canopy with emergent rimu, while the montane forests on their summits typically contain kaikawaka and podocarps such as miro, Hall's totara and toatoa. Kokako are present on Pirongia and the park is close to the northern limit of the more or less continuous Wanganui–King Country habitat for the North Island brown kiwi. West of Pirongia (and south of Karioi) lie the isolated Aotea and Kawhia harbours, both very important feeding and breeding habitats for native fish and coastal birds, especially waders. Aotea Harbour is more remote than Kawhia, its clear waters contrasting with the less pristine west coast harbours in Northland. The Aotea Dunefield on the northern entrance to the estuary is a nationally important dunefield, supporting a healthy community of the rare sand-binding plant, pingao. An area of 500 ha of this wild coastal landscape is protected as Aotea Heads Scientific Reserve, and large parts of the margins of the estuary are still in coastal forest. Kawhia Harbour and its catchment are an important habitat for a number of threatened birds (bittern, New Zealand dotterel and banded rail), some unusual threatened plants (including the king fern, *Marattia salicina*), and notable for a large number of key fossil sites interpreting the Mesozoic Era in our geological history.

South of Kawhia Harbour lie the Taharoa Dunelands, now greatly modified by mining of their titanomagnetite sands. However, the 50 km of coastline from here to the mouth of the Awakino River is particularly wild. Cliffs

100 m high (reaching 300 m at Moeatoa) straddle the coast, interrupted only by a small number of sandy river mouths, at Marokopa, Kiritehere and Waikawau. Inland from the cliffs, the land rises sharply to the peak of Whareorino and the 700–800 m crest of the Herangi Range. Most of this country is still covered in rimu/tawa, rimu/tawa/beech, and montane podocarp/broadleaf forest and, despite extensive damage from browsing animals there are still opportunities for protecting vegetation sequences from the coast to the subalpine crest of the Herangi Range. Furthermore, these forests are the habitat of a number of

The coastline south of Kawhia Harbour to the mouth of the Awakino River is particularly remote and wild. Much of it is cliffed but this section between the mouth of the Marokopa River and Kiritehere Stream is an excellent coastal walk provided it is traversed around low tide. There are many fossilised clams, mussels and the scallop-like *Monotis* in the sedimentary rocks.

threatened and endangered species, including Archey's and Hochstetter's frogs. This landscape of wild coastline and forest (in both public and Maori land) has high value for remoteness seekers.

THREATS AND CONSERVATION PRIORITIES

Marine Reserves: Potential on Auckland's Wild West Coast

The four small marine reserves in the Auckland region – Cape Rodney–Okakari Point, Long Bay–Okura, Motu Manawa–Pollen Island, and Te Matuku Bay – lie along the eastern coastline or within Waitemata Harbour. There are no marine reserves along Auckland's west coast. Increasing frustration at the inability of local and regional government to protect the marine and coastal values of the west coast led to an exciting marine park conservation initiative in 2001. Since then, a local west coast working group and Forest & Bird have undertaken wide stakeholder consultation on the ideal mix of marine reserve, rahui, mataitai and/or taiapure that would provide strict protection for biodiversity 'hot spots' between Papakanui Spit at the entrance to Kaipara Harbour and the mouth of the Waikato River, while still allowing recreational fishing (excluding set netting) at certain beaches. A key part of the marine park idea is a marine mammal sanctuary extending 12 nautical miles offshore to protect the 100 or so Maui's dolphin, an endangered subspecies of Hector's dolphin and reputedly the smallest dolphin in the world.

Restoration of Key Habitats

Although so much of the natural landscape has been degraded, the region's large population has provided plenty of conservation visionaries and an enthusiastic pool of volunteers who have set about 'restoring the dawn chorus' in a number of key habitats. The outstanding example of successful restoration has been the replacement of former pasture by shrub forest as habitat for the 'open sanctuary' of Tiritiri Matangi Island in the Hauraki Gulf. Here visitors can now experience takahe, saddleback and stitchbird, and the island even has its own supporters' group and trust group directing the restoration. Other Hauraki Gulf island restoration programmes are well established on Motuora and Motutapu. There are many successful programmes on the mainland too. Well-publicised examples are:

- the *Ark in the Park* joint project between Auckland Regional Council, Forest & Bird, other contributing organisations, and hundreds of volunteers – in 1000 ha of Cascades Kauri Park in the Waitakere Ranges. Since 2004, intensive pest control has allowed the re-introduction of whiteheads/popokatea, North Island robins/toutouwai and stitchbirds/hihi;
- pohutukawa rehabilitation all around the Auckland and Coromandel coastline through Project Crimson;
- formation of the National Wetland Trust in the Waikato,

Sundews (*Drosera* spp.) are a group of plants, widespread throughout the Waikato wetlands, that trap insects on their sticky hairs and gradually absorb them.

and its intention of establishing a wetland interpretation centre at Rangiriri;
- replanting kauri on the Coromandel Peninsula through the volunteer efforts of Kauri 2000, and the establishment of a viable kiwi population on the Moehau Range.

The success of these community efforts stems from a symbiosis between enthusiastic local volunteers (often Forest & Bird members, or school groups) and professionals in DOC and local government. Success can breed success, and confidence grows as networks develop and experiences are shared. Consequently, more ambitious projects can be envisaged. One such Waikato project has been the building of a vermin-proof fence around the 3500 ha Maungatautari Scenic Reserve, an 'ecological island' on the forested old volcanic cone of Maungatautari.

A West Waikato Conservation Park (Kawhia to Awakino)

The idea of a conservation park in the ranges of the western King Country was formally proposed to DOC by Forest & Bird in 1989 but it received only lukewarm advocacy in the 1996-2006 Waikato Conservation Management Strategy. The proposed park would recognise the biodiversity and remote recreation values of the forested country extending south from Te Kauri Scenic Reserve (east of Kawhia Harbour) to the Awakino River mouth. It would centre on the Whareorino and Tawarau forests but would ideally involve covenanted Maori land and other private indigenous forests. Walking access along the wild coastline south of Marokopa would be an associated attraction.

Pakoka River plunges 55 m over a resistant band of basalt rock to form the aptly-named Bridal Veil Falls, in Bridal Veil Falls Scenic Reserve between Pirongia Forest Park and Raglan.

ABOVE Pukatea and nikau palm forest interior, Pirongia Forest Park. RIGHT A smooth green stick insect (*Clitarchus laeviusculus*) on lichen, Hauturu/Little Barrier Island (ROD MORRIS). Unlike many overseas adult stick insects, New Zealand stick insects are wingless.

LEFT The threatened endemic brown teal or pateke (*Anas aucklandica*) was formerly widely distributed in wetlands and swamp forests from Northland to Stewart Island/Rakiura. Its stronghold is now on Great Barrier Island/Aotea, with around 1200 thriving in Whangapoua Estuary and other wetlands around the island. Once again, the pateke's decline on the mainland was probably through predation by cats, dogs and mustelids. BELOW The colony of Australasian gannet (*Morus serrator*) at Muriwai spread to the mainland during the 1980s when the breeding sites on adjacent Oaia and Motutara islands were all occupied. Gannet-watching at this very accessible site has become popular with Aucklanders, particularly because of the bird's impressive ability to dive for prey at high speed from heights of 30 m above the surface of the sea.

CHAPTER FOUR

VOLCANIC LANDS OF THE CENTRAL NORTH ISLAND

At the centre of the North Island lies Lake Taupo, the glistening jewel nestling in the navel of the Volcanic Plateau. For Lake Taupo occupies the caldera of the huge Taupo Volcano, a 'super-volcano' which has erupted intermittently for the past 330,000 years and is considered to have produced the largest volcanic eruption on Earth during the last 7000 years. Vulcanicity is the unifying environmental feature of this region, with Lake Taupo lying near the centre of what geologists call the Taupo Volcanic Zone, a rift valley full of volcanic cones and domes, lake-filled calderas and high lava plateaux. This 250 km zone of crustal weakness extends in a line of impressive volcanic landscapes running south-west to north-east from the highpoint of Mt Ruapehu (2797 m) to White Island in the Bay of Plenty. At the geographic extremities of the Taupo Volcanic Zone, the volcanoes of Tongariro National Park and White Island are among the most continuously active in the world. Like the Alpine Fault (see Ch.1, p.11), New Zealand's other great tectonic landform associated with the collision of the Pacific and Australian plates, the Taupo Volcanic Zone is natural heritage of international significance.

Volcanic activity giving rise to the complex of landforms in the Taupo Volcanic Zone probably began about two million years ago. The two main volcanic landmarks in Pureora Forest Park, Titiraupenga and Mt Pureora date from these early eruptions. However, the most extensive landforms on the Volcanic Plateau are not the volcanoes themselves but the sheets of ignimbrite (literally 'fire rock'), formed from the welding together of extremely hot particles of rhyolitic ash ejected at great speed during cataclysmic eruptions as a ground-hugging avalanche of gas and molten lava. These ignimbrite plateaux now border the Taupo Volcanic Zone depression, as the heavily forested Hauhungaroa Range and Mamaku Plateau in the west and the Kaingaroa Plateau in the east. Impressive cliffs of this ignimbrite rock are exposed along the banks of the Waikato River, especially around Lakes Whakamaru and Arapuni.

From these volcanic uplands flow four of the main rivers of the North Island – the Waikato (and its major tributaries, the Tongariro and the Waipa), the Rangitaiki, the Mohaka, and the Whanganui (including two major tributaries, the Ongarue and the Manganui-o-te-Ao). A highly attractive feature of these rivers in their upper reaches is the clarity of their water. Although volcanic ash soils are very prone to erosion if their vegetation cover is removed, their raw, sandy nature ensures that any water turbidity after rainfall is short lived – a key factor in establishing the Volcanic Plateau rivers (and Lake Taupo) as self-sustaining trout fisheries of international repute.

Most of the present-day volcanic activity is concentrated within two locations: Tongariro National Park–Lake Taupo and the Rotorua Basin. At the former, Mt Ruapehu erupted violently throughout the winters of 1995 and 1996 and the Crater Lake refilled to the point where the sudden release of its melt-waters sent an impressive lahar down the Whangaehu River on 18 March 2007. The Rotorua Basin contains the greatest concentration of New Zealand's geothermal phenomena, especially the spectacular range of geysers, fumaroles, hot springs, sinter deposits and mud pools in the Whakarewarewa, Waimangu and Waiotapu geyser fields. In addition, the rhyolitic dome of Mt Tarawera on the south-east margin of the basin was the site of the short-lived but violent Tarawera Eruption in the early hours of 10 June 1886; an event that had devastating human and

Mt Ruapehu during the 1996 series of eruptions.

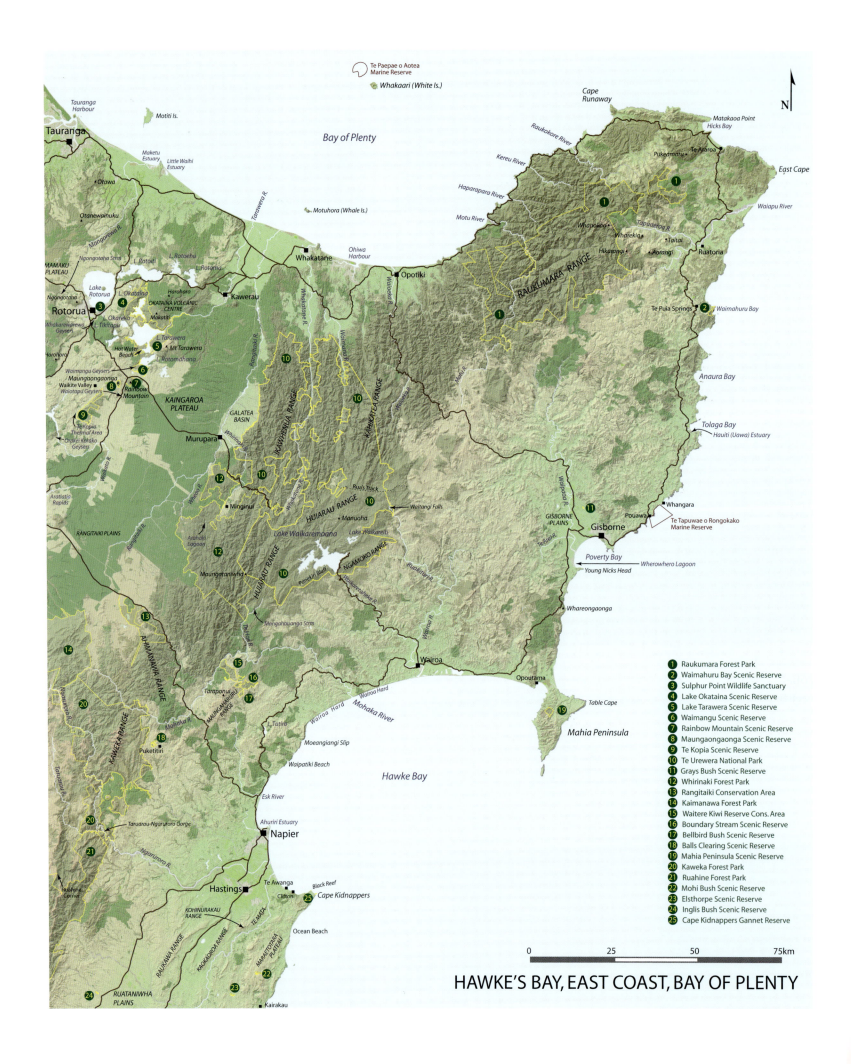

Te Paepae o Aotea
Marine Reserve

Whakaari (White Is.)

Bay of Plenty

Tauranga
Tauranga Harbour

Motiti Is.

Maketu Estuary
Little Waihi Estuary

Otawa

Otanewainuku

MAMAKU PLATEAU

Ngongotaha Stm

Ngongotaha

Rotorua

Lake Rotorua

L. Rotoehu
L. Rotoiti
Rotoma

L. Okataina

OKATAINA VOLCANIC CENTRE

Harohoro

Makatiti

Whakarewarewa Geysers

L. Okareka
L. Tikitapu

Horohoro

Hot Water Beach

L. Tarawera
Mt Tarawera

L. Rotomahana

Waimangu Geysers
Maungaongaonga
Waikite Valley
Waiotapu Geysers

Rainbow Mountain

KAINGAROA PLATEAU

Te Kopia Thermal Area
Orakei Korako Geysers

Aratiatia Rapids

Maketu Estuary

Mongorewa R.

Tarawera R.

Motuhora (Whale Is.)

Whakatane

Kawerau

Opotiki

Whakatane R.

Waioeka R.

Cape Runaway

Raukokore River

Kereu River

Haparapara River

Motu River

Matakaoa Point
Hicks Bay

Te Araroa

Pukeamaru

East Cape

Waiapu River

RAUKUMARA RANGE

Whapokoo
Wharekia
Tapuaeroa R.
Taitai
Hikurangi
Aorangi
Ruatoria

Te Puia Springs
Waimahuru Bay

Anaura Bay

Tolaga Bay
Hauiti (Uawa) Estuary

GALATEA BASIN

Murupara

RANGITAIKI PLAINS

Minginui

Rangitaiki R.

Whirinaki R.

Waiau R.

KAWHINUA RANGE

KAHIKATEA RANGE

Rua's Track

Manuoha

Waitangi Falls

HUIARAU RANGE

Arahaki Lagoon

Lake Waikaremoana

Lake Waikareiti

Maungataniwha

Panekiri Bluff

NGAMOKO RANGE

Ruakituri R.

Waikaretaheke R.

Mohaka River

AHIMANAWA RANGE

Taraponui

MAUNGAHARURU RANGE

Mangahouanga Stm

Tutira

Taharua R.

KAWEKA RANGE

Puketitiri

Taruarau R.

RUAHINE RANGE

Ruahine Corner

Ngaruroro R.

Taruarau-Ngaruroro Gorge

Moeangiangi Slip

Esk River

Waipatiki Beach

Ahuriri Estuary

Napier

Ngaruroro R.

Te Awanga
Clifton
Black Reef
Cape Kidnappers

Ocean Beach

KOHINURAKAU RANGE

TE MATA

RAUKAWA RANGE

KAOKAOROA RANGE

MARAETOTARA PLATEAU

Hastings

RUATANIWHA PLAINS

Kairakau

GISBORNE PLAINS

Gisborne

Te Arai R.

Te Tapuwae o Rongokako
Marine Reserve

Whangara

Pouawa

Poverty Bay
Young Nicks Head
Wherowhero Lagoon

Whareongaonga

Wairoa R.

Wairoa
Opoutama

Table Cape

Mahia Peninsula

Wairoa Hard
Wairoa Hard

Mohaka River

Hawke Bay

1 Raukumara Forest Park
2 Waimahuru Bay Scenic Reserve
3 Sulphur Point Wildlife Sanctuary
4 Lake Okataina Scenic Reserve
5 Lake Tarawera Scenic Reserve
6 Waimangu Scenic Reserve
7 Rainbow Mountain Scenic Reserve
8 Maungaongaonga Scenic Reserve
9 Te Kopia Scenic Reserve
10 Te Urewera National Park
11 Grays Bush Scenic Reserve
12 Whirinaki Forest Park
13 Rangitaiki Conservation Area
14 Kaimanawa Forest Park
15 Waitere Kiwi Reserve Cons. Area
16 Boundary Stream Scenic Reserve
17 Bellbird Bush Scenic Reserve
18 Balls Clearing Scenic Reserve
19 Mahia Peninsula Scenic Reserve
20 Kaweka Forest Park
21 Ruahine Forest Park
22 Mohi Bush Scenic Reserve
23 Elsthorpe Scenic Reserve
24 Inglis Bush Scenic Reserve
25 Cape Kidnappers Gannet Reserve

0   25   50   75km

HAWKE'S BAY, EAST COAST, BAY OF PLENTY

environmental consequences with the loss of more than 150 lives and the destruction of the world-famous Pink and White Terraces (considered at that time to be the best geothermal sinter formations in the world).

The Taupo Volcanic Zone extends out into the waters of the Bay of Plenty beyond Whakatane, and includes the volcanic landmarks of Motuhora/Whale Island and highly active White Island/Whakaari. Pumice (a soft, light-coloured, frothy rhyolitic rock with the appearance of a sponge) was erupted in vast quantities from the Taupo and Rotorua volcanic centres and spread across the plateaux. This friable, unconsolidated pumice was subsequently eroded off the uplands and deposited by river as alluvium in the Waikato Basin and the Bay of Plenty. The Rangitaiki Plains were once dotted with wetlands of very high significance as wildlife habitats, but virtually all have been drained for farm development. The four main estuaries (Tauranga Harbour, Ohiwa Harbour, and the Little Waihi and Maketu estuaries) are the most important remaining wildlife habitats in the Bay of Plenty.

Prior to the arrival of humans, the combined effect of volcanic eruptions, natural fires, coarse pumice soils and a cold winter climate made most of the Volcanic Plateau an inhospitable place for native plants and animals. The harsher sites would have carried a heathland of manuka and monoao, a natural landscape that now remains only as 'frost flats' in a few areas of the upper Rangitaiki, mainly protected in the 5110 ha Rangitaiki Conservation Area. Repeated burning by Polynesian inhabitants maintained this heathland over the drier pumice lands. Attempts to develop pastures on the pumice soils led to stock suffering from the puzzling malady of 'bush sickness', its cause eventually identified by soil surveys in the mid-1930s as soil cobalt, selenium and copper deficiencies which were then rectified with fertilisers. But many of the pumice lands had already been planted with exotic conifers, especially on the Kaingaroa Plateau from 1901 to 1936.

Yet outstanding remnants of the once widespread dense podocarp forests of the central North Island did survive around the margins of the Volcanic Plateau – at Pureora, Whirinaki, Kaimai–Mamaku, Otawa–Otanewainuku, Mangorewa, and on the Erua–Pokaka–Ohakune sector of the Mt Ruapehu ringplain. During the years 1970–1985, three of these forests – Kaimai–Mamaku, Pureora and Whirinaki – became synonymous with a nationwide campaign to preserve the remaining indigenous forests of the North Island from logging. They were literally conservation battlegrounds on which the drama of New Zealanders' hard-

ening attitudes towards traditional timber exploitation was acted out between the NZ Forest Service and local forest communities and the emerging urban-based, activist conservation movement.

TONGARIRO NATIONAL PARK AND TONGARIRO FOREST

Tongariro stands pre-eminent among New Zealand's 14 national parks. Protected within its 79,670 ha is the volcanic 'roof' of the North Island, especially the peaks of Tongariro (1968 m), Ngauruhoe (2291 m) and the highest peak in the North Island, Ruapehu (2797 m). The gifting of the volcanic peaks to all the people of New Zealand by Horonuku Te Heu Heu Tukino of the Ngati Tuwharetoa iwi on 23 September 1887 laid the foundation for New Zealand's first national park – a concept so new that Tongariro was at that time only the fourth national park in the world and the first gifted by an indigenous people. The park is also one of New Zealand's three current World Heritage sites, listed twice on the UNESCO World Heritage list because of its outstanding universal value – first in 1990 as a 'natural property' for its uniquely active composite volcanoes, and again in 1993 as a 'cultural property' because of its significance to tangata whenua as a 'cultural landscape'.

Mt Ruapehu is a large, complex strato-volcano which has been built up from successive eruptions of andesitic lava and tephra over at least 200,000 years. It still carries glacier remnants, although they have greatly diminished in extent over the last 50 years. Ruapehu is the only active volcano in New Zealand to have a lake (Crater Lake) in its summit crater. During periodic eruptions, the waters of the lake are violently ejected as the magma rises in the throat of the volcano; this occurred with the 1945 and 1995 eruptions when the lake completely disappeared. However, the cycle resumes once the eruption begins to subside. Crater Lake is capable of refilling to a level where its impounding tephra barrier can collapse, leading to a lahar flowing down the Whangaehu River (and even spilling over into the Tongariro River, as has occurred historically). The lahar hazard from Mt Ruapehu's crater lake is very significant, with at least 60 lahars flowing down the Whangaehu valley since the 1860s. The most devastating was the one that washed away the Tangiwai rail bridge and passenger train on the night of 24 December 1953, with the loss of 151 lives.

Mt Ngauruhoe is the youngest volcano in the park, being only about 5000 years old, so it still retains its perfect conical shape. It is really a 'daughter cone' of the old Tongariro volcano. Ngauruhoe produced spectacular lava

flows in 1949 and 1954, followed by regular ash eruptions during the mid-1970s. The Tama Lakes at the southern foot of Ngauruhoe are explosion craters formed about 10,000 years ago. Mt Tongariro is a very complex old volcano, with eight craters of different shape and depth. Further north, Lake Rotoaira is impounded by three old volcanic cones – Kakaramea, Tihia and Pihanga, which make up an outlier of the park above the southern shores of Lake Taupo.

The vegetation of Tongariro National Park is a sometimes puzzling mosaic of bare alpine gravelfields, tussock grasslands and mossy herbfields, impenetrable shrublands, and different forest communities dominated by both beech and podocarp trees. The long history of volcanic eruptions is written in this dynamic vegetation pattern, with woody species continuously trying to colonise the bare slopes of tephra and the fire-induced grasslands. Consequently, the volcanic landscape is very susceptible to weed invasion: witness the deliberate introduction of heather in 1913, a game sport folly which has inexorably led to the loss of most of the park's red tussock landscape. Likewise, most of the open areas below 2000 m would now be a pine forest if the wilding trees of lodgepole pine (*Pinus contorta*), escapees from an ill-advised plantation experiment in Karioi State Forest, had not been painstakingly removed by volunteers (and the Army) for the past 40 years.

On the north-west flanks of the park, decades of government-sanctioned non-sustainable logging of podocarps seriously degraded the forest structure of Tongariro Forest, so much so that the Forest Service and the Department of Land & Survey tried to convert the area to pine plantations and farmland. From the early 1980s, retention in public ownership of a regenerating indigenous Tongariro Forest was the goal of another of the North Island forest conservation campaigns. Today it is known as Tongariro Forest Conservation Area (21,470 ha) and valued as an important habitat for North Island brown kiwi, fernbird and blue duck/whio (in the Whakapapa River and Mangatepopo Stream). Tongariro Forest is also a very important site for a variety of recreational pursuits (such as mountain-biking, hunting, horse-riding and 4WD motoring) which are either forbidden or discouraged within the national park.

LEFT Sunrise touching the eastern slopes of Mt Ngauruhoe (2291 m), the youngest volcanic cone in Tongariro National Park. In the distance is the large strato-volcano of Mt Ruapehu, the highest point in the North Island at 2797 m.

LAKE TAUPO AND THE TONGARIRO RIVER

Lake Taupo, with an area of 622 km², is the largest of New Zealand's many natural lakes. It is a high and deep caldera lake (357 m above sea level and up to 160 m deep), historically with very high water quality. It is not circular like the classic caldera lake of Rotorua, because the Taupo Volcano had several different eruption centres. Taupo Volcano is considered by many vulcanologists to be the most frequently active and 'productive' (in terms of volume of material ejected) rhyolitic volcano in the world, spreading ignimbrites and tephras over much of the central and eastern North Island. The present shape of the caldera was largely determined by one of the largest eruptions in New Zealand's volcanic history – the Oruanui Eruption of around 26,500 years ago. This eruption was so large and violent that if it happened today it would devastate most of the North Island and the northern part of the South Island. Close to the Oruanui eruption vent, the ignimbrite and tephra was 200 m deep; tephra was deposited 1 m deep in coastal Hawke's Bay, and 10 cm of ash even reached the Chatham Islands, 1200 km to the south-east. Ignimbrite sheets from the Oruanui Eruption formed the cliffs which today ring the Western Bay of Lake Taupo, a popular location for rock-climbers.

The margins of the lake contain many special plant communities that are not specifically protected. These include cliff vegetation and lakeshore herbfields. The South Taupo Wetland extends from the lower Waimarino River to the delta of the Tongariro River (a classic 'bird's foot' delta, possibly the best example of this type of landform in the country). This unprotected wetland is a mosaic of vulnerable swamp and bog vegetation, the habitat of a number of threatened plants and birds. The Tongariro River rises in the Kaimanawa Mountains as the Waipakihi River (see Ch.7), before it is joined by a succession of streams draining the eastern slopes of Tongariro National Park. The Tongariro is a large, wild, mountain river, internationally celebrated for the fighting quality of its rainbow trout, its dramatic scenery (especially the Waikato Falls, Tree Trunk Gorge and the Pillars of Hercules), and opportunities for white-water rafting and kayaking.

But it was the Taupo Eruption of around AD 181 that left the overwhelming volcanic imprint on the landforms, soils, vegetation and waters of the natural landscape. Although there were no humans present to witness its awesome power, scientists consider it produced eruption columns reaching 50 km in height, and deposited enormous quantities of pumice and ash up to 50 m in depth on the eastern margin

ABOVE Red Crater is the most active of Mt Tongariro's many craters and vents. The red and purple hues in the rocks are due to the variety of minerals in the ejected andesitic tephra. The Emerald Lakes can be seen in the middle distance, with Blue Lake beyond – all water-filled craters and depressions on the complex topography of this old, composite volcano. RIGHT Peripatus, a velvety grayish-green caterpillar-like forest floor animal is one of New Zealand's most unusual creatures, another 'missing link' with claims of an ancient lineage back to Gondwana. It is a zoological oddity, neither worm, centipede, nor caterpillar, but with an affinity to all three.

CLOCKWISE FROM TOP LEFT The colourful subalpine shrublands of Tongariro National Park are one of its botanical delights – mountain tauhinu (*Cassinia vauvilliersii*), inaka (*Dracophyllum longifolium*), mountain koromiko (*Hebe odora*), bog pine (*Halocarpus bidwillii*), mountain celery pine (*Phyllocladus alpinus*), golden olearia (*Olearia nummulariifolia*) and dozens of other shrubs are tightly woven together. *Thismia rodwayi* (sometimes called 'fairy lanterns') are small, uncommon, parasitic plants usually half-buried in the forest floor litter – these specimens occurred in rimu forest on the slopes of Mt Ruapehu (ROD MORRIS). Helm's butterfly (*Dodonidia helmsii*), sometimes called the 'forest ringlet', is a rare endemic butterfly shown here feeding on koromiko (*Hebe*) flowers. It has become more endangered because of predation by introduced wasps (ROD MORRIS). Drifts of the large yellow buttercup, *Ranunculus insignis*, thrive in the splash zone beside a waterfall near Soda Springs.

of the lake, best seen in the white cliffs exposed just north of Hatepe. Lake Taupo empties into the Waikato River, which flows only a few kilometres downstream before spectacularly plunging 22 m over the Huka Falls escarpment. Close by lies the Wairakei locality which was a wild geothermal landscape prior to its subjugation for energy generation. Huka Falls and the Craters of the Moon/Karapiti geothermal field remain, but the Aratiatia Rapids and the Spa and Wairakei geothermal fields have been destroyed or harnessed. Aratiatia is the first of nine hydro stations harnessing the waters of the Waikato, a 'run of the river' scheme allowing the rocky riverbed to embrace the surging Waikato waters only in scheduled performances, a daily environmental circus strictly timed to suit both the hydropower planners and the bustling tourist.

Lake Taupo occupies the huge caldera of the Taupo super-volcano. With an area of 622 km², Taupo is the largest of New Zealand's many natural lakes.

PUREORA AND WHIRINAKI FOREST PARKS

At the margins of the Volcanic Plateau lie the two great podocarp forest wildernesses of the North Island – Pureora and Whirinaki. Pureora Forest extends along both east and west flanks of the Hauhungaroa Range and the Waikato River slopes of the Rangitoto Range, from around 500 m to the montane podocarp/broadleaf forest on the volcanic highpoints of Pureora (1165 m) and Titiraupenga (1042 m). The dense lowland podocarp forests of Whirinaki lie at an altitude of 400–600 m in the middle reaches of the Whirinaki River. Further inland, towards the main Huiarau Range in the steeper, higher country, there are increasing amounts of broadleaf species like kamahi, tawa and black maire. Above 750 m in the east and the south, beech forest (red, silver and mountain) is dominant – probably refugia that escaped destruction in the volcanic eruptions. As with Pureora, there is stunted montane podocarp forest (Hall's totara, mountain toatoa and pink pine) on the highest ridgecrests, up to the high point of Maungataniwha at 1374 m.

At Pureora, a fascinating buried forest site has preserved all the trees that were blown flat by the Taupo Eruption blast, their bases pointing towards Taupo 50 km away. Furthermore, the buried vegetation assemblage at Pureora (containing around 50 plant species) was not incinerated by the metre of Taupo pumice covering it, indicating that the tephra had cooled by the time it reached the western Hauhungaroa Range. These tephra deposits blocked the local stream, causing the waters to pond and cover the devastated site, preserving the forest intact for 1800 years. The dominant tree in the buried forest is celery pine/tanekaha (*Phyllocladus trichomanoides*), one of the podocarps that can thrive on infertile, acidic soils, whereas today in Pureora the emergent podocarps in the lower-altitude (500–600 m) indigenous forest on deep tephra are more likely to be magnificent specimens of rimu, matai, totara and miro. At Whirinaki, the dense podocarp forest also seems to be associated with deep accumulations of tephra and, in addition to these four main podocarp trees, there are superb kahikatea reaching up to 65 m in height.

During the 1970s and 1980s when the indigenous forest conservation battles of the North Island were at their height, there was a great deal of scientific debate about why such dense stands of rimu, matai, kahikatea, miro and totara had survived so long. The conventional wisdom (as then expressed by the NZ Forest Service as justification for replacing them with fast-growing exotic trees) was that the forests were 'over-mature': the podocarps were long-lived relics of even-aged stands that sprang up after the eruptions – doomed to senescence because of their poor ability to regenerate under their own canopy, while more shade-tolerant trees like tawa and kamahi gradually invaded and became dominant. Yet much ecological evidence ran counter to this argument, for there were places in both forests where vigorous podocarp regeneration was taking place. The depth of erupted tephra and subsequent soil rejuvenation seem to be the key factors; the deeper the deposits of Taupo pumice, the denser the podocarp forests.

Whirinaki, along with Pureora, is one of the last remaining podocarp forest wildernesses in the North Island. Whirinaki Forest Park contains a forest sanctuary and five ecological areas.

In the Whirinaki Basin the dense podocarp stands, many around 600–700 years old, may have been rejuvenated by two events: cultivation and fires associated with early Maori occupation; and airfall deposits of Kaharoa ash emanating from the Okataina Volcanic Centre near Tarawera 680 years ago, which reached Whirinaki, but not Pureora.

Both Pureora and Whirinaki forests have a special place in New Zealand's conservation history and folklore. Here the forestry ideology of indigenous inferiority was squarely confronted by many brave protesters and scientists. National media attention was drawn to Pureora for several weeks in 1978 when radical protesters perched high in the canopy of large trees that were about to be felled. The government responded to the Pureora protests later that year by designating the remaining scattered blocks of indigenous forest as Pureora Forest Park (74,178 ha). While conversion to exotic plantations continued, the NZ Forest Service responded to public pressure by scientifically delineating specially protected areas within the park. In all, 10 ecological areas (totalling nearly 30,000 ha), representative of all major vegetation types, were set aside. These included not only the impressive dense podocarp forest in the Waihaha, Waipapa and Pikiariki ecological areas, but others such as rare tanekaha forest (Waimonoa Ecological Area), rata for-

est (Rata-Nunui Ecological Area), and frost flats containing the rare shrub *Pittosporum turneri* (Whenuakura Ecological Area). The 1977–1984 anti-logging campaign in Whirinaki was even more bitter, because it threatened the livelihood of the population of Minginui village. Again, a Whirinaki Forest Park (54,921 ha) was designated in 1984, and this included a forest sanctuary and five ecological areas. All indigenous logging ceased when control passed to the new Department of Conservation (DOC) in 1987.

Today, Pureora and Whirinaki forest parks are important habitats for a number of threatened native birds – kiwi, kaka, kakariki, blue duck/whio, New Zealand falcon/karearea and kokako – as well as the short- and long-tailed bats. Indeed, monitoring of kokako in Waipapa Ecological Area during 2003 found 77 breeding pairs, probably the most significant population of this endangered species in the country. Their wilderness recreation value, and remoteness from the main natural icons of interest to tourists, make Pureora and Whirinaki attractive to local trampers, and especially hunters. It is hard to believe that in the space of only 15–20 years Minginui has become a ghost village; the mill is derelict and even DOC has relocated its visitor centre to SH 38 near Murupara. Although DOC has upgraded the Whirinaki Track (and even developed a purpose-built mountain-biking trail), there is an overwhelming feeling that both Pureora and Whirinaki have been forgotten – the battles were won and a new generation has moved on to new conservation priorities somewhere else, far from these ancient forest relics of Gondwana.

ROTORUA LAKES AND GEOTHERMAL FIELDS

Rotorua is one of the geothermal wonders of the world. Its geysers, fumaroles, hot springs and boiling mud pools are attractions visited by 90 per cent of the tourists who come to New Zealand each year. The high-temperature geothermal phenomena found throughout the Taupo Volcanic Zone are rare, and found on this scale in only a few other places in the world. Geysers are the most spectacular features and these are in their greatest concentration in the Whakarewarewa geyser field at Rotorua. There are also small geysers at Orakei–Korako, Waikite and Waiotapu, while the Waimangu geothermal field has the distinction of being another international rarity – a major geothermal field formed in historic times (as a result of the 1886 Tarawera Eruption). Both Waimangu and Waiotapu geothermal fields contain a number of unique phenomena of international importance: in Waimangu, the remarkable inverse relationship

LEFT Kahikatea (*Dacrycarpus dacrydioides*) trees standing at the edge of Arahaki Lagoon in Whirinaki Forest Park; ABOVE Male long-tailed bat (*Chalinolobus tuberculatus*) on bark (ROD MORRIS).

between the levels of Inferno Crater Lake and the rate of hot-water discharge from Echo Crater (Frying Pan Lake) 500 m distant; in Waiotapu, the colourful metallic sulphide sinters of Champagne Pool, Artist's Palette and Primrose Terrace, as well as the remarkable Mud Volcano on Loop Road. In addition, the geothermal fields are habitats for a number of highly specialised plants capable of withstanding the steam, hot and acidic soils, and toxic minerals in the geothermal ground waters. The most obvious specialised plant is a kanuka (*Kunzea ericoides* var. *microflora*), no longer a tree but a prostrate shrub, its flattened branches hugging the ground surface and its roots penetrating only a few centimetres into the hot soil. There are also frost-intolerant 'thermal ferns', plenty of clusters of the primitive fern ally *Psilotum nudum* overhanging hot streams, and attractive displays of sun orchids (*Thelymitra* species) and bearded orchids (*Calochilus* species), especially *C. robertsonii* which seems endemic to the geothermal area.

Lake Rotorua (7978 ha) is the largest of 10 lakes over 400 ha in size – almost all of them occupying calderas created through past volcanic eruptions in the Rotorua Basin. Although the lakes constitute a world-renowned trout fishery and support notable populations of New Zealand scaup, New Zealand dabchick, New Zealand shoveller and several species of shag, they suffer from acute environmental problems stemming from poor management of their water quality and the introduction of highly aggressive exotic lake weeds. This is not surprising when agriculture,

ABOVE Pohutu Geyser is the most famous of the many geothermal phenomena in the Whakarewarewa geyser field at Rotorua. Whakarewarewa has one of the highest concentrations of geysers in the world, with seven geysers (including Pohutu as a centrepiece) closely aligned along Te Puia (Geyser) Flat. In total, Whakarewarewa has around 500 hot springs displaying most forms of geothermal activity. Pohutu erupts spectacularly about 14 times each day, to a height of 18 m but occasionally to twice that height. RIGHT One of the many sinter deposits around a geothermal vent in Whakarewarewa geyserfield.

LEFT Manuka (*Leptospermum scoparium*) in Tokaanu thermal area, adjacent to the southern shore of Lake Taupo. Manuka is one of the hardy plants which can survive heat and geochemicals toxic to many plants.
BELOW Champagne Pool is the largest hot spring in the Waiotapu geothermal field (covering an area of 2000 m²). The hot alkaline chloride water filling this 900-year-old explosion crater gives off carbon dioxide and deposits a raised rim of bright orange silica sinter around the margins of the water.

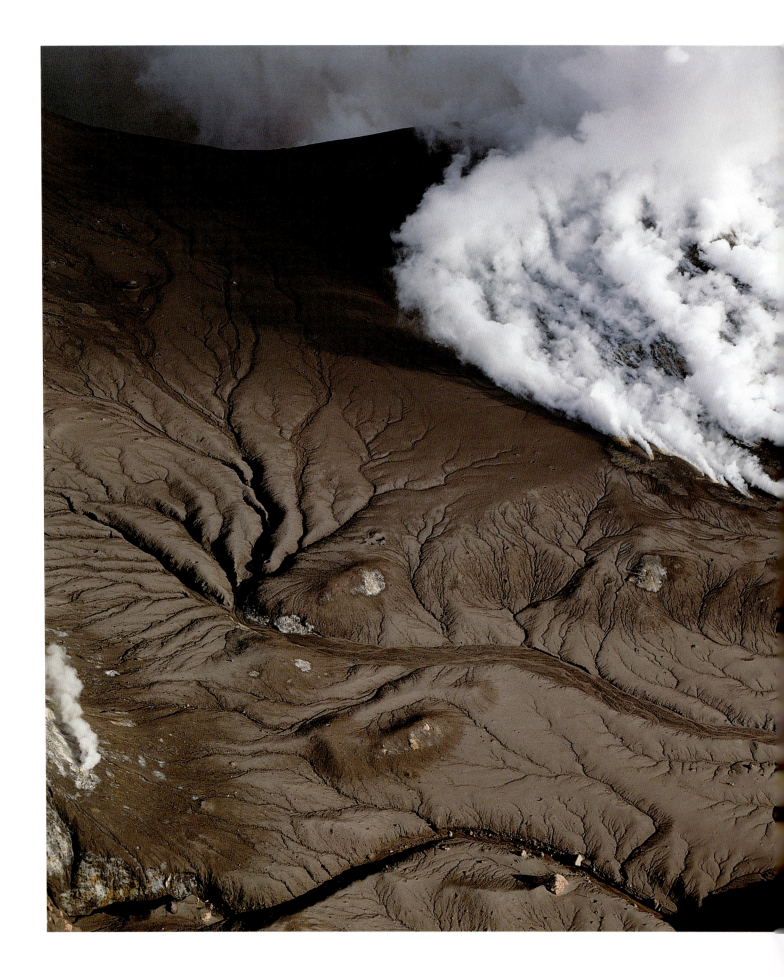

plantation forestry and urban residential are the main land uses in the catchments of the Rotorua Lakes; only two of the lakes (Okataina and Tarawera) still retain more than 50 per cent of their catchment in native forest.

The other major landforms associated with past eruptions are the rhyolitic lava domes which dominate the skyline – Ngongotaha (which looms over the city of Rotorua itself), Haroharo, Makatiti, Horohoro and Tarawera. Mt Tarawera consists of three large domes (the highest 1111 m above sea level), their summits rent by the 7 km long rift of the 1886 eruption. The spectacular and colourful view along Tarawera's chain of craters is a highlight of any flight over the Okataina Volcanic Centre, with the red-purple of the basaltic scoria contrasting with the white rhyolitic pumice beneath. Only 15 per cent of the Rotorua region now remains in native forest, and most of this is in three blocks of podocarp/broadleaf forest – the hill country between Lake Rotoehu and the Tarawera River (an important kokako habitat), the Tarawera–Lake Okataina scenic reserves, and the headwaters of Ngongotaha Stream.

WHITE ISLAND AND TUHUA: BAY OF PLENTY VOLCANIC ISLANDS

White Island/Whakaari is a small (238 ha) volcano 50 km offshore in the Bay of Plenty, at the north-eastern extent of the Taupo Volcanic Zone. Although it is only 321 m high, it is the most active volcano in New Zealand. White Island/Whakaari is unusual compared to the other andesitic volcanoes of the North Island because its vent is below sea level, but sealed from contact with sea water. The magma source is very shallow and the violent thermal activity (boiling pools, and vents of steam and other gases) is caused by rainwater seeping down and making contact with the magma. There is no vegetation within the crater of White Island but pohutukawa forest has managed to establish itself on the sheltered northern coastal fan. Nor does volcanic activity deter the Australasian gannet and grey-faced petrel, which have now established breeding colonies on headlands. The island has been uninhabited since 1934 when sulphur mining ceased because of site danger (a volcanic catastrophe killed 11 miners in 1914). White Island/Whakaari is private land but now protected as a scenic reserve, and a guided visit is an unforgettable adventure, as close as one would ever want to get to a wilderness volcano experience.

Tuhua/Mayor Island is much larger (1276 ha) than White Island/Whakaari and, although not currently active,

Eroded rills in the volcanic ash in the main crater of White Island/Whakaari.

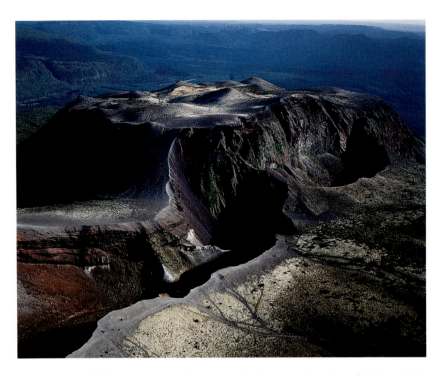

Mt Tarawera, site of the devastating Tarawera Eruption of 10 June 1886. It is one of many volcanic and geothermal features around Rotorua worthy of protection as a World Heritage site because of their outstanding universal value.

is just as internationally significant a part of New Zealand's volcanic heritage. It has a large, well-preserved caldera, with steep walls up to 200 m high enclosing forest-covered lava flows and domes as well as two crater lakes. Large sections of the coastline are formidable, with spectacular brightly-coloured cliffs 100–150 m high. The island is completely covered in coastal forest with a canopy dominated by kanuka, pohutukawa and rewarewa. Although this vegetation was modified during its long Maori occupation, it still supports a good population of bellbirds, kaka and other forest birds. But it is the interesting chemistry of the rocks of Tuhua/Mayor Island that is of universal interest. Its rhyolitic rocks are high in silica content and, unlike the other rhyolites of the Taupo Volcanic Zone, are unusually high in sodium. One of these rocks, obsidian (or 'volcanic glass'), was extremely important to tangata whenua because of its utility as a cutting tool; it was fought over and traded widely throughout Aotearoa in pre-European times. The island is also known internationally as the type locality for tuhualite, a unique purplish-blue mineral discovered there in 1922. There is close co-operation between DOC and the trust board representing the Maori owners, with a 1075 ha conservation area to be managed as if it were a national park.

Both White Island/Whakaari and Tuhua/Mayor Island are surrounded by a rich marine environment. They are situated in the warm East Auckland Current in moderately deep water. Tuhua/Mayor Island is at the edge of the continental shelf, and White Island/Whakaari is isolated in the Pacific Ocean where it was not linked to the mainland during the low sea levels of the Last Glaciation. The marine flora and fauna around both islands are diverse, with both subtropical affinities and volcanic influences. In addition, Tuhua/Mayor Island is internationally famous for its big-game fishing. A 1060 ha Mayor Island Marine Reserve has been established around the northern quarter of the island, but it is rather inaccessible to the public and considered quite inadequate for conserving this important marine habit.

THREATS AND CONSERVATION PRIORITIES

Geothermal Features: the Need for Greater Protection and Recognition

Whereas there were five major geyser fields within the Taupo Volcanic Zone 120 years ago, today there is only one – Whakarewarewa. The other four, all irreplaceable geological heritage of international importance, have been destroyed through natural events, or to feed our society's insatiable appetite for energy:

- Rotomahana in the 1886 Tarawera Eruption;
- Taupo Spa by construction impacts;
- Wairakei by geothermal power generation;
- Orakei–Korako, largely inundated by damming of the adjacent Waikato River for hydroelectricity generation.

Incredibly, despite the overwhelming significance of Whakarewarewa as a taonga of the Te Arawa iwi, and its importance to the Rotorua tourist industry, it too was nearly lost by the over-exploitation of the Rotorua geothermal field for residential and industrial heating within the city. Faced with the prospect of extinction of the once magnificent geysers of Geyser Flat – Pohutu, Prince of Wales Feathers, Kereru, Waikorohihi and Mahanga – the government fortunately intervened in 1987, closing all bores within a 1.5 km radius of Whakarewarewa and requiring the Rotorua District Council to exercise stricter control of bores outside this core area.

For far too long the management of the Rotorua geothermal areas and lakes has been an uncoordinated mess. From a conservation perspective, it is hard to understand why their heritage values have never been recognised with national park status. In 1872 far-sighted explorers moved quickly to have the geothermal wilderness of the Great Geyser Basin of Wyoming designated as the world's first national park, Yellowstone. Unfortunately, the same idea did not take root when William Fox, explorer, artist and oft-times premier of New Zealand, tried to convince Premier Julius Vogel in 1874 to adopt the American park model to forestall private speculation and exploitation of the geothermal wonders of Taupo and Rotorua. Instead, this extraordinary natural resource has been balkanised, progressively carved up by tourist enterprises, government-sponsored energy generators and municipal consumers. Most of these exploiters showed little regard for protecting tikanga Maori values or conserving the ecosystem integrity, geodiversity and biodiversity that was once present in our Rotorua–Taupo geothermal heritage.

The dominant geothermal paradigm in New Zealand has been for energy development. Even government's policy framework for geothermal resources, prepared by the Ministry of Energy in 1986, espoused the primacy of exploitation of most geothermal fields; since then, the privatisation of electricity companies has resulted in a scramble for new geothermal generating stations. Environment Waikato and Environment Bay of Plenty (BOP), who have responsibility under the Resource Management Act 1991 to plan for the future of the geothermal sites in the Taupo Volcanic Zone, have largely failed to produce a conservation vision. DOC, too, has failed to acquire any in-house geothermal expertise and clout; successive Ministers of Conservation and Environment have preferred to hide behind ownership hurdles, such as waiting for Treaty claims to be settled, instead of aggressively advocating greater protection and coordinated management of this whole geothermal heritage. Without this political leadership, DOC has largely restricted its efforts to overseeing the leased geothermal scenic reserves (the most important of which is Waimangu) and a number of less iconic geothermal features: Rainbow Mountain (Maungakakaramea), Hot Water Beach on the shores of Lake Tarawera, the small but biologically important Sulphur Point Wildlife Sanctuary, and two smaller geothermal fields which are protected from tourism facilities – Te Kopia and Maungaongaonga.

Yet, fragmented as the Rotorua geothermal heritage is, it is still worthy of natural (and perhaps cultural) World Heritage status because of its 'outstanding universal value'. The Bay of Plenty Conservation Board has recognised the acute need for better conservation of the entire geothermal resources of Rotorua, and it is to be hoped that it can

Energy development has been a constant threat to the integrity of the geothermal wonders of the central North Island. The harnessing of the Wairakei geothermal field destroyed the Geyser Valley and Spa Springs but had the effect of increasing the extent of steaming ground and fumarole activity at the adjacent Craters of the Moon/Karapiti locality (pictured).

provide the leadership to get all communities of interest to focus on the wider picture. The geothermal heritage of Rotorua is of international scientific importance, and of the utmost significance to tangata whenua. A World Heritage listing would require all parties – Te Arawa as tangata whenua, Rotorua District Council, Environment BOP, the tourism industry, the energy industry, and DOC – to put aside their sectoral interests and instead concentrate on protection and coordinated management of those geothermal features that remain in a natural state (or that are capable of rehabilitation).

Declining Water Quality in Lake Taupo and the Rotorua Lakes

The Rotorua Lakes have been in trouble for some years, with decreasing water quality and occasional algal blooms. Now it is clear that Lake Taupo is heading for trouble too. There are unmistakable signs that Lake Taupo's health is slowly declining, with the increasing nitrogen content of the inflowing groundwaters and rivers feeding the growth of free-floating algae and thus decreasing water clarity in the lake. Potentially toxic algae bloomed in the lake for the first time in 2001 and again in 2003.

Although there are many pockets of protected riparian forest around the western shores of Lake Taupo, over the past 40 years a range of agricultural and residential development has been unwisely sanctioned throughout the catchment. In the late 1970s, DSIR scientists warned the government of the environmental dangers of extensive agricultural development of the remaining pumicelands around the western and northern shores of the lake, but these concerns were ignored. Pressure from land developers for more pockets of residential development throughout the lake's catchment is intense, especially in the north around Whakaipo Bay. Elsewhere, large areas of pine forest are being felled so that the land can be converted to dairying, the resultant nutrient acceleration placing the Waikato River under further environmental stress – an ecological folly encouraged by the failure of current government policies. Given the natural and cultural heritage significance of the near-pristine waters of the lake, the short-sightedness and ecological insensitivity of successive central and local governments in allowing polluting development amounts to incompetent political leadership on a monumental scale.

Fortunately, Environment Waikato, Taupo District Council, Ngati Tuwharetoa iwi and central government agencies are belatedly taking action; in late 2003, they launched the Protecting Lake Taupo Strategy. This is an $83.5 million package funded by national taxpayers and local ratepayers, mainly using incentives to try to slow water deterioration through land-use changes in the Lake Taupo catchment. But water quality trends will take decades to reverse, because Taupo is a deep, low-nutrient lake, and so great is the lag time for groundwaters to enter the lake system that the increased levels of nitrogen currently entering the lake are considered to be due to the land cover change from indigenous forest and shrubland to pastoral agriculture 30–40 years ago.

Nevertheless, Lake Taupo and its associated volcanic phenomena are of outstanding international vulcanological significance, of high economic importance to the tourist industry, and cherished by Tuwharetoa, the iwi with mana whenua for the lake and its catchment, and who own title to the lake bed. It is hard to understand why all parties did not adopt environmentally sustainable policies decades ago, and then submit the globally outstanding natural features of Lake Taupo to UNESCO for consideration as a natural World Heritage site.

Public outcry over the declining quality of Lakes Rotorua and Rotoiti resulted in the diversion of Rotorua's sewerage to land-based waste disposal in 1990. Efforts have also been made to retire land from grazing and exclude cattle from the margins of Lake Rotoehu, one of the more polluted lakes. But these measures have yet to improve the water quality to acceptable standards for the four large lakes with eutrophication problems – Rotorua, Rotoehu, Rotoiti and Okareka. More severe measures will probably be required, such as stopping dairying, retiring much more land from grazing, and placing stricter controls on residential subdivisions to minimise nutrients coming from stormwater and septic tank discharges. These sorts of restrictions are going to be just as important to maintain the ecological and recreational values of the more natural lakes – Tarawera, Rotoma, Okataina, Rotomahana and Tikitapu.

Managing the Impacts of Tourism

The wild landscapes of the Volcanic Lands are the most visited natural areas of the North Island. Visitors range from skiers and mountaineers on the alpine slopes of Tongariro National Park, to rafters on the Tongariro and Kaituna rivers; from anglers on Lake Taupo and the Rotorua Lakes, to hunters in Whirinaki Forest Park; from tourists marvelling at Huka Falls or the display of Pohutu Geyser, to mountainbikers on the 42-Traverse through Tongariro Forest. Tourism is burgeoning in the localities of Rotorua, Taupo and Tongariro National Park. Tourist numbers are increasing so rapidly that there are severe pressures on the natural landscapes of the region, and better planning is needed to minimise their environmental impacts.

The management response in Tongariro National Park is a good pointer to what is required. The greatest conservation challenge to the integrity of the park today is the need to balance preservation with public use. On the one hand, to not resile from the imperative to 'preserve in perpetuity' the natural landscape and respect the sacredness of the gift area; on the other, to somehow manage the sharply increasing numbers of visitors to the skifields in winter and the Tongariro Crossing Great Walk throughout

the rest of the year. The three skifields on Mt Ruapehu now attract around 350,000 skiers in a good season – about 50 per cent of annual visitors to the park. The alpine Tongariro Crossing, over-promoted by some tourist operators as 'the greatest volcanic day walk in the world', is traversed by up to 80,000 visitors per year (and has even attracted an extraordinary 1200 walkers in one day). A comprehensive park management plan has been developed over the decades to handle the conservation of the park's natural and historic heritage, and to regulate this ever-increasing pressure for development and enhanced visitor safety. Major challenges being addressed are: treating sewerage from the Iwikau ski village; efficient and sensitive management of the Turoa and Whakapapa skifields; better management of the Tongariro Crossing; and the commissioning

Blue Lake, filling an old crater on the eastern flanks of Mt Tongariro, is one of the many volcanic landforms encountered on the Tongariro Crossing, one of the most popular alpine tramps in Tongariro National Park.

of a comprehensive lahar early-warning system (and other 'non-engineering' hazard responses outside the park). The effectiveness of the latter non-intrusive approach was demonstrated with the avoidance of any loss of life or major infrastructure when the anticipated lahar finally surged from the Crater Lake in March 2007. Careful management of these and a legion of other developmental pressures are of fundamental importance for maintaining opportunities for wilderness recreation and sustaining the future of ecotourism in the central North Island.

CHAPTER FIVE

TARANAKI, WANGANUI, MANAWATU

The Taranaki–Wanganui–Manawatu region is not widely recognised by overseas tourists for those iconic natural landscapes considered essential to visit – with the notable exception of Mt Taranaki or Mt Egmont[1], the symmetrical volcanic cone that dominates the skyline of Taranaki. There are no lakes, except the string of small, shallow, nutrient-rich water bodies hidden away in the Manawatu–Horowhenua sand country. Pastoral agriculture long ago replaced most of the magnificent podocarp/broadleaf forests of the Taranaki, Wanganui, Rangitikei and Manawatu lowlands. Today, the unimpeded vista across the pastoral landscape reveals the wealth of outstanding natural landforms in the region, such as:

- flights of uplifted marine terraces between Waverley and Marton, the best in the country save for those at Waitutu in southern Fiordland (which are difficult to visit because they are very remote and densely forested);
- cut-off meanders in the Whanganui River (at Atene) and Rangitikei River (at Ohingaiti);
- parallel dunes and parabolic dunes with dune flats in the Foxton sand country (the most extensive dunelands in the country);
- debris avalanche mounds on the western part of the Mt Taranaki/Egmont ringplain;
- alluvial terraces of the lower Rangitikei and Manawatu rivers (the best examples in New Zealand).

In addition, the variety of large rivers is an impressive landscape feature of the region. The hundreds of clear, fast-flowing rivers that radiate out across the ringplain of

Mt Taranaki/Egmont contrast sharply with the silt-laden, serpentine rivers (like the Waitara, Whanganui, Mangawhero and Whangaehu) that thread their way through the soft mudstones (papa) of the King Country and Wanganui hill country. One of the major rivers rising on the slopes of Mt Taranaki/Egmont, the Patea, graphically illustrates these two different characteristics. As it passes from the edge of the volcanic ringplain just east of Stratford into the sedimentary hill country of East Taranaki, it loses its clarity and changes to a sinuous course. Further riverine diversity is provided by a number carrying large quantities of hard greywacke shingle in their beds, namely, the upper Rangitikei and Manawatu rivers, the Pohangina River and the Otaki River, respectively draining the Kaimanawa Mountains and the Ruahine and Tararua ranges (see Ch.7) in the far east of the region. The Manawatu River cuts its way through the greywacke bedrock between the Ruahine and Tararua ranges, forming the wild landscape of the Manawatu Gorge. This is New Zealand's best-known antecedent river gorge (i.e. a gorge formed by a river that is not deterred from its original course by the steady rising of the land – in this case, the backbone of Te Ika a Maui, the axial ranges of the North Island).

Even though the coastline from the mouth of the Mokau River to Paekakariki is 375 km long, much of it is inaccessible from the road. There are very few rocky headlands or incised estuaries, and only Kapiti Island and the Sugar Loaf Islands stand off the arcs of the North Taranaki and South Taranaki bights. Sand and wind characterise the dynamic, high-energy coastal landscape from Patea to Paekakariki. Here gale-force WNW winds, pronounced wave surges and a strong south-easterly longshore drift effectively transport

---

[1] Abbreviated to 'Mt Taranaki/Egmont' throughout the rest of the chapter.

The beautiful symmetrical cone of the dormant andesitic volcano Mt Taranaki or Mt Egmont stands out from every direction in Taranaki.

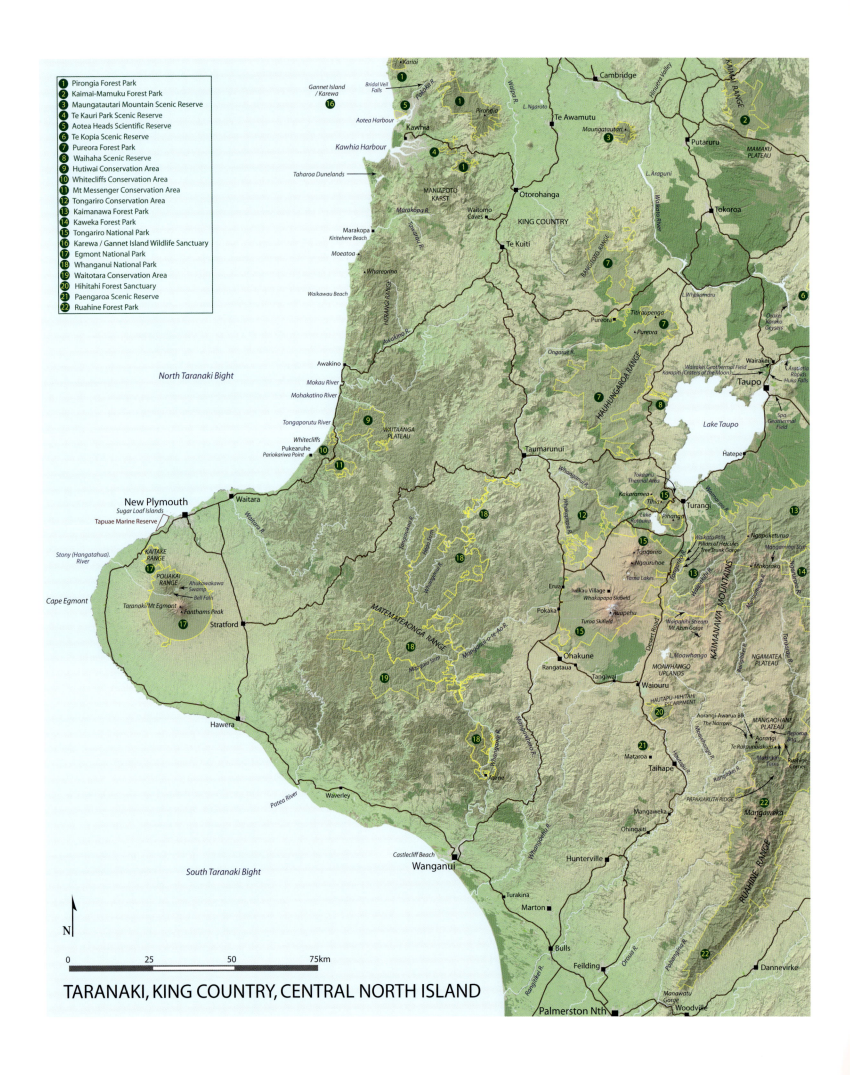

1 Pirongia Forest Park
2 Kaimai-Mamuku Forest Park
3 Maungatautari Mountain Scenic Reserve
4 Te Kauri Park Scenic Reserve
5 Aotea Heads Scientific Reserve
6 Te Kopia Scenic Reserve
7 Pureora Forest Park
8 Waihaha Scenic Reserve
9 Hutiwai Conservation Area
10 Whitecliffs Conservation Area
11 Mt Messenger Conservation Area
12 Tongariro Conservation Area
13 Kaimanawa Forest Park
14 Kaweka Forest Park
15 Tongariro National Park
16 Karewa / Gannet Island Wildlife Sanctuary
17 Egmont National Park
18 Whanganui National Park
19 Waitotara Conservation Area
20 Hihitahi Forest Sanctuary
21 Paengaroa Scenic Reserve
22 Ruahine Forest Park

North Taranaki Bight

South Taranaki Bight

N

0   25   50   75km

TARANAKI, KING COUNTRY, CENTRAL NORTH ISLAND

the vast quantities of sediment carried down the many rivers entering the South Taranaki Bight. Close to the coast, the sand dunes run parallel with the shoreline; further away, they are oriented with the prevailing WNW winds, extending as parallel strands for up to 20 km inland between the Turakina and Manawatu rivers. Long sections of this wide, sandy shoreline feel truly remote from civilisation, with lots of sea, sky and sand, and the cries of coastal birds, and only the distant Tararua Range and Kapiti Island on the horizon. West of Wanganui, the dunelands perch on top of the marine terraces that the sea has eroded into 30–40 m high cliffs. The cliffs are largely inaccessible on foot but present a spectacular sight from the air, extending unbroken for 130 km to Cape Egmont.

The dry dunes and damp flats of the sand country contain a host of rare and endangered plants, and the estuaries are important habitats for wading birds, including Arctic migrants like plovers, knots and godwits. The Manawatu River Estuary is particularly important and has recently been given the international accolade of a 'wetland of international importance' (a Ramsar site), through the efforts of Forest & Bird and the local community. The estuary is the largest in the lower North Island, sheltering a number of native fish, and is one of our most diverse habitats for coastal wading birds. To date, birdwatchers have counted 93 species, not only native threatened species like wrybill, fairy tern and shore plover, but also exotic migrants such as curlews, tattlers and sandpipers. The upper part of the estuary is also frequented by our rare swamp birds – bitterns, crakes and fernbirds.

Four natural areas – Egmont National Park, the North Taranaki forests, the Moawhango uplands and Whanganui National Park – stand out because of their qualities of remoteness, their biodiversity or geodiversity value, and the recreational opportunities which they provide.

EGMONT NATIONAL PARK

Egmont National Park (34,170 ha) protects the andesitic volcanic cones of Taranaki – the Kaitake Range, the Pouakai Range and the classically shaped 2518 m Mt Taranaki/Egmont (with its parasitic cone of Fanthams Peak). The concentric bands of vegetation on Mt Taranaki/Egmont are one of the best examples of altitudinal zonation of natural vegetation in New Zealand. The park's lowland forest is mainly a canopy of kamahi, with many rimu and rata, which completely covers the Kaitake Range and up to about 750 m altitude on the slopes of Mt Taranaki/Egmont

Lake Papaitonga near Levin is one of the series of small, shallow dune lakes strung in a line parallel to the coastline throughout the Manawatu–Horowhenua sand country.

and the Pouakai Range. Above 750 m the montane forest is kamahi, mountain totara, pahautea and broadleaf – the 'goblin forest' of tourist brochures, so-called because of its gnarled nature and the profusion of mosses, filmy ferns and lichens clinging to the branches. At around 1000 m, the montane forest merges into nearly impenetrable subalpine shrublands dominated by leatherwood, which above 1250 m gives way to red tussock grasslands and many small flowering herbs. The largest mire in the park, Ahukawakawa Swamp, nestles in the montane basin between the northern slopes of Mt Taranaki/Egmont and the Pouakai Range, at an altitude of 920 m. It contains 260 different species of higher plants, about one-third of the total number of higher plants in the park – all confined in an area of only 30 ha.

The flora of Egmont National Park is unusual in that while it has almost a full complement of lowland plants, its montane and alpine flora lack many of the more common plants of these higher altitudes. The best-known absentee is beech, but at least 100 other plant species widespread on North Island mountains are missing, including most of the subalpine podocarps. This distinctive mountain flora of Mt Taranaki/Egmont is probably the result of its isolation from other mountain ranges (the nearest mountain, Mt Ruapehu, is 130 km away; the Tararua Range 200 km; and the Tasman Mountains of Kahurangi National Park 220 km distant across the South Taranaki Bight and Golden Bay).

ABOVE Bells Falls (30 m) lie in the upper reaches of the Stony/Hangatahua River, one of the largest of the 300 or so streams draining radially off Mt Taranaki and the other volcanic landforms in Egmont National Park. RIGHT Pahautea or mountain cedar (*Libocedrus bidwillii*) trees are a prominent feature of the montane forests and subalpine shrublands of Egmont National Park.

LEFT Whio or blue duck (*Hymenolaimus malacorhynchos*) frequent the clear, fast-flowing waters of tributaries of the Whanganui River such as the Manganui-o-te-Ao and Whakapapa. In recent years juvenile whio have been released in Egmont National Park in an attempt to re-establish this interesting bird in one of its former mountain river habitats. BELOW From Holly Hut at 1000 m altitude, the 2518 m summit of Mt Taranaki/Egmont towers above. The montane forest here (consisting of kamahi, mountain totara, pahautea and broadleaf) can be seen merging upslope into nearly impenetrable subalpine shrublands and, above 1250 m, red tussock grasslands with many small flowering herbs.

The eminent botanist Tony Druce concluded that the park had an 'island flora', with most of its alpine plants having arrived by chance (mostly on the wind or carried by birds) after eruptions had destroyed the previous alpine vegetation.

Egmont National Park is of very high importance for the protection of native wildlife, for the park is the only large tract of indigenous forest remaining in western Taranaki. It is a habitat not only for the more common forest birds such as tomtits, tui, bellbirds and riflemen, but also for rarer birds like the North Island brown kiwi, fernbird and the New Zealand falcon. In recent years, the transfer of blue duck/whio juveniles from the Manganui-o-te-Ao River tributary of the Whanganui River has established a small

The Taranaki coastline between the mouth of the Tongaporutu River and Pukearuhe is a spectacular line of cliffs, archways and stacks carved into the sedimentary rocks by the constant surge of the Tasman Sea.

population within the park. And because the park protects the headwaters of more than 300 streams of high water quality, it is an outstanding habitat for New Zealand's indigenous fish species.

In winter, the alpine slopes of Mt Taranaki/Egmont can provide the best ice-climbing in the North Island. The high rainfall and severe winds regularly experienced by visitors to the park add substantially to its reputation as a wilderness landscape which should never be underestimated.

NORTH TARANAKI COAST AND FORESTS

North Taranaki is the only part of the region where natural landscape still extends to the coastline. For 10 km between Pukearuhe and the mouth of the Tongaporutu River, the forested hill country is abruptly terminated in a dramatic line of cliffs cut into a narrow band of elevated marine terraces. This locality, known as Whitecliffs (Parininihi to tangata whenua), is a sinuous line of 40–60 m high cliffs which block all coastal travel except at low tide. Here, in Whitecliffs Conservation Area (1856 ha), the terrace surface and clifftops still retain a rich broadleaved coastal forest of predominantly kohekohe, karaka, puriri, pukatea and ngaio, which grades a short distance inland into hard beech forest – a superb forest type that has long gone from the rest of the coastal lower North Island through clearance for farming.

Inland from Whitecliffs, the Mt Messenger Conservation Area (2900 ha) protects the attractive broadleaf forest around SH 3, while the much larger Hutiwai Conservation Area (10,680 ha) ensures protection for the forest, which extends inland to the Waitaanga Plateau. Gradually the warmth- and nutrient-loving plants of the coastal forest give way to hill-country forests dominated by tawa, hinau, rewarewa, rimu (and other podocarps) and northern rata. Here, on the poorer, shallower soils of the steep slopes and ridge-crests at around 400–500 m altitude, hard beech, kamahi and mountain totara become more common, and there are pockets of silver beech on the Waitaanga Plateau. Geological diversity (in the form of limestone, coal measures and hard sandstone) also contributes to the botanical diversity of this forest wilderness, which extends from the coast into the heart of the King Country, not as a contiguous forest tract, unfortunately, but more like a patchwork quilt of indigenous forest clothing the network of ridges.

The main rivers draining this forested hinterland – the Mokau, Mohakatino, Tongaporutu and Waitara – all have high ecological values. The scenic Mokau River also has very high historical and recreational values, for the most part protected in a string of riparian reserves and a 10,000 ha forest block purchased through the Nature Heritage Fund. The estuaries of the rivers are important breeding habitats for native fish and resting areas for a wide range of migratory wading birds. The marine biodiversity values are also very high and a marine reserve extending out from the Whitecliffs coastline was proposed in 1995. Overall, there is a natural integrity to North Taranaki, which is not yet reflected in its protective status.

The Mokau is the largest of several rivers draining the forested hinterland of North Taranaki, its scenic, historical and recreational values protected in recent years by a string of riparian reserves.

MOAWHANGO TUSSOCKLANDS AND RANGITIKEI UPLANDS

The tussock grasslands and wetlands of the remote Moawhango Basin and upland plateaux extending across the Rangitikei gorges to the north-western Ruahine Range are wilderness landscapes unique in the North Island. They are arguably the least visited natural corners of the region, a fascinating mixture of greywacke uplands exhumed from the soft marine sediments in the ancient sea of the Wanganui Basin, which once reached its northernmost extent here at the southern end of the Kaimanawa Mountains – with tephra erupted from the nearby Tongariro Volcanic Zone smoothing the uplands.

This is the largest area of tussock grassland in the North Island, induced through millennia of fires caused by eruptions and more recent Polynesian and European burning. Yet a high degree of naturalness remains, with tens of thousands of hectares of tall red tussock (and shorter silver and hard tussock) still containing a mosaic of forest remnants and extensive montane wetlands. Here, far from the main highways lie some of the most dramatic landforms in the region:

- the meandering upper Moawhango River, with its wetland basins separated by a series of striking greywacke gorges (such as Mt Azim Gorge);

- the Hautapu–Hihitahi Escarpment;
- the Mangaohane Plateau with its wetlands (Reporoa Bog and Makirikiri Tarns) and sinkholes (dolines);
- the forested butte of Aorangi (1236 m);
- the spectacular 25 km long gorge of the Rangitikei River between The Narrows below Mt Aorangi and its confluence with the Moawhango River, a near-continuous series of 100 m high cliffs carved into the sandstone, limestone and mudstone strata. The wild and scenic values of the middle and upper reaches of the Rangitikei River above Mangaweka have been recognised and are protected with a National Water Conservation Order.

In biodiversity terms, the Moawhango–Rangitikei uplands contain the region's greatest range of indigenous plants, and a concentration of rare and endangered plant species. Most of these grasses and herbs (the latter including forget-me-nots and buttercups) occur in the Moawhango and Mangaohane wetlands. There is also a botanical enigma in the relatively small (102 ha) Paengaroa Scenic Reserve beside the Hautapu River at Mataroa. Within this well-preserved kahikatea/matai forest there are more than 30 species of divaricating shrubs, including 10 trees that have a divaricating form as juveniles. Furthermore, the reserve's assemblage of more than 220 higher indigenous plants (extending across 500–700 m of altitude) lacks common broadleaf trees like titoki, tawa, kamahi, northern rata, beech species, rewarewa and hinau; instead,

LEFT The Rangitikei River has carved out a sheer-walled gorge in the soft sedimentary rocks in its middle reaches. Above Mangaweka, its waters are protected as a 'wild and scenic river'. ABOVE The tussocklands of the Moawhango uplands are of high plant biodiversity value.

The Whanganui River drains the largest lowland wilderness in the North Island and is surrounded by Whanganui National Park for 170 km of its sinuous course.

it resembles forests usually found only on the eastern side of the North Island axial ranges.

The 80,000 ha of Moawhango tussock grasslands (mostly under New Zealand Army management) suffered severe overgrazing from herds of Kaimamawa wild horses for many decades, until DOC moved to bring them under proper management in the early 1990s. A bitter stand-off with horse-lovers ensued. Four years of investigation and consultation led to a plan whereby horse numbers are now controlled at an optimum of 300–500 in an 18,000 ha southern sector of the tussocklands.

WHANGANUI NATIONAL PARK (AND THE WAITOTARA CONSERVATION AREA)

Between the Patea River in the west and the Whangaehu River in the east lies the largest lowland wilderness in the North Island, a homogenous maze of deeply entrenched streams, narrow flat-topped ridges and dense indigenous forest. The Whanganui River drains most of this hill country, and for 170 km its sinuous course is surrounded by Whanganui National Park (74,321 ha), although the bed of the river is Maori land. Much of the surrounding forested hill country is conservation land (mostly in Waitotara Conservation Area), of such high value that 90,000 ha were recommended for addition to the park by the NZ Conservation Authority in 1995. Off-track travel through the Wanganui hill country and Matemateaonga Range is difficult because the very soft mudstones have been eroded into an intricate, random pattern of gullies and streams. Instead, the Whanganui River is the main artery through the park, its volume of water and gentle gradient allowing Maori and European settlers to navigate far into the interior. During the latter part of the 19th century, tourists used the river as the most scenic route to Mt Ruapehu and the Volcanic Plateau. It remains as New Zealand's longest navigable river – a wild river mostly used by canoeists, and a taonga of enormous cultural significance to tangata whenua.

The park's forests have a pattern of podocarp, broadleaf and beech trees very closely related to topography and soil depth/fertility. Rimu and tawa are most common on the hill slopes, with scattered rewarewa, kamahi and hinau. Terraces are limited in extent, with kahikatea and pukatea on wetter sites and totara and matai on well-drained river terraces. Black beech predominates on the drier, shallow soils of the narrow ridge crests. This vast lowland forest is an important habitat for most native forest birds, with notable populations of brown kiwi, robin, kaka, New Zealand falcon/karearea and yellow-crowned parakeet. One of the clear tributaries of the Whanganui, the Manganui-o-te-Ao River, is a very important habitat for blue duck/whio.

THREATS AND CONSERVATION PRIORITIES

There are myriad threats to the integrity of the wilderness heritage of the Taranaki–Wanganui–Manawatu region, and thousands of priority conservation actions that are being (or could be) undertaken. The following conservation priorities stand out.

Extension of Successful Biodiversity Conservation Programmes

Successful animal pest control programmes have been completed throughout Egmont National Park, first for goats and then for possums. Until recently, the forests of North Taranaki were free of deer, and the excellent efforts by DOC to mount an inter-agency co-operative approach to hunting down small herds of deer and isolated escapees before they established in large numbers is a pointer to the

sort of proactive and targeted pest management required. The threat of deer and possums to the upland forests of the Rangitikei–Moawhango (especially Hihitahi Sanctuary) has been countered by aerial 1080 poison drops for more than a decade, and vegetation responses are now very apparent. Goats and possums remain an acute problem in the vast forests of the rugged Wanganui hill country, however, and it is hard not to be pessimistic about the conservation future of this geologically vulnerable landscape.

Despite the animal pest threat to the Wanganui hill-country forests, they are still the habitat of one of the country's three major populations of North Island brown kiwi, as well as important populations of bats, kaka, North Island robin, NZ falcon and kakariki. The North Taranaki forests are also important kiwi habitat but kiwi populations here and in Whanganui National Park are steadily declining because of stoat predation. Predator control and translocation programmes for blue duck/whio are showing great promise for this interesting bird, whose numbers are now probably fewer than 2500 nationally and whose international conservation status was raised to 'endangered' by the World Conservation Union (IUCN) in 2002.

Weeds are a ubiquitous problem in the forest margins, wetlands and sand country. The scourge of old man's beard and other smothering vines remains in the Taihape locality. Despite the notable success in removing weeds from Paengaroa and other targeted key reserves, the huge source of weed seed on private land needs to be confronted. Riparian forests, especially the reserves along the mid-Rangitikei, are a high priority for more intensive conservation management.

One of the biggest challenges is to maintain the health of the unique Moawhango tussocklands and upland wetlands. This will involve not only continued tight management of the reduced Kaimanawa wild horse herds and halting the advance of alien heather and *Pinus contorta* (which have largely eliminated red tussock in Tongariro National Park) but also contemplating controlled burning to perpetuate the grassland landscape. 'To burn or not to burn' the tussocklands poses a real dilemma for scientists and managers. The invasion of tussockland by woody shrubs and trees in this wetter environment is a natural process, which has been held in check historically by volcanic fires and past fires of human origin. The increasing dominance of *Hieracium pilosella*, pasture grasses, lotus and other weeds is a serious threat to the survival of tussockland herbs like *Ranunculus recens*, *Euchiton ensifer*, *Myosotis* 'glauca' and so on. Burning is likely to aggravate this weed problem, but without fire the tussocks will eventually be overwhelmed by invading woody shrubs, like manuka and species of *Dracophyllum* and *Hebe*.

More Representative Protected Areas and Increased Protective Status

The existing Protected Natural Area network is not representative of the natural ecosystems in this region, especially dunelands, wetlands and tussocklands. For example, the natural character and biodiversity value of the Foxton sand country has been severely degraded through many decades of ecologically insensitive agriculture, roading and beach settlement. The coastal forest that once covered the older dunes has virtually disappeared (save for small remnants like Himatangi Bush and Pakipaki Bush) and the dynamic process of dune formation halted by exotic tree plantations. Although the coastline does have some outstanding examples of 'pure' spinifex dunes (such as those at Castlecliff Beach), this native sand-binding grass and the striking golden sedge, pingao, have been largely replaced by planted marram grass and tree lupin, and a host of weed plants. In addition, many of the dune lakes are now polluted by nutrients from municipal wastewater and agriculture.

Ecological surveys have indicated a wide range of recommended areas for protection, especially in the upland tussock grasslands and wetlands of the Mangaohane Plateau, and the remnants of indigenous vegetation on the Manawatu–Rangitikei lowlands. The incremental loss to agriculture over the last 30 years of the tussock landscape around the Inland Patea Road (where it crosses the upper Rangitikei River and Ngamatea Plateau) is one of the great indigenous landscape tragedies of the North Island. A close working relationship needs to be maintained by DOC with the New Zealand Army to protect the Moawhango Basin – the last significantly sized red tussock landscape left in the North Island. At the same time, all effort should be made to protect the Reporoa Bog–Makirikiri Tarns uplands and to negotiate a long-term protective covenant with tangata whenua for the superb Aorangi–Awarua kaikawaka/podocarp forest block nearby.

A number of protected area initiatives seem to have bogged down – especially the 90,000 ha addition of hill-country forest in Waitotara Conservation Area to Whanganui National Park, and the delineation of a conservation park and adjacent marine reserve in the Whitecliffs locality of North Taranaki. The management of the Whanganui River is a sensitive issue for DOC and tangata whenua but it is to be hoped that the spirit of co-operation shown in the upgrading of Tieke Marae, a key recreational visitor site within the park, will carry through into a National Water Conservation Order for the river one day. Several factors argue for the designation of a North Taranaki Conservation Park and a much better level of recreational facilities and interpretation:

- diverse opportunities for wilderness tramping and hunting in the North Taranaki forests;
- the spectacular Whitecliffs coastline (traversed by the Whitecliffs Walkway);
- fishing, whitebaiting and birdwatching attractions of the Mokau and other estuaries.

In addition, enhancing the water quality of the rivers, dune lakes and estuaries through better agricultural practices and urban planning is one of the biggest conservation challenges facing the district and regional councils. The pollution so evident in the lower Manawatu and Whanganui rivers is little cause for regional pride.

Improved Public Access to Wilderness Landscapes

More needs to be done to negotiate public access over private lands to some of the key wilderness landscapes in the region. This is particularly so for the Moawhango and Mangaohane tussock grasslands and wetlands, sections of the Rangitikei, Waitara and Mokau rivers, and the forests of North Taranaki and the Wanganui hill country. The forest margins of the latter contain many old logging roads and farm vehicle tracks which are ideal for mountain-biking and horse-riding, recreational activities discouraged in national parks and sensitive conservation areas. The Whitecliffs Walkway and the Matemateaonga Walkway are the only two walkways that give access across private land into parts of these wild North Taranaki and Wanganui landscapes. There is scope for walkway development in the North Taranaki–Mokau hill country to provide better opportunities for tramping. However, it is important to retain sufficient undeveloped areas for wilderness recreation – similar to the Heao and Mangaio Remote Experience zones maintained within Whanganui National Park.

TOP The North Island variety of the brown kiwi (*Apteryx australis*) still survives in significant numbers in the Wanganui and North Taranaki hill country but it is increasingly under threat from stoats (ROD MORRIS). LEFT A nesting adult female fernbird (*Bowdleria punctata*) at the Manawatu River estuary (ROD MORRIS). ABOVE The katipo spider (*Latrodectus katipo*), seen here with a dead sand scarab in the Foxton sand country, has a venomous bite and is usually found under driftwood in sand dunes (ROD MORRIS).

CHAPTER SIX

EAST OF THE RANGES
GISBORNE, HAWKE'S BAY AND WAIRARAPA

The lowland and hill country east of the North Island axial ranges extends for 500 km from Hicks Bay to Palliser Bay. There are so many geological and climatic similarities within the regions historically known as Gisborne, Hawke's Bay and Wairarapa that it is convenient to treat them as one ecological 'super-region'.

The similarity in the geological character of the region is twofold: a pronounced north-east–south-west trend to the coastal basins and hills, and the relatively young sedimentary origins of most of the rocks. In the southern and central parts of the region, the inland valleys and coastal hills lie parallel to the axial ranges on their western boundary. In tectonic terms they can be thought of as furrows and wrinkles in the earth's surface, all oriented along roughly parallel faults, as the eastern North Island part of the Australian Plate is compressed like a concertina as the Pacific Plate is forced under it. Most of the sedimentary rocks of this coastal hill country are soft marine sandstones and siltstones of Tertiary age, often surrounding bands of harder sandstone or limestone. Many of the latter stand out as spectacular hill landscapes of parallel hogbacks and cuestas. The limestone cuesta topography is quite pronounced in central Hawke's Bay and northern Wairarapa, where the Te Mata, Raukawa, Kaokaoroa, Kohinurakau and Puketoi ranges, and the Three Kings cuestas, stand out like ribs running SW–NE. The limestone stratum dips gently north-westward, with the sheer scarp face generally facing south-east. Further south, in coastal Wairarapa, a line of spectacular sandstone peaks (known locally as taipos) stand out boldly in the landscape, their harder rocks resisting the erosive forces that have reduced the surrounding sedimentary strata to gentle hills.

Another outstanding geological feature of these eastern lowlands is a remarkably rich record of ancient life preserved as fossils in the widespread sediments and conglomerates. Most of these fossils are at the more youthful end of the geological time-scale, Miocene to Holocene in age. They are especially accessible in coastal exposures such as:
- Pourerere (foraminifera);
- Cape Turnagain (rare fossil crabs in siltstone);
- Castlepoint (over 70 fossil species in limestone, reflecting past changes from cold to warmer seawater);
- the 8000-year-old fossil totara forest at the mouth of the Kaiwhata River.

At the other extreme, inland at Mangahouanga Stream (a tributary of the Te Hoe River) lies New Zealand's best-known site of fossil dinosaurs, of Cretaceous age. This site is of international importance not only for its dinosaurs but also because of its record of fossil turtles, plesiosaurs, early fish and New Zealand's oldest known fossil insect.

The region's climate is characterised by very warm summers with a pronounced dryness extending through into autumn. Most rain falls in winter, but heavy rainstorms can occur at any time of the year – for example, the devastating Cyclone Bola of March 1988. The combined effect of unstable geology and climatic extremes has predisposed the region to historical cycles of severe natural erosion. Sediment from climatic or earthquake events over the millennia caused riverbeds to build up naturally, but the rate of erosion accelerated markedly after European farmers began to fell large areas of native forest from the 1880s onwards. The hill country between Hawke Bay and Ruatoria was probably the most severely affected. The Gisborne

Putangirua Pinnacles, just inland of the Palliser Bay coastline, are probably the best example of a 'badlands' erosion landform in New Zealand.

Napier

Clifton
Black Reef
Cape Kidnappers

Hastings

Te Awanga

Ocean Beach

KOHINURAKAU RANGE

RAUKAWA RANGE

KAOKAOROA RANGE

TE MATA

MARETOTARA PLATEAU

Aorangi-Awarua Blk
The Narrows

MANGAOHANE PLATEAU

Repaton Bog
Aorangi
Makaturi Tarns
Te Rakaunuiakuna
Ruahine
Corner

Ngaruroro R.

Mataroa

Taihape

Hautapu R.

Moawhango R.

Rangitikei R.

Mangawhero R.

Whangaehu R.

Atene

Waverley

Castlecliff Beach

Wanganui

Turakina

Marton

Mangaweka

Ohingaiti

Mangaweka

PAPAKIAKUTA RIDGE

RUAHINE RANGE

Hunterville

Kairakau

Waipukurau

RUATANIWHA PLAINS

Takapau

Bulls

Feilding

Oroua R.

Pohangina R.

Dannevirke

Pourerere

Aramoana

Blackhead

Te Angiangi Marine Reserve

Rangitikei River

FOXTON SAND COUNTRY

Palmerston North

Himatangi Bush

Manawatu River

Foxton

Manawatu Gorge

Woodville

Pahiatua

Porangahau Lagoon

Cape Turnagain

Levin

Lake Papaitonga

Eketahuna

PUKETOI RANGE

Otaki River

Otaki

Pukemoremore

Bruce Strm

Arete

Girdlestone

Mitre

Bruces Hill

Mauriceville

Kapiti Island Marine Reserve

Kapiti Island

Waikanae

Table Top

Mt Hector

Alpha

TARARUA RANGE

CONE RIDGE

Masterton

Whakataki

Castlepoint

Paekakariki

Kaitoke Regional Park

Carterton

Whareama River

Porirua

Upper Hutt

Featherston

WAIRARAPA PLAINS

Lower Hutt

RIMUTAKA RANGE

L. Wairarapa

Martinborough

Kaiwhata River

Flat Point

WELLINGTON

Pencarrow Head
Baring Head
Turakirae Head

East Harbour Regional Park

L. Onoke

Lake Ferry

Ruamahanga River

Palliser Bay

Putangirua Pinnacles
Whatarangi Bluff

AORANGI RANGE

Honeycomb Rock

Pahaoa River

Pararaki Stream

Ngawi

White Rock
Ngapotiki Fan
Waitetuna Stream

Kupe's Sail

Cape Palliser

N

1 Whanganui National Park
2 Hihitahi Forest Sanctuary
3 Cape Kidnappers Gannet Reserve
4 Paengaroa Scenic Reserve
5 Kaweka Forest Park
6 Ruahine Forest Park
7 Mohi Bush Scenic Reserve
8 Elsthorpe Scenic Reserve
9 Inglis Bush Scenic Reserve
10 Kapiti Island Nature Reserve
11 Tararua Forest Park
12 Pukaha / Mt Bruce National Wildlife Centre
13 Carter Scenic Reserve
14 Rimutaka Forest Park
15 Rocky Hills Sanctuary Area
16 Aorangi Forest Park

0   25   50   75km

WELLINGTON, MANAWATU, SOUTHERN HAWKES BAY

Plains suffered 10 major floods in the 1932–42 decade. Soil and rock debris up to 20 m deep choked the bed of the Waipaoa River, and rivers of mud formed during high rainfall. Government responded in the 1960s by retiring from farming 150,000 ha of critical headwaters from the Waipaoa to the Waiapu, and progressively planting the area in exotic forests during the next 25 years. Nevertheless, the removal of the original forest must rank as one of New Zealand's most costly environmental disasters, one which has blighted the economy, and the biodiversity, of the region for more than a century.

In terms of indigenous biodiversity, this eastern region is now one of the more impoverished regions in New Zealand. This is primarily because of the virtual wholesale removal, for pastoral agriculture and intensive horticulture, of indigenous vegetation from the lowlands and wetlands. What is left of the original character is now best appreciated in three landscapes:

- the immediate coastal zone;
- some small but superb pockets of lowland podocarp/broadleaf forest that survive on the flood plains and low hills;
- southern Wairarapa, where sizeable forest and wetland habitats remain in the Aorangi Range and Lake Wairarapa.

A SPECTACULAR, DYNAMIC COASTLINE

There is a wildness and scenic grandeur to the long eastern coastline, all the way from Matakaoa Point in the north to Lake Ferry in Palliser Bay. Pacific Ocean swells pile up to provide some of the best surfing waves in the country. The soft pale siltstone and mudstone has been carved into clean lines of impressive cliffs and headlands, many of them out of sight, but some icon landmarks like Young Nicks Head (Poverty Bay), Cape Kidnappers, Cape Turnagain, Castlepoint and Whatarangi Bluff (Palliser Bay) can be seen or reached from highways. Along this dynamic coastline the sea is constantly eroding the soft cliffs, keeping the exposed sediments free of vegetation that would otherwise obscure the strata. At the same time, the rivers are continually depositing fresh sediment, carried down from the same soft-rock hinterland, to build up fertile floodplains behind the major bays, especially Tolaga Bay, Poverty Bay and Hawke Bay. Marine habitats have not been as damaged as terrestrial habitats, but they are significantly modified by the same sediments smothering bottom-dwelling marine life, and by over-fishing and the wholesale poaching of crayfish and shellfish.

Fossils are a feature of the sedimentary rocks east of the axial ranges. This skull of *Tuarangisaurus keyesi*, a late Cretaceous age dinosaur, was found in Hawke's Bay (PETER E. SMITH, NATURAL SCIENCES IMAGE LIBRARY).

Coastal forests of pohutukawa, tawapou, puriri, wharangi, kohekohe and karaka now remain as only small scattered remnants. The best can be found (from north to south) between Hicks Bay and Te Araroa, Waimahuru Bay directly east of Te Puia, Anaura Bay, Whareongaonga and Waipatiki. Some coastal areas, like the 1931 earthquake slump feature of Moeangiangi Slip in Hawke's Bay, are regenerating in manuka and could eventually develop into coastal forest. Although the coastal forests have largely gone, the unstable slips and cliffs are still a suitable habitat for many interesting, rare and biogeographically significant shrubs and herbs. The kakabeak/kowhai ngutukaka, with its clusters of striking red flowers, was once plentiful in this habitat between East Cape and Tolaga Bay but is now very rare. Other notable plants include:

- a shrub daisy, raukumara (*Brachyglottis perdicioides*), and a small, rosette herb (*Plantago spathulata* var. *picta*);
- divaricating shrubs like matagouri (rare in the North Island), *Muehlenbeckia astonii* and *M. ephedroides*, and *Teucridium parvifolium*;
- the rengarenga lily (*Arthropodium candidum*), found only at Kairakau throughout this entire coastline;
- Cooks scurvy grass (*Lepidium oleraceum*), now very rare on mainland New Zealand;
- *Chionochloa flavicans*, a coastal cliff tussock member of this primarily subalpine snowgrass genus.

Estuaries are not a major feature of the coastline; the two largest are Ahuriri and Porangahau. As a result of the

devastating 1931 Hawke's Bay earthquake, 1300 ha of the inner Ahuriri Lagoon was lost, exposed as dry land when its bed was lifted 2–3 m. Nevertheless, the 450 ha remnant is still one of the most significant estuaries for wildlife in the North Island, particularly because of its high educational value through its proximity to the Napier–Hastings urban population. Porangahau Estuary is the largest and least modified on the east coast of the North Island south of Ohiwa Harbour in the Bay of Plenty. It has an intact dune flat/ridge system of national significance because of its conservation values, and is an important wintering and feeding area for migratory wading birds, notably wrybill, banded dotterel and Caspian terns.

Two coastal landscapes – Cape Kidnappers and Mahia Peninsula – are widely appreciated, both for their outstanding landforms and wildlife significance. Cape Kidnappers is a well-known tourist destination because of the scenic quality of its sedimentary geology and the presence of the largest mainland gannet colony in New Zealand (the other

Gable ends, such as this ridge-end near East Cape, are common coastal landform features in the vertical sedimentary strata along the east coast of the North Island.

two being at Farewell Spit and Muriwai). Along the 7 km coastal walk from Clifton to the gannets at Black Reef and the cape, the 100 m high sea cliffs are an impressive sight, with alternating layers of sediments (and tephra). The different coloured layers include: sandstone, siltstone, greywacke gravels, shells (white), peat (dark), and volcanic ash (white) from eruptions in the Taupo Volcanic Zone – all deposited between one million and 500,000 years ago.

Mahia Peninsula, forming the northern extremity of Hawke Bay, is one of the most prominent landmarks on the eastern coastline of the North Island. Mahia has been progressively uplifted from the sea floor over the past five million years, first as an island and, in the last 10,000 years (since the end of the Last Glaciation), as the peninsula we know today – through sand building up the tombolo

connecting Mahia to Opoutama. The extensive marine terraces and raised beaches at Table Cape and elsewhere around the peninsula are of international significance; some consider them the best-preserved and most accessible sequence of uplifted late Quaternary marine terraces in New Zealand. Mahia Peninsula Scenic Reserve, one of the largest (374 ha) tracts of coastal forest remaining, has a wide range of broadleaf trees (tawa, kohekohe, karaka, ngaio, rewarewa, tarata) and podocarps (rimu, kahikatea and matai). Mahia's wildlife significance is focused on Opoutama Beach, which has the dubious distinction of having the world's second highest recorded rate of whale strandings.

FOREST REMNANTS EAST OF THE AXIAL RANGES
Only remnants of the once extensive indigenous forests east of the axial ranges now remain, most of very high conservation value despite their small size. Four in particular – the group of forests on the Maungaharuru Range, Waingake Waterworks Bush, Balls Clearing Scenic Reserve and Rocky Hill Sanctuary Area – survived because they occupy rugged landforms distant from the main centres of agricultural development.

The blue penguin or korora (*Eudyptula minor*) is the smallest and most common of the 13 penguins found in the New Zealand region (ROD MORRIS).

The Maungaharuru Range separates the deep valley of the Mohaka River from the northern Hawke's Bay hill country around Lake Tutira. The crest of the range is a spectacular plateau of uplifted sedimentary rocks, reaching an altitude of 1308 m at Taraponui. It is not surprising that some significant forest remnants survived in this landscape of abrupt escarpments, deep gorges, tomos and subterranean streams, and weathered limestone outcrops; notable remnants are Boundary Stream Scenic Reserve (704 ha), Bellbird Bush Scenic Reserve (182 ha) and Waitere Kiwi Conservation Area (1662 ha). The crest of the range has an unusual broadleaf cloud-cap forest, with the attractive 'mountain holly', *Olearia ilicifolia* (one of the tree daisies), and scattered red tussock. Boundary Stream is a podocarp/kamahi forest which has assumed high conservation importance as a mainland island. After intensive pest control, North Island brown kiwi have been re-introduced (shortly after the local population died out from the cumulative effects of a more than a century of habitat

The worldwide myrtle family is best represented in New Zealand by the 12 species of the *Metrosideros* genus, the best known being the coastal pohutukawa (*Metrosideros excelsa*). Its crimson flowers, made up from many erect stamens, are very typical of the genus, and the copious nectar is relished not only by birds and bats but also insects and lizards. Pohutukawa now grows in most coastal locations throughout New Zealand but its natural distribution is on the east coast of the North Island north of Gisborne and the west coast north of New Plymouth (ROD MORRIS).

The New Zealand red admiral or kahukura (*Vanessa gonerilla*) is an endemic butterfly found throughout the country wherever its food source, the large stinging nettle ongaonga (*Urtica ferox*), is common (ROD MORRIS).

LEFT An Australasian gannet (*Morus serrator*) about to land in its colony. BELOW The 13 ha Cape Kidnappers Gannet Reserve in Hawke's Bay is claimed to be the largest accessible mainland gannet colony in the world. Since 1880, when around 50 birds were first observed to be breeding at the site, numbers have grown to almost 7000 breeding pairs in four sub-colonies. In addition to New Zealand's two other mainland breeding sites (Muriwai and Farewell Spit), there are another 21 offshore gannetries, the largest of which are the Three Kings Islands, Gannet Island (offshore between the mouths of Raglan and Aotea harbours), and White Island/Whakaari (ROD MORRIS).

fragmentation and predation), along with North Island robins and kokako.

Waingake Waterworks Bush (1106 ha) lies in the headwaters of the Te Arai River south-west of Gisborne. This catchment was set aside in the 1880s to protect Gisborne's water supply; it now has additional protection under a Queen Elizabeth II Trust covenant. This little-known catchment is probably the most important forest remnant on soft-rock hill country in the region. Primary forest covers 90 per cent of the area, with a 100–720 m altitude range – from semi-coastal tawa/kohekohe forest, to rimu/tawa/kamahi forest with black beech forest strips on stable ridges at mid-altitudes, and rimu/red beech/tawa and red/silver beech forest at the higher altitudes.

Balls Clearing Scenic Reserve (135 ha) lies 65 km northwest of Napier beyond Puketitiri at 600 m altitude; remote, but so impressive that it is the stuff of conservation legend. It was protected in the 1930s after strong public opposition to milling the last Puketitiri forests. Today, a walk through the 36 ha of unlogged forest in the reserve is an unforgettable experience, conjuring up visions of how New Zealand's primeval forests must have been. The podocarp trees are exceptionally dense, with kahikatea and rimu reaching heights of over 35 m, rivalling trees in the two great North Island podocarp forest wildernesses, Tihoi in Pureora Forest Park and Whirinaki Forest Park (see Ch.4, pp.84–87). Prior to 1954, the clearing was a botanically significant 46 ha natural enclave of red tussock, herbs and sedges. However, as manuka began to colonise the clearing, the then-managers of New Zealand's public lands, the Department of Lands and Survey, became apprehensive about fire hazard. Unfortunately, they lacked the expertise to understand the ecological harm they caused when they panicked and, without consultation with the scientific community, cultivated and grassed the clearing.

The fourth remote remnant, Rocky Hills Sanctuary Area (404 ha), is the only area of protected indigenous forest in the eastern Wairarapa taipo landscape. This rather inaccessible sanctuary lies across three 550–600 m high pinnacles of hard sandstone (known locally as the Rough Taipos) in the headwaters of the Pahaoa River. The forest is broadleaf/podocarp (miro, totara and rimu), now quite rare in the Wairarapa.

A few lowland forest remnants are worthy of especial note because they are rare forest types on alluvial landforms. Grey's Bush near Gisborne is small (12 ha) but of very high conservation significance as the only remnant of the tall kahikatea forest that once covered the highly fertile

ABOVE AND LEFT Grey's Bush near Gisborne is the only remnant of the tall kahikatea forest that once covered the fertile flood plain of the Waipaoa River. The kahikatea trees in the left photo are over 40 m high.

flood plain of the Waipaoa River. The 40 m high kahikatea trees, around 500 years old, are mixed with puriri, giving an unusual and nationally rare forest association. Broadleaf trees like pukatea, tawa and kohekohe add to the attractiveness of this priceless forest remnant. The semi-swamp forest in Carter Scenic Reserve (on terraces beside the Ruamahanga River, not far from Carterton) varies markedly with the soil water table. It has a wide range of forest and swamp habitats, and contains more than 200 indigenous plant species – a very high number for an area of only around 20 ha. Kahikatea forest fringes the wetland, but this changes to titoki forest (with scattered kahikatea and matai) as drainage improves; on the terrace slopes, where the soil is well drained, totara is the dominant podocarp in

TOP The clear streams running from the eastern side of the North Island axial ranges are a habitat for native fish, like this threatened dwarf galaxias (ROD MORRIS). ABOVE The kingfisher or kotare (*Halcyon sancta*) frequents the forest edges and stream margins of the lowlands east of the ranges.

the forest. Another Wairarapa remnant, Fanshaw Reserve northwest of Carterton, is owned by Forest & Bird and contains beech as well as dense stands of kahikatea.

Several outstanding podocarp forest remnants also remain on the Maraetotara Plateau in central Hawke's Bay. Two of these, Mohi Bush and Elsthorpe scenic reserves, contain magnificent kahikatea, miro and matai, and are accessible by track from country roads. They are important for sustaining forest bird populations, especially tui and kereru, and the excitement of the flocks of birds feasting

on the berry-like fleshy cones of kahikatea in autumn is such that the dislodged and/or digested ripe berries can literally rain down on visitors. Mohi Bush is also notable for its population of the diminutive rifleman/titipounamu, far from its major habitat in Ruahine and Kaweka forest parks to the west. Further south lie the scattered forest remnants of Seventy Mile Bush which once extended unbroken from Takapau to Woodville, until government-sponsored Scandinavian settlers in the 1870s were encouraged to convert the dense forest to farmland.

The best of many forest pockets remaining on the Ruataniwha Plains is Inglis Bush Scenic Reserve beside the Tukituki River: it contains dense kahikatea over an understorey of tawa and titoki, and is notable for its population of long-tailed bats. Still further south, between Pahiatua and Mauriceville, Forty Mile Bush has long gone, save for a 500 ha remnant around Bruces Hill (716 m). This locality is better known as Mt Bruce, because of the location of the Pukaha Mt Bruce National Wildlife Centre here in podocarp/kamahi forest beside Bruce Stream and SH 2. The Mt Bruce Centre was the first place in New Zealand where the captive breeding of threatened wildlife was pioneered. Today, it is also important as an educational facility where DOC's conservation efforts for a number of threatened endemic birds are interpreted, and the surrounding forest is now being managed as a mainland island.

LAKE WAIRARAPA, THE AORANGI RANGE AND PALLISER BAY

Lake Wairarapa, Lake Onoke and their associated wetlands (and some scattered forest remnants) make up the largest wetland ecosystem in the lower North Island. The total protected area is 9500 ha, with a National Water Conservation Order recognising the outstanding wildlife habitat of Lake Wairarapa and the former lower reaches of the Ruamahanga River (now cut off by flood protection works). Lake Onoke, a 650 ha lake at the mouth of the Ruamahanga, is separated from Palliser Bay by an impressive 3 km long shingle spit. At times of high water level, the lake is open to the sea and is tidal (hence the historical name of 'Lake Ferry' in reference to the need to cross the dangerous outlet by small boat). Further upstream, Lake Wairarapa is quite shallow, mostly less than 2.5 m deep. Despite being subject to water-level fluctuation and wind-driven waves, its wide eastern shoreline is an important habitat for the feeding and breeding of many native birds. Twelve freshwater fish species are known to inhabit the wetlands, which are also of high recreational value to duck-shooters and fishers.

The Pararaki Stream enters Palliser Bay from its greywacke-choked stream bed. The forested Aorangi Range (the core of Aorangi Forest Park) can be seen in the distance.

To the east of the Lake Wairarapa wetlands, the Aorangi Range rises up as an isolated massif of greywacke basement rock. The range ends in the dramatic landscape of Cape Palliser, where the eastern hill country terminates in gale-swept Cook Strait. The Aorangi Range is relatively free of the fog and low cloud that is the scourge of the wetter Tararua and Rimutaka ranges to the west (see Ch.7). Snowfall is infrequent, but severe southerly winds in winter make it an inhospitable place. The forests, much of which have been damaged by deer, goats and wind, are a mixture of four species of beech (red, black, hard and silver) plus a wide range of podocarp and broadleaf trees. Of particular interest are many large specimens of hinau, matai and miro scattered along the ridge crests. The easiest access is via the pronounced radial pattern of stream drainage. Much of the range is protected as Aorangi Forest Park (19,382 ha),

although it is probably the least visited of the 20 or so forest (conservation) parks managed by DOC; the isolation and lack of track maintenance means that it is rapidly reverting to a recreational wilderness – which is probably not a bad consequence.

The coastal flanks of the Aorangi Range contain a number of interesting geological features and landforms. The best known are the Putangirua Pinnacles in Palliser Bay, the prime example of 'badlands' erosion in New Zealand. Here rain has washed away the silty matrix of the old alluvial conglomerate uplifted long ago from the seabed, forming hundreds of individual earth pillars (technically

ABOVE A wave-cut platform in the sedimentary rocks of Mahia Peninsula. Mahia Peninsula is one of many coastal localities that need to be
given better protection because of their landforms and biodiversity
features. RIGHT Castlepoint on the remote Wairarapa coast is a locality
of high recreational and scientific interest. Its limestone and sandstone
rocks contain over 70 different fossil species. The prominent reef enclosing the lagoon is oriented along local faults.

known as hoodoos); each 60–90 m high pillar is protected by a cap, usually a boulder or a cemented gravel layer. Close by, the narrow road to Cape Palliser has to negotiate Whatarangi Bluff, where rainfall continually causes deep gullying in the soft, grey, muddy sandstone cliff. Beyond the fishing village of Ngawi, the road takes a precarious path between the surf and the base of Kupe's Sail Nga ra o Kupe, a huge slab of sandstone which is tilted at an angle of about 45 degrees.

Cape Palliser is a place of special significance to tangata whenua as well as to science. The coastal fringe was forcibly taken by the Crown in 1897 for the building of Cape Palliser lighthouse, but returned to the tangata whenua, Ngati Hinewaka hapu, in 1993. The hapu has designated this 20 ha as an open-space covenant, Matakitaki-a-Kupe, to protect a number of features associated with Kupe, waahi tapu and once important fishing grounds. The area includes the pillow lava reef at Cape Palliser and the main North Island breeding colony of the New Zealand fur seal. In addition, a number of rare and endangered plants, including *Muehlenbeckia astonii* and *M. ephedroides* and the local endemic coastal tussock *Chionochloa beadiei*, occur on the coastal cliffs and beach gravels.

The entire Cape Palliser locality is one of the wildest parts of the eastern North Island coastline. For here the steep eastern slopes of the Aorangi Range plunge 800 m down to the huge Ngapotiki Fan, a typical greywacke fan reminiscent of the mountains of Marlborough or Canterbury, yet quite enigmatic on the otherwise soft eastern coastline. The wildness of the aspect is completed by two other impressive landforms at opposite ends of the fan: the ravine and waterfalls of Stonewall Stream/Waitetuna to the south, and the jagged limestone reef of White Rock to the north. This unique combination of wilderness landscape and biological interest in the southern Aorangi Range around Cape Palliser is well summed-up in the words of the eminent botanist, Tony Druce: 'If any area on the southern North Island coastline should be declared a National Coastline Park, this is it.'

THREATS AND CONSERVATION PRIORITIES

Greater Protection for Coastal Landscapes and Marine Ecosystems

Most of the coastal ecosystems throughout the region currently lack protected area status. There are a few notable exceptions, like narrow sections of the coastal cliffs at Cape Kidnappers and Castlepoint, parts of the Ahuriri Estuary,

Waimahuru Scenic Reserve east of Te Puia, and Earthquake Slip Conservation Area – 8 km of coastal cliffs around the 1931 earthquake-induced Moeangiangi Slip on the northern side of Hawke Bay. There are only two marine reserves: Te Tapuwae o Rongokako (3450 ha) between Whangara and Pouawa on the Tairawhiti coastline north-east of Gisborne, and the small Te Angiangi (446 ha) between Aramoana and Blackhead in central Hawke's Bay.

Considering the dynamic and scenic nature of this coastline, the lack of any comprehensive network of coastal and marine protected areas is a colossal historical oversight by both central and local government. The oversight is even more puzzling considering that the isolation and highly eroding nature of the coastline has rendered much of it unsuitable for settlement. With the notable exception of controversial proposals to establish a luxury tourist lodge above the gannet colony at Cape Kidnappers, and to subdivide a natural coastline near Ocean Beach, much of the region's coastline has been free of the intense real-estate speculation and tourist-resort development plaguing other parts of the eastern coastline of the North Island. So it is an urgent priority for DOC and local government to work closely with landowners and iwi to identify the key landscapes and natural values needing protection within this coastal and marine environment.

In particular, the region's district councils, in association with tangata whenua, need to develop coastal conservation strategies under the Resource Management Act 1991, to protect a number of features of geological importance as well as the biodiversity remaining in coastal wetlands, estuaries, sand dunes and coastal forest remnants. Some key coastal and marine localities are a priority:

- East Cape wetlands and dunelands;
- Hauiti (Uawa) Estuary (Tolaga Bay);
- Wherowhero Lagoon (Muriwai);
- Mahia and the 'Wairoa Hard';
- Ahuriri Estuary;
- the cliffs, inter-tidal reefs, and dune systems from Te Awanga, around Cape Kidnappers, to Ocean Beach (north);
- Porangahau Estuary and dune systems;
- Cape Turnagain fossil sites and diverse coastal vegetation communities;
- Whakataki shore platform (alternating mudstone–sandstone 'grooves');
- Kaiwhata River mouth (fossil trees);
- Honeycomb Rock on the Glenburn Coast.

CHAPTER SEVEN

AXIAL RANGES OF THE NORTH ISLAND

The axial ranges are the single most dominant physical feature of the North Island. They extend from Pukeamaru above Hicks Bay in East Cape to Turakirae Head east of the entrance to Wellington Harbour. Their beautiful Maori names resonate like a waiata extolling a remote wilderness of forest and turbulent rivers – Raukumara, Ikawhenua, Huiarau, Ahimanawa, Kaweka, Kaimanawa, Ruahine, Tararua and Rimutaka. Even though the axial ranges extend right through the traditional central, eastern and southern provinces of the North Island, they are considered here as a discrete region because they have ecological and recreational values common to what is, in effect, one 500 km long, largely forested mountain chain.

The geological unity of the region lies in its greywacke and argillite bedrock. There is landform unity in the deeply incised nature of the ranges, all oriented NE–SW parallel with the plate boundary. Their summits stand 1500–1750 m above sea level, uplifted by enormous tectonic forces caused by compression of the continental Australian Plate from the subducting Pacific Plate (see Ch.1), and they have a common mountain climate: typically, significant cloud and fog, high rainfall, severe winds and cold temperatures with winter snowfalls. There are other common soil and botanical similarities: highly variable steepland soils, often podzolised and low in available nutrients, and montane rainforests dominated by species of that ubiquitous denizen of cool, wet, infertile and unstable environments – southern beech (*Nothofagus*). All five taxa of *Nothofagus* are found throughout the ranges, sometimes as almost pure stands but often in competition with broadleaf trees at lower altitudes; montane conifers (such as mountain toatoa, Hall's totara and kaikawaka) occur on higher, poorly drained or less-fertile soils.

The axial ranges contain the forested headwaters of some of the largest rivers of the North Island:
• the Waiapu, Waipaoa, Wairoa, Mohaka, Ngaruroro, Tukituki, Manawatu and Ruamahanga in the east;
• in the west, the Motu, Waioeka, Whakatane, the Waipakihi headwaters of the Tongariro–Waikato, the Rangitikei, the Oroua and Pohangina tributaries of the Manawatu, and the Otaki;
• in the south, the Hutt River flowing into Wellington Harbour from its source on the southern slopes of the Tararua Range.

The flood plains which these rivers have built up in the lowlands all carry agricultural, horticultural or residential developments of vital importance to New Zealand's economy. Cyclone Bola's devastating impact on the East Coast hill country in 1988 points to the fundamental environmental and economic importance of maintaining the forests of the axial ranges for water and soil conservation, and the protection of downstream amenities.

Historically, most of the indigenous forests of the axial ranges were too remote and difficult to clear for farmland, although the lower reaches of some valleys were logged for their larger podocarp trees. Consequently, most of the steepland was retained as public land – 'protection forests' managed by the NZ Forest Service, although the outstanding scenic attractions of the Lake Waikaremoana locality led to the designation of Te Urewera National Park in 1954. There was an unsuccessful campaign in Wellington to mark the 1940 New Zealand Centennial by designating the Tararua Ranges as a national park, but it was not until the emergence of a post-World War Two generation of trampers and hunters that the wilderness recreation

Sunrise on snow tussock and leatherwood above the bushline on the Tararua Ranges (ROB BROWN).

Looking into the rugged peaks of Raukumara Wilderness Area from the summit of Mt Hikurangi. Whanokao (1625 m) is the highest peak in the distance (SHAUN BARNETT/BLACK ROBIN).

value of most of the axial ranges began to be more widely appreciated. Tramping clubs became popular and their members developed networks of huts and tracks, later reinforced by the NZ Forest Service's extensive deer culler hut- and track-building programme of the 1960s. Further pressure for national park designation was countered by the NZ Forest Service with its very successful forest park concept, with recreational use accorded a higher priority (although management was still primarily for water and soil conservation). The first forest park in the axial ranges was Tararua, established in 1967; others quickly followed: Kaimanawa (1969), Rimutaka (1972), Kaweka (1974), Ruahine (1976) and Raukumara (1979) (see also Ch.1).

The axial ranges are the outstanding wilderness heritage of the North Island, and their wild character is best described in more detail by considering four clusters, from north to south:

- Raukumara Range;
- Huiarau Range and Te Urewera National Park;
- Kaimanawa Mountains and the Kaweka and Ruahine Ranges;
- and the Tararua and Rimutaka Ranges.

RAUKUMARA RANGE AND THE MOTU RIVER

The Raukumara Range is arguably the most remote and rugged forested wilderness in the North Island. Compared with the other ranges in the chain, the Raukumara is very difficult to penetrate on foot along the rivers because of the severity of their gorges. The 115,044 ha Raukumara Forest Park protects the crest of the range and the upper reaches of the wilderness rivers that flow down the western slopes to the Bay of Plenty – the remarkable Motu and the Haparapara, Kereu and Raukokore rivers. In its upper reaches the Motu River meanders across the farmland of the Matawai district on the south-western flanks of the Raukumara Range. But at the Motu Falls, 115 km from the sea and 460 m above sea level, the river begins to change dramatically and, for the next 85 km, it twists and tumbles its way through a maze of sheer gorges and unrelenting rapids unparalleled in the North Island for their scenery and wilderness canoeing/rafting challenges. The Motu is

New Zealand's classic 'wild and scenic' river, a conservation *cause célèbre*. During the decade 1975–1985, a sustained campaign for the protection of the wilderness values of the Motu was jointly led by the NZ Canoeing Association and the Federated Mountain Clubs of NZ, in the face of government investigations of sites for two or more large dams for hydroelectricity generation. Public pressure for the protection of the waters of wild and scenic rivers like the Motu, Whanganui and Buller eventually led to Parliament in 1981 passing an amendment to the Water and Soil Conservation Act 1967 allowing 'water conservation orders'. The Motu became the conservation test case under the new legislation; early in 1984 a National Water Conservation Order preserved the entire Motu (including all of its wild tributaries) from the Motu Falls to the SH 35 bridge (4 km upstream from the sea). It took another four years before the first real wilderness area in the North Island – the Raukumara Wilderness Area (39,650 ha) – was legally established within the heart of Raukumara Forest Park.

The most spectacular peaks in the Raukumara Range

The Motu River, draining the south-western slopes of the Raukumara Range, was the first Wild and Scenic River protected by a Water Conservation Order (SHAUN BARNETT/BLACK ROBIN).

rise at its north-eastern extremity, the so-called Waiapu Mountains – Hikurangi (1752 m), Whanokao (1625 m), Aorangi (1272 m), Wharekia (1106 m) and Taitai (677 m). Each of these peaks has a characteristic shape, with an exceptionally steep craggy summit area standing on a pedestal with only moderate slopes. Each is steeped in Maori tradition and the creation legend of Te Ika a Maui (the North Island). They are a spectacular sight looking up the Tapuaeroa River valley from Ruatoria. Hikurangi is the highest non-volcanic peak in the North Island and has the highest silver beech treeline in New Zealand. There are a number of endemic plants in this locality, and Whanokao, in particular, carries a very interesting assemblage of montane podocarp forest, shrubland and subalpine vegetation. The damp forests of the Raukumara Range are also notable for populations of two ancient Gondwana animals

– Hochstetter's frog and the Raukumara tusked weta. The latter was not discovered until August 1995, no doubt because of remoteness and difficult access. It is the third species of this highly distinctive weta group found only in the North Island (the other two being in Northland and on the Mercury Islands).

HUIARAU RANGE AND TE UREWERA NATIONAL PARK

Te Urewera National Park (212,673 ha) is by far the largest wilderness park in the North Island, and the fourth largest of New Zealand's national parks. It is centred on the heavily forested Huiarau, Ikawhenua and Kahikatea ranges, and the maze of broken hill country around the upper Whakatane, Waimana and Ruakituri rivers – a vast jumble of ranges wedged between the Taupo Volcanic Zone in the west and Hawke Bay in the east. The western and northern part of the park is rugged greywacke hill country like the rest of the axial ranges; however, the eastern and southern margin of the park consists of softer sedimentary rocks, uplifted and eroded into a broken sandstone escarpment 500–600 m high, with well-known spectacular landmarks like Panekiri Bluff and the Ngamoko Range above Lake Waikaremoana. The lake itself owes its origin to a large landslide around 2200 years ago, when 2 km³ of the south-western end of the Ngamoko Range broke away and slid into the then gorge of the Waikaretaheke River, forming a debris dam through which the lake subsequently drained underground. A few kilometres to the north-east, a much earlier and even more massive landslide of soft rocks off the ridges near Mt Manuoha formed the hummocky landscape around Lake Waikareiti (892 m above sea level). This odd landscape is a confusing wilderness on the ground, a colourful mosaic of forested knolls and wetlands, the latter sometimes referred to as the 'Kaipo tundra' because of their resemblance to the permafrost tundra of the Arctic.

The forests of the southern half of the park and the Kahikatea Range are dominated by species of beech (mainly red and silver), with many rimu emergent above the canopy up to about 950 m altitude. Kamahi is common, and there are local pockets of mountain, black and hard beech. The summits of the heavily forested Huiarau Range are generally only 1000–1200 m in altitude, except for Manuoha (1392 m), the highest point in the park and the only locality just above the treeline. The forested islands in Lake Waikareiti are particularly interesting, for they are still untouched by possums, and deer only rarely make the effort to swim out to them; consequently, the islands, albeit small

in area, carry one of the most pristine montane forests in the North Island and feature three species of mistletoe.

In the northern half of the park, tawa (along with a wide range of broadleaf trees) becomes more common as the forest canopy, with increasing amounts of warmth-loving kohekohe and pukatea in the margins closest to coastal Bay of Plenty. These northern forests are the site of DOC's largest 'mainland island' biodiversity restoration project – a joint project which has thrived on a close partnership between DOC and the tangata whenua of Te Urewera, the Tuhoe people to whom the forests and their wildlife have always been a taonga. Here the restoration approach has used labour-intensive ground trapping by local people. Four core areas (with a total area of around 5000 ha) have been intensively trapped for possums, rats and stoats, but only possums are trapped in the vast 50,000 ha of background forests surrounding the core sites. The results have been initially encouraging for the key species targeted for restoration – mistletoe, kokako and North Island brown kiwi. Other threatened birds like kaka, kereru and North Island robin, as well as tui, bellbird and other more common forest birds, have also benefited from this approach. But the cost effectiveness of this hands-on approach (compared with the aerial spreading of 1080 poisoned bait over much wider remote areas) is being debated. One disappointing feature has been the loss of radio transmitter-carrying kiwi to pig-hunting dogs.

The wilderness character of Te Urewera National Park was formally recognised late in 2003, when 23,547 ha of montane beech forest on the south-eastern slopes were designated as the Ruakituri Wilderness Area. Most of the wilderness area is in the isolated upper catchment of the Ruakituri River above the spectacular Waitangi Falls. The remote terrain is not difficult but does require experienced visitors to have good bushcraft skills and to navigate the forest carefully – wilderness travel on nature's terms, on foot, without tracks and huts. The overwhelming experience is of solitude, allowing an appreciation of how vast the North Island's forest wilderness once was. Although the forest is bisected by Ruas Track, this lightly marked route is still maintained because of its historic and recreational value, and is not considered to compromise the integrity of the wilderness area.

The North Island kokako (*Callaeas cinerea wilsoni*) is the iconic bird of the North Island's forested wilderness). Once widespread, this magnificent wattlebird has been eliminated from all of its axial ranges habitats except the northern Urewera forests (ROD MORRIS).

RIGHT Mist filters through the silver beech (*Nothofagus menziesii*) forest on the highest ridges of the Huiarau Range in Te Urewera National Park. BELOW The hummocky landscape around Lake Waikareiti (centre) was formed thousands of years ago by a massive landslide of soft rocks off the ridges near Mt Manuoha and today it is a wilderness of lake-filled hollows, wetlands and forested knolls; Lake Waikaremoana can be seen in the distance.

TOP Hochstetter's frog (*Leiopelma hochstetteri*) is one of New Zealand's four species of endemic frogs belonging to the primitive Leiopelmatidae family, a group of frogs probably widespread in Gondwana but now extinct everywhere except in New Zealand. Unlike Hamilton's frog and Archey's frog, it is often found close to water, particularly along stream banks in the Coromandel, Raukumara and Huiarau ranges (ROD MORRIS).

CENTRE Our ancient short-tailed bat (*Mystacina tuberculata*), pictured here feeding on the nectar of *Dactylanthus* flowers, has evolved a number of unique features because of its long freedom from mammalian predators. It not only eats insects like other bats but also nectar, pollen and fruit; and it has adapted its wings, tail and hind legs to enable it to forage on the forest floor (whereas most other bats can only hang upside down from the roof of a cave or hollow tree) (ROD MORRIS).

BOTTOM The wood rose (*Dactylanthus taylorii*) is a very unusual plant of the forest floor. It is New Zealand's only fully parasitic flowering plant and seems to have co-evolved with the short-tailed bat which pollinates its flowers (ROD MORRIS).

The highest peaks in the Kaimanawas and Kawekas are more than 1700 m above sea level but they are very different in landscape character. The Kaweka Range has a superficial similarity to the greywacke ranges of Canterbury – extensive screes, deep V-shaped valleys, and beech forests severely depleted by past fires. The Kaimanawa Mountains, however, are much closer to the eruption centre of the ancient Taupo Volcano, and volcanic deposits are widespread, softening the contour of the mountains. Indeed, the tephra-choked basins in the head of the Mohaka, Ngaruroro, Mangamaire, Taruarau and Moawhango rivers are unique in the North Island; they lie 800–1000 m above sea level, and often contain wetlands and montane red tussock grasslands, with a variety of interesting indigenous plants (see Moawhango Tussocklands, p.103).

The main recreational attractions of the Kaimanawa–Kaweka mountains are:

• their open wilderness character;
• the outstanding trout fishing in the major rivers (rainbow in the upper Rangitikei and Ngaruroro; brown in the Mohaka);
• the only large wild herd of sika deer in the Southern Hemisphere.

The northern part of Kaimanawa Forest Park was gazetted a recreational hunting area (RHA) in 1982, because of the popularity of the sika deer herd with recreational hunters at a time of high levels of commercial venison recovery by helicopter. Today, it is one of only two remaining RHAs still managed by DOC in the entire country.

The Ruahine Range also rises to more than 1700 m above sea level (the highest peak is Mangaweka, 1733 m), but the range is long and narrow, extending NE–SW for 100 km from the Taruarau–Ngaruroro Gorge in the north to the Manawatu Gorge in the south. The southern 30 km of the Ruahine Range is only 10 km wide and just above 1000 m in altitude, its crest covered in impenetrable montane leatherwood shrubland (*Olearia* and *Brachyglottis* species). In the north, the range is up to 25 km wide, with its western slopes carrying moutain cedar/kaikawaka forest once extensive throughout the upper Rangitikei (remnants still remain in Hihitahi Sanctuary (2352 ha) and in the privately owned Aorangi/Awarua block around Mt Aorangi (see Moawhango Tussocklands, p.103). The juxtaposition of this conical-shaped high-altitude forest alongside the red tussock grasslands of the Mangaohane Plateau is one of New Zealand's special natural landscapes. However, past high numbers of deer and possums have devastated this

The Rangitikei River rises in the Kaimanawa Mountains and is protected as a 'Wild and Scenic' river. The surrounding forests and ranges are managed as a de facto wilderness area (SHAUN BARNETT/BLACK ROBIN).

KAIMANAWA MOUNTAINS, THE KAWEKA AND RUAHINE RANGES

In the centre of the North Island, the Kaimanawa Mountains, the Kaweka Range and the northern Ruahine Range extend in a huge semi-circle enclosing the headwaters of the Rangitikei and Ngaruroro rivers. The recreational significance of the Kaimanawa, Kaweka and Ruahine ranges is very high with most of the area included in three large forest parks – Kaimanawa (77,888 ha), Kaweka (59,340 ha) and Ruahine (95,268 ha).

Dusk settling over the Kaweka Range. Most of the severely-eroded range lies within Kaweka Forest Park (SHAUN BARNETT/BLACK ROBIN).

kaikawaka/mountain totara forest, with up to 50 per cent of the larger trees dying and the canopy opening up, inducing thickets of horopito and other unpalatable shrubs. There is now clear evidence that the once puzzling dieback of the attractively shaped montane cedar is due to possums browsing the leading leaf shoots, causing whole trees to die. For many trampers and hunters, penetrating into this mountain fastness is a unique wilderness experience in the North Island. A week can be spent traversing east from the Desert Road, through the beech forests and clear waters of the upper Waipakihi and Rangitikei Rivers, to the open mountain tops of Makorako (1727 m) or Ngapuketurua (1517 m), or on to the Ngaruroro Valley and the distant Kaweka Range via the Mangamingi Stream. The core 30 per cent of this wilderness of beech forest and tussockland is private land owned by the East Taupo Lands Trust, who historically granted the public the privilege of free access to this wilderness heart of the Kaimanawas.

At the New Zealand Wilderness Conference in May 1981, the Federated Mountain Clubs of NZ proposed a Kaimanawa–Kaweka Wilderness Area for approximately 47,000 ha of the central Kaimanawa and western Kaweka Ranges. The idea of a formal wilderness area was initially supported by the NZ Forest Service but it was never achieved. Instead, the Rangitikei River headwaters have since then been managed as a Remote Experience Zone without facilities. However, over the past decade public foot access to the private land core of the central Kaimanawa has become more difficult. To get a financial return on their land, the Maori owners leased recreational access to the remote core area to air charter operators, who helicopter in fee-paying hunters, fishers and rafters. Initially, foot entry from the surrounding forest parks was tolerated, but public access became progressively restricted. DOC was able to advocate an arrangement whereby, since 2001, trampers could enter some of the private mountain land on payment of a permit to the lessees. However, this system has engendered criticism of DOC for failing to take enough initiative in resolving how reasonable public access to the wilderness resource can be restored.

TARARUA AND RIMUTAKA RANGES

The Tararua Range is a very rugged landscape, and has a notorious reputation for severe mountain weather. The highest peaks are Mitre (1571 m) in the northern group and Mt Hector (1529 m) in the southern group. In contrast to the V shape of most of the valleys, the headwaters of the rivers which rise around the central peaks of Mitre, Arete and Girdlestone retain the pronounced U profile typical of past glaciation. Like most of the axial ranges, the Tararua Range is aligned along faultlines, primarily the active Wairarapa and Wellington faults (the latter responsible for the orientation of the Hutt River and the prominent escarpment along the western side of Wellington Harbour and the Hutt Valley). The southern end of the Rimutaka Range is being uplifted probably faster than any other North Island mountain range, leaving a superb chronological record of uplift chiselled in the eastern Wellington Harbour coastline. Notable landforms are the internationally important raised beaches of Turakirae Head (where the Rimutaka Range abruptly terminates on the shores of Cook Strait) and the series of uplifted marine terraces around Baring and Pencarrow heads. In the most recent catastrophic earthquake, on 23 January 1855, the Rimutaka Range and the Turakirae raised beaches rose by nearly 3 m.

The Tararua and Rimutaka ranges act as major barriers to the north-westerly gales that sweep through Cook Strait, and both also share with the Seaward Kaikoura Range a high degree of exposure to the cold southerly winds that move up the east coast of the South Island each winter. The Tararua Range is one of the windiest areas in New Zealand, with the prevailing north-westerlies particularly strong on the slopes above the Manawatu Gorge, as well as descending, foehn-like, to scourge the Wairarapa Plains. Mist is the constant subalpine companion of Tararua trampers, demanding of them a high level of navigational skill in the alpine tops. It has been estimated that mist and cloud shroud the Tararua summits for around 200 days a year; on average, there are fewer than 80 clear days each year.

The vegetation of the Tararua Range is mainly verdant rainforest, changing from podocarp/tawa or podocarp/kamahi forest in the lowlands, through montane podocarp/beech, then subalpine pure beech (forming a sharp treeline), to alpine tussock grasslands. The absence of

Sunrise touches the snow tussocks, *Celmisia*, and other alpine herbs on the Papakiakuta Ridge of the Ruahine Range in Ruahine Forest Park (ROB BROWN).

beech from the northern Tararuas is an enigma. The most likely explanation is that they were eliminated during earlier unfavourable warmer climatic conditions and have not yet managed to reinvade. There are also some interesting comparisons between the Tararua forests and those of adjacent ranges. The Ruahine Range to the north has montane forests dominated by mountain beech and mountain cedar – both absent from the Tararuas. In the south and east, the Tararuas have a closer affinity with the forests of the Marlborough Sounds, rather than the neighbouring drier Rimutaka and Aorangi ranges. The tops of the Tararua Range, like the Kaimanawa and Ruahine ranges, are well covered in snow tussock grasslands and herbfields. In spring and early summer, the delicate flowers of many alpine herbs, such as *Celmisia* (mountain daisy), *Ranunculus* (buttercup), *Gentiana* (gentian) and *Leucogenes* (edelweiss), shelter among the tussocks.

Most of the Tararua Range is protected in Tararua Forest Park, at 116,536 ha the largest forest park in the North Island. Rimutaka Forest Park is much smaller (19,919 ha), for much of the Rimutaka Range is protected as water catchment reserves vested in the Greater Wellington Regional Council. Similarly, 2500 ha of superb beech/rimu/rata forest in the headwaters of the Hutt River on the southern slopes of the Tararua Range were off limits to trampers and hunters for decades because of the Hutt's water supply status. However, in recent years, advances in water treatment and management enlightenment have seen the area transformed into Kaitoke Regional Park, the most natural of Wellington's five regional parks.

Like the Ruahine Range, the Tararua Range has a remarkably well-developed network of tramping tracks and over 50 huts. Indeed, the 'Southern Crossing' of the Tararua Range is almost synonymous with the sport of tramping in New Zealand. This classic crossing involves 6–8 hours of alpine travel between Table Top and Mount Alpha, with superb views to the south of Wellington Harbour, Marlborough Sounds and the Kaikoura Ranges. The main Tararua Range between Pukematawai and Bridge Peak is the remote core of Tararua Forest Park. It has a rugged wilderness character but there are no formal wilderness areas in the park, although the upper Otaki and Waiohine valleys are managed as 'remote experience areas'.

Sunrise on red tussock and adjacent kaikawaka forest on the slopes of Te Rakaunuiakura, from Ruahine Corner at the northern end of Ruahine Forest Park (ROB BROWN).

Snow tussock and flowering speargrasses (*Aciphylla* sp.) on the slopes of Pukemoremore in Tararua Forest Park (SHAUN BARNETT/BLACK ROBIN).

THREATS AND CONSERVATION PRIORITIES

The Deer Problem

Three species of deer, introduced for sport hunting around 100 years ago, have established themselves in the forests, shrublands, tussock grasslands and herbfields of the axial ranges:

- red deer demonstrated a remarkable ability to thrive on New Zealand's indigenous vegetation and had spread throughout the entire mountain chain by the mid-1960s;
- sika deer are still mainly confined to the Kaimanawa, Kaweka and Ahimanawa ranges, having spread from their point of liberation at Poronui Station on the eastern side of Lake Taupo;
- rusa deer have not really thrived, spreading into the

western Ikawhenua Range only since they were released near Galatea.

By the mid-1950s, red deer (and goats) were clearly devastating the interior of the forests, and the NZ Forest Service undertook a series of scientific surveys to establish the nature and extent of deer and goat damage to the vegetation. The most seriously affected communities were the montane silver beech forests, the recovering vegetation on open sites like slip faces and gully heads, leatherwood shrublands and the alpine tussock grasslands.

The detrimental effect of possums was also becoming clearer, particularly in rimu/rata/kamahi forests where their browsing accentuated the damage already caused by deer, leading to widespread forest canopy collapse, especially in the Ruahine Range. The NZ Forest Service developed a comprehensive hut, bridge and track network throughout the axial ranges during the 1960s in order to make all the affected habitats readily accessible to ground hunters. But by the late 1970s, the era of the government deer hunter (termed a 'deer culler' at that time) was largely at an end. The advent of helicopters opened the ranges to the commercial hunting of deer – both live capture and killing for carcass recovery – but deer population control through this type of commercial hunting is now over. However, helicopters are widely used by recreational hunters for access to remote huts and campsites in most of the ranges. In more recent times, the role of increasing populations of sika deer in the onset of canopy collapse of mountain beech forests in the central axial ranges has become very evident. By the late 1990s, about 90 per cent of Kaweka Forest Park's 20,000 ha of mountain beech forest exhibited clear regeneration failure (that is, there were few or no mountain beech seedlings). The severe damage that deer browsing causes to many indigenous ecosystems is irrefutable. Yet eliminating deer (let alone other serious pests like rats, possums and stoats) throughout the entire axial ranges of the North Island is well-nigh impossible – even if enough political will could be mustered to finance such a gargantuan task. For deer are not only alien pests – they are also highly regarded as game animals by a significant section of the New Zealand back-country community. This sharp polarisation of public opinion about deer is recognised in DOC's 2001 *Policy Statement on Deer Control*, a rather lightweight document which seeks to 'reduce the impact of deer' and 'restrict the feral range of deer', but is very vague about exactly what level of control will be acceptable, and about where and whether DOC will itself

fund any specific deer-control programmes. The department wishes to encourage recreational hunting of deer, but even in the Kaimanawa Recreational Hunting Area (RHA), where the pressure from recreational hunters during the mid-1990s was seven times the national average, this was insufficient to stem the progressive loss of highly palatable plants. Elsewhere many deer are killed (variously 10–70 per cent of herd numbers) as a 'by-catch' of aerial 1080 possum poisoning operations, but these numbers are too low (and aerial operations too infrequent) to bring about either long-term animal control or significant improvement in the protection of highly palatable plants.

The short-term prospects for satisfactory deer control in the North Island axial ranges do not look promising. The commercial helicopter hunting industry has largely collapsed under the combined effect of export disincentives and hygiene issues. DOC claims that recreational hunting has proved insufficient for controlling deer to levels that allow desirable vegetation recovery – yet it could also be said that DOC has failed to work closely enough with recreational hunters (even in RHAs) to develop detailed control plans that give a measure of 'win-win' for both camps. The crux of the control problem for DOC and conservation advocates is more social than biological – a large number of New Zealanders just do not consider wild deer (and, to some extent, pigs) to be vermin, like possums, rats and stoats. Until these attitudes change (and they are unlikely to), the problem of deer control will continue to paralyse the Minister of Conservation and DOC – the 'venison in the sandwich', wedged between Forest & Bird on the one hand and recreational hunters on the other.

Access to the Central Kaimanawa Mountains
Public ownership of most of New Zealand's natural landscapes, especially mountain wildlands and beaches, is so fundamental to the Kiwi way of life that it is too easily taken for granted. There was once a more respectful, tolerant and less commercial era when trampers, hunters, mountaineers and fishers could obtain permission to freely enter private land like the central Kaimanawa Mountains, or climb Mt Tarawera, or pass through the pastoral leasehold runs of the eastern South Island high country to reach the alps beyond. While DOC is charged with fostering the use of public land for recreation where this is '… not inconsistent with its conservation', the department has been much less enthusiastic publicly about using its financial resources and advocacy powers to facilitate public access through natural private lands to the back country. The Walkways

Act 1975 has played a role in the past in facilitating walking access through private rural lands closer to urban centres, but a 'day-tripper' walkway concept just doesn't fit with the wilderness challenges of the central Kaimanawa Mountains.

The need for improved public access to and through the park was a key issue in the review of the Kaimanawa Forest Park Management Plan. In the 2007 draft plan, DOC has committed itself to continue to maintain the wilderness integrity of the Rangitikei Remote Experience Zone, and to make efforts to negotiate a payment to the lessees of the private land in return for free public access. If this fails, then DOC will have to consider the costly alternative of re-routing some of the tracks to ensure that they are entirely within the park.

On the other hand, the Nga Whenua Rahui fund offers an ideal mechanism for Maori owners to approach the Minister of Conservation to negotiate a covenant

Cone Ridge, south-eastern Tararua Range. The mist and gnarled silver beech 'goblin forest' are constant companions of trampers on the higher ridges in Tararua Forest Park (ROB BROWN).

(kawenata) to both protect the conservation values of their land and allow conditional public access for recreation. Such a kawenata was agreed upon in August 2003 for a key part of the Kaimanawa wilderness – nearly 7000 ha of beech forest and mountain tops known as The Needles Block that lies between the Waipahihi Stream and the lower Waipakihi River, both major tributaries of the Tongariro River. This was an important agreement, indicating how with good will private back-country access rights can be purchased as a public good. It is to be hoped that it foreshadows similar 'win-win' solutions to the central Kaimanawa access conundrum.

CHAPTER EIGHT

COOK STRAIT AND MARLBOROUGH

Anyone lucky enough to stand on Mt Omega's summit at the southern end of the Tararua Range at sunset on a clear winter's day gains a remarkable visual insight into the vast tectonic forces that have sliced up the rugged landscapes of Wellington and Marlborough. The trace of the Wellington Fault lies in deep shadow as a straight black line, sweeping down the Eastern Hutt River to the escarpment of the western side of the Hutt Valley and Wellington Harbour, cleaving Wellington City in two between Hawkins Hill and Makara Hill, before leaping across Cook Strait to the Awatere Valley and deep into the mountains of South Marlborough. The sharp mountain silhouettes of the Inland and Seaward Kaikoura ranges stand end on, accentuating their height and the depth of the fault-controlled valleys separating them. The NE–SW orientation of the mountains is common to both islands, leading one to assume that the great faultlines of Marlborough continue across Cook Strait and into the axial ranges of the lower North Island (see Ch.7, p.125). But it is not quite so straightforward, for Cook Strait poses one of the great geomorphic enigmas in the long story of how New Zealand achieved its present shape. Why should two large mountainous islands[1] be separated by the extraordinarily wild stretch of water which is Cook Strait – more than 1000 m deep in Cook Strait Canyon, yet only 22 km wide at its narrowest point ('The Narrows')?

Climatic extremes are distinctive features of both Cook Strait and inland Marlborough. The traditional deep

respect of Maori for Raukawa (Cook Strait) meant that anyone attempting to cross this most dangerous stretch of water for the first time submitted to a blindfold so that they could paddle continuously without seeing the wild seascape around them. The spring nor'wester gales are legion, as James Cook found in 1773 on his second visit to the strait, when the Resolution battled them for 10 days while trying to reach the haven of Queen Charlotte Sound. But it is the large waves generated by periodic southerly storms sweeping through the strait that have caused most shipwrecks and heavy loss of life – the sinking of the inter-island ferries Penguin (1909) and Wahine (1968) being the most notorious. The 'Wahine Storm' generated winds up to 298 km/h, and contributed to the sinking of this new ferry at the entrance to Wellington Harbour while a traumatised Wellington population could do little to rescue the stricken ship and its passengers. Further south, the Kaikoura mountains and inland basins of South Marlborough experience the climatic extremes of both summer dryness and winter cold. This remote rainshadow area is so different from the rest of the South Island in its geodiversity and biodiversity that it is both an important centre of endemism and a unique wilderness landscape.

THE WATERS AND WHALES OF COOK STRAIT AND KAIKOURA

The geological history of Cook Strait is still being unravelled, but what is becoming clearer is the extraordinary power of the tidal forces which surge through the strait. Indeed, Cook Strait may be the largest erosional feature in the greater New Zealand 'mini-continent'. Even at the peak of the Last Glaciation around 20,000 years ago (when

---

[1] The North Island is 11.5 million hectares in area, is very hilly and has many ranges up to 1500 m in height; the South Island is 15.4 million hectares, with the Southern Alps and many mountain ranges above 2500 m.

The tail of a sperm whale (*Physeter macrocephalus*) flips as it begins its dive into the Kaikoura Canyon off Kaikoura (DENNIS BUURMAN).

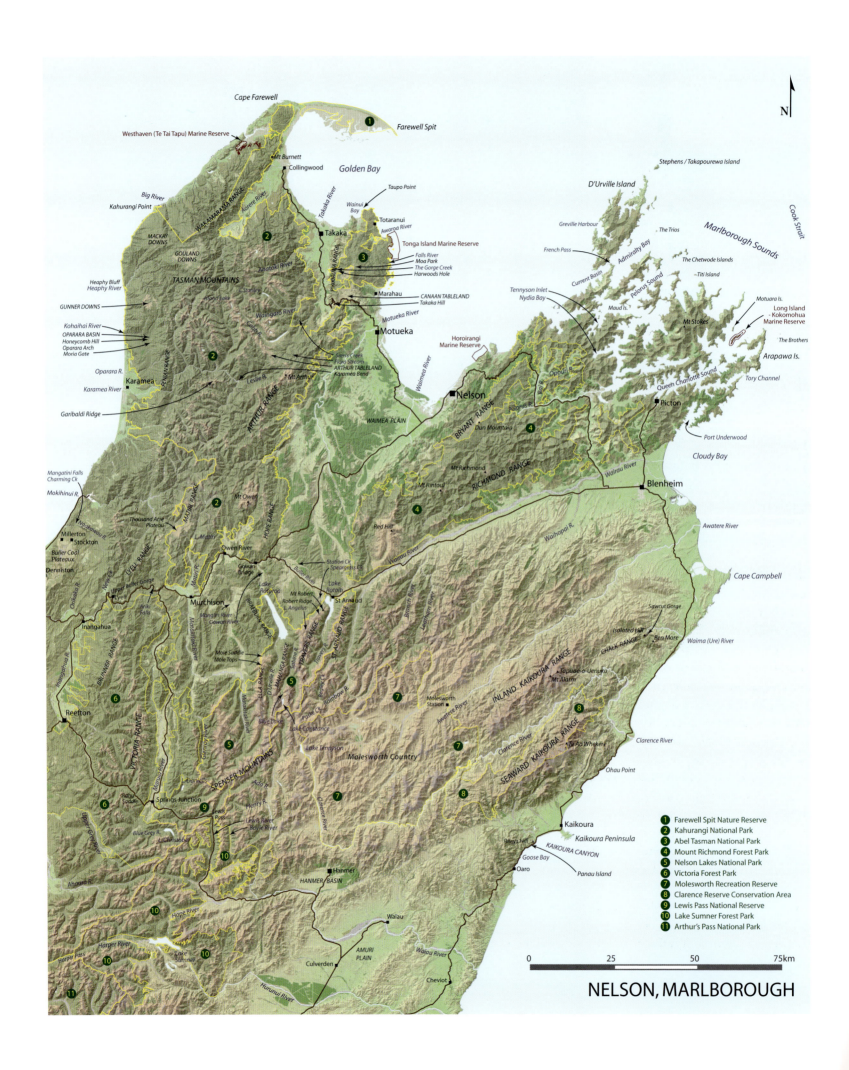

N

Cape Farewell
Farewell Spit
Westhaven (Te Tai Tapu) Marine Reserve

Golden Bay

Stephens / Takapourewa Island

D'Urville Island

Marlborough Sounds

Cook Strait

Mt Burnett
Collingwood

Big River
Kahurangi Point

Taupo Point
Wainui Bay
Totaranui
Awaroa River

Takaka

Greville Harbour
French Pass
The Trios

Admiralty Bay

The Chetwode Islands

~Titi Island

MACKAY DOWNS
GOULAND DOWNS

WAKAMARAMA RANGE

Tonga Island Marine Reserve
Falls River
Moa Park
The Gorge Creek
Harwoods Hole

Current Basin

Motuara Is.
Long Island - Kokomohua Marine Reserve

Heaphy Bluff
Heaphy River

TASMAN MOUNTAINS

C.Stanley
Anatoki River

Marahau

CANAAN TABLELAND
Takaka Hill

Tennyson Inlet
Nydia Bay

Maud Is.

Mt Stokes

The Brothers

GUNNER DOWNS

Iron Lake

Waingaro River

Motueka River

Pelorus Sound

Arapawa Is.

Kohaihai River
OPARARA BASIN
Honeycomb Hill
Oparara Arch
Moria Gate

Oparara R.

Leslie R.

Mt Arthur

Sam's Creek
Flora Stream
ARTHUR TABLELAND
Karamea Bend

Motueka

Horoirangi Marine Reserve

Nelson

Rai R.

Opun R.

Queen Charlotte Sound

Tory Channel

Karamea

ARTHUR RANGE

Picton

Karamea River

Garibaldi Ridge

WAIMEA PLAIN

BRYANT RANGE

Pelorus R.

Dun Mountain

Port Underwood

Cloudy Bay

Mt Richmond

RICHMOND RANGE

Wairau River

Blenheim

Mangatini Falls
Charming Ck

Mokihinui R.

Mt Owen

Thousand Acre Plateau

MATIRI RANGE

HOPE RANGE

Mt Rintoul

Red Hill

Awatere River

Millerton
Stockton

LYELL RANGE

Matiri R.

Owen River

Gowan Bridge

Station Ck
Speargrass Ck

Buller Coal Plateaux

Denniston

Ariki Falls

Lake Rotoroa

Buller River

Waihopai R.

Cape Campbell

Upper Buller Gorge
Lyell

Lake Rotoiti
Mt Robert
Robert Ridge
L.Angelus

Branch River

Wairau River

Leatham River

Sawcut Gorge

New R.

Murchison

St Arnaud

Isolated Hill

Inangahua

Mangles River
Gowan River

CHALK RANGE

Ben More

Waima (Ure) River

BRUNNER RANGE

Mole Saddle
Mole Tops

MANINGA RANGE

ELLA RANGE

TRAVERS RANGE

ST ARNAUD RANGE

INLAND KAIKOURA RANGE

Tapuae-o-Uenuku
Mt Alarm

Molesworth Station

Awatere River

Reefton

D'Urville R.

Blue Lake

Lake Constance

Clarence River

SEAWARD KAIKOURA RANGE

Te Ao Whekere

VICTORIA RANGE

Glenroy River

SPENSER MOUNTAINS

Lake Tennyson

Molesworth Country

Clarence River

Clarence River

Ohau Point

Kahu Saddle
Springs Junction

L.Daniells

Ada R.

Henry R.

Lewis Pass
Lewis River
Boyle River

Kaikoura

Upper Grey River

Blue Grey R.

L.Christabel

Kaikoura Peninsula

KAIKOURA CANYON

Ahaura R.

Hope River

Hanmer

HANMER BASIN

Riley's Hill
Goose Bay
Oaro

Panau Island

Harper River

Harper Pass

Lake Sumner

Walau

AMURI PLAIN

Culverden

Waiau River

Cheviot

0   25   50   75km

1 Farewell Spit Nature Reserve
2 Kahurangi National Park
3 Abel Tasman National Park
4 Mount Richmond Forest Park
5 Nelson Lakes National Park
6 Victoria Forest Park
7 Molesworth Recreation Reserve
8 Clarence Reserve Conservation Area
9 Lewis Pass National Reserve
10 Lake Sumner Forest Park
11 Arthur's Pass National Park

NELSON, MARLBOROUGH

The highly acrobatic dusky dolphin (*Lagenorhynchus obscurus*) occurs in large groups, from several hundred to over 1000, in the shallower waters off Kaikoura and in the Marlborough Sounds (ROSS ARMSTRONG).

the North and South Islands were joined by the 150 km long landbridge sandspit of Farewell Rise extending from Cape Farewell to Taranaki), tidal scour was still sufficient to maintain deep water in Cook Strait itself. Today, the high-tide bulges that sweep twice daily around New Zealand's coastline have the effect of creating, at certain times of the day, very different sea levels at opposite ends of the strait. Consequently, twice a day powerful currents flow north-ward through the strait at flood tide and southward at the ebb, reaching speeds of 9 km/h. This is sufficient to pump the millions of tonnes of sediment carried into the western basins by the Whanganui, Rangitikei, Manawatu and West Coast rivers, through The Narrows and into the deep sub-marine canyons in the east. Indeed, there is evidence that this tidal scouring is causing constant headward erosion of the Cook Strait canyons, extending them north-westwards into the shallower western basins – just as some waterways erode upstream on land.

Cook Strait is also notable for its historical importance as a whale habitat, with probably more than 30 different whale species once migrating through its turbulent waters.

The best known are the large baleen whales – humpback, right and blue – which 'filter-feed' on small crustaceans they sieve out of the sea. Humpback whales use Cook Strait as a major migration route, travelling north from their Antarctic feeding grounds to their breeding grounds around Tonga and other South Pacific island groups during winter, and returning during spring. Right whales used to breed in the calmer bays around the strait, and were so common in Port Nicholson (Wellington Harbour) during the early 1840s that the first European settlers complained that their loud, low-frequency moans kept them awake at night! New Zealand's first permanent commercial whaling station was established in 1827 at Te Awaiti near the mouth of Tory Channel in the Marlborough Sounds. Others quickly followed in Port Underwood and Cloudy Bay, part of an explosion of 80–100 whaling stations between East Cape and Stewart Island/Rakiura, along with more than

100 competing 'bay whaler' ships – all contributing to the unsustainable slaughter which followed. By the late 1840s the right whale population was all but gone.

Decades later, in 1909, the Perano family established Tory Channel's most famous shore whaling station to hunt humpback whales passing through Cook Strait. Since then, a combination of unsustainable shore-based whaling around New Zealand and illegal Russian whaling in Antarctica has severely depleted the humpback whale population that historically migrated through the strait. Whereas 500 humpbacks were sighted in the strait in 1953, the numbers dropped sharply over the next decade, and all whaling in New Zealand waters ceased after the Peranos harpooned their last whale (a sperm whale off Kaikoura) in December 1964. Today, there is good evidence that humpback whale populations are slowly recovering from the devastating effect of that commercial exploitation, with numbers increasing steadily since 1990. Over 15 days during late June 2004, the first systematic whale survey conducted in Cook Strait in 40 years counted 53 whales (of which 47 were humpbacks; the others blue and sei whales). The most recent survey in June 2007 counted 27 humpback whales in 12 days. These numbers are encouraging, indicating that numbers passing through the strait are at least now back to what they were at this time of year during the 1950s.

Just as the underwater topography of Cook Strait plays a major role in allowing the passage of migrating whales, so does the sea floor just off Kaikoura provide ideal conditions for adolescent male sperm whales. Sperm whales are the largest of the toothed whales, and their huge bulbous heads carry tonnes of oil which seems to be involved in the intriguing sonar location of their main prey, giant squid, often located more than 1000 m below the surface of the sea. But why Kaikoura? Because, just offshore, the deep Hikurangi Trough terminates in the Kaikoura Canyon which is over 1500 m deep. This is a unique location on the entire South Island coastline, the place where deep water comes closest to shore – as deep as 1000 m just 3 km off Goose Bay. These waters off Kaikoura are particularly nutrient-rich because of the upwelling of the deep waters from the trench and their mixing with the converging cold Southland Current and the warm East Cape Current. Here the sperm whales surface for a few minutes every 50 minutes before 'upping tail' to begin another remarkable dive to the ocean depths. Fortunately, in the mid-1980s, a few conservation-minded entrepreneurs in the Kaikoura community had the vision to appreciate that the days of hunting whales were gone forever, and that watching these magnificent whales (as well as dusky dolphins, seals and albatross) could instead become the basis of a thriving maritime eco-tourism industry.

COOK STRAIT SANCTUARIES:
KAPITI ISLAND AND STEPHENS ISLAND/TAKAPOUREWA

Kapiti Island and Stephens Island/Takapourewa lie 80 km apart at the northern end of Cook Strait, the former only 5 km off the heavily populated Kapiti coastline of the North Island, the latter 3 km off the northern tip of D'Urville Island at the western extremity of the Marlborough Sounds. Both islands have very rugged topography, and both are often isolated by the gales that regularly whip through Cook Strait. Yet each island has played a remarkable historic role as a sanctuary protecting New Zealand's endangered fauna.

Kapiti is by far the larger island, an isolated block of greywacke almost 2000 ha in area, with an impressive line of cliffs rising to a high point of 521 m on its western side. Much has been done to heal Kapiti's environmental scars, stemming from inter-tribal Maori warfare, whaling, the invasion of serious pests like Norway rats and possums, and failed farming endeavours (which led to the clearing of 75 per cent of the island's coastal broadleaf forest). Kapiti Island was designated as one of New Zealand's first bird sanctuaries in 1897, and it gradually regenerated to a forest of kanuka, kohekohe, northern rata and tawa. But possums and rats had completely overrun the island by the late 1970s, severely limiting its value as a safe haven for vulnerable native birds. Official scepticism towards the likelihood of eradicating possums was eventually overcome, largely through the vision and perseverance of a number of Wildlife Service officers and DSIR scientists.

In 1982, a dedicated team of trappers began an extraordinary seven-year campaign, cutting an intensive network of tracks for the traps, and using dogs and a single aerial 1080 poison drop to track down the last of an estimated 22,000 possums. The response from the vegetation was immediate, most notably a profuse flowering of kamahi and rata. While for some years Kapiti had been a stronghold for weka and New Zealand's only remaining viable population of little spotted kiwi, the pest control allowed a number of endangered birds – North Island saddleback, takahe, stitchbird, brown teal and kokako – to be progressively introduced. Encouraged by the success of the possum eradication, Kapiti achieved another conservation milestone at the end of 1996, with the world's first eradication of rats

– both Norway and Pacific rats/kiore – from an island of such large size and rugged topography. This aerial poisoning operation (with brodifacoum) was carried out while some of the more vulnerable birds were taken off the island. Since then, the population of hole-nesting birds like saddlebacks, bellbirds and kakariki has increased markedly, and the island has become a key location for DOC's threatened species recovery work.

Another conservation achievement was the establishment in 1992 of Kapiti Marine Reserve (1825 ha in the east, extending to the mainland at the Waikanae Estuary, and a 342 ha sector off the north-western cliffs). Kapiti Island is influenced by both the cold Canterbury Current

The biodiversity of Kapiti Island has responded to the elimination of possums and rats, with numbers of hole-nesting birds like saddlebacks and kakariki increasing sharply.

passing northwards through Cook Strait and the warmer D'Urville Current of the Taranaki Bight. Consequently, the waters around the island are unique marine habitats on the western coast of the North Island. The designation of a marine reserve was strenuously opposed by the more conservative sector of the Kapiti District's recreational fishing fraternity, but today the abundance of crayfish, blue cod, butterfish, perch and moki is welcomed by local fishers, iwi and conservationists.

CLOCKWISE FROM OPPOSITE TOP LEFT A fairy prion (*Pachyptila turtur*) breeding pair outside their burrow on Stephens Island/Takapourewa. Fairy prion on Stephens Island often share their burrows with tuatara, a risky business resulting in the loss of about 25% of the eggs and chicks to tuatara predation (ROD MORRIS). Maud Island frogs (*Leiopelma pakeka*) share the distinctive features that make our endemic frogs unique: having no slit eyes, croak, or tadpole stage. An adult male little spotted kiwi (*Apteryx owenii*) foraging on Kapiti Island. The little spotted is the smallest of our four kiwi species and many of the Kapiti population have been successfully transferred over the years to predator-free islands like Red Mercury, Hen/Taranga, and Tiritiri Matangi (ROD MORRIS). A Wellington tree weta (*Hemideina crassidens*) pair during courtship (male above). They are the most widely distributed of the tree wetas, from Mt Ruapehu, through the islands of Cook Strait, to South Westland (ROD MORRIS). A mating pair of Stephens Island tuatara (a subspecies of the Cook Strait tuatara, *Sphenodon punctatus*). Tuatara are the sole surviving members of the Sphenodontia, one of the four orders of reptiles (the others being turtles; crocodiles; lizards and snakes), which was represented by many other species 200 million years ago.

Stephens Island/Takapourewa is much smaller (150 ha) than Kapiti but just as rugged and windswept. Its outstanding conservation importance is twofold:
- the high level of endemism in its fauna;
- its very large population of tuatara (*Sphenodon punctatus*), the sole survivor of an ancient order of reptiles that became extinct elsewhere in the world about 65 million years ago (see also Ch.1, p.19).

Like Kapiti Island, Stephens Island/Takapourewa lost most of its forest over a century ago, in this case for farm animals introduced to feed the lighthouse-keeper's family.

The Marlborough Sounds have a long, intricate coastline and a hilly interior which is regenerating to native forest under controlled conservation management.

Unlike Kapiti, however, little forest has regenerated, and much of the island is pasture and open shrubland. In addition, the island has remained surprisingly free of rats (although the role of the lighthouse-keepers' cats in the extinction of possibly as many as 14 of its land bird species in the space of 20 years is one of New Zealand's conservation history horror stories). The tuatara have an interesting co-existence with the many seabirds nesting on the island, often occupying tunnels dug in the soil by fairy prions. They also seem to have benefited from improved egg incubation in the warmer non-forest soils – so much so that their population has steadily grown to more than 50,000. In the most favourable forest habitats it has been estimated to reach an extraordinary density of up to 2000 tuatara per hectare. Other notable fauna are seven species of skink and gecko; a population of probably the rarest frog in the world, the Stephen's Island variety of the endemic Hamilton's frog (*Leiopelma hamiltoni*) (the other related population is on Maud Island in the Marlborough Sounds); and many large beetles, weevils and weta, including the Stephens Island tree weta and giant weta.

A number of other small pest-free windswept islands of high significance for the conservation of native fauna lie along the southern margin of Cook Strait, to the south-east of Stephens Island/Takapourewa:

- The Brothers, spectacular rocky islets which are habitat for New Zealand's largest gecko, *Hoplodactylus duvaucelii*, and a separate species of tuatara;
- The Trios, noted for their diversity of sea birds (blue penguins, shearwaters, fairy prions and petrels) and the density of their burrows;
- The Chetwode Islands, with their flocks of kakariki, kaka, bellbirds and other forest birds;
- Titi Island, blessed with plentiful forest birds and seabirds.

THE MARLBOROUGH SOUNDS

The Marlborough Sounds are New Zealand's classic example of a drowned valley landform – flooded in part through a rise in sea level but primarily because the Earth's crust here is collapsing as the Pacific Plate is subducted below the Australian Plate. The result is a coastline with an intricacy unmatched elsewhere in the country – indeed, this small corner of Marlborough is estimated to contain 15 per cent of New Zealand's entire coastline. The highest point is Mt Stokes between Pelorus and Queen Charlotte sounds; at 1203 m above present sea level, it is the only small part of the Sounds landscape above the treeline. At the other extreme, at French Pass the former ridgeline is barely submerged, and the tidal forces resulting from converging currents can generate flows as high as 7 knots between Admiralty Bay and Current Basin.

Gone now are most of the luxuriant coastal podocarp/broadleaf forests that once nurtured the bellbirds, tui and other forest birds whose dawn chorus so captivated Cap-

The spotted shag or parekareka (*Stictocarbo punctatus*) breeds in the Marlborough Sounds and on the Kaikoura coast, favouring the marine environment off rocky coasts.

tain James Cook and his naturalists at their Queen Charlotte Sound anchorages. Between 1860 and 1870, most of the lower slopes were burnt and cleared for sheep farms, and the superb forests on the river flats of the Pelorus, Rai and Opouri valleys were milled for timber. But steep slopes, infertile soils, isolation and the 1930s Depression all contributed to the eventual failure of farming on 50 per cent of the cleared land around the Sounds. Many of the beech forests above 500 m altitude survived the fires, but fire still remains a major threat to the extensive shrubland and second-growth forest that has slowly regenerated around the coastline of the inner Sounds. Gradually attitudes changed, and the creation of a network of shoreline reserves and conservation of the remaining natural landscapes and marine ecosystems became a priority. The designation of a short-lived Marlborough Sounds Maritime Park in 1976 was also a belated recognition of the national importance of the Sounds for water-based recreation, especially the outstanding opportunities for boating, kayaking, fishing and diving in a vast labyrinth of comparatively calm waterways with myriad sheltered coves and anchorages.

Yet even severely modified natural landscapes can play an important part in the conservation of endangered fauna – especially when they happen to be pest-free islands sufficiently distant from mainland shores. Maud Island, near the entrance to Tennyson Inlet in Pelorus Sound, is a good example. This rather small, nondescript scientific reserve seems an unlikely location for an extraordinarily rich fauna of large endemic insects (especially the *Carabidae* family), except that the island has historically been free of major insect predators like tuatara and introduced rodents. But Maud Island is better known for the key role it played for 30 years in the recovery of New Zealand's unique 'night parrot', the kakapo. However, kakapo breeding occurred only in one year (1998) and the last birds were relocated in 2003 to the larger, forested islands around Fiordland and Stewart Island/Rakiura (see Ch.13). Nevertheless, the kohekohe/mahoe forest remnants of Maud Island still remain the largest habitat for the rarest of New Zealand's endemic frogs, the small primitive Hamilton's frog. Rodent eradication campaigns by DOC have also converted the Chetwode, Trios and Rangitoto islands, as well as Titi Island, Long Island and Motuara Island, into important biodiversity sanctuaries, havens for endangered fauna as varied as tuatara and green gecko, giant weta, and two of New Zealand's rarest species of kiwi and frog,

SOUTH MARLBOROUGH: KAIKOURA MOUNTAINS, CLARENCE RIVER AND MOLESWORTH COUNTRY

The Wairau River is one of the most significant topographic and geological boundaries in the northern South Island. It flows in a straight line for almost 100 km from near Lake Rotoiti in Nelson Lakes National Park to Cloudy Bay near Blenheim. This course follows the Wairau Fault, the northeastern extension of the great Alpine Fault which runs along the western foot of the Southern Alps/Ka Tiritiri o te Moana. The river effectively cuts Marlborough in two: the Sounds and the Richmond and Bryant ranges to the north; and the scree-streaked and sparsely vegetated mountains around the Awatere and Clarence rivers to the south. Up until 10 million years ago, most of the local crust deforma-

tion associated with the subduction of the Pacific Plate was absorbed by movement along this Wairau Fault, but since then the Pacific and Australian plates seem to have become locked together under Marlborough. The resultant 'tectonic wrestling' has fractured South Marlborough along several active faults and pushed up a series of parallel ranges. The most dramatic of these are the Inland and Seaward Kaikoura ranges, the highest mountain ranges in the country outside the Southern Alps.

The greywacke rocks of the Kaikoura Ranges began rising about 5 million years ago, a period of intense mountain-building activity (termed the 'Kaikoura Orogeny' after these ranges) considered by geologists to be continuing unabated today. The uplift of the Kaikoura Ranges is an impressive 10 mm per year (or a metre per century), sufficient to deny the wild Clarence River the opportunity to spread out and form terraces and flood plains. Instead, its energy has been spent in continual down-cutting as it twists and turns through the faulted depressions. This is especially so for the turbulent 80 km where it is wedged between the walls of the Inland and Seaward Kaikoura ranges as it seeks a route to the Pacific Ocean. The highest point in the Inland Kaikoura Range (and indeed the top half of the South Island) is Tapuae-o-Uenuku (2885 m); Te Ao Whekere (2596 m) is the most prominent peak in the Seaward Kaikoura Range when viewed from near the mouth of the Clarence River. However, the most spectacular landforms have been etched out of the younger limestone rocks – the straight line of the Chalk Range hogback and Sawcut Gorge and other impressive canyons near Isolated Hill.

But the Kaikoura Ranges and the Molesworth country are not only notable for their tectonic features; they are also a major centre of biodiversity, with a wonderful range of endemic alpine plants (to date, more than 60), especially those clinging to inhospitable bluffs and screes. The best known are the diverse mountain daisies – both shrubs and herbs. Among the shrubs, the Kaikoura Ranges are the stronghold of all five species of the showy Marlborough rock daisy (*Pachystegia*) and three of New Zealand's five species of *Heliohebe* (or 'sun hebe'), as well as a number of endemic *Helichrysum*, *Cassinia* and *Olearia*. There are 16 endemic daisy family herbs, most belonging to the genera of *Brachyscome*, *Celmisia*, *Craspedia* (woollyhead), *Haastia* and *Raoulia* (vegetable sheep), *Senecio* and *Leucogenes*

The Clarence River twists and turns as it seeks to pass between the mountain walls of the Inland and Seaward Kaikoura ranges on its journey to the Pacific Ocean.

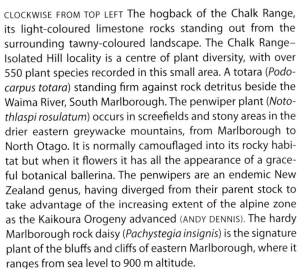

CLOCKWISE FROM TOP LEFT The hogback of the Chalk Range, its light-coloured limestone rocks standing out from the surrounding tawny-coloured landscape. The Chalk Range–Isolated Hill locality is a centre of plant diversity, with over 550 plant species recorded in this small area. A totara (*Podocarpus totara*) standing firm against rock detritus beside the Waima River, South Marlborough. The penwiper plant (*Notothlaspi rosulatum*) occurs in screefields and stony areas in the drier eastern greywacke mountains, from Marlborough to North Otago. It is normally camouflaged into its rocky habitat but when it flowers it has all the appearance of a graceful botanical ballerina. The penwipers are an endemic New Zealand genus, having diverged from their parent stock to take advantage of the increasing extent of the alpine zone as the Kaikoura Orogeny advanced (ANDY DENNIS). The hardy Marlborough rock daisy (*Pachystegia insignis*) is the signature plant of the bluffs and cliffs of eastern Marlborough, where it ranges from sea level to 900 m altitude.

ABOVE The threatened black-eyed gecko (*Hoplodactylus kahutarae*) of the Seaward and Inland Kaikoura ranges has been called New Zealand's only true alpine gecko (although since its discovery other species of gecko have been found in the alpine zone of the Takitimu Mountains, Fiordland, and the Southern Alps). But the black-eyed gecko seems to frequent the highest alpine habitat (up to 2200 m), and is considered to be one of the more recently evolved of New Zealand's 40 or so geckos. Because they inhabit remote mountain wilderness, there may be more alpine geckos awaiting discovery – most likely by interested mountaineers and climbers (ROD MORRIS).

LEFT The endemic Hutton's shearwater (*Puffinus huttoni*) has a population of more than 160,000 breeding pairs, but until 1965 its breeding location was a mystery. This adult was photographed in snow on the Seaward Kaikoura Range, where the birds' breeding colonies are scattered across the mountainside at an altitude of 1400–1800 m (ROD MORRIS).

(edelweiss). The Kaikoura mountains also carry possibly the most diverse flora of scree plants in the South Island, including the spectacular penwiper plant (*Notothlaspi rosulatum*), willowherbs (*Epilobium* species) and a harebell (*Wahlenbergia cartilaginea*). There are three endemic *Hebe* and six different species of South Marlborough's flowering glory – the pink brooms, coastal tree broom and weeping tree broom of the *Carmichaelia* genus. Plant diversity is particularly marked in the dry limestone landscapes of the Chalk Range, Isolated Hill and Ben More in the east, with more than 550 indigenous species (a remarkable 25 per cent of our total flora).

Nor is the species diversity of South Marlborough limited to the plants. The diversity of lizards is very high (eight geckos and four skinks), possibly reflecting the habitat diversity in the open tussock, scree and shrubland landscape. The mountains are also the main habitat for black-eyed gecko, one of New Zealand's unique group of alpine geckos, rarely seen because it is nocturnal and found only on rocky bluffs above 1250 m. Likewise, the mountains have a diverse invertebrate fauna, including three giant weta and a scree weta. The rocky mountain slopes are also important habitat for kea (the easternmost population of this distinctive mountain parrot) and the threatened New Zealand falcon/karearea. But the most unusual avian inhabitants are seabirds: Hutton's shearwaters, which burrow into the snow tussock on the higher (1400–1800 m) slopes of the Seaward Kaikoura Range – their only mainland nesting colony.

The Molesworth country – remote inter-montane tussock basins locked away in the heart of South Marlborough – lies to the west of the Inland Kaikoura Range. This is a rainshadow environment with continental climatic features: hot and dry in summer; snow and dry cold in winter. The beech forest that existed before human occupation was burnt off, leaving a montane grassland with many screes on the greywacke mountain slopes. Molesworth Station (180,476 ha) is the largest farm in New Zealand, amalgamated from a number of failed sheep runs which were abandoned by their lessees by 1938. A combination of plagues of rabbits and the ruinous farming practices (burning and overstocking with sheep) of the lessees led to such near collapse of the depleted grassland ecosystem that the government had to step in. Over the

Molesworth is the heart of inland Marlborough. Here over 180,000 ha of mountains, rivers, and lakes are managed by DOC for biodiversity conservation and recreation while co-existing with the largest farm in New Zealand.

The Marlborough pink broom (*Notospartium carmichaeliae*) is one of the botanical glories of the South Marlborough back country. It can grow to a small tree 3–4 m high, preferring bluffs and steep places (ROD MORRIS).

Conservation Challenges in the Marlborough Sounds

The marine biodiversity of the Sounds is still sorely lacking in protection. There is only one small marine reserve of 619 ha (Long Island/Kokomohua) in outer Queen Charlotte Sound. At the other extreme, within the Sounds there are now around 600 ha of marine farms, an industry which is known to have a huge detrimental impact upon the immediate marine environment. The Marlborough Sounds Maritime Planning Scheme places restrictions on marine farming development within Queen Charlotte Sound, and these need to be vigorously implemented. Oil spillage and shipwreck are major biodiversity risks in both Cook Strait and the Sounds, and a high state of preparedness needs to be maintained to deal with the consequences of any such catastrophes. Within the confines of the Sounds there are ongoing shoreline erosion impacts from the wake of Cook Strait ferries and the increasing number of bulk carriers. In this respect, the eventual transfer of the Picton passenger and freight terminals to an open coast site like Clifford Bay would have major recreational and conservation benefits for the Sounds. The proliferation of further structures such as jetties, power poles, boat sheds and seawalls on the foreshore of the Sounds needs to be resisted. Rigorous fire control and the eradication of wild pigs, which are causing considerable damage to shrublands and forest floors, are key measures for promoting the steady regeneration of indigenous vegetation throughout the Sounds. The Marlborough Sounds do not provide wilderness tramping opportunities, but the Nydia Track and Queen Charlotte Walkway have increased steadily in popularity. The latter is now held up as the prime national example of how a walkway (over both public and private land) can be sustainably managed – with a high level of community involvement in maintenance of the facility, and a management partnership between DOC and private providers of transport and accommodation.

D'Urville Island: Forgotten Back Country

D'Urville Island (Rangitoto ki te Tonga), with an area of 16,700 ha, is the sixth largest of New Zealand's minor islands – after Stewart/Rakiura, Chatham, Auckland, Great Barrier/Aotea, and Resolution (in descending size). Yet it is a somewhat overlooked island, due to its remote location at the northern extremity of the Marlborough Sounds and its difficult access by both land and sea. The conservation value of the island could be given greater recognition, particularly

next 50 years, the land was rehabilitated by soil and water conservation measures and by replacing sheep with cattle. Molesworth came to be regarded as a shining example of high-country management, blending environmental sustainability with profitability, and all, ironically, managed by a government agency (rather than the family-run pastoral leases throughout most of the South Island high country). But even though the land had reverted to the Crown, the Department of Lands and Survey virtually excluded the public from this wild landscape until the newly formed Department of Conservation in 1987 negotiated agreements for protected areas and limited public access. Since then, Molesworth has continued to function as a farm, but up to 7000 people annually have had the privilege of visiting this superb landscape.

because it is free of possums, Norway and ship rats, and goats, though it does have stoats, feral cats and mice.

The purchase by the Nature Heritage Fund in 2006 of Moawhitu, 1,764 ha of spectacular landscape around Greville Harbour, was an important step in this direction. The area needs rehabilitation after a century of farming but it still retains an impressive range of habitats – duneland, coastal flats and wetland, cliffs, coastal kohekohe forest, pockets of pukatea and nikau forest in the gullies, and steep forested hills (covered in four beech species, with emergent rimu) reaching up to montane cloud forest at its highest point (693 m). Moawhitu is contiguous with the existing 4072 ha D'Urville Island Scenic Reserve, thus giving a complete west–east transect of protected land across the trunk of the island. Although D'Urville Island is poorly served with tracks and huts, there is road access to the splendid coastal camping opportunities provided by Moawhitu. DOC now has the opportunity to develop a shared vision with the tangata whenua, Ngati Koata, to restore this wild, remote place of high cultural value to something like its former integrity and richness of biodiversity.

Molesworth and a Kaikoura Ranges National Park?

Very significant conservation and wilderness recreation gains have been made in the Kaikoura Ranges and in the Molesworth country in the past 15 years. In 1994, tenure review of the 52,000 ha Clarence Reserve (the largest pastoral lease in Marlborough) led to the purchase through the Nature Heritage Fund of 41,000 ha of the Seaward Kaikoura Range and its retirement from grazing. Another 10,000 ha of lower hill country and flats adjacent to the mid-Clarence River were also returned to public ownership but made available for periodic grazing under much stricter conditions than under the former pastoral lease. And thousands of hectares of land of high conservation value between the Seaward Kaikoura Range and the sea have been purchased by the Nature Heritage Fund.

But the key piece of the South Marlborough conservation lands jigsaw fell into place in July 2005 when a campaign spearheaded by Forest & Bird and Federated Mountain Clubs of NZ convinced government to pass Molesworth Station to DOC for management. This was an outstanding conservation step by government – part of its vision for a new network of high-country parks and reserves throughout the tussocklands ranged along the eastern side of the main divide of the South Island. Although about one-third of Molesworth continues to be grazed, DOC management allows:

- greater protection for the biodiversity contained in the screefields, tussocklands and herbfields in the higher areas;
- better control of pests and wilding pines ;
- greater recreational opportunity, especially tramping and mountain-biking, with up to 12 weeks of vehicle access via the Acheron road.

In 2002, Forest & Bird proposed a Kaikoura Ranges National Park, based on a 68,000 ha core (including all of the Clarence Reserve mountainland) on the Seaward Kaikoura Range. However, this proposal was later withdrawn when the society began to question whether a national park was the best option to protect the area. A variety of factors make the Kaikoura Ranges and Molesworth an unlikely national park candidate:

- the isolation and difficult road access;
- the biological impacts of 150 years of grazing and pest infestation;
- the political, commercial and even ecological requirement to continue some level of cattle grazing at lower altitudes;
- the need for intensive management to avoid fire and further weed invasion.

Molesworth will probably need to be managed as a farm park, but the Kaikoura Ranges could become a wilderness area or another of the eastern South Island's tussockland conservation parks. The wilderness values of the Kaikoura Ranges are indeed impressive: there is very little in the way of huts, tracks and bridges, and their climatic extremes and exposure through lack of forest shelter make them a serious proposition for visitors, who definitely need to be self-sufficient. It is precisely this challenge of remoteness and wildness that makes rafting or kayaking the Clarence River, or climbing Mts Alarm, Mitre or Tapuae-o-Uenuku in winter, so appealing to the back-country adventurer or remoteness-seeker.

A Marine Reserve for the Kaikoura Coast?

The geomorphology and marine biodiversity of the rocky Kaikoura coastline, from the mouth of the Clarence River to Oaro, is generally recognised as outstanding by scientists, conservationists and tourists. In addition to the marine diversity outlined above, one of the largest breeding colonies of the New Zealand fur seal on the South Island coast occurs beside SH 1 at Ohau Point (with smaller colonies and 'haul-out' groups on Kaikoura Peninsula and around

Panau Island and the scenic rocky coastline below Rileys Hill). The seals seem to thrive on the nocturnal hunting of lanternfish (a non-commercial fish) and their numbers in the Ohau Point colony continue to grow. There is impressive landform diversity around the Kaikoura Peninsula too, with limestone and siltstone eroded by waves, forming an extensive offshore reef and a variety of pools, channels, stacks and limestone cliffs. All make spectacular sights from the popular Kaikoura Walkway.

A very small Kaikoura Marine Reserve around the peninsula was proposed by Forest & Bird in 1992 but it was probably premature, albeit well-intentioned. Substantial opposition was mounted by Ngai Tahu iwi who were concerned at the lack of other more culturally acceptable marine conservation protection mechanisms (taiapure and mataitai), not only at Kaikoura but throughout their long coastal rohe around Waipounamu (South Island). Like many others, this Kaikoura marine reserve proposal has been bogged down, partly because of the narrowness and scientific exclusiveness of the Marine Reserves Act 1971. DOC has explored other options for marine protection with the Kaikoura runanga and various stakeholders, but progress (if any) seems painfully slow. However, with government adopting a new Marine Protected Areas Policy in December 2005, it is to be hoped that all parties can work together to establish acceptable protected areas in this remarkable coastal/marine ecosystem. In the meantime, at the very least there should be a complete ban on set nets to protect Kaikoura's population of Hector's dolphin.

The Seaward Kaikoura Range and Kaikoura coastline at sunrise.

CHAPTER NINE

NELSON

The Nelson region contains some of the most diverse wild lands in New Zealand. It is ringed by mountain ranges, watered by clear, fast-flowing rivers, and blessed with a long and varied coastline. It has one of the country's best climates, far from the winds that scourge Cook Strait and sheltered from the westerlies by the great mountain fastness of Kahurangi National Park. Nelson's geological and topographic diversity has resulted in geographic fragmentation of the landscape, historically creating difficulties for settlement because of the isolation of the small pockets of lowland suitable for agriculture. Four Nelson parks today retain some of the largest areas of wilderness remaining in New Zealand.

KAHURANGI NATIONAL PARK

Kahurangi National Park (452,889 ha) became New Zealand's second largest national park when it was designated in 1996; prior to that it was already one of the country's most important wilderness landscapes. The park is centred on the Tasman Mountains in the north-west corner of Nelson, with two major outliers, the Arthur Range in the east and the Matiri Range in the south. Kahurangi extends right down to the Tasman Sea in the west, is bounded by the gorges of the Buller River in the south, and its interior is drained by four main rivers: the Takaka (especially its Cobb, Waingaro and Anatoki tributaries), Aorere, Heaphy and Karamea. Although no peaks are higher than 2000 m and there are no present-day glaciers, the park is a complex maze of mountains, remote from the main chain of the Southern Alps/Ka Tiritiri o te Moana.

Kahurangi National Park is priceless not only because of its wilderness heritage but also because it has very high scientific values. No other protected area in New Zealand has such a diversity of geological history and rock types, landforms and plant communities. It contains an extraordinary level of endemism in both its flora and its invertebrate, giant land snail and native fish fauna – a result of the tectonic history of the area, coupled with its role as a refuge for isolated local plant and animal communities during the ice age glaciations.

The geodiversity of Kahurangi is the most complex of any of New Zealand's national parks and the variety of rock types responsible for many visually appealing landforms:

- the rolling tussock-covered downlands of the Mt Arthur Tableland, Gouland Downs and Gunner Downs (old peneplain surfaces);
- the spectacular cliffs of Garibaldi Ridge and the mesa-like plateaux around the Matiri Range (especially the Thousand Acre Plateau);
- the alpine glaciated landforms around the Cobb Valley and Island Lake, including cirque lakes, hanging valleys, and ice-polished resistant bedrock;
- earthquake-dammed lakes (like Lakes Matiri and Stanley) – more than a dozen such lakes were created in the park by the magnitude 7.8 (Richter scale) Murchison earthquake of 1929 – along with large areas of earthquake-induced landslides in the Karamea, Mokihinui and Matiri valleys;
- the wild, cliffed coastline between Kahurangi Point and the Heaphy Bluff.

In particular, the park is renowned for its karst landforms, especially the glaciated alpine karst in the marble of

Honeycomb Hill arch across the Oparara River is one of the many impressive karst landforms in Kahurangi National Park.

Mt Owen and Mt Arthur. Other remarkable karst features include the Oparara Arch (the largest of its kind in Australasia), Moria Gate and the other arches of the Oparara Basin, and the limestone cliffs of the lower Heaphy Valley. Furthermore, the Honeycomb Hill cave system in the Oparara Basin contains outstanding sub-fossil deposits of extinct birds (including a giant eagle), amphibians and reptiles.

The diversity of rock types, soils, topography and climates throughout Kahurangi has produced an equally remarkable array of natural vegetation communities – descending from alpine fellfields, screefields, tarns and alpine bogs, down through snow tussock grasslands and herbfields, the subalpine shrublands and montane beech rainforests, to humid coastal rainforests (comprising podocarps, rata and nikau palms), dunelands, estuaries and swamps. The alpine areas contain an exceptionally high proportion

ABOVE The 1000 Acre Plateau partly covered in winter snow at the southern end of Kahurangi National Park. It is one of a number of upland mesa-like plateaux found on the Matiri Range. LEFT Spectacular fluting in the limestone cliffs of Garibaldi Ridge is just one of many outstanding geodiversity features of Kahurangi National Park. Acidic water flowing from the peaty plateau and over the escarpment slowly dissolves the rock, especially where there are crevices or fractures in the limestone.

(80 per cent) of New Zealand's alpine plant species, and around 40 of these plants are endemic to Kahurangi. Another group of very distinctive montane plants, mountain neinei or 'pineapple scrub' (species of *Dracophyllum*), are found on the wet, infertile soils in the granite areas. The park is the most important remaining large habitat for the great spotted kiwi; there are also significant populations of kea, blue duck/whio, kaka and rock wren.

Due to the long isolation of the different karst systems,

the park has a diverse cave fauna, including a number of different cave weta and at least 12 cave beetles. The cave weta are preyed on by another specialist, the endemic Nelson cave spider (New Zealand's largest spider, with a leg span of about 12 cm). The park also contains many endemic freshwater insects (caddisflies and stoneflies) as well as the rare Nelson alpine weta (one of the smallest of New Zealand's 11 giant weta species) and two large tree weta species. But the real standard-bearers of Kahurangi's wildlife are *Powelliphanta*, colourful giant land snails, some with shells 10 cm in diameter. *Powelliphanta* are carnivorous and have a very ancient lineage, tracing their origins back more than 80 million years. There are more than 27 distinct forms of this giant land snail within the park out of a nationwide total of around 64. They are most common in the cool, wet montane beech forests or the snow-tussock grasslands of the downlands.

The recreational value of Kahurangi National Park is also important, mainly because of its large size and diversity of natural landscapes. The park has a network of more than 500 km of maintained tracks and 60 huts; most of these (except for the Heaphy Track and the Arthur Tableland) escape the severe pressures that overseas backpackers and day trippers currently place on the coastal parts of Abel Tasman National Park. Of fundamental conservation and recreation importance is the protection of Kahurangi's predominant wilderness character, especially the 87,000 ha Tasman Wilderness Area interior of the park, which was set aside for wilderness recreation in 1988 after

LEFT The high rainfall and warmer temperatures in the Oparara Basin produce a rainforest where the trees are draped in epiphytes and mosses. ABOVE The insectivorous Nelson cave spider (*Spelungula cavernicola*), our largest spider, is restricted to the cave systems of the Oparara Basin and Paparoa National Park (ROD MORRIS).

TOP The great spotted kiwi or roa (*Apteryx haastii*) is the largest of our four kiwi species. This adult male would weigh around 2.8 kg. The forests, downlands, and pakihi wetlands of Kahurangi National Park are their major stronghold (ROD MORRIS). RIGHT There are more than 27 distinct forms of the colourful and carnivorous *Powelliphanta* giant land snails within Kahurangi National Park. This one, the Oparara land snail (*Powelliphanta annectens*), inhabits the Oparara cave localities (ROD MORRIS).

LEFT The subalpine shrublands of Kahurangi National Park contain a range of colourful papery-barked small trees, such as *Olearia lacunosa* (left) and mountain neinei (*Dracophyllum traversii*). BELOW The Gouland Downs are the largest of several tussock and shrub covered uplands in Kahurangi National Park. The Gouland Downs and the nearby Mackay Downs are remnants of a peneplain, an ancient land surface worn down by millions of years of erosion. The downs are crossed by the Heaphy Track, one of New Zealand's Great Walks.

Clematis marmoraria is a rare and endemic prostrate subshrub, found naturally in only two sites on alpine marble karrenfield in Kahurangi National Park (ROD MORRIS).

a decade or more of campaigning by the Federated Mountain Clubs of NZ. Tasman is New Zealand's second-largest wilderness area (see map of wilderness areas on p.29). It protects not only outstanding opportunities for wilderness tramping but also the Karamea River, one of the best wilderness rafting/kayaking and fishing rivers in the South Island. Although the entire 50 km length of the river has a wild character, it is the 20 km within the wilderness area – from below the junction with the Leslie River at Karamea Bend to where the river turns sharply to the south to get around the Fenian Range – that is free of tracks, huts and helicopter incursions.

Kahurangi has another outstanding dimension – underground – to its variety of wilderness recreation opportunities. The cave systems under Mt Owen and Mt Arthur are especially challenging to cavers and speleologists because of their great length and depth. These are considered to be some of the most extensive cave systems in the Southern Hemisphere, and include the longest (Bulmer, 55 km), deepest (Nettlebed, almost 900 m) and oldest (at least 700,000 years) caves in New Zealand.

With this amazing geo/biodiversity and range of wilderness recreation opportunities, the obvious question is why it took so long for the area to be recognised as a national park. The recreational attractions of the area were appreciated by the NZ Forest Service which gazetted the area as North-West Nelson Forest Park in 1970, but its remoteness meant that it was not well known to the public. The Heaphy Track was probably the only feature of national prominence at that time, partly because mountain clubs and Forest & Bird

were campaigning against plans to convert it to a road (part of a mooted link between Collingwood and Karamea). By the mid-1970s, however, the park was caught up in the forest conservation, mining and hydro-dam controversies that raged throughout New Zealand at that time. The Native Forest Action Council highlighted the destructive logging occurring on the private Tai Tapu Estate lying on the western slopes of the Wakamarama Ranges. In addition, the public were appalled by the NZ Forest Service's economic lunacy in attempting to convert the magical Oparara Basin into an exotic plantation. Their 'scorched earth' approach using helicopters to drop napalm generated particularly wide opposition; their fires incinerated not only the clear-felled indigenous trees but all remaining wildlife (especially the great spotted kiwi and *Powelliphanta* land snails which were distinctive biodiversity features of the area). Other exploitation proposals which galvanised public support for greater protection as a national park were:

- the bulldozing of the historic Flora Track;
- opposition of the mining industry to the wilderness area and the whole national park concept;
- Buller Electricity's attempt to exclude the Mt Owen–Matiri area from any park in order to realise its energy pipedream of linking the waters of Lake Matiri to a flooded Ngakawau Valley.

The NZ Conservation Authority finally initiated the formal move towards national park status in June 1991, yet it took another five years of consultation and argument before New Zealand's 13th national park, Kahurangi, became a reality. But despite the overwhelming majority of the 1000 submissions supporting a national park, the horse-trading over the final boundary went on, leading to the exclusion of the 28,500 ha Tai Tapu Estate and nearly 60 other land parcels around the periphery of the proposed park (an area of 16,000 ha in total, including the Mt Burnett dolomite mine and the Sam's Creek gold prospect). Achieving national parks, along with politics, is indeed very much the 'art of the achievable'!

ABEL TASMAN NATIONAL PARK AND FAREWELL SPIT

Abel Tasman National Park in the south and Farewell Spit Nature Reserve in the north enclose Golden Bay, so named because of the colour of the quartz-rich sands that have weathered out of the granite hinterland and now grace its superb beaches. Abel Tasman is the smallest of New Zealand's national parks (22,689 ha) and its name

Kahurangi National Park extends to the Tasman Sea coastline between Big River and Kohaihai. This coastal forest in the lower reaches of Big River has a subtropical look, with nikau palms and profuse bunches of climbing kiekie.

commemorates its historical association with the Dutch navigator Abel Janzoon Tasman, who attempted to land off Taupo Point in 1642. Prior to its designation as a national park in 1942 (the 300th anniversary of Tasman's visit) through the efforts of Perrine Moncrieff, one of New Zealand's most notable woman conservationists, easy sea access had allowed some of the coastal landscape to be subdivided and severely modified by fire and weed invasion. Yet the park has a well-deserved international reputation because of its coastal scenery. The Abel Tasman coastline has one of the highest tidal ranges in the country (up to 4 m), and the granite sands have been swept into an intricate network of sandspits and beaches all the way from Wainui Bay to Marahau.

But there is much more to the park than walking the Abel Tasman Coastal Track or cruising in the multitude of water craft that ply the coast. The park interior, traversed by the Awaroa and Falls rivers, is very rugged, with many narrow gorges, steep rapids and waterfalls. A particularly interesting vegetation feature of the park is the occurrence of all five types of beech (*Nothofagus*) in the forest cover – quite a rarity for one small region. Black beech clings to the dry and exposed ridge crests and headlands close to the sea, with hard beech downslope where there is more soil moisture; moving into the park interior, at about 350 m altitude red beech becomes the dominant canopy tree; and silver beech predominates as the higher,

wetter parts of the Pikikiruna Range are reached (around 700–1000 m), along with mountain beech on the more poorly drained soils and frost hollows.

Between the southern end of the Pikikiruna Range and Takaka Hill lies the marble Canaan Tableland. The Canaan area also has many interesting karst features, and is particularly important because its many stream sinks and dolines link with other cave systems within the park. Lying at the western edge of Canaan, Harwoods Hole is an outstanding karst feature, a gaping hole in the surrounding marble landscape, with its 176 m vertical cave shaft the deepest in New Zealand. From a safe lookout nearby there are impressive views of the hole and the surrounding landscape, including the deep defile carved by Gorge Creek and the razor-sharp flutings on the marble, so hard and smooth that plants are quite unable to establish themselves.

ABOVE Sand ripples on Awaroa Beach in Abel Tasman National Park. RIGHT The sandy arc of Farewell Spit extends for almost 30 km, enclosing over 11,000 ha of inter-tidal sandflat habitat at the western end of Golden Bay.

To protect the Canaan catchment, and secure continued public access into Harwoods Hole and the higher parts of the park around Moa Park, in 2004 government purchased the 758 ha Canaan Downs property through the Nature Heritage Fund. The irony of the occasion did not escape many of Nelson's long-suffering taxpayers. Canaan Downs is a former Crown lease property that was freeholded in the early 1970s; subsequently most of its beech forest cover was clear-felled, and the land grassed and fenced – all with the assistance of the environmentally ruinous supplementary stock-subsidy schemes of the Muldoon administration.

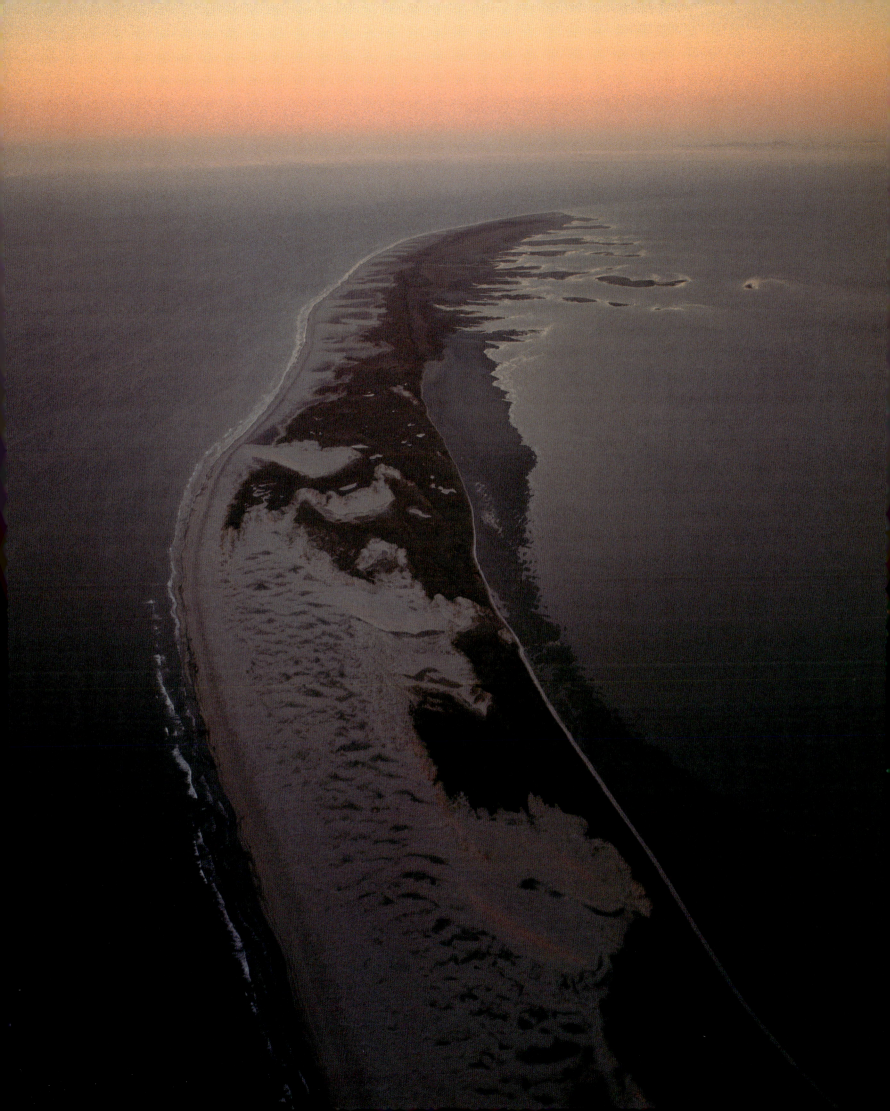

Northern rata (*Metrosideros robusta*) flowering in Golden Bay. Never far from the coast, northern rata will tend to dominate the forests on alluvial plains in the north-west corner of the South Island.

tidal seascape is a habitat for billions of molluscs, crabs, shrimps, sand-hoppers and other small creatures – and is a vast smorgasbord for the tens of thousands of wading birds that advance and retreat with the turning of each tide. Around 90 different bird species are known to frequent Farewell Spit Nature Reserve, earning it international recognition as a Ramsar site (a Wetland of International Importance). Many of these are migratory waders that breed in Siberia and the Arctic, and flock to the spit between our spring and autumn. Three of these species – the bar-tailed godwit, the knot and the turnstone – account for around 50,000 of the birds (or around 90 per cent of the total). Twenty-five years ago, Australasian gannets established their most recent mainland breeding colony on the spit. On a darker note, however, the geography of Farewell Spit and the northern end of Golden Bay is such that dolphins and whales regularly become stranded in the shallows; pilot whales seem most susceptible, but sperm, minke, fin and beaked whales have all been victims at times (see also Mahia Peninsula in Ch.6).

Now the taxpayer is paying twice for this folly but it will take much longer for the downs to regenerate into beech forest than the 30 years it took to establish the pasture.

Farewell Spit is a complete landscape contrast, a low, kilometre-wide arc of sand that extends out from Cape Farewell for almost 30 km, enclosing a band of inter-tidal sandflats up to 7 km wide along its southern edge. The spit and inter-tidal sandflats together make up Farewell Spit Nature Reserve (11,423 ha). On most days the spit is a wild place, where strong north-westerly winds constantly swirl the sand that accumulates there. This vast amount of sand, of West Coast origin, is being deposited along the spit as the Westland Current meets the opposing currents through Cook Strait (see Ch.8), and is estimated to be around 3–4 million m³ per annum. Most of the sand, once trapped, seems to be blown across into the leeward shallows of Golden Bay instead of lengthening the spit, thereby maintaining an outstanding habitat for a wide variety of shore birds.

The subtle changes in salinity and tidal depth across such a wide sand plain have produced one of the country's best examples of inter-tidal vegetation zonation. Closest to the dunes there are jointed rushes, then sea-rush and salt-marsh (with coastal plantain, sea-primrose and glasswort turfs); beyond the salt-marsh, a vast swathe of *Zostera* eelgrass extends out to the low-tide limit. This 10,000 ha

NELSON LAKES NATIONAL PARK

Nelson Lakes National Park straddles the Spenser Mountains (in effect, the northern end of the Southern Alps/ Ka Tiritiri o te Moana). Its name derives from the twin lakes – Rotoiti and Rotoroa – that are the major sources of the Buller River. The lakes occupy the lower end of troughs carved through the greywacke mountains by past glaciers, their valleys now drained by the Travers, Sabine and D'Urville rivers. The Spenser Mountains themselves are truncated by the Alpine Fault, a great diagonal SW–NE slash across the park – from Lake Daniells near the head of the Maruia River, through the floor of the Glenroy Valley, and down Station Creek to cross the Matakitaki Valley and Mole Saddle, past the head of Lake Rotoroa, through Speargrass Creek, and across the lower end of Lake Rotoiti to the Wairau Valley. When the park was formed in 1956 it was a simple affair, 140,000 acres (about 55,000 ha) centred on the mountain catchments of the two lakes. Some of the frontal country (such as Mt Robert, the Mole Tops and the floor of the lower Travers Valley) were already severely modified by fire and stock-grazing. However, the beech forests of the main Travers, Sabine and D'Urville valleys were ideal for multi-day 'pass-hopping' tramping trips, and the glacier-free peaks of the Ella, Mahanga, Travers and St Arnaud ranges provided many easy climbs (relative to the higher, glacier-mantled peaks of the Southern Alps south

Winter snows in Nelson Lakes National Park. This view from Robert Ridge above the Travers Valley shows the sharp beech treeline, though broken in many places by snow-covered shingle slides.

of Arthur's Pass). The park board of the day even made a brave if naïve attempt to establish a wilderness area around Lake Constance and Blue Lake in the head of the west branch of the Sabine River. This is a delightful mountain valley, but so small that it soon became trampled underfoot by all who came to seek the solitude of wilderness; by the late 1960s, the authorities had to respond by revoking its wilderness area designation and building a proper track up the West Sabine with a hut at Blue Lake! It was a salutary lesson about the impending 'back-country boom' in the New Zealand outdoors and the dangers of making the experience of wilderness too easy.

The original Nelson Lakes National Park was very much a product of the sort of protected area thinking that gave rise to the National Parks Act of 1952. But there was always a feeling that it lacked something, that it could be the core of a much larger, more diverse park. In the early 1970s, the Federated Mountain Clubs of NZ proposed that the park be doubled in size by incorporating the main Spenser

Mountains to the south, as well as the more open montane tussock grasslands of the east and south – parts of Rainbow Station (Begley and Paske valleys), the headwaters of the Wairau, Lake Tennyson and the upper Clarence (all part of Molesworth Station) and the upper Waiau (St James Station); but the proposal fell on deaf ears in the Department of Lands and Survey, so powerful was the pastoral farming industry at that time.

But another 1970s issue kept the idea of a more representative national park alive: the NZ Forest Service's South Island Beech Utilisation Scheme. The beech scheme sought to fell many of the more accessible beech forests of the upper Buller, Matakitaki and Maruia valleys for wood chips; only the ensuing bitter forest conservation controversy saved most of them. Some became part of Victoria Forest Park

when it was formed in 1981, and 43,000 ha of beech forest in the Glenroy and Matakitaki valleys was then added to Nelson Lakes National Park in 1983. This addition brought the park up to its present, more substantial size (101,872 ha), but the irony of it all was that the National Parks and Reserves Authority of that time completely failed to use the 'scientific representativeness' provisions of the new National Parks Act of 1980. To many, the Matakitaki and Glenroy beech forests were the soft option, just more of the same, whereas the grasslands and wetlands of Rainbow, Molesworth, and St James pastoral runs in the east would have added really significant ecosystem diversity to the park.

Red and mountain beech forest in the West Sabine Valley, Nelson Lakes National Park. All four beech (*Nothofagus*) species, often in mixed associations, are found in the park. The understorey of this forest has been eaten out in past times by deer.

Essentially, the park is valued today as back country with moderately challenging tramping and mountaineering opportunities. The park has a good hut and track system which, save for the Lake Rotoiti–Lake Angelus–Robert Ridge circuit, is far from the Great Walks and the masses of overseas backpackers who clog the more accessible back country of the Nelson region.

MOUNT RICHMOND FOREST PARK

Mount Richmond Forest Park (New Zealand's second-largest conservation park, with an area of 163,836 ha) lies between Nelson City and the Waimea Plains in the west and the Wairau Valley in the east. Its largest feature is the Richmond Range, which effectively forms the topographic boundary between Nelson and Marlborough; the highest peaks, Mt Richmond (1760 m), Mt Rintoul (1731 m) and Red Hill (1790 m), are prominent skyline features from both sides. Three major rivers, the Motueka, Waimea and Pelorus, have their headwaters in the park. The Pelorus River, flanked by the Bryant Range in the west and the Richmond Range in the east, flows through the heart of the park; many of its tributaries are untracked and heavily forested, giving this core area a wilderness character. The park is heavily forested with all varieties of beech present, often mixed with podocarp and broadleaved trees at lower altitudes. An interesting feature of the forests along the Richmond Range is the exceptionally high altitude of the beech forest treeline – almost as high as that in the Branch and Leatham tributaries across the Wairau River, which at 1550 m are considered the highest in the country.

Part of the Bryant Range behind Nelson is known as the Nelson Mineral Belt (technically the Dun Mountain Ophiolite Belt, after Dun Mountain, the most prominent peak, so named because of its colour). These ultramafic rocks lack silica but are very high in magnesium and iron, and sometimes contain nickel- and chromium-bearing minerals. They weather to a reddish-brown colour (a kind of iron oxide rust), and the high levels of magnesium in the soils tend to be toxic to most plants, hence the absence of forest or shrubland on the mineral belt. The other part of the Nelson Mineral Belt lies in the south-western corner of the park, around Red Hill and the headwaters of the right branch of the Motueka River. Elsewhere in the park only the highest peaks of the Richmond Range carry small cirques as evidence of past glaciation, but here the ultramafic rock has been carved by a 10 km long glacier, and the lack of vegetation means that the truncated spurs and cirque basins are clearly visible. The ophiolite belt has been very important in unravelling the structural geology of the South Island, for the same rocks are also found around Red Mountain in Mount Aspiring National Park in north-west Otago – but on the opposite side of the Alpine Fault. So the two outcrops of red rock, 500 km distant from each other, are distinctive markers of New Zealand's geological history, indicating the enormous extent of sideways displacement of the Pacific and Australian plates over millions of years

An outcrop of ultramafic rock (with a high content of magnesium and iron) in the Red Hills locality in the south-western corner of Mount Richmond Forest Park.

along the Alpine Fault. The Nelson Mineral Belt is also notable for its unusual flora. Whereas its toxic soils deter the establishment of tall forest, these so-called 'serpentine soils' are instead colonised by a number of shrubs normally only found in the harsh subalpine environment. In all, there are 21 varieties of shrubs, herbs and grasses (such as *Myosotis laeta*, *Craspedia* 'Hacket' and *Geranium* 'Red Hills') which are endemic to the mineral belt. Their conservation is a priority, especially because the belt is being steadily over-run by wilding exotic conifer trees.

THREATS AND CONSERVATION PRIORITIES

Tourism Impacts on the Abel Tasman National Park Coastline

Abel Tasman National Park does not extend out to the low-water mark along its scenic coastline. Save for the 1835 ha Tonga Island Marine Reserve, the coastline has long been a management no-man's land, with at one time 17 water-taxi companies disgorging thousands of visitors onto what was once a quiet and secluded seascape. In addition, there have been summer holiday peaks of up to 500 kayaks and scores of motorised boats in the waters between Totaranui and Marahau. The growth of holiday home and tourism developments on private coastal land enclaves has also added to the problem, although this threat was met to

ABOVE The South Island kaka (*Nestor meridionalis meridionalis*) was once widespread in the forests around the shores of Lakes Rotoiti and Rotoroa in Nelson Lakes National Park. Both kaka and bellbirds (see opposite page) have suffered from the competition of alien wasps for one of their main food sources – the honeydew exudate on the bark of the beech trees. The conservation efforts in the Lake Rotoiti mainland island project are beginning to pay off for kaka, which are now beginning to increase in number (ROD MORRIS). RIGHT The South Island tomtit or ngiru-ngiru (*Petroica macrocephala*) has a yellower breast than its North Island cousin but both are frequently found in beech forests.

ABOVE The endemic bellbird or korimako (*Anthornis melanura*) is our outstanding songbird. Like the other honey-eaters (tui and stitchbird), the bellbird has a brush-tipped tongue for reaching deeply into flowers for nectar. This male, in Nelson Lakes National Park, is using its tongue to feed on drops of honeydew exudate on the bark of beech trees (ROD MORRIS). BELOW Blue Lake at the head of the West Sabine Valley, Nelson Lakes National Park. Blue Lake was once the centrepiece of a wilderness area, but its status had to be revoked because so many people wanted to visit the area. As a consequence a track system and hut had to be built.

some extent by the purchase as a park extension of the 1700 ha Hadfields block in Awaroa Inlet in 2006 by the Nature Heritage Fund.

Past attempts by DOC to incorporate the entire Abel Tasman foreshore within the park were frustrated by powerful vested fishing industry and tourism interests. Most tourist transport operators admitted to a serious problem which needed addressing, but a solution was stalled for years by the national foreshore and seabed controversy. The impasse was finally overcome late in January 2007, when a compromise was reached and government gazetted all 70 km of Abel Tasman foreshore adjoining the national park and private land as scenic reserve. The challenge now is for the foreshore joint managers – DOC and Tasman District Council – to quickly develop a reserve management plan, bylaws

The beautiful Abel Tasman National Park coastline was in a management limbo until the foreshore became a scenic reserve in 2007.

to control anti-social behaviour and polluting activities, and regulation of tourist operators through concessions.

Pest Control and the Re-introduction of Threatened Indigenous Species

The usual range of animal pests is an ever-growing threat to the indigenous wildlife and flora of Nelson's wilderness. For park visitors, two of the most obvious impacts over the last 20 years have been the loss of kaka from the shoreline forests of Lakes Rotoiti and Rotoroa, and a drastic reduction in the numbers of blue duck/whio from the swiftly flowing streams (like Flora Stream) in Kahurangi National Park. The problem is so widespread and pervasive that researchers have been hard-pressed to develop strategic approaches that emphasise an integrated ecological approach to solving this decline in indigenous biodiversity. Nor are DOC's and volunteers' efforts helped by stupid, short-sighted biosecurity lapses – like allowing fitch farming in Golden Bay; when this small industry collapsed the ferrets were released and have since decimated the rock wren population in the park.

One of the longest-running and encouraging biodiversity research programmes has been in the 825 ha Lake Rotoiti mainland island restoration project. Tiny scale insects in the bark of the beech trees of the area produce large quantities of a sweet exudate called 'honeydew', which is a key component of the forest food chain, supporting not only birds like kaka, tui and bellbird but also lizards, native bees and soil bacteria. But major alien pests – Northern Hemisphere wasps – thrive on the honeydew. They have invaded the forests en masse, endangering the energy flow of the whole ecosystem. So, for more than a decade, scientists and volunteers have worked on controlling wasps, as well as possums, mustelids, rodents, cats and deer in the mainland island. Their dedicated efforts have resulted in a marked recovery in the most threatened organisms in the forest – kaka, yellow-crowned parakeet, tui, bellbird, robin, long-tailed bat and mistletoe – as well as a much better understanding of the surges in animal populations (both indigenous and pest) in those years (called 'mast' years) when the beech trees seed. Furthermore, the relationship between pest predators themselves is complex; for example, controlling stoats can lead to an upsurge in rats. However, by 2004, the improved level of security against pests at Lake Rotoiti was considered sufficient for the release of nine great spotted kiwis in the area, followed by another 10 in 2006. Eventually, the chatter of saddlebacks/tieke, red-crowned parakeets and even yellowheads/mohua could also once again be heard in these beech forests.

Tasman Wilderness Area: Maintaining its Integrity

The Tasman Wilderness Area, centred on the Tasman Mountains in Kahurangi National Park, is the largest legal wilderness area in the top half of the South Island. It was established after years of consultation, especially over its boundaries (primarily to allow the Heaphy Track to pass along its northern boundary, and recreational rafters and fishers to have adequate helicopter access to the upper reaches of the Karamea River). But there has been constant pressure on DOC from tourist interests to allow helicopter access for fishers and recreational hunters – in

The middle reaches of the Karamea River and Garibaldi Ridge (in the distance) lie within the Tasman Wilderness Area of Kahurangi National Park.

contravention of the park management plan and wilderness policy. In addition, DOC has in the past allowed virtually unrestricted year-round access for commercial helicopter hunting. While this has provided necessary control of deer, it has also diminished the solitude and natural quiet that is such an essential ingredient of the visitor's wilderness experience. As the profile of Kahurangi National Park increases, the value of maintaining the integrity of the wilderness core should be obvious. Consequently, DOC needs to insist on greater co-operation from the helicopter and wild animal recovery industries to restrict the number of helicopter hunting operators, limit the seasonal duration of their permits and enforce the prohibition of landings within the wilderness area.

CHAPTER TEN

WEST COAST

The West Coast has an overwhelming wilderness character. No other region in New Zealand has such a unique combination of natural features:

- a long, narrow strip of land, geographically isolated west of the Southern Alps/Ka Tiritiri o te Moana;
- a wet but generally mild climate;
- a remarkable array of glacial and riverine landforms, in many places extending unbroken from the mountains to the sea;
- an almost continuous green mantle of forest and wetland vegetation extending the entire 550 km length of the coast, from Kahurangi Point to Awarua Point.

Human settlement has always been on nature's terms and even today the population is little more than 30,000. SH 6 is a narrow thread of civilisation allowing tens of thousands of fascinated tourists to travel the length of the West Coast each year. However, the mountains are crossed by roads at only three passes: Lewis Pass, Arthur's Pass and Haast Pass/Tioripatea. On either side of the mountain highways there is usually wildness, with nature seemingly anxious to fill any vacuum, diligently trying to re-vegetate slips and fresh shingle deposited beside streams – indeed, any of the bare ground constantly generated in such a dynamic landscape.

The Alpine Fault is the largest and most internationally significant geological feature in the West Coast. On land it can be traced as a straight line (clearly visible from space) for 450 km from the mouth of the John O'Groats River near Milford Sound to Springs Junction, where it splinters into several faultlines in the Marlborough Fault Zone. This great faultline cleaves the West Coast in two lengthwise; the coastal lowlands lie to the west and, to the east, the main divide of the Alps rearing up as high as 3497 m at Mt Tasman, New Zealand's second highest peak. (The highest, Aoraki/Mt Cook, actually lies on the Mt Cook Range, an eastern outlier of the Alps.)

The Alpine Fault is one of only four places where the collision of the Earth's great tectonic plates can be seen on the land surface (the other three are also notorious for their earthquakes and mountain-building – the Karakoram–Himalaya Mountains, the Andes Mountains and the San Andreas Fault of California). Along the Alpine Fault not only are the Pacific and Australian plates grinding past each other but the Pacific Plate is also being pushed up over the Australian Plate to form the Southern Alps/Ka Tiritiri o te Moana. Even though the Alps are rising at the rate of 10–20 mm per year, they have probably maintained more or less the same height throughout the last several million years because the high rates of erosion on the western slopes match the rate of mountain uplift. Enormous amounts of eroded sediment are transported in flood to the narrow coastal flood plain, for the mountains of the West Coast are among the wettest in the world, in places drenched in up to 18,000 mm of precipitation annually. Some rivers, like the Landsborough, carry as much as 15,000 tonnes of sediment per square kilometre of catchment (in comparison with only 1600–2000 tonnes per square kilometre of catchment for the adjacent Dobson and Hopkins rivers on the eastern rainshadow side of the Alps). After rain, the short, turbulent rivers rise as quickly as they subside again, a phenomenon well known to wilderness trampers and anyone who has to work and travel in the mountainous West Coast back country.

Fox Glacier/Te Moenga o Tuawe plunges down into the West Coast rainforest from its névés on the western side of the Southern Alps/Ka Tiritiri o te Moana.

1. Kahurangi National Park
2. Victoria Forest Park
3. Paparoa National Park
4. Paparoa Wilderness Area
5. Saxton Ecological Area
6. Molesworth Recreation Reserve
7. Clarence Res. Conservation Area
8. Lewis Pass National Reserve
9. Lake Sumner Forest Park
10. Arthur's Pass National Park
11. Craigieburn Forest Park
12. Castle Hill Conservation Area
13. Korowai–Torlesse Tussocklands Park
14. Eyrewell Scientific Reserve
15. Adams Wilderness Area
16. Bankside Scientific Reserve
17. Aoraki / Mount Cook National Park
18. Hakatere Conservation Park (proposed)

NORTH WESTLAND, CANTERBURY

0   25   50   75km

The two accessible glaciers of the West Coast (Franz Josef Glacier/Ka Roimata o Hine Hukatere and Fox Glacier/Te Moenga o Tuawe) and the Pancake Rocks of Punakaiki are internationally famous tourist icons. Many visitors also flock to see the Cape Foulwind seal colony and the white herons of Waitangiroto Lagoon. But just as significant are the Coast's many unparalleled opportunities for back-country and wilderness recreation: white-water rafting on the Karamea, Buller and Landsborough rivers; kayaking the solitude of Okarito Lagoon, Ohinetamatea River and the Tawharekiri Lakes; caving in the Oparara or Paparoa karst country; tramping through the beech forests of the upper Buller and Maruia; or mountaineering around the Garden of Eden and Garden of Allah – and any of the hundreds of ranges and glaciers which extend throughout the length of the West Coast. It is no surprise, then, that most of New Zealand's limited number of wilderness areas lie along the western side of the South Island divide: the Tasman, Paparoa, most of Adams, Hooker–Landsborough and Olivine wilderness areas. Furthermore, New Zealand's wilderness exploration literature is rich in the romance of those who always wondered what lay beyond that last blue West Coast ridge; of those who penetrated so many fear-some gorges – like the Poerua or the Douglas, the Waiatoto or the Ten Hour Gorge of the Arawhata – to reach hidden hanging valleys high in the mountains beyond.

It is not surprising, then, that the West Coast contains the greatest area of legally protected landscape in any of New Zealand's regions – over two million hectares, or more than a quarter of the protected land in New Zealand. This includes all, or large parts, of five of New Zealand's 14 national parks (Kahurangi, Paparoa, Arthur's Pass, West-land/Tai Poutini and Mount Aspiring). Indeed, over 80 per cent of the West Coast is managed by DOC and most of this still has a wilderness character, making the Coast pre-eminent in the conservation of New Zealand's wilderness heritage.

The vast indigenous forests of the West Coast are the most significant in the country. While most of the diverse lowland forests of New Zealand's fertile coastal and allu-vial soils were elsewhere long ago cleared for agriculture and settlement, large areas fortuitously survived intact on the West Coast. Here remain most of our magnificent ka-hikatea forests and the largest areas of dense, unmodified rimu terrace forest.

In addition, South Westland (the least affected part of the West Coast) stands alongside Stewart Island/Rakiura as the only part of the country with large areas of freshwater

A narrow fault scarp defile cut by waterfalls in the mountainside. The rocks were worn smooth by the ice of the Franz Josef Glacier/Ka Roima-ta o Hine Hukatere when its level was much higher than today.

wetlands intact. Outstanding examples are Kini Swamp behind Bruce Bay, the Tawharekiri Lakes near Haast, and the Okuru Swamp and Burmeister Morass on the Haast Coastal Plain. Furthermore, many coastal wetlands and estuaries are still in a natural state, including the large Salt-water and Okarito lagoons. Consequently, this wealth of natural habitats makes the West Coast of enormous impor-tance for biodiversity conservation. The forests are notable for harbouring three species of kiwi – great spotted kiwi/roa, the Okarito brown kiwi/rowi and the Haast brown kiwi/tokoeka. In addition, the region is a stronghold for kea, kaka, blue duck/whio and mohua, as well as coastal wildlife like the Westland petrel, Fiordland crested pen-guin/tawaki and Hector's dolphin.

Lake Christabel lies in the headwaters of the Blue Grey River, surrounded on all sides by the beech forests of Victoria Forest Park.

THE BULLER, VICTORIA FOREST PARK AND THE SOUTH ISLAND BEECH SCHEME

The Buller, by the time it reaches Westport, is New Zealand's third largest river in volume; it is also notorious for having the highest ratio of peak flood to normal flow (up to 20 times the mean flow). The Buller River has shown a tenacious ability to maintain its westward flow over the millennia, twisting and turning and cutting several impressive gorges through the Hope–Braeburn, Lyell–Brunner and Mt William–Paparoa ranges as they were uplifted and barred its way. It rises in the clear, cool waters of the twin Nelson lakes, Rotoiti and Rotoroa, quickly gathers up the Hope and Owen rivers from Kahurangi National Park, rests momentarily to receive the Mangles, Matakitaki and Matiri at the Four Rivers Plain around Murchison, and then embarks on the long sinuous path to the sea through the scenic Upper and Lower Buller gorges. En route, the Buller is joined by the beautiful Maruia River, and finally the Inangahua, Orikaka and the Ohikanui, the latter a pristine river flowing out of the heart of the Paparoa Wilderness Area. Sections of the Buller system are highly valued for their challenging kayaking and rafting, especially the rapids of the Gowan and Matakitaki, and the earthquake-formed drops in the Upper Buller Gorge, such as impressive Ariki Falls (locally known as Upthrust Falls or Fantail Falls).

By any standards the Buller is a Wild and Scenic River, but in the mid-1970s, when hydro-power planners were still

paramount, they devised a scheme to divert the wild headwaters of the Wairau, Clarence and Waiau rivers via tunnels under the Spenser Mountains into the Buller catchment, leaving the Gowan and Buller above Gowanbridge completely dry. They also planned to dam the Buller at Lyell and Hawks Crag, inundating both the upper and lower gorges. All that stopped these planners and engineers was the sheer cost of handling the awesome flood peaks of the river (up to 450,000 cumecs) and the high risk of earthquakes in this seismically active locality. The 'Save the Buller' campaign began in earnest in 1986, with Nelson–Marlborough Fish and Game applying for a Water Conservation Order over the river and its tributaries. It took another 15 years of legal process before the main Buller and most of the headwater reaches of its tributaries were protected by the order – a resounding victory for a broad cross-section of New Zealand's conservationists, anglers, kayakers and rafters. But this victory is becoming tarnished through didymo infestation and pollution of the Buller's waters as dairying agri-business proliferates throughout the catchment.

North of the lower Buller and perched above the Tasman coastline lies a little-known and strange landscape of fog-bound heathland, tussockland and shrubland called the 'Buller Coal Plateaux'. Geologically the plateaux are quite distinct, with hard quartzose sandstone exposed on the surface and seams of coal in the rock types, collectively known as the Brunner Coal Measures, which form the basis of Westport's coal industry. Coal was taken from the plateaux via engineering masterpieces like the Denniston Incline, Millerton Incline and the Charming Creek tramway, all part of the rich historic coal-mining heritage of the West Coast. With so few visitors, concern for the conservation of the unique landforms and vegetation communities of the coal plateaux was slow to materialise, and then only as a result of the threatened inundation of the impressive Ngakawau Gorge and Charming Creek Walkway for hydro-electricity generation and the expansion of coal mining into the wild upper Waimangaroa Valley.

The plateaux landscape is a colourful, scattered assemblage of stunted and prostrate shrubs like pink pine, manuka and *Dracophyllum densum*, all interspersed with sandstone outcrops. The shrubs are often very old, and slow growing because of the extreme infertility of the acidic soils, the high rainfall (up to 6000 mm annually) and poor drainage, and the low sunshine levels. The most notable plant of the grasslands is a local endemic tussock, *Chionochloa juncea*; the area is also a stronghold for the great spotted kiwi and

contains many species of endangered giant carnivorous land snails. The best-known river track in this landscape is the Charming Creek Walkway, which works its way through the spectacular lower Ngakawau Gorge, passing Mangatini Falls and the defile where the Ngakawau River emerges from its deeply incised upper gorge. However, the ecological attractions of the plateaux can be best appreciated by a trek into the red tussock grasslands and manuka shrublands of the upper Waimangaroa River, reached via the mining roads through Denniston–Burnetts Face or Stockton. The crest of the Mt William Range can be traversed by mountain bike along the pylon track through Orikaka Forest, a 2–3 day trip from New Creek just downstream from the upper Buller Gorge, across to Burnetts Face, Coalbrookdale and Denniston.

The upper reaches of the Buller were protected as a Wild and Scenic River after a 15-year 'Save the Buller' campaign.

Victoria Forest Park is New Zealand's largest conservation park (206,827 ha). It is mainly a rugged mountainous landscape, based on the Victoria and Brunner ranges lying between the Maruia River in the east and the Inangahua River in the west. The rocks making up these mountains are old, hard granites and greywackes, quite different from the nearby Southern Alps/Ka Tiritiri o te Moana. The Victoria Range and the May Tops between Rahu Saddle and the upper Grey/Mawheranui River are very bold in outline, with numerous hanging valleys and cirque lakes retained in the hard rock after glaciers retreated from the crest of the range. This part of the park has a wild character and is virtually

Mt Rochfort (1038 m) is a prominent landmark at the southern end of the little-known landscape of fog-bound heathland, tussockland and shrubland called the 'Buller Coal Plateaux'. Note the conglomerate rocks and layered sedimentary rocks, all part of the Brunner Coal Measures.

devoid of tracks and huts. Below the treeline, the forests of the park and the nearby Maruia Valley consist almost wholly of beech species. Superb tall red and silver beech predominate on the valley floors and lower slopes, even forming a canopy over scenic SH 7 in the upper Inangahua, across Rahu Saddle, and beside the upper Maruia through Lewis Pass National Reserve. In the south-east, the park extends across to the main divide east of the Alpine Fault; here lies the only large lake in the park, Lake Christabel in the headwaters of the Blue Grey River.

The Maruia Valley is enshrined in New Zealand's turbulent conservation folklore. Its forests were central to the North Westland part of the South Island Beech Scheme of the 1970s – the NZ Forest Service's plan to log about 80 per cent of the largely 'unutilised' lowland beech forest of the

Buller and Grey catchments. The NZ Forest Service hoped that some of the felled red and silver beech forest could be managed on a sustainable basis to supply both a pulp mill and a beech furniture industry; at the same time, large areas of hard beech and mountain beech of inferior timber quality would have been converted to exotic softwoods and hardwoods. Ironically, it was the beech scheme, rather than the traditional ecologically destructive milling of the West Coast's rimu forests, which ignited public opinion into a raging forest conservation/utilisation conflagration, polarising the West Coast and the rest of the country for the next 15 years. The bold vision of an eventual end to the felling of not just beech but all of New Zealand's indigenous forests took shape in the winter of 1975 on the banks of the Maruia River. A previously fragmented forest conservation campaign now coalesced around the Native Forest Action Council, with their six objectives outlined in a petition which took its name from this beautiful threatened valley. When the 'Maruia Declaration' was eventually delivered to Parliament in 1977, its 341,159 signatures were the largest number ever collected in New Zealand's history, and signalled a sea-change in public attitudes towards the use and/or conservation of our natural resources. The ripples touched every indigenous State Forest throughout the entire West Coast, and eventually led to the dissolution of the NZ Forest Service. But more than that, it also led to the fulfillment of the Declaration's prayer to government that 'our remaining publicly owned native forests … be placed in the hands of an organisation that has a clear and undivided responsibility to protect them'.

The Department of Conservation (DOC) was established in 1987 with that forest protection mandate, and more – although it was not until the year 2000 that DOC was given conservation of the last 130,000 ha of West Coast indigenous forest that had been earmarked for timber production and vested in Timberlands West Coast Ltd. Reefton's dream of a high-quality beech product industry dissipated when a succession of industry bids was little more than the usual crude New Zealand primary industry approach to the use of natural resources – in this case, chipping of the beech forests for export to Japan and Korea.

One positive outcome of the Beech Scheme was an intense scientific investigation of these forests and a commitment to achieve the protection of *representative* reserves which, in total, encompassed all the natural ecosystems of a region. As a consequence, DOC inherited 24 representative 'ecological areas' (totaling 116,000 ha) in and around Victoria Forest Park. Furthermore, many of these ecological areas are quite large and were key components of what became known as the 'North Westland Wildlife Corridor' – a mountains-to-the-sea continuum of natural forested wildlife habitat. The corridor was enhanced with forest additions from the former Timberlands West Coast Ltd after 2000 (see above) and now extends from the main divide (Lewis Pass National Reserve and Lake Sumner Forest Park), through Victoria Forest Park and the Grey–Inangahua Depression, to the Paparoa Range and the Tasman Sea coastline.

PAPAROA NATIONAL PARK AND PAPAROA WILDERNESS AREA

The Paparoa Range extends for 75 km as an unbroken rocky spine from the lower Buller Gorge to the Brunner Gorge of the lower Grey/Mawheranui River. Its rugged crest is a succession of pinnacles, bluffs and jagged spires, carved in the very old and hard granite and gneiss rocks by glaciers long past – creating shapes reminiscent of the spectacular Fiordland landscape. Rivers like the Ohikanui and Otututu which drain the interior of the range run through U-shaped valleys, their near-vertical walls still reflecting the enormous power of those glaciers. The western coastline is no less spectacular, but here the sheer headlands, stacks and wild beaches between the mouth of the Fox River and Razorback Point are cut into a variety of limestone, mudstone and marine gravels. The most famous landmark is Dolomite Point, with the Pancake Rocks and blowholes now visited by more than 600,000 people each year. Hidden behind this scenic coastline is an impressive karst landscape, which includes the canyons of the Pororari and Fox rivers and Bullock Creek. The diversity of landforms between the crest of the Paparoa Range and the Tasman coastline (nowhere more than 15 km distant) is so impressive that it is probably unmatched anywhere else in New Zealand. The 'West Coast Conservation Management Strategy' describes it very well: 'towering coastal bluffs, a superb sequence of vertical-walled canyons, large natural arches and overhangs, sinkholes and slots of every shape and size, blind valleys, self-draining basins, rivers and streams that are "captured" by adjacent catchments, complex patterns of underground drainage, numerous caves, sculpted creekbeds, and patterns of surface etching sometimes on a very intimate scale and sometimes covering whole cliff faces.'

Paparoa National Park (38,823 ha) was formed in 1987 after a bitter decade-long campaign initiated by the Native Forest Action Council (and then taken up by the broadly-based Joint Campaign on Native Forests) to protect the unique Paparoa limestone landscape from being logged and mined. In many ways this national park was the first of a more modern and scientific era ushered in by the passing of the 1980 National Parks Act. Although small, the boundaries of Paparoa were carefully chosen to give the best cross-section of landforms and vegetation communities from the mountains to the sea on the western side of the range. The park's vegetation reflects the wide variety of both topography and soils deriving from the different geological parent materials. Notable features include:

• the lush, super-humid forest in the limestone canyons,

with their northern rata, nikau palms and broadleaf trees draped in kiekie vines;

- the stunted forests of rimu, silver pine and yellow-silver pine fringing the pakihis beside the Tiropahi/Four Mile River;
- the extraordinary diversity of podocarp/beech/broadleaf forest associations – 25 alone identified in the Pororari Basin;
- the curious 'temperature inversions' of plants, the result of cold air draining down into hollows such as valleys and even sinkholes – an associated phenomenon is the large number of alpine plants found at low altitudes;
- the low altitude of the treeline (often only 800 m), possibly the result of low radiant energy because of the frequency of cloud cover – on the coal measures at the southern end of the range, the low treeline is a consequence of the low soil fertility.

The park is also an important wildlife habitat, particularly for great spotted kiwi/roa, kaka, blue duck/whio, bats and a number of endemic weta, land snails and specialised cave fauna. The coastal hills between the Punakaiki River and Lawson Creek contain the only breeding sites of the endemic Westland black petrel. Petrels are oceanic birds which usually dig their burrows in the soil of predator-free islands, so the Punakaiki colony of several hundred birds is of particular ornithological interest.

A Paparoa Wilderness Area was first proposed in 1979 by the Federated Mountain Clubs of NZ for the northern and central parts of the Paparoa Range. For the next 20 years this rugged and remote area was managed as a de facto wilderness area for wilderness recreation. Finally, in August 2002, government approved the establishment of a 30,768 ha Paparoa Wilderness Area around the Ohikanui, Ohikaiti and Otututu (Rough) river catchments in the northeast. Unlike the national park, the wilderness area includes most of the crest of the range and is contiguous with the park only on the south, from just north of Mt Priestley to the head of Bullock Creek. During the same period, the lowland diversity of the park itself was increased by the addition of around 4000 ha of the former Charleston Forest previously managed for indigenous timber production by Timberlands West Coast Ltd. This addition, around the Waitakere (or Nile) River, is important because it contains

The Pancake Rocks at Dolomite Point are the iconic symbol of the wild coastal landscape of Paparoa National Park. The constant pounding of the Tasman Sea at Punakaiki has eroded the layered limestone and mudstone into stacks of 'pancakes' interspersed with blowholes.

ABOVE The gneiss rock spine of the Paparoa Range extends for 75 km from the lower Buller Gorge to the Brunner Gorge of the lower Grey/Mawheranui River. Its wilderness of pinnacles, bluffs and tarns is rarely visited because of the physical difficulty of foot travel. The crest of the range forms the boundary between Paparoa National Park to the west, and the Paparoa Wilderness Area to the north and east. RIGHT A lady's slipper orchid (*Winika cunninghamii*) in Paparoa National Park. This orchid is the only member of an endemic genus and it is considered to be the most beautiful of our native orchid flowers.

BELOW The endemic Westland black petrel (*Procellaria westlandica*) breeds only in the densely-forested coastal hills of the Paparoa Range, just south of the Punakaiki River. BOTTOM A pied adult South Island fantail or piwakawaka (*Rhipidura fuliginosa*) displaying its tail (ROD MORRIS).

TOP A large clump of neinei (*Dracophyllum townsonii*) growing among beech forest in Paparoa National Park. ABOVE A male South Island robin or toutouwai (*Petroica australis australis*) on the beech forest floor (ROD MORRIS).

PREVIOUS PAGE The Sheila Face of Aoraki/Mt Cook (right), looking north-west to Mt Tasman (centre, left). ABOVE The Southern Alps/Ka Tiritiri o te Moana reflected in the waters of Lake Matheson at sunset, in West-land/Tai Poutini National Park. The prominent peak on the left is Mt Tasman and that on the right is Aoraki/Mt Cook. Lake Matheson is the best known of many lakes fringed with dense podocarp rainforest in the glacial outwash lowlands of the park. RIGHT Mist clearing from Lake Mapourika in Westland/Tai Poutini National Park is a typical West Coast scene, with the lowland lake fringed with flax and kahikatea trees.

as many caves as does the rest of the park, and these are unique for the richness of their seabird fossils. In a historical sense, the highly publicised tree-top protests by a new generation of young conservation activists, which stopped the logging of Charleston Forest, marked the end of a 25-year-long fight by conservationists to have all the publicly-owned West Coast indigenous forests protected.

WESTLAND/TAI POUTINI NATIONAL PARK

Westland/Tai Poutini National Park is New Zealand's classic mountains-to-the-sea park. The original 85,089 ha park was formed in 1960, Westland's centennial year (marking the Arahura Purchase – James Mackay's purchase of virtually the entire West Coast on behalf of the Crown). At that time the rationale for the park was the protection and public enjoyment of the icon landscapes of the 'Glacier Country' – the Franz Josef Glacier/Ka Roimata o Hine Hukatere, Fox Glacier/Te Moenga o Tuawe, and other glaciers and mountainous valleys between the Alpine Fault and the crest of the Southern Alps/Ka Tiritiri o te Moana. In the lowlands west of the fault, the only significant natural features included in the park were Lakes Matheson, Mapourika and Wahapo, and a token corridor of forest beside the road to Gillespies Beach; noticeably absent were the vast podocarp forests of the old moraines and outwash terraces stretching out to Okarito Lagoon and the coast. This exclusion was all the more extraordinary given the lowland forests' scientific importance in interpreting the beech gap – the absence of beech from West Coast forests between the Taramakau and Paringa rivers. The beech gap is generally attributed to beech's slow re-invasion of the area – even many thousands of years after Ice Age glaciers swept out across the lowlands and completely eliminated all forest vegetation. Instead, the park's montane forests consist of rata/kamahi/mountain cedar associations. When in flower in December/January, these rata were a wonderful sight from the highway where it passes through the Omoeroa and Waikukupa valleys but in recent years they have suffered from possum damage.

In the 1960s and 1970s, Harihari and Whataroa were thriving timber towns. By and large, the West Coast community then believed that once the podocarp forests of Ianthe, Poerua and Waitaha state forests were logged out (however wastefully and unsustainably), the millers would just move progressively south. Consequently, the podocarp forests adjacent to the park – Saltwater, Waitangi, Okarito and Waikukupa state forests – came under threat. But by

The Okarito brown kiwi or rowi (*Apteryx mantelli* 'Okarito') is a critically endangered subspecies of brown kiwi. Its podocarp forest habitat lies between the Okarito and Waiho rivers in Westland/Tai Poutini National Park and its numbers have dropped to about 100 birds (ROD MORRIS).

1980 attitudes were changing; the revised National Parks Act of 1980 gave much greater emphasis to the protection of ecosystem diversity, and the widespread opposition to the Beech Scheme had galvanised a Joint Campaign on Native Forests which fought for a cessation to logging in South Westland. Another bitter forest conservation battle ensued. In 1982, government agreed to add around 25,000 ha of terrace podocarp and hill-country forest in the southern part of Okarito Forest and all of Waikukupa Forest to the park – making the park's 117,547 ha much more representative of the range of glacial landforms and vegetation communities extending from the Alps to the Tasman Sea. However, the northern part of Okarito Forest, 6000 ha of dense rimu-dominated terrace podocarp forest adjacent to Okarito Lagoon, was retained for selective logging. Perhaps the final chapter in the organic growth of Westland/Tai Poutini National Park was the addition of this superb northern Okarito Forest to the park in 2002, another consequence of government deciding to stop the logging of the indigenous forests formerly vested in Timberlands West Coast Ltd. This addition has increased the park to 127,165 ha, protecting all the lowland forest between the Waitangitaona and Cook rivers.

Westland/Tai Poutini National Park is a very wild landscape that is quite challenging to traverse on foot. Save for the Copland Track, there are none of the back-country hut and track systems that are the hallmark of other national parks. The moraine and terrace landscapes of the lowlands and the Waikukupa Plateau are a forest and wetland wilderness, untracked and only really accessible to visitors

via short walks beside SH 6, or the side roads to Gillespies Beach or Okarito Lagoon. While hundreds of thousands of tourists each year throng to view the terminals of the two great glaciers, the climbers and ski-mountaineers who stay in the alpine huts on the névés generally only reach them via aircraft. The untracked coastline has a pronounced wilderness character, but the turbulent rivers are as much a barrier to today's remoteness-seekers as they were the bane of the blacksand miners of the 19th century. Kayaking is probably the best way of appreciating the tranquillity of the forests and waterways in the park: Okarito Lagoon (and Saltwater Lagoon just outside the park); accessible lakes like Mapourika; and the meandering Ohinetamatea River which can be navigated from the highway out to the Tasman Sea.

Not surprisingly, kayaking can also allow an intimate appreciation of the wildlife that frequents the lakes, freshwater swamps and lagoons: the white heron/kotuku and other herons, crested grebe, royal spoonbill, New

LEFT Sunset at Bruce Bay/Mahitahi, South Westland. Even-aged and densely packed rimu trees (*Dacrydium cupressinum*) line the foredunes, while the pakihi of Kini Swamp occupies the hollow behind. ABOVE The white arc of Ohinemaka Beach curves southwards, while inland lies a mosaic of pakihi and forested dunes.

Zealand kingfisher, fernbird, New Zealand scaup and pukeko. These wetlands are also one of the most important habitats in the country for native freshwater fish. To date 16 species have been found, including the threatened giant and short-jawed kokopu, torrent fish and the lamprey. The podocarp forests of Okarito are considered to have the densest populations of forest birds in Central–South Westland: wood pigeon/kereru, falcon/karearea, kakariki, South Island robin/toutouwai and kaka – although the latter seem to be declining in numbers. But Okarito's most threatened forest birds are a very small population (probably no more than 100) of rowi, the Okarito brown kiwi. The rowi of the park are now being intensively managed to help this genetically interesting kiwi survive; actions include intensive control of two of the many pests (possums and stoats), and the artificial hatching of eggs. The chicks are then reared in 'creche' sites, before being released back into their Okarito habitat when they have reached the age of one year, at which stage they are capable of protecting themselves from stoat attack.

Looking north-east into the upper Landsborough Valley, the heart of the Hooker/Landsborough Wilderness Area in South Westland. The high peaks in the distance are Aoraki/Mt Cook (left) and Mt Sefton (centre).

HOOKER–LANDSBOROUGH WILDERNESS AREA AND THE OHINEMAKA COAST

The Hooker–Landsborough Wilderness Area (41,000 ha) is one of the five wilderness areas on the West Coast. Its central feature is the wild Landsborough River, the main source of the Haast River. The Landsborough rises in the high peaks around the main divide at the southern end of Aoraki/Mount Cook and Westland/Tai Poutini national parks. It then flows south-west for 50 km enclosed in a narrow valley between the Southern Alps/Ka Tiritiri o te Moana in the east and the Hooker and Solution ranges in the west. Mt Hooker (2652 m), at the apex of the Hooker and Solution ranges, is the highest of many glaciated peaks (others include Mt Dechen, Mt Strachan and Fettes Peak). The Hooker Range is an interesting western outlier of the

Southern Alps/Ka Tiritiri o te Moana, in height more than matching this section of the main divide, as well as being more impressively glaciated because its more westerly position allows it to intercept the moisture-laden westerly winds. Marks Flats below Mt Hooker is the source of the Clarke River and is one of the most isolated and charming montane grassy river flats in South Westland. The Landsborough and the headwaters of the Paringa, Otoko, Mahitahi and Makawhio/Jacobs rivers in the west have always had an attraction for wilderness mountaineers and hunters. The latter are attracted by the opportunity of hunting Himalayan thar, which have always threatened to establish themselves in sufficient numbers to seriously damage the alpine areas. The Hooker–Landsborough area is also notable as the location of one of DOC's most sustained aerial 1080 possum control operations; the three-yearly poisoning efforts showing marked improvements in biodiversity, especially for birds and browse-vulnerable plants like rata, fuchsia, mountain cedar, and mistletoe.

The Ohinemaka Coast is a term coined to describe the wonderful mosaic of sandy beaches and rocky headlands, wetlands, rivers and lakes, and forested moraines lying between the Alpine Fault and the coastline, from the mouth of the Cook River in the north to Lake Moeraki and Knights Point in the south. The Paringa River marks the southern boundary of the enigmatic West Coast beech gap. The highway touches this coastline only at Bruce Bay/Mahitahi, allowing all too brief glimpses of the majesty of row after row of stately rimu standing against the Tasman Sea. This area, too, is the stronghold of the last great swamp kahikatea forests of New Zealand, especially on the floodplains between the Ohinetamatea and Ohinemaka rivers.

These kahikatea forests of South Westland are considered to be the world's best remaining representatives of the Mesozoic swamp forests of the ancient super-continent of Gondwana. After decades of controversy and indecision, government in 1989 moved to preserve these superb South Westland swamp kahikatea and terrace rimu forests by designating them 'conservation land'. This landmark conservation decision in South Westland freed up the last piece of the West Coast's natural heritage jigsaw. It opened the way for UNESCO to then give World Heritage status in 1990 to the entire south-west of the South Island as Te Wahipounamu (South West New Zealand) World Heritage Area (an area of 2.6 million hectares, or 10 per cent of New Zealand's total area – see map p.30).

HAAST COASTAL WETLANDS AND THE OLIVINE WILDERNESS AREA

The valleys that drain the western side of Mount Aspiring National Park between the Haast and Cascade rivers are the West Coast's great wilderness landscape, and are surpassed in wildness only by Fiordland. For 90 years after the first ill-fated attempts at a European 'Jackson's Bay special settlement', the Haast area was isolated from the rest of the West Coast; ships and aeroplanes had to suffice in transporting most supplies until the Haast–Paringa road was completed in 1965. As a consequence, large areas of podocarp forest still cover the Haast coastal plain. The most impressive are by no means tall but, rather, are squat, tightly clustered stands of rimu densely lined behind the coastal dunelands – their trunks swept free of ferns and epiphytes and their canopies closely knitted to withstand the westerly winds. The forests of the plain are also interesting for the fringing kowhai around the coastal lagoons, delighting flocks of bellbirds, tui and wood pigeon/kereru each spring. But it is the extent of the freshwater wetlands which is the outstanding ecological feature of the Haast lowlands. The Hermitage Swamp in the lower Cascade Valley, the Tawharekiri Swamp complex between the lower Waita and Haast rivers, the Waiatoto and Okuru swamps, and the aptly named Burmeister Morass all make up the greatest extent of unmodified wetlands remaining in mainland New Zealand. From the air they are an arresting sight: long ribbons of water and swamp strung out within a series of parallel forest-covered dunes. Each duneline marks a former shoreline, with the coastline moving westwards by around 10 km over the past 6000 years as sediments were progressively deposited by the Haast, Waiatoto and Arawhata rivers. Here, in the swamps of the coastal plain, lie the best prospects for conserving the most threatened of our aquatic fauna, like the short-jawed and giant kokopu. The coastal plain is the habitat of another seriously threatened wildlife icon – the Haast tokoeka species of brown kiwi. To try to save this threatened species of probably no more than 200 birds, the Haast Tokoeka Kiwi Sanctuary was created between the Waiatoto and Arawhata rivers in 2001, and similar attempts are being made to ensure its survival as for the Okarito brown kiwi further north (see above).

Inland from Jackson Bay/Okahu lie three of the main wilderness rivers of South Westland – the Waiatoto, Arawhata and Cascade. All three rise on the western side of the Southern Alps/Ka Tiritiri o te Moana: the Waiatoto in the magnificent Volta and Therma glaciers on the flanks of Mt Aspiring/Tititea; the Arawhata in the Olivine Ice Plateau and the glaciers strung along the Barrier Range;

ABOVE An intricate mosaic of wetlands, forested dunes and glaciated knolls is a striking visual feature of the Haast coastal plain. This view eastwards across the largest of the Tawharekiri Lakes shows a band of low pakihi vegetation rising to dense podocarp forest (mainly rimu) on the relatively dry slopes of Bayou Hill. RIGHT The white heron or kotuku (*Egretta alba*) is widespread in Asia and the Pacific but rarely seen in New Zealand. Its only breeding site (with around 30 breeding pairs) is in a few trees beside Waitangiroto Lagoon near Okarito. OPPOSITE Looking south along the Red Hills Range to the ultramafic massif of Red Mountain. In the left distance across the Arawhata Valley (in shadow) is the Olivine Range and the Olivine Ice Plateau. Most of the landscape in the photo lies within the Olivine Wilderness Area on the western margin of Mount Aspiring National Park.

and the Cascade from hanging valleys high on the Olivine and Red Hills ranges. The Arawhata and Cascade rivers are routes to the mountainous Olivine Wilderness Area in the interior of Mount Aspiring National Park; but there are formidable challenges to foot travel, like the Ten Hour Gorge of the Arawhata, the Cascade Gorge and Durward Falls, and many difficult river crossings. Explorers, surveyors, prospectors and mountaineers have left a rich literature of their attempts to traverse this wilderness, among them:

- Alphonse Barrington's diary telling of the privations suffered by him and his companions while searching for gold;
- 'Arawata Bill' O'Leary's quest for a lost ruby mine;
- the maps and reports of Charles 'Mr Explorer' Douglas;
- the romantic writings of Robert Paulin and many others.

Attracted by the talk of a mineral belt and a 'glowing red mountain', many prospectors sought nickel, chromium and asbestos in this band of distinctive red rock which extends for 70 km from the head of the Jackson River, through the Cascade and Pyke, to Serpentine Saddle above the Hollyford River. (See 'Mount Richmond Forest Park', p.175, for accounts of these ophiolite belt rocks).

THREATS AND CONSERVATION PRIORITIES

Protecting the geodiversity, biodiversity and historic heritage of more than two million hectares of conservation land on the West Coast is a huge responsibility for DOC, particularly as the department in the past has often lacked the support of the local population. For too long the Coast lacked community leadership that could look beyond the region's pioneering history (with its unsustainable exploitation of seals, gold and native timber) to the need to plan for a future based on sustainable tourism. The West Coast's tourism industry is largely dependent on conservation of the region's outstanding wilderness heritage, yet the greatest conservation threat looming may be from tourism itself. The challenge for DOC's West Coast managers is to encourage the burgeoning number of tourists to have a 'West Coast Experience' that does not destroy the very fragile wilderness values which they are seeking.

The Threat of Wide-scale Mining

The West Coast has a long and colourful gold- and coal-mining history, and its environmental legacy is still very apparent: large areas of weed-infested coastal dunelands and river terraces impoverished from sluicing; the Buller Coal Measures Plateaux scarred with open-cast mines; and the Reefton quartz country pock-marked with shafts. But although most of the back country was prospected, remarkably few past industrial mining operations penetrated far into the mountain wilderness. One that came close was the charlatan prospecting company, Nickel Spoon Mining Company, which made grossly exaggerated claims about the mineral bonanza to be found in the Red Mountain ophiolites adjacent to what is now the Olivine Wilderness Area. In a major management failure, the NZ Forest Service in 1973 allowed a mining bulldozer train to blaze its way from the Jackson River for 100 km into this wilderness. After years of prospecting and controversy, their dreams of an asbestos mine on the Red Hills Range came to nothing. Although New Zealand then needed an asbestos industry as much as it needed an outbreak of foot and mouth disease, and despite the subsequent incorporation of much of this mineral belt into Mount Aspiring National Park, the whole Red Mountain debacle was an early lesson in how environmentally unaccountable the mining industry was, especially on the West Coast.

Although national parks are no longer open for surface mining, conservation land on the West Coast has in recent years been the focus of a number of major and controversial mining ventures. These include: proposals to mine the ilmenite-rich sands of the Barrytown Flats and dunelands; GRD Macraes' hard-rock gold mine behind Reefton; the Pike River Coal Company's 12 km access road through the Saxon Ecological Area and trucking of coal from under Paparoa National Park; and government-owned Solid Energy extending coal mining from the environmental wasteland of their existing Stockton Mine into a new open-cast mine in Cypress Creek in the head of the Waimangaroa Valley, the habitat of the rare giant land snail *Powelliphanta patrickensis*. Solid Energy admits to past poor environmental management of its mines (which have already polluted the Ngakawau River) and there are fears that the Waimangaroa River could suffer the same degradation. In addition, the mine could see the loss of one of the best parts of the wild Buller Coal Measures Plateaux, with its striking sandstone outcrops, unique plants and rare wildlife. The future operations of the Reefton, Pike River and Cypress Creek mines need to be watched closely by environmental authorities, for the credibility of government's economic development agencies, and the mining industry itself, is very much on trial in North Westland.

The Detrimental Impact of Tourist Flights on Wilderness Values

There is a high level of concern at the disruption of natural quiet in Westland/Tai Poutini National Park. The drone of aeroplanes and helicopters is now almost constant above the glaciers. Indeed, the noise of aircraft is even worse in Franz Josef/Waiho, where the once-pleasant alpine village character is now completely overwhelmed by the onslaught of poorly planned tourist infrastructure. DOC and the Grey District Council are also under pressure to allow helicopters to buzz the Pancake Rocks and the iconic coastline of Paparoa National Park for sightseeing tourists. The Civil Aviation Authority (CAA) shows no interest in regulating overflights of wilderness, and DOC is under increasing pressure for air access through buffer zones in order to land at the very edge of the Coast's wilderness areas. For example, white-water rafting is popular on the middle reaches of the Landsborough, so parties are taken by helicopter upriver to the boundary of the Hooker–Landsborough Wilderness Area – another manifestation of the 'wilderness adventure tourism' oxymoron, the irony of which is seemingly lost on participants in such commercial air access approaches to back-country adventure. Indeed, the experience may seem the Shangri-La of the thrill-seeker, but is likely to leave a thirst in those seeking, but not knowing how to find, a true wilderness experience. And the solution? Clearly, DOC, CAA and the West Coast Conservation Board need to take a much higher profile in engaging with the air tourism industry, publicly encouraging them to confine their flights to corridors and areas stipulated in management plans, and rigorously policing 'no flight' and 'no landing' zones by prosecuting offenders.

The Chimera of the Hollyford–Cascade Road

Each decade or so, tourism advocates on the West Coast raise the idea of a tourist road linking Haast with the Milford Road, via the Hollyford, Pyke and Cascade valleys. Such a road would be enormously expensive, destroy the values of the last lowland wilderness in South Westland, and provide few real scenic rewards for those who would travel it (but considerable losses – such as forgoing the sights experienced from SH 6 as it passes beside Lakes Hawea and Wanaka and through the Makarora and Haast valleys). Fortunately, each new proposal has so far been stymied because sectoral tourist interests in Te Anau, Queenstown, Wanaka and South Westland have been squabbling over the issue, for some of them would be financial losers if this roading chimera were ever to materialise.

The great mountain buttercup (*Ranunculus lyallii*), shown here beside the Copland Track, is the most spectacular of the alpine herbs that grace the snow tussock/herbfields of the Southern Alps in summer. It, and other mountain flowers, are grazed by introduced red deer, chamois and Himalayan thar.

Impacts of Thar on the West Coast's Alpine Wilderness

In the early part of the 20th century, Himalayan thar were released in the Franz Josef/Waiho and Aoraki/Mt Cook localities in order to provide trophy game for tourist hunters. Since then, thar have spread throughout the alpine regions between Whitcombe Pass and Haast Pass, where they have had severe grazing impacts on snow tussocks and a number of vulnerable alpine herbs, such as beautiful mountain buttercups (like *Ranunculus lyallii* and *R. grahamii*) and gentians. In 1992 DOC released its Himalayan Thar Control Plan which became a source of dispute between hunters, DOC and conservationists. Under the plan, the thar population must be maintained at no more than 10,000 animals; but Forest & Bird considers that thar numbers are now higher than this and that the goal should be to progressively work towards eradicating thar completely from the high country – a position considered impractical by DOC, which maintains that thar are subject to rigorous and sustained control, at least on the West Coast part of their range.

CHAPTER ELEVEN

CANTERBURY AND THE SOUTHERN ALPS

Wilderness in Canterbury is synonymous with the high country: tawny tussock grasses waving under a nor'west arch sky, the horizon crowded with scree-streaked greywacke mountains and clouds of loess whipped up from the beds of the braided rivers that thread their way out to the Canterbury Plains. Canterbury shares the highest peaks of the Southern Alps/Ka Tiritiri o te Moana with central Westland and, although the great ice sheets that mantled the high country have long gone, the landform imprint of past glaciations is easily seen in a largely treeless landscape. Four great glacier-fed rivers – the Waimakariri, Rakaia, Rangitata and Waitaki – have carried vast quantities of coarse greywacke detritus out of the mountains, building the gently sloping fans which eventually coalesced into the lower Waitaki Plain and the Canterbury Plains (at 750,000 ha, the largest alluvial plain in New Zealand). So great was this outwash of glacier-derived rock fragments that during the peak of the Last Glaciation (around 20–25,000 years ago) the fans reached present-day Banks Peninsula – itself the eroded remnant of two overlapping and long extinct volcanoes, and an island for most of its 10-million-year history.

Most overseas tourists arriving for the first time in Christchurch in winter easily mistake the snow-covered frontal ranges along the western margin of the Canterbury Plains for the Southern Alps/Ka Tiritiri o te Moana. However, the real Alps lie 50–100 km to the west, hidden behind an outer wall of the Puketeraki, Torlesse, Craigieburn, Two Thumb, Kirkliston and myriad other frontal ranges. Enclosed within the Alps and these outer mountain ranges are a series of inter-montane basins which give the Canterbury high country so much of its landscape character. The largest and best known is the Mackenzie Basin

in the upper Waitaki. Other smaller basins provide relief to travellers on the highways to the West Coast – Amuri and Hanmer en route to Lewis Pass, and the Waimakariri Basin on the highway to Arthur's Pass. A string of beautiful lakes lies within these basins: Lakes Sumner, Pearson, Coleridge, Heron, Tekapo, Alexandrina, Pukaki and Ohau are the largest, but there are hundreds of smaller lakelets and tarns, all reflecting the surrounding peaks and tussock grasslands.

The dynamic history of eastern Canterbury's indigenous vegetation since the end of the Last Glaciation 14,000 years ago is worth summarising in simple terms. As the climate warmed, a windswept and dry landscape dominated by tussock grasses was gradually re-colonised by cold-tolerant shrubby podocarps (especially celery pine and bog pine); later, tall podocarp forest (especially matai and totara) established itself, along with more drought-tolerant broadleaf trees like kowhai, ngaio, *Hoheria* and the many fascinating divaricating shrubs (small-leaved, tangle-branched – see Ch.1, p.15), especially those of the *Coprosma*, *Olearia*, *Pittosporum* and *Melicytus* genera. This rather open forest/shrubland was extremely susceptible to fire. Following settlement by Maori, widespread fires destroyed most of the woody vegetation and led to the rapid re-establishment of grasslands. Short tussocks (such as *Festuca* and *Poa* species) spread from remnant pockets in riverbeds in the semi-arid locations and, in the wetter west, snow tussocks (*Chionochloa* species) moved down into the valleys from the alpine zone. The combined effect of habitat loss through fire, hunting by Maori and predation by Pacific rat/kiore had a devastating effect on forest birds, including moa. European settlement had an even greater biological impact, for

Snow tussock landscape at Lindis Pass in the South Island high country.

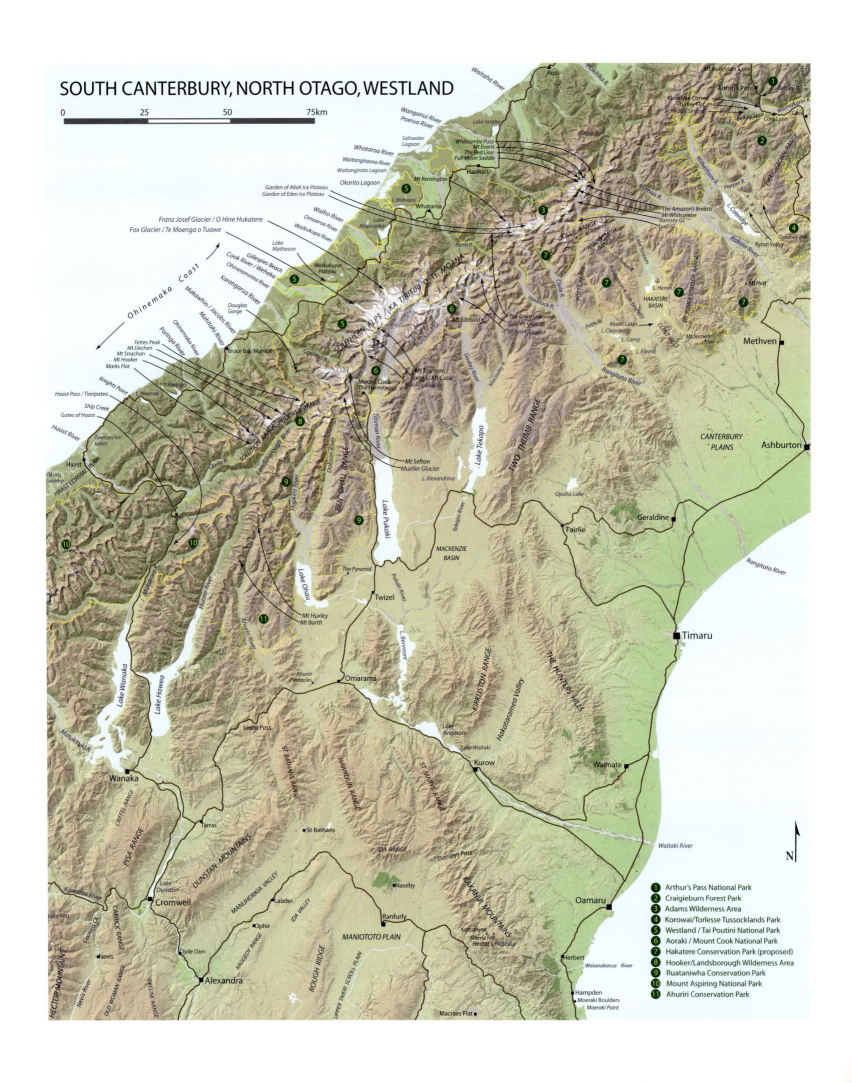

SOUTH CANTERBURY, NORTH OTAGO, WESTLAND

0   25   50   75km

Waitaha River
Ross
Hokitika R.
Mt Rolleston
Arthur's Pass
Klondyke Corner
Turkey Flat
Jordan Stream
Bealey Spur
Cass
Coral Lynn
Waimakariri R.
CRAIGIEBURN RANGE
Wanganui River
Poerua River
Lake Ianthe
Cronn R.
Wilberforce R.
Harper R.
L. Coleridge
Whataroa River
Saltwater Lagoon
Whitcombe Pass
Mt Evans
The Red Lion
Full Moon Saddle
Mathias R.
Waitangitaona River
Waitangiroto Lagoon
Okarito Lagoon
Mt Kensington
Adams R.
The Amazon's Breasts
Mt Whitcombe
Ramsey Gl.
Lyell Gl.
Ryton Valley
Godney Hill
Rakaia River
Garden of Allah Ice Plateau
Garden of Eden Ice Plateau
L. Wahapo
Whataroa
Harihari
JOLLIE RANGE
Mt Hutt
Waiho River
Omeoroa River
Waikukupa River
Lake Mapourika
Perth R.
Carleton R.
L. Heron
ARROWSMITH RANGE
Lake Stream
Mt SOMERS/STAUR RANGE
Franz Josef Glacier / O Hine Hukatere
Fox Glacier / Te Moenga o Tuawe
Lake Matheson
POTTS RANGE
Ashburton River (south branch)
HAKATERE BASIN
Gillespies Beach
Cook River / Weheka
Ohinetamatea River
Waikukupa Plateau
Havelock R.
Karangarua River
Mt Sibbald
The Great Unknown
Godley Glacier
Classen Glacier
Maori Lakes
L. Clearwater
L. Camp
L. Emma
Mt Somers
Methven
Makawhio / Jacobs River
Douglas Gorge
Mahitahi River
Bruce Bay/Mahitahi
SOUTHERN ALPS / KA TIRITIRI O TE MOANA
Fettes Peak
Mt Dechen
Mt Strachan
Mt Hooker
Marks Flat
Ohinemaka River
Paringa River
Copland R.
Mt Tasman
Aoraki / Mt Cook
Hooker Glacier
Mount Cook
The Hermitage
Godley River
Macauley R.
Cass River
Rangitata River
Knights Point
L. Paringa
L. Moeraki
Haast Pass / Tioripatea
Ship Creek
Gates of Haast
Mt Sefton
Mueller Glacier
L. Alexandrina
Lake Tekapo
TWO THUMB RANGE
CANTERBURY PLAINS
Ashburton
Haast River
HOOKER RANGE
SOLUTION RANGE
Landsborough River
Tasman River
Dobson River
BEN OHAU RANGE
Haast
Okuru Swamp
HAAST COASTAL PLAIN
Towharekiri Lakes
Clarke R.
Hopkins River
Lake Pukaki
Ohinemaka Coast
Makarora R.
Hunter River
Ahuriri River
Mt Huxley
Mt Barth
Lake Ohau
The Pyramid
Pukaki River
MACKENZIE BASIN
Twizel
Geraldine
Fairlie
Opuha Lake
Rangitata River
Lake Wanaka
Lake Hawea
Ahuriri Pinnacles
Omarama
L. Benmore
Lindis Pass
Lake Aviemore
Lake Waitaki
KIRKLISTON RANGE
Hakataramea Valley
THE HUNTERS HILLS
Timaru
Matukituki R.
PISA RANGE
CRIFFEL RANGE
Tarras
ST BATHANS RANGE
HAWKDUN RANGE
Kurow
Waimate
Wanaka
Lake Dunstan
DUNSTAN MOUNTAINS
St Bathans
IDA RANGE
ST MARYS RANGE
Danseys Pass
Waitaki River
N
Cromwell
MANUHERIKIA VALLEY
Lauder
Ophir
IDA VALLEY
Naseby
MANIOTOTO PLAIN
Ranfurly
KAKANUI MOUNTAINS
Kaitothyst
Siberia Hill
Hector's Plateau
Oamaru
Kawarau River
HECTOR MOUNTAINS
Lake Alta
Nevis
Doolans Ck.
CARRICK RANGE
RAGGEDY RANGE
Clyde Dam
ROUGH RIDGE
UPPER TAIERI SCROLL PLAIN
Herbert
Waianakarua River
Hampden
Moeraki Boulders
Moeraki Point
Nevis River
OLD WOMAN RANGE
OBELISK RANGE
Alexandra
Macraes Flat

1 Arthur's Pass National Park
2 Craigieburn Forest Park
3 Adams Wilderness Area
4 Korowai/Torlesse Tussocklands Park
5 Westland / Tai Poutini National Park
6 Aoraki / Mount Cook National Park
7 Hakatere Conservation Park (proposed)
8 Hooker/Landsborough Wilderness Area
9 Ruataniwha Conservation Park
10 Mount Aspiring National Park
11 Ahuriri Conservation Park

the remaining indigenous vegetation of the Canterbury Plains and Banks Peninsula underwent an almost wholesale conversion to an exotic landscape, and introduced pests eliminated most of the remaining indigenous birds and reptiles. In all, it is a fascinating story of continual ecological adjustment to environmental change in the lowlands and along the coastline – leading to the situation today where wilderness in Canterbury has retreated far up into the mountains of the west.

Now only tattered remnants of the region's once rich biodiversity remain on the plains, coastline and Banks Peninsula. On the plains, the braided rivers are the only important habitats for migratory fish species and threatened birds like the wrybill and banded dotterel. Riccarton Bush is a small but magnificent remnant of the kahikatea forest that once dominated the low-lying swamps around the Heathcote and Avon rivers; Bankside and Eyrewell scientific reserves protect remnants of kanuka forest; and Travis Swamp is the only remnant of the wetlands that once existed where Christchurch city now stands. Lake Ellesmere/ Te Waihora and Kaitorete Spit are important wildlife habitats on the coast; the ecological values of the former are protected by a water conservation order, and the latter is a remarkable coastal barrier spit with interesting shrub and grassland communities (including a fine community of the sandbinder sedge, pingao) which protect a variety of endemic moths and skinks. Banks Peninsula remains an outstanding Canterbury landform with its radial pattern of drowned valleys where the sea has flooded back into the interior of the two volcanoes. However, most of the indigenous forest and tussockland of the peninsula has gone, and most remnants lack legal protection. While efforts have been made to protect Hector's dolphin through the Banks Peninsula Marine Mammal Sanctuary, only tiny (215 ha) Pohatu Marine Reserve (around Flea Bay) protects the other important marine features around the peninsula.

LEWIS PASS–ST JAMES–LAKE SUMNER FOREST PARK

The mountains and valleys between Lewis Pass and Harper Pass are some of the most accessible in Canterbury for tramping and hunting. Lewis Pass (863 m) is crossed by SH 7, the northernmost of the four state highways crossing the main divide of the South Island (the other three are Arthur's Pass, Haast Pass and The Divide on the Milford Road). From the junction of the Boyle and Lewis rivers in the east to Springs Junction in the west, the highway passes through Lewis Pass National Reserve, almost 20,000 ha of

The threatened endemic yellowhead or mohua (*Mohoua ochrocephala*) now survives in only a few places in Canterbury, especially in Lake Sumner Forest Park and Arthur's Pass National Park (ROD MORRIS).

highly attractive beech forest in a superb mountainous setting. Lewis Pass is also the starting point for the popular St James Walkway, an easy 4–5 day tramp through 67 km of the upper Maruia, Ada, Henry and Boyle rivers. The eastern sector of the walkway is through grassy river terraces beside tributaries of the upper Waiau River in part of St James Station, the largest pastoral lease in Canterbury. To the south-west of Lewis Pass around the headwaters of the Boyle, Hope and Hurunui rivers lies Lake Sumner Forest Park, at 107,222 ha the largest conservation park in Canterbury.

Lake Sumner Forest Park has the richest population of forest birds in Canterbury: kaka, kea, great spotted kiwi, yellowhead/mohua, orange-fronted parakeet, New Zealand falcon, blue duck/whio and weka are of particular note. Because the forests of the park are a mosaic of red, silver and mountain beech, there are also plentiful South Island robins, riflemen, brown creepers, grey warblers and tomtits. All the valleys in the park provide easy tramping

A mountain tarn surrounded by beech forest at Lewis Pass, Lewis Pass National Reserve.

through grassy flats and beech forest; none of the peaks are higher than 1800 m; and the tops provide excellent off-track travelling for the wilderness tramper or hunter. Because the upper Hurunui contains mature beech forests that are broadly representative of those throughout Canterbury, 12,000 ha have been intensively managed by DOC since 1995 as a 'mainland island'. This is the largest of the mainland island experiments, covering two parallel catchments of the Hurunui River: the south branch where farm stock is excluded, and stoats and possums poisoned; and a similar area of around 6000 ha in the north branch which is used as a control (monitored for comparison purposes, but with no active pest control). Results to date indicate that possums and stoats can be managed to a level where bird populations (especially of mohua and parakeet) and mistletoe will benefit.

ARTHUR'S PASS NATIONAL PARK AND THE WAIMAKARIRI BASIN

Like most of our national parks, Arthur's Pass National Park (114,839 ha) had its origins in a public clamour for landscape protection in the face of increasing destruction of wilderness – in this case the completion of the Otira Tunnel of the Midland Railway in 1923. The eminent ecologist Leonard Cockayne had been effective 20 years earlier in urging the reservation of much of the mountain land in the head of the Waimakariri River because of its fine 'transalpine flora'. However, it was the subsequent impact of an upsurge of visitors via popular train excursions from Christchurch to Arthur's Pass village that sufficiently alarmed a wide range of Canterbury citizens for them to press the government for a national park. So, in August 1929 a core area of the upper Waimakariri, Bealey, Otira and Deception valleys was legally designated New Zealand's third national park. The park's diversity of landforms and ecosystems was enhanced subsequently by the addition of:

- the Otehake catchment and the southern side of the Taramakau up to Harper Pass in 1938;
- the Hawdon and Poulter valleys in 1950;
- the Cox–Binser area in 1994, after decades of bureaucratic procrastination.

A small page of wilderness conservation history was opened in Arthur's Pass National Park in 1955, when scientist/conservationist Lance McCaskill convinced the park board and government of the day to gazette the first wilderness area in our national park system – the 12,000 ha Otehake Wilderness Area. Unfortunately, subsequent management agencies failed to maintain the area's integrity, and Otehake (always marginally small in terms of the wilderness policy) had its status as a wilderness area revoked.

Arthur's Pass National Park is the quintessential little trans-alpine national park, with greywacke shingle screes and open braided rivers in the east, and steep gorges in the west. The peaks are uniformly about 2000–2200 m in height, and 10 small glaciers (the northernmost in the South Island) cling precariously to the main peaks above the Waimakariri and Bealey headwaters. The forests in the east are completely dominated by beech, with mountain beech ubiquitous. In the wetter west, the forest pattern is more complex; there are more red and silver beech, and podocarps (including rare matai/totara forest) are widespread in the lower Taramakau and Otira valleys. The flowering of southern rata in the Otira Valley is a joy to behold in a good summer; it is probably the best southern rata in the South Island, having been maintained through a sustained 45-year possum poisoning effort with 1080. There are also plentiful kamahi, mountain cedar/kaikawaka and Hall's totara on the higher slopes.

Two mountain landforms are distinctive landmarks within the park: the first is the series of perfectly shaped alluvial fans extending down the Waimakariri Valley – in particular, at Jordan Stream (Turkey Flat), Bealey Spur–Cora Lynn,

ABOVE The upper Otira River flows through a hanging valley below Mt Rolleston (2275 m) before turning abruptly to the west and plunging down the steep Otira Gorge. This landscape is very typical of the alpine zone in Arthur's Pass National Park. The park straddles the Southern Alps/Ka Tiritiri o te Moana but most of the peaks are around 2000–2200 m high. The forests in the east are mainly mountain beech (with other beech species) but in the wetter west the forest pattern is more complex, with podocarps mingled with red and silver beech.

LEFT South Island edelweiss (*Leucogenes grandiceps*), with its mats of soft silvery leaves and conspicuous flowers, is a delight to mountain wilderness travellers. Its preferred habitats are rock outcrops or dry fellfields where it can shelter between the rocks.

Hawdon River and Poverty Stream. The other remarkable landscape feature is the widespread occurrence of huge rock avalanches; the most visible are seen from the sweep of the road viaduct across the upper Otira Gorge, but the most impressive is the collapse of the entire north-western side of Falling Mountain. Triggered by the destructive 1929 Murchison Earthquake, an estimated 60 million m³ of rock piled up in a 3 km long jumble of debris which still chokes the head of the west branch of the Otehake River.

The Waimakariri Basin lies downstream from the national park, tucked within the embrace of the Craigieburn, Torlesse and Puketeraki ranges. At Porters Pass the Arthur's Pass highway, SH 73, enters this wonderful open montane landscape of scree-draped greywacke mountains, limestone tors and caves, and lakes ponded by post-glacial fans that have dammed local streams. As the Waimakariri River comes into view just above Cass, the intricate pattern of its silver braids and the smooth lines of its impressive flights of alluvial terraces and fans complete a magnificent natural panorama of ice- and water-derived symmetry. Before the highway leaves the basin where it crosses the river and enters the beech forests of the Bealey Valley at Klondyke Corner, it has traversed 50 km of probably the best diversity of mountain landforms in the South Island – an educational delight, warranting the highest quality of roadside natural heritage interpretation.

The Waimakariri Basin is also of historical heritage importance, a special place where science unravelled many of the mysteries about ecological processes in Canterbury's mountains. Study of the ecology of alpine plants and soils around Porters Pass advanced our understanding of their genesis, development and destruction over the past 14,000 years. Other key research into climate, scree stability and sediment movement in the Kowai River catchment of the Torlesse Range gave deeper insights into the processes of mountain erosion. This sum of new knowledge led to a revolutionary reversal in thinking – a gradual realisation that the screes which give these mountains their barren appearance are indeed a natural phenomenon, probably dating back thousands of years to post-glacial times. Until then, conventional wisdom preached constantly by the NZ Forest Service and catchment boards held that most of this erosion was induced by humans. Salvation of the land could be achieved only by adhering to the doctrine of redemption through fast-growing plants, usually exotic conifers – many of which have now become the source of wilding conifers plaguing the Canterbury high-country landscape.

In recent years, the basin's diversity of scree and dry rock outcrop plants has been better understood. Whereas the annual precipitation in the peaks above Arthur's Pass is as high as 8000 mm, the eastern rain-shadow effect is so pronounced throughout the Waimakariri Basin that the figure drops to only 1000 mm in the Kowai River at the foot of the Torlesse Range. So, the screes and outcrops of the Torlesse Range (and other dry ranges like the Candlestick and Puketeraki ranges) support some unusual members of our native alpine flora. These include specialised scree plants that have evolved complex root systems and fleshy, furry leaves to withstand the extremes of diurnal temperature, desiccation and scree movement: the willowherbs (*Epilobium*), scree daisies (*Cotula* and *Leptinella*), Haast's scree buttercup (*Ranunculus haastii*), scree lobelia (*Lobelia roughii*) and the remarkable succulent penwiper plant (*Notothlaspi rosulatum*). Large patches of vegetable sheep (species of *Raoulia* and *Haastia*) are also highly visible and distinctive features of these dry mountains.

Fortunately, the designation in 2001 of New Zealand's first dry mountains conservation park – the 20,328 ha Korowai/Torlesse Tussocklands Park – at last protected much of the basin's dry mountain natural heritage. Further high-country conservation progress in the Waimakariri was made in 2004 when government used the Nature Heritage Fund to purchase three-quarters of Castle Hill Station (more than 8500 ha). Not only did this protect the iconic roadside vista around the limestone tors in Kura Tawhiti/Castle Hill Conservation Area but it also linked Korowai/Torlesse Tussockland Park with the beech forests of Craigieburn Forest Park, giving a corridor of protected wild land back to the main divide in Arthur's Pass National Park.

RAKAIA–RANGITATA BASINS AND THE ADAMS WILDERNESS AREA

The Rakaia and Rangitata rivers drain the real mountain wilderness of Canterbury. And between them they enclose one of the most delightful of Canterbury's inter-montane basins – the Hakatere Basin containing Lake Heron and a dozen smaller lakes, collectively known as the Ashburton Lakes. Far out on the lower Canterbury Plains, both the Rakaia and Rangitata are crossed each day by thousands of travellers on SH 1, few of whom would realise that more than half the length of each of these magnificent braided rivers lies above their distant gorges, where they break out of the frontal ranges and onto the plains. In the Rakaia Basin above the Rakaia Gorge, the strands of the Rakaia River surge from side to side across a 3 km wide bed of fresh greywacke gravels. The upper Rakaia

gathers up similarly turbulent tributaries – the Mathias, Harper and Wilberforce rivers – before sweeping past Lake Coleridge, now perched 100 m above the river, lying stranded in the trough of what was once the Wilberforce Glacier. Lake Coleridge has a superb landscape setting among ice-carved mountains; there are razor-backed ridges, conical hills, *roches moutonnées* and numerous small lakes of glacial origin. And here, at the eastern margin of the basin, lie two internationally significant landforms illustrating the catastrophic forces sometimes shaping our mountains – the Ryton Valley debris flow and the Goldney Hill rock avalanche. The latter is considered the largest rock avalanche in the Alps, a staggering 500 million m³ of debris which collapsed from the western flanks of the Craigieburn Range around 350 years ago.

The Rangitata River above the Rangitata Gorge has an open, braided character similar to the upper Rakaia. Between the Rakaia and the Rangitata lies a maze of wild high country, with the jagged barrier of the Jollie, Arrowsmith and Potts ranges in the west, and the frontal ranges run-

Looking from the Arrowsmith Range down the Cameron Valley towards Lake Heron. This mountain and inter-montane basin landscape is the heart of the proposed Hakatere Conservation Park.

ning from Mt Hutt to Mt Somers in the east. Here lie the lakes, wetlands and tussock-covered terraces of the Hakatere Basin in hollows shaped and planed by branches of the ancient Rakaia and Rangitata glaciers, as well as by the ice which would have streamed down the valleys now occupied by the local rivers like the Cameron, Potts, and south branch of the Ashburton. Lake Heron (with an area of 686 ha) is the largest of the 12 lakes and, unlike the others, it drains northwards through Lake Stream swamp into the Rakaia. Lake Clearwater and Lake Emma are the largest of the other lakes, draining with similar but smaller kettlehole lakes to the south branch of the Ashburton River. Collectively, the Hakatere Basin lakes and red tussock wetlands are considered to be the most important wetland complex for wildlife in the eastern South Island high country. Lake Heron and the Maori Lakes are protected

tion during 2002, government accepted that 56,000 ha of conservation land met the stringent criteria, and the Adams Wilderness Area came into being.

The kea (*Nestor notabilis*) is the world's only alpine parrot, its curiosity and amusing antics making it the court jester of the alpine realm.

as nature reserves, and Lake Clearwater and Lake Camp as wildlife refuges; they are habitats for wetland birds as diverse as crested grebe, New Zealand scaup, grey duck, shoveler, grey teal, marsh crake, pukeko and bittern. The wide, braided beds of both the Ashburton (south branch) and Rangitata rivers are particularly important as breeding habitats for a number of special birds such as the threatened wrybill plover, as well as banded dotterel, pied stilt and South Island pied oystercatchers. In all, the Rangitata River is a habitat at different times of the year for a remarkable 80 species of native birds.

But it is in the alpine headwaters of the Rakaia and Rangitata where the real wilderness lies – far up the Lyell and Ramsay, Clyde and Havelock. Here, during the 1930s, young mountaineers from the fledgling Canterbury Mountaineering Club sought a different *Erewhon* from Samuel Butler and the high-country pastoralists. Fine peaks, passes and névés became known to the outside world – with evocative names like Mt Whitcombe, Full Moon Saddle, Mt Evans, The Amazon's Breasts, The Red Lion, Garden of Eden, Garden of Allah, Mt Kensington and The Great Unknown. The main divide at the head of the Rakaia and Rangitata was crossed, and the headwaters of the severely gorged Wanganui, Adams and Perth rivers of the West Coast explored. The wilderness character of this remote and difficult mountain country led the Federated Mountain Clubs of NZ in 1981 to propose its protection as the Adams Wilderness Area. Finally, after wide public consulta-

AORAKI/MOUNT COOK NATIONAL PARK AND THE MACKENZIE BASIN

Aoraki/Mount Cook National Park (70,699 ha) is New Zealand's outstanding alpine park. Aoraki is central to the Maori creation traditions for Te Waipounamu, the South Island. Aoraki, the first-born son of Raki (the Sky Father), and his three brothers went on a great voyage in their canoe, *Te Waka o Aoraki*. The canoe capsized and became the land Te Waipounamu, while Aoraki and his brothers were embodied in the highest peaks in the Southern Alps/Ka Tiritiri o te Moana – Aoraki (Mt Cook), Rakiroa (Mt Dampier), Rakirua (Mt Teichelmann) and Rarakiroa (Mt Tasman). When Ngai Tahu's Treaty of Waitangi claims against the Crown were settled in 1998, the name of Aoraki was restored to New Zealand's highest peak by changing 'Mount Cook' to 'Aoraki/Mt Cook' and the name of the park to 'Aoraki/Mount Cook National Park'.

The first mapping and scientific exploration of the glaciers and rivers at the head of Lakes Tekapo, Pukaki and Ohau was by Julius von Haast and Arthur Dudley Dobson in 1862. Edward Sealy's alpine exploration and excellent photography throughout the late 1860s gave further publicity to the alpine glories of the area. Mountaineers soon followed, opening a golden era in alpine climbing in the latter part of the 19th century. In the summer of 1894–45, first Aoraki/Mt Cook was climbed (by the amateur New Zealanders Tom Fyfe, Jack Clarke and George Graham) and then Mts Tasman and Sefton (by the Englishman E. A. Fitzgerald and his Swiss guide Mattias Zurbriggen). Tourists were encouraged to visit by the establishment of an accommodation house which became known as 'The Hermitage'; by 1921 tourist bus transport and accommodation were being provided by the Mount Cook Motor Company. The value of the area for tourism had resulted in recreation reserves being created in the Hooker, Mueller and Tasman valleys in the late 1880s. These were later renamed Aorangi Domain and Tasman Park – but both were placed under the control of the Minister of

RIGHT The Hooker River and the south face of Aoraki/Mt Cook (3754 m). The name Aoraki was restored to New Zealand's highest peak in recognition of its place in Maori creation traditions for Te Waipounamu (the South Island). OVERLEAF Looking north across Mt Tasman (3491 m) into the mountain wilderness of the Southern Alps/Ka Tiritiri o te Moana. The 28 km long Tasman Glacier, the largest in New Zealand, can be seen in the right of the photo.

Tourist and Health Resorts and were not managed in any conservation sense.

During the 1920s public concern grew over both the impact of pastoralists burning the Tasman Valley landscape and the leasing of the public land in the reserves to a private company (which then tried to charge mountaineers for access, even though they were not staying at The Hermitage). The doyen of the NZ Alpine Club, A.P. Harper, had for years been urging the government to license alpine guides and not to renew the Mount Cook Company's lease and, instead, to designate a national park (see also Ch.1, p.25). The Godley and Classen glaciers were added to the Tasman Park in 1927, but it was not until 1953 (after the passing of the National Parks Act 1952) that the reserves were combined and given full protective status as Mount Cook National Park. In 1986 the 'outstanding universal value' of both Mount Cook and Westland national parks was recognised by UNESCO, when they were jointly designated as a World Heritage site. In 1991 both parks were then incorporated into Te Wahipounamu (South-West New Zealand) World Heritage Area – the vast 2.6 million ha World Heritage site encompassing the natural landscapes and biodiversity of the entire south-west of New Zealand.

What would those pioneer 19th-century visitors think of the park today? The first change they would notice is the shrinking of the most approachable glaciers, the Tasman, Mueller and Hooker – a process that has been going on since the onset of the present inter-glacial warming period. At the peak of the Last Glaciation, the terminal of the Tasman Glacier would have been several kilometres downstream of the present outlet to Lake Pukaki; further up-valley, the Hermitage site would have been buried under an extraordinary 600 m depth of ice. Since then the glacier has retreated 60 km to its present position. But the pace of wasting seems to have accelerated over the past 100 years; rapid ablation of the glacier surfaces has left them covered with a grey veneer of rock, and the once-striking terminal faces have now collapsed and melted into the wide Tasman, Mueller and Hooker terminal lakes. The other change they would notice would be the crush and noise of tourism. Aoraki/Mount Cook National Park no longer has any real wilderness; it does not have the large expanses of forest which can absorb the visual impact of visitors in our other parks. Sightseeing and ski planes drone incessantly up valleys where once the only sound was the crack of avalanches. And Mount Cook Village, including a much-enlarged Hermitage and DOC's visitor centre, is jammed to capacity with foreign tourists.

The tussock grasslands of the Mackenzie Basin provide the perfect landscape setting for the peaks of the park. At 200,000 ha, the Mackenzie is by far the largest of Canterbury's inter-montane basins. Despite the visual intrusion of hydro schemes, shelterbelts and intensified pastoral farming, the basin is large enough to provide solitude in an uncluttered vista of short tussock and braided river landscapes. From the air the surface texture of the basin – the silver-grey braids of the current riverbeds and the intricate pattern on the tussocky terraces of river channels abandoned long ago – looks as if it has been painted in giant brush strokes.

THREATS AND CONSERVATION PRIORITIES

Braided River Habitat Conservation

For too long Canterbury's outstanding braided river landscape heritage has been undervalued and taken for granted. Yet this type of river landscape is globally rare, restricted to only a few other temperate regions of the world where sufficient mountain uplift and glacial activity occur, such as the Hindu Kush–Pamir–Kun Lun–Karakoram–Himalaya mountain knot, Siberia, Alaska and Patagonia. As expected for such a dynamic habitat, the braided rivers are inhabited by a number of specialised native plants and animals. These include:

- plants which are able to establish themselves in raw gravels (from cushions of *Raoulia* to clumps of willowherbs and low shrubs of native broom and matagouri);
- a number of native freshwater fish (especially some rare species of *Galaxias* which appear to spend their entire lives in the braided rivers rather than migrating to sea, like the whitebait group of galaxiids);
- many birds – not only the black stilt/kaki, wrybill and terns, but also oystercatchers, dotterels and herons.

Maintaining an open riverbed habitat is important for the specialised riverbed birds: some rely on camouflaging their eggs and chicks among the greywacke stones; others need a clear view in order to distract predators away from the nest (often just a scraped hollow in the shingle) with their 'broken wing' diversionary ploy.

Winter snows highlight the numerous braids, formed by abandoned stream channels, in the bed of the Godley River in Aoraki/Mount Cook National Park.

RIGHT A pair of the endangered black stilt or kaki (*Himantopus novaezelandiae*) at their nest in the bed of the Tekapo River in the Mackenzie Basin. Once widespread throughout the braided rivers of the high country, the numbers of this endemic wader were reduced to less than 50 through loss of habitat and predation. Project River Recovery has undertaken intensive management of their habitat in the Ahuriri and the deltas of the Pukaki and Tekapo rivers, resulting in a sharp recovery in their numbers (ROD MORRIS). BELOW A paradise shelduck (*Tadorna variegata*) with its chicks, surviving despite snow covering the banks of the Tasman River.

ABOVE The New Zealand falcon or karearea (*Falco novaeseelandiae*) is New Zealand's only endemic raptor. It is widespread in the Alps and Canterbury high country, with good hunting opportunities provided along beech forest edges besides streams or open tussockland. Falcons are fiercely territorial during their breeding season and trampers and mountaineers often experience frightening dive attacks if they happen to pass too close to the bird's nest. LEFT The rare wrybill (*Anarhynchus frontalis*) is one of New Zealand's most unusual endemic birds. The end third of its long bill is angled to the bird's right, allowing it to sweep in a clockwise motion under stones for invertebrates. They breed in the Canterbury and inland Otago high country, particularly on the braided riverbeds of the Waimakariri, Rakaia, Rangitata, and upper Waitaki.

But the open spaces of the riverbeds have been steadily invaded by alien species. Numerous weeds have been able to quickly establish themselves, especially crack willow and the nitrogen-fixing exotics like lupins, broom and gorse; and now there is the very serious threat of didymo – another ecological catastrophe wrought on our once pristine fast-flowing rivers by overseas tourist users. The worst animal pests are cats, followed by ferrets and hedgehogs (the latter eating eggs as well as lizards and insects). The plight of the black stilt/kaki epitomises what is happening to the biodiversity of the high country's braided rivers. This distinctive-looking endemic wader was once widespread throughout the South Island's riverbeds, but predation and habitat loss have reduced its wild population to fewer than 50 birds. Most of them are confined to the Mackenzie Basin, especially the bed of the Ahuriri River. Project River Recovery was set up by DOC in partnership with Meridian Energy in 1991 to attempt restoration of the threatened braided river habitats of the black stilt and other native species in the Mackenzie Basin. Weed control (especially

Looking across the terminal lake of the Ramsay Glacier to the braided bed of the upper Rakaia River and the Jollie Range (right), at the eastern end of the Adams Wilderness Area.

the removal of willows) and predator management have been priorities, especially in the Ahuriri and the delta of the Pukaki and Tekapo rivers at the head of Lake Benmore; in addition, captive breeding and electronic monitoring of black stilts has led to a remarkable recovery in their numbers. But these restoration programmes need to be continued and extended, probably over the next 20 years, if these very distinctive ecosystems are to continue to contribute significantly to New Zealand's indigenous biodiversity.

The Mackenzie Basin contains the greatest concentration of braided river habitat in New Zealand – almost 20,000 ha in the combined beds of nine tributaries of the Waitaki: from east to west, the Godley, Macaulay, Cass, Tekapo, Murchison, Tasman, Hopkins, Dobson and Ahuriri. A major problem is the failure of government to give conservation land status to most of the riverbeds, the real threat of dairying replacing traditional dryland pastoral use (and the consequent ecological insanity of dairy wastes polluting these high quality waters), and the difficulty of achieving wild river conservation through the Resource Management Act procedures. The Rakaia River was protected by a National Water Conservation Order (NWCO) in 1988 because of its 'outstanding wildlife habitat … fisheries … recreational, angling, and jet boating features', and the Ahuriri was similarly protected in 1990 for its 'outstanding wildlife habitat'. The Rangitata River has been under threat of water abstraction for irrigation for the last 50 years – one proposal involved the construction of a 550 m wide rock dam above the Rangitata Gorge which would flood back for 18 km, inundating much of the braided bed of the upper Rangitata. It took decades of tribunal hearings for the Rangitata to be finally recommended for NWCO protection late in 2004 – again because of its outstanding wild scenery, its special birdlife and its recreational fishing (in this case, salmon).

Role of the Nature Heritage Fund in Protecting Dryland and Valley-floor Ecosystems

The Nature Heritage Fund committee has done an excellent job in the Canterbury high country over the past 15 years by convincing government to purchase outright a range of non-forest ecosystems, particularly valley-floor grasslands, shrublands and wetlands. Perhaps because they lack the aesthetic appeal of montane forests and snow-tussock grasslands, areas of Canterbury's short tussock grassland (*Festuca* and *Poa* species, with scattered native brooms and speargrasses) and 'grey scrub' of divaricating plants like matagouri were overlooked for too long. Now with a series of pastoral lease purchases, such as Benmore, Avoca, Castle Hill, Clent Hills and the Poplars, these shrubland and wetland communities are rightly taking centre stage in the evolving network of Canterbury high-country conservation parks. Furthermore, for generations high-country farmers had allowed their cattle to range widely from their valley-floor pastoral leases (or pastoral occupational licences) out into surrounding forests, wetlands and riverbeds on public conservation land. DOC managers have, by and large, a sorry record of failing to deal firmly with these illegal and destructive incursions, but this is not surprising given the social standing and political clout of the high-country lessee community. The strategic value of the ongoing high-country valley-floor purchases by the fund should make it much more difficult for this type of illegal grazing to continue with impunity.

Conservation of Canterbury's High Country through Pastoral Retirement

The Crown Pastoral Land Act of 1998 opened the way to speeding up the process of rationalising the use of Canterbury's high-country leasehold land through tenure review (see p.309 for a fuller account of the controversial elements of this policy). Compared with Otago, tenure review was slower to take off in the Canterbury high country. Ben Ohau Station in the Mackenzie Basin was the first to be resolved, with mixed results for conservation: wetlands and black stilt habitat are now part of the conservation estate, but an obvious landmark, The Pyramid, was excluded. This indicated the vexatious nature of tenure review and the difficulty of satisfying all parties that the final agreement is 'win-win' for both conservation and the lessees. Whole leasehold property acquisition by purchase, where possible, is a far more satisfactory option. This was the situation when the Minister of Conservation used the Nature Heritage Fund to purchase the entire 23,783 ha Birchwood pastoral lease in the upper Ahuriri Valley. Birchwood is an outstanding addition to the conservation estate: it has extensive wetlands, tussock grasslands, beech forest, alpine herbfields, and mountain crests including major peaks like Mt Barth (2456 m) and Mt Huxley (2695 m) – all open to public access since January 2004. Since then, tenure reviews of adjacent Quailburn and Ben Avon stations have added thousands more hectares to what has become an outstanding public entity in the high country–Ahuriri Conservation Park.

Later in 2004, both conservation and high-country farmers benefited when the review of the Clent Hills pastoral lease beside Lake Heron was completed. A number of adjacent farmers purchased some of the lower land to improve the viability of their pastoral operations, while the major portion of Clent Hills became conservation land – including wetlands and lakes supporting a significant population of southern crested grebe, braided riverbeds and tussock grasslands. But perhaps of most importance to those interested in wilderness recreation, the purchase enables a key piece of natural landscape to be soon designated as Hakatere Conservation Park. An outstanding portion of Canterbury's high country will now be protected, extending all the way from the mountain crests of the Adams Wilderness Area and the Arrowsmith Range, through the Hakatere Basin and out to Mt Somers. If the braided riverbeds and wetlands of the Rakaia and Rangitata are included, it could make an outstanding candidate for World Heritage status, such is the global significance of its natural heritage values.

OPPOSITE PAGE The Clay Cliffs (or 'Ahuriri Pinnacles') are a landmark in the middle reaches of the Ahuriri Valley in the Mackenzie Basin. The weakly-consolidated sedimentary deposits have been eroded by rain and wind into spires and deep gullies. ABOVE The braided bed of the Ahuriri River at the southern end of the Mackenzie Basin is one of the most important breeding habitats for the endangered black stilt (see p.220). LEFT One of the most visual consequences of possum control is the reappearance of the rare red- and yellow-flowered mistletoes throughout our forests. All mistletoes are parasitic, like this red mistletoe (*Peraxilla tetrapetala*) growing on a beech tree near Lake Ohau (ROD MORRIS).

CHAPTER TWELVE
OTAGO

Like Canterbury, Otago lies in the eastern rain shadow of the Southern Alps/Ka Tiritiri o te Moana. It too has a landscape moulded by the alternating cold/warm climates of the past two million years, with its former mixed indigenous forests, shrublands and grasslands largely converted to grasslands through the impact of Maori fires which began around 700 years ago (see Ch.1, p.21). Again like Canterbury, Otago has many inter-montane basins – Strath Taieri, Maniototo, Manuherikia, Ida and upper Clutha – but there much of the similarity ends. For inland Otago has a unique landscape character, and the reasons are both geological and geographical.

Geologically, inland Otago has a different bedrock; a metamorphic rock, schist, which cleaves into very distinctive flat 'plates' and usually contains many glistening flakes of mica minerals. In the absence of trees for timber, most of the historic buildings of Central Otago were constructed from these ideal schist building blocks. Central Otago's schist mountains are also quite different in shape from the scree-streaked greywacke ranges of Canterbury. Geomorphologists call them 'block mountains', a series of ranges with broad summits aligned along parallel faults and separated by basins which are also oriented along the faultlines; indeed, so regular is this topography that it is often referred to as 'basin and range country'. These block mountains are remnants of the ancient Otago Peneplain, a surface worn down through millions of years of erosion. In addition, where schist is the bedrock, the block mountain summits all carry spectacular tors, isolated towers of more resistant bedrock (some up to 20 m high), while their slopes can have a 'fretted' appearance because of the jagged lines of smaller tors. Historically, this tor landform phenomenon

was recognised in the apt names given to many the ranges by early European explorers: Rock and Pillar, Knobby, Raggedy, Pisa, Old Man and Old Woman.

The geographical distinctiveness of inland Otago is related to its great distance from the sea. The Manuherikia Valley, the most continental climatic environment in New Zealand, is 120 km from the Otago coast and 140 km from the Tasman Sea – and sheltered from moisture-bearing winds from both directions by a maze of uplands and mountain ranges. Consequently, Central Otago's lowlands have a semi-arid climate, with hot dry summers and cold dry winters. Rainfall can be as low as 350 mm per annum near Alexandra, and places like Lauder and Ophir have the distinction of being among both the hottest and coldest places in the country. Tussock grasslands (both the *Festuca* and *Poa* short tussocks and *Chionochloa* tall snow tussocks) and drought-resistant bracken fern and shrubs have thrived here since fires (of both natural and moa-hunter origin) progressively eliminated the matai/totara/bog pine/toatoa forests. Beech forests, however, survived most of the fires in the wetter western mountain valleys draining into Lakes Hawea, Wanaka and Wakatipu, and relict stands still persist in the Cardrona, Kawarau and Lindis valleys.

Inland Otago has many important centres of biodiversity, and in this sense it mirrors Kahurangi National Park (see Ch.9, p161) in its co-evolution of landforms and species. Both inland Otago and Kahurangi have a complex tectonic history, with a large number of old mountain ranges isolated from each other; but in inland Otago they are separated by broad basins. Like Kahurangi, most of the Central Otago ranges were probably able to remain as refuges for plants and animals during the ice ages. They too escaped

Mt Aspiring/Tititea (3033 m) from the west, with the setting sun still touching the Therma Glacier (left) and Bonar Glacier (right).

FIORDLAND, WESTERN SOUTHLAND, SOUTH WESTLAND

0   25   50   75km

- ① Mount Aspiring National Park
- ② Fiordland National Park
- ③ Eyre Mountains / Taka Ra Haka Conservation Park
- ④ Takitimu Conservation Area

Jackson Bay / Okahu

Arawhata R.
Waitoto R.
Waiototo Swamp
Haast R.
Cascade River
CASCADE PLATEAU
Burmeister Moraes
Hermitage Swamp
Jackson R.
Arawhata R.

RED HILLS RANGE
Ten Hour Gorge
Mystery Col
Limbo Glacier
Olivine Ice Plateau

OLIVINE RANGE
HAAST RANGE

Big Bay

Forgotten River

Martins Bay

Lake McKerrow

Volta Glacier
Therma Glacier
Bevan Col
Mt Aspiring / Tititea
Bonar Glacier

Fiery Col
Serpentine Saddle
Ngapunatoru Plateau

BARRIER RANGE
Dart River
FORBES RANGE

Matukituki R.

Lake Wanaka

John O'Groats R.
Mt Pembroke
Milford Sound / Piopiotahi
Mitre Pk
Sinbad Valley
Gulliver Valley
Esperance Valley

Mt Tutoko
Mills Pk

DARRAN MOUNTAINS

Mt Earnslaw / Pikirakatahi
Rees River

RICHARDSON MOUNTAINS

Wanaka

Routeburn Valley

HARRIS MOUNTAINS

Arthur R.

WICK MOUNTAINS

Hollyford River

Key Summit
Ngatimamoe

HUMBOLDT MOUNTAINS

Sutherland Sound

Bligh Sound

EARL MOUNTAINS

Eglinton Valley

LIVINGSTONE MOUNTAINS

Shadow River

PISA RANGE

George Sound

FRANKLIN MOUNTAINS

Queenstown

Kawarau River

Caswell Sound

STUART MOUNTAINS

Lake Wakatipu

THE REMARKABLES
Lake Alta
Double Cone

Rastus Burn

Nevis

CARRICK RANGE

Doolans Ck

Gold Arm, Charles Sound
Nancy Sound
Gaer Arm, Bradshaw Sound
Thompson Sound
Secretary Island

MURCHISON MOUNTAINS

Lake Te Anau

Von River

Mavora Lakes

HECTOR MOUNTAINS

Boating Lies Ck

OLD WOMAN RANGE

Bauza Is.
Doubtful Sound / Patea

Malaspina Reach

KEPLER MOUNTAINS

Jane Peak
Eyre Peak

EYRE MOUNTAINS

Mataura River

Nevis River

GARVIE MOUNTAINS

Nokomai Wetlands

Gorge Creek
Blue Lake
Lake Gow

Dagg Sound

Te Anau

Oreti River

Garston

UMBRELLA RANGE

Breaksea Sound
Wet Jacket Arm
Breaksea Is.
Gilbert Is.
Resolution Island

Lake Manapouri

Maratoa River

Mossburn

WAIMATE MTNS

HUNTER MOUNTAINS

TAKITIMU MOUNTAINS

Lumsden

Five Fingers Peninsula

WAIMEA PLAINS

HOKONUI HILLS

Anchor Is.
Dusky Sound

L. Monowai

L. Hauroko

Oreti River

Aparima River

Winton

Gore

Mataura River

Chalky Inlet
Chalky Is./Te Kakahu
Preservation Inlet
Coal Is.
Puysegur Point

Lake Poteriteri

SOUTHLAND PLAINS

Waitutu Terraces

Lake Hakapoua
Waitutu R.
Wairaurahiri River

Waiau River

Tuatapere

Long Sound

N

Solander Islands

Te Waewae Bay

Riverton

Invercargill

the devastating impact of piedmont ice sheets or large valley glaciers; instead, there were only small cirque glaciers along the summits of the Hawkdun, St Bathans, Pisa and Old Man ranges, the Garvie and Hector mountains and The Remarkables.

Plenty of wilderness landscapes still remain in the Otago high country, mainly because severe winters limit pastoral use of the upper parts of the block mountains to summer rangeland only. The wildest areas are in the far north-west in Mount Aspiring National Park, and in the mountains around the periphery of Central Otago – the Garvie and Hector mountains in the west, and the St Bathans and Hawkdun ranges in the north. But even the settled Otago coastline has stretches that are still natural, although not remote. The only remaining wild river of any length is the Taieri, for the magnificent swirling blue Clutha/Mata-au River was systematically dammed and ultimately sacrificed on the altar of Think Big by Robert Muldoon and Bruce Beetham, leaving New Zealand the costly folly of the Clyde Dam and Lake Dunstan.

Blackhead, one of several locations around the old 'Dunedin Volcano' where long ago thick layers of basaltic lava cooled and formed masses of jointed columns.

OTAGO'S COASTLINE: FROM THE WAITAKI TO THE CLUTHA/ MATA-AU RIVER MOUTHS

The schist rocks which make up so much of Otago's interior are not apparent on the Otago coast. Instead, the scenic coastline consists of prominent headlands and peninsulas of volcanic origin, alternating with softer sediments which have been eroded to form a variety of interesting coastal landforms. The latter include, from north to south:
* the near-perfect arc of the Waitaki River delta fan with its sheer 20 m cliffs of alluvium;
* the spectacular concretions, the Moeraki Boulders, on Moeraki Beach;
* beautiful Katiki Beach and Blueskin Bay inlet;
* cliffs near the Taieri River mouth, which are being eroded back rapidly by undercutting waves from the southerly storms that regularly lash the Otago coast.

The prominent volcanic headlands include Cape Wanbrow, the Moeraki Peninsula and Otago Peninsula itself – the deeply-eroded remnant of a basalt volcano which erupted 13 million years ago in the Port Chalmers and Portobello locality. The peninsula is a deceptive landscape, for although its old domes and cones are gentle in outline when viewed from Otago Harbour, they hide a wild, outer coastline fronting the full force of the Pacific Ocean. Here, from Taiaroa Head to Maori Head, the sea has carved both cliffs and isolated beaches, and breached the old volcano in two places to form the tidal Hoopers and Papanui inlets.

The Otago coastline is well known for both its diversity and number of seabirds and marine mammals. Blue penguins/korora nest in their thousands around Oamaru Harbour, cherished as Oamaru's own special wildlife tourism attraction. Further south lies Shag Point/Matakea, a promontory of major biogeographical significance (and cultural significance to southern Maori). Here the Kakanui Mountains plunge down to the coast, effectively separating the flora of Canterbury from that of Otago. Curiously, around Shag Point/Matakea a range of alpine plants and insects (especially moths) survive at sea level – along with profuse maritime life, such as breeding colonies of fur seals, shags, gulls and yellow-eyed penguins. The Katiki mudstones of marine origin at the point are also famous for their Cretaceous-age fossils, especially the plesiosaur, a 7 m long extinct marine reptile with an extremely long neck – a 'sea serpent' from the Age of the Dinosaurs.

But it is the teeming wildlife on the cliffs and beaches of Otago Peninsula – the 'Wildlife Capital of New Zealand' – which is the pride of maritime Otago. Like Kaikoura, Otago Peninsula is one of those places on the east coast of the South Island where cold, nutrient-rich, deep oceanic water comes close to the land – allowing a profusion of

RIGHT The Moeraki Boulders lie scattered along the Otago coastline between Hampden and Moeraki. They are concretions, unique in New Zealand for their large size and roundness, which began to form deep in the ocean sediments around 60 million years ago and have subsequently been uplifted and exposed by wave action. BELOW The wild Otago Peninsula is an important habitat for threatened wildlife, especially the yellow-eyed penguin, the royal albatross (with a breeding colony at Taiaroa Head), New Zealand fur seal and New Zealand (Hooker's) sea lion.

TOP The endangered yellow-eyed penguin or hoiho (*Megadyptes antipodes*) is very vulnerable to predation by ferrets, stoats, dogs and cats, and to human interference. During the 1980s the number of breeding pairs dropped sharply but conservation work by the Dunedin-based Yellow-eyed Penguin Trust over the past 20 years has helped secure the bird's main habitats on the Otago coastline. MIDDLE A parent northern royal albatross or toroa (*Diomedea epomophora sanfordi*) feeding its chick at Taiaroa Head, Otago Peninsula. Around 100 of these magnificent birds congregate on the headland each spring, in the world's only mainland albatross colony (ROD MORRIS). BOTTOM This young bull New Zealand fur seal (*Arctocephalus forsteri*) at Moeraki Point is just one of many thousands of these marine mammals attracted to the Otago coastline because of the plentiful food supply (ROD MORRIS).

sea and coastal wildlife to thrive. The royal albatross/toroa colony on Taiaroa Head is the most famous feature, and its 100 or so birds, in the world's only mainland colony, have been well studied and managed for 70 years. Living for more than 60 years, and with a wing-span of around 3 m, this remarkable bird is a fleeting but tangible symbol to all land-bound New Zealanders of the great wilderness that is the Southern Ocean. Otago Peninsula is also the best-known habitat for the yellow-eyed penguin/hoiho. The plight of this large, scientifically interesting but rather solitary bird has been well publicised over the past 20 years. The Dunedin-based Yellow-eyed Penguin Trust has led a widespread effort to protect it from predators like mustelids (ferrets and stoats), dogs and cats, to research its periodic and catastrophic decline in numbers, and to minimise the threat of fire and visitors to its coastal duneland habitat. Other notable seabirds occupy different ecological

Snow mantles the broad summits of the Dunstan Mountains – one of the many block mountain ranges in Central Otago.

niches on the peninsula: blue penguins in rock crevices or burrows in the sand dunes; Stewart Island shags in their noisy, smelly, dense colonies with impressive elevated nests of mud-cemented seaweed; spotted shags nesting high on narrow rocky ledges along the cliffs; and, at dusk, sooty shearwaters/titi as they return from the day's harvest out on the ocean to the safety of their burrows in the sandy soils of headlands. Marine mammals, too, are attracted to the waters in and around the peninsula by the plentiful food supply. New Zealand fur seal breeding colonies are now scattered all around the peninsula, with about 2000 seal pups born each year and the total population probably beginning to stabilise at around 5000 animals. Dusky, common and bottlenose dolphins often frequent the more sheltered waters of the harbour, and right whales and orca are sometimes seen offshore. A particularly exciting conservation development on the peninsula is the reappearance in significant numbers of Hooker's sea lion (or the New Zealand sea lion), which was exterminated around our mainland shores long ago by Maori and European hunters. Over the past 15 years the sea lions seem to have begun migrating back from their Auckland Islands stronghold, building up to a population of 60–70 on the peninsula and another 30 or so on the Catlins coast further south. Most of them are males, but a small number of females have begun to breed, raising hopes that the Otago coastline will eventually harbour a viable breeding population of these endearing and fearless marine mammals – the largest and rarest of the world's five sea lion species.

NORTH OTAGO DRY MOUNTAINS: KAKANUI MOUNTAINS, HAWKDUN AND ST BATHANS RANGES

The long east–west arm of the Kakanui Mountains links the Otago coast at Shag Point/Matakea to the Hawkdun and St Bathans ranges. Further inland still lie the mountains around Lindis Pass and the Lindis River, and further west the Barrier Range and the range between the Ahuriri and Hunter rivers (the watershed between the Waitaki and Clutha river systems). This great sweep of high country is unique in the South Island, the only place where a mountain chain extends from the main divide right out to the east coast. The Kakanui Mountains are an old peneplain of greywacke and semi-schist rocks, rising through a steep escarpment above the Waihemo/Shag River at the eastern margin of the Maniototo Plains. At its eastern end lies Trotters Gorge, a scenic gem of spectacular cliffs carved long ago in the greywacke conglomerate at a time when Trotters Creek was much larger than it is now. The basaltic lava landscape around Siberia Hill (1272 m) is one of the most interesting summit features of the Kakanui Mountains. Here black boulder fields spill out across the smooth peneplain surface known locally as Hector's Plateau, and impressive 60 m high basaltic columns form the summit of nearby Kattothyrst. Large areas of intact *Chionochloa macra* and *C. rigida* snow tussock grassland, fellfield, bluff/scree and alpine wetland plant communities extend along the top of the range. The three branches of the Waianakarua River catchment draining to the north-east contain the only significant areas of native forest in coastal North Otago. Because most of the range has been so long in pastoral lease tenure, public access has been limited and its

The tussock uplands of the broad Lammerlaw and Lammermoor ranges contain many alpine wetlands, like these cut-off meanders of the Taieri River near Lake Onslow.

conservation values and opportunities for wilderness recreation (including cross-country skiing in suitable years) are largely unrecognised.

Further west and inland, the Hawkdun, Ida, St Bathans, and St Marys ranges are often known as the 'dry' mountains of North Otago. The heights of their summits range from around 1800 m in the Hawkdun Range, to 2000 m in the St Marys Range and over 2100 m in the St Bathans Range. The striking feature of both the Hawkdun and St Bathans

ranges is their steep, 1200 m high western escarpments, which are topped by remarkably flat summits. They make an impressive sight in winter from the Ranfurly–Alexandra highway where it passes through the basins in the head of the Manuherikia River and Ida Burn – an uncluttered mountain vista celebrated in many a Grahame Sydney painting. But the north-eastern slopes of these ranges are much gentler, with extensive areas of alpine plateaux and some associated cirque basins, and wetlands between the Hawkdun–Ida mountain crests, ultimately draining to the Waitaki River system via tributaries of the Otematata River. The winding road through the snow tussock landscape around Danseys Pass gives visitors a tantalising glimpse into the wild upland of the St Marys Range, but little idea of how vast in both breadth and length these remote North Otago dry mountains are, extending another 75 km north-west to the iconic tussock landscape of Lindis Pass (where it is crossed by SH 8).

The undulating summit of the Pisa Range, with isolated schist tors standing above the old peneplain surface.

The eastern crest of the Hawkdun Range also boasts an impressive series of cirques, reflecting the influence of past small-scale local glaciations. Indeed, the orientation of the Hawkdun Range directly across the path of the cold south-westerly winds that prevail in winter seems to regularly produce a lower snowline and more reliable snow cover than in the adjacent St Bathans or St Marys ranges. Coupled with the undulating nature of the topography, and the lack of fences and buildings, this makes the Hawkdun Range an outstanding place for wilderness cross-country skiing. Together, these North Otago dry ranges have distinctive alpine vegetation, reflecting both their cold, dry climate and their geology, the latter a transition from the greywackes of Canterbury to the schists of Otago. Their mountain landforms are therefore rather hybrid in nature: although they lack the distinctive tors of the schist block mountains of Central Otago, they still have the same broad summits (exhumed relics of the ancient Otago peneplain), yet screes are widespread on their flanks. The screes and rocky fell-fields are habitats for species of *Notothlaspi*, *Ranunculus*, *Epilobium*, *Leucogenes*, *Raoulia*, *Leptinella* and other specialist alpine plants so characteristic of the mountains of Marlborough and Canterbury, many reaching their southern limits here. Rolling tussocklands of *Chionochloa rigida* (up to 1000 m) and *C. macra* (above 1000 m) are widespread, especially where loess has accumulated and soil development has continued uninterrupted by the fire, wind erosion and rabbit invasions which have plagued the drier basins of Central Otago.

SCHIST BLOCK MOUNTAINS OF CENTRAL OTAGO

The schist block mountains are the unique landform feature of Central Otago. Like giant prehistoric lizards, the Dunstan Mountains, Rock and Pillar, Pisa and Old Man–Old Woman ranges, and Taieri and Rough ridges stretch out in the summer heat haze, their limbs tightly enclosing the middle reaches of the Clutha/Mata-au River, as well as the entire Manuherikia and Taieri river catchments. The Taieri River is well known to the residents of Dunedin and Mosgiel where it flows sluggishly across the Taieri Plain, but its tortuous 200 km route to Taieri Mouth from its source on the Central Otago block mountains is a largely unsung epic of riverine tenacity. It rises at around 1100 m in the snow tussock uplands between the Lammerlaw and Lammermoor ranges before wending its way through a maze of short schist gorges to emerge into the Styx Basin and then the Maniototo Basin. These basins contain the Upper Taieri Scroll Plain, a remarkable series of tight meanders, ox-bow lakes and abandoned channels which the river has developed over thousands of years. And then, confronted by the barrier of the Kakanui Mountains, the Taieri circumnavigates the Rock and Pillar Range by swinging 180° SSW through another schist gorge to the Strath Taieri Plain, and then the main Taieri Gorge, before emerging at Outram.

In sharp contrast to the mountains around Lakes Wakatipu, Wanaka and Hawea, the dry block mountains of Central Otago did not carry extensive glaciers during the Last Glaciation. However, they certainly had (and still have) a severe periglacial environment, with the ground frozen for up to six months of the year. Over the millennia, the pronounced diurnal or seasonal freeze-thaw cycles have generated widespread rock and soil creep, producing a fascinating tableau of patterned ground on the undulating summits. This patterned ground phenomenon is probably best developed on the wide summits of the Dunstan Mountains and the Old Man Range. Features include soil stripes and hummocks, stone nets, and solifluction terraces and lobes – the latter frozen in time on the slopes below the range crests like icing that has flowed before setting on the sides of a giant mountain cake. From the air the soil stripes and furrows look like vast ploughed alpine paddocks. The hummocks and hollows have their own intricate cushion-plant communities attuned to this tundra-like micro-environment: the green leaves of the mountain daisy *Celmisia viscosa* choke the furrows and hollows while our smallest turpentine shrub, *Dracophyllum muscoides* and pale mats of *Raoulia hectorii* are draped across the tops of the stripes and hummocks. All of this alpine community sits atop deep, friable, chocolate-coloured soils which, albeit frozen for half the year, would be the envy of horticulturalists far below in the semi-arid valleys.

The schist tor landscape is ubiquitous throughout Central Otago, with tors marching in geometric ranks across the summit of the Rock and Pillar Range and the Dunstan Mountains, and giving a fretted appearance to the flanks of the Pisa and Old Man ranges. Some tors are outstanding landmarks – such as Leaning Rock on the southern end of the Dunstan Mountains; Hyde Rock on the Old Man Range; and The Obelisk, an impressive 25 m high tor standing alone above the flat schist-slab paving of the Obelisk Range. It stands like a relic of some geological Ozymandias, remaining as a 'vast and trunkless leg of stone' while the block mountain summits 'boundless and bare … stretch far away'. Nowhere else in New Zealand is this strange mountain micro-topography better developed. So, why does it occur here in Central Otago? Probably two factors combine to create the necessary very cold, yet glacier-free, environment:

- first, the rainshadow location, where annual precipitation as both rain and snow is only 1500–1800 mm, compared with 4000–12,000 mm in the axial mountains of the North Island, the Southern Alps/Ka Tiritiri o te Moana, or Fiordland;
- second, they have generally lower altitudes than the glaciated mountains of western Otago (most of the inner ranges of Central Otago reach only 1200–1600 m, while the lightly glaciated outer ranges, like the St Bathans Range, Pisa Range and the Hector Mountains, are up to 1900–2100 m).

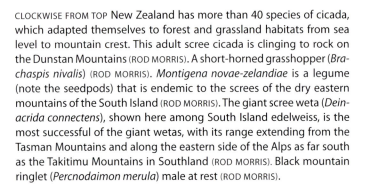

CLOCKWISE FROM TOP New Zealand has more than 40 species of cicada, which adapted themselves to forest and grassland habitats from sea level to mountain crest. This adult scree cicada is clinging to rock on the Dunstan Mountains (ROD MORRIS). A short-horned grasshopper (*Brachaspis nivalis*) (ROD MORRIS). *Montigena novae-zelandiae* is a legume (note the seedpods) that is endemic to the screes of the dry eastern mountains of the South Island (ROD MORRIS). The giant scree weta (*Deinacrida connectens*), shown here among South Island edelweiss, is the most successful of the giant wetas, with its range extending from the Tasman Mountains and along the eastern side of the Alps as far south as the Takitimu Mountains in Southland (ROD MORRIS). Black mountain ringlet (*Percnodaimon merula*) male at rest (ROD MORRIS).

ABOVE Large tors of erosion-resistant schist rock stand like obelisks on the broad summit of the Old Man Range. Despite the lack of glaciation and an altitude of not much more than 1600 m, this is one of the most severe alpine environments in New Zealand. In the foreground of the photo, the gently-sloping surface is slightly furrowed from freeze-thaw activity, yet tiny, hardy cushion plants like *Dracophyllum muscoides* are still able to survive even though the soil is frozen for six months of the year. LEFT The Otago skink (*Oligosoma otagense*) was once widespread throughout the Otago high country, but is now endangered and restricted to two tussockland habitats in the Lindis Valley and the Macraes–Middlemarch locality. Despite the climatic severity of the Central Otago environment, the area seems to be a centre of exceptional diversity for lizards. However, there are few protected areas in this landscape and their habitat is under threat from a wide range of human activities and introduced predators. There are fears that both the endemic Otago skink and its other tussockland companion, the grand skink (*O. grande*), could be extinct in another decade if urgent conservation measures are not undertaken.

These mountains today stand as biodiversity islands, probably due to their stability over a long period. The stability is primarily because of their geographic isolation and lack of catastrophic soil and vegetation community disruption and rejuvenation (usually an ecosystem-disrupting by-product of glaciation). As a consequence, the Central Otago mountains are notable habitats for many endemic species. While the Tasman Mountains in Kahurangi National Park are rich in their diversity of land snails (see Ch. 9, p.165), Central Otago is especially noted for its diversity of lizards (at least 14 species to date). The rarest and largest lizards are the Otago skink (*Oligosoma otagense*) and the grand skink (*O. grande*) which have their stronghold in the Taieri Ridge–Macraes district. There are also a number of newly discovered geckos, including what may be a new group restricted to foggy mountain slopes.

In addition, Central Otago seems to be a centre of diversity for those indigenous species which have to date not been well studied – native fish (especially galaxiids), beetles and moths. This insect fauna is still in the process of being documented but is known to include a wide variety of beetles, cicadas and grasshoppers. There are three known weta species, including the large striped mountain weta (*Hemideina maori*) and the giant scree weta (*Deinacrida connectens*), which seems to reach its south-eastern limit in the screes of the dry North Otago mountains. The prolific moth fauna is said by experts to consist of at least 200 species in the alpine zone of each of Central Otago's mountain ranges; many of them are day-flying, coloured and hairy. In contrast, butterflies are quite limited in number and distribution. As more field surveys are completed, scientific experts are concluding that Central Otago may have the most diverse and spectacular insect fauna of any New Zealand region.

GARVIE AND HECTOR MOUNTAINS AND THE REMARKABLES

The Frankton escarpment of The Remarkables, rising 2000 m sheer from the shores of Lake Wakatipu, is one of New Zealand's iconic mountain landscapes. The Remarkables are contiguous with the Hector Mountains, which extend for another 30 km along the south-eastern shores of Lake Wakatipu. The northern section is a wild landscape of jagged ridges and deep, narrow valleys with alpine tarns nestling in their cirqued headwaters. The Remarkables Skifield road into the head of the Rastus Burn gives walking access to Lake Alta, a beautiful cirque tarn nestled under Double Cone (2319 m) – probably the easiest place in Otago from which to appreciate the glaciated landscapes of the western mountains. Passes above Lake Alta lead to the tarn-studded basins in the head of Wye Creek and Doolans Creek, superb country for summer mountaineering and winter cross-country skiing. The southern Hector Mountains are more remote but less rugged, providing opportunities for Nordic skiing, particularly the last 20 km where the range slopes gently down to the pass crossed by the Garston–Nevis Road.

East of the Hector Mountains lies the most extensive winter wilderness in Otago – the Garvie Mountains extending for 60 km northwards into the Old Woman Range. The barrier formed by the Hector–Garvie–Old Woman–Carrick mountains shields Central Otago from the rain-bearing south-westerly winds; consequently, these wetter mountains show more evidence of past glaciation. Indeed, the Garvie Mountains are of national importance as New Zealand's best example of a glaciated peneplain remnant. The glaciated eastern side of the Garvie crest (1700–1900 m), especially in the headwaters of Gorge Creek, carries an impressive line of cirques containing many tarns (some, such as Blue Lake and Lake Gow, more than 1 km in length). In contrast, the western slopes have no recent glacial landforms; instead, over the last 7000 years, at around 1350 m in the headwaters of Roaring Lion Creek and the Dome Burn, an extensive low-alpine patterned mire has developed on peat. These Nokomai Wetlands cover more than 500 ha, a visual wonderland of string bogs, stepped pools and raised islands whose vegetation comprises different sphagnum mosses and a variety of sedges, herbs and grasses. A product of both gentle topography and a cool, moist climate, the Nokomai is one of very few Southern Hemisphere subarctic-like patterned mires (there are some similar mires in Tierra del Fuego), unique in New Zealand and of international ecological importance.

MOUNT ASPIRING NATIONAL PARK–OLIVINE WILDERNESS AREA

The mountains around the wide glaciated Dart, Rees, Matukituki and Makarora valleys at the head of Lakes Wakatipu and Wanaka attracted Otago's mountaineers as early as the 1890s. The Otago section of the NZ Alpine Club formulated the first proposals for a national park centred on these valleys and the beautiful peak of Mt Aspiring/Tititea (3033 m) as early as 1936. But Otago climbers had little appreciation of the vast wilderness lying west of the main divide. It was only during the Depression years of the early 1930s that mountaineers, most of them students

from Otago University, began to explore and map in better detail its confusing topography – filling the blank spaces on rudimentary maps of this 'Olivine Country' with intriguing names like Mystery Col, Forgotten River and Limbo Glacier. The Federated Mountain Clubs of NZ continued to promote the idea of a national park over the next 25 years but progress was slow. Today, it is hard to understand the degree of opposition that then existed to the conservation of this magnificent landscape as a national park. A myriad of vested interests – high-country runholders, and government mining and forestry agencies – carved away at the park concept. Consequently, when Mount Aspiring was eventually designated as New Zealand's tenth national park in 1964, its area of just under 200,000 ha consisted only of the alpine interior, the spine of the Southern Alps/ Ka Tiritiri o te Moana. Virtually all lands of any commercial potential for grazing, forestry or mining were excluded. So unenthusiastic was the government of the day that, at the

Mt Aspiring/Tititea from the east, looking west along the Coxcombe Ridge from the Volta Glacier. Although Tititea's mana is supposed to be recognised with a topuni status, commercial helicopter and climbing activity is encroaching onto its flanks.

park opening ceremony, the officiating Minister of Lands smugly commented that Mount Aspiring would be the 'last of New Zealand's national parks'.

Successive conservation campaigns since 1964 have sought to protect the western wilderness and improve Mount Aspiring National Park's landscape and biodiversity representativeness; these fleshed out the original skeletal boundaries with an additional 155,000 ha. Gradually and grudgingly, small pieces of public land on the West Coast side of the main divide were added – the headwaters of the Waiatoto and Arawhata rivers in 1970, Fiery Col in 1972, and the Waipara River and Haast Range in 1989. The most protracted campaign, however, was to protect

TOP One of the showy, large mountain daisies, *Celmisia coriacea*, which prefers the poorly-drained, peaty soils in the snow tussock/herb-fields (ROD MORRIS). RIGHT The snow marguerite (*Dolichoglottis scorzoneroides*) is one of the most profusely flowering of our mountain herbs, often seen in moister sites like snow-banks or stream margins (ROD MORRIS). BOTTOM One of the highest flowering plants in Mount Aspiring National Park is *Ranunculus buchananii*. This remarkable buttercup can be found on inaccessible ledges and bluffs, where it cannot be eaten by chamois and thar, up to an altitude of 2400 m.

LEFT A native insect on a mountain buttercup petal. BELOW The little male rock wren (*Xenicus gilviventris*) weighs only 16 g but its diminutive size belies its antiquity, robust nature and tenacity in carving out a niche in the harsh alpine zone. The rock wren does not move down the mountain slopes in winter but remains in its subalpine or alpine territory all year. They are a true mountain wilderness bird, their high-pitched song and bobbing dance while flicking their wings delighting many a weary mountaineer. The rock wren and the forest-dwelling rifleman are the only survivors of New Zealand's endemic family of wrens, a group which molecular biologists now consider may have been the ancestral type for many of the world's songbirds.

the wilderness values of the remote Olivine Country and the remarkable Red Hills Mineral Belt. Most of this unique ultramafic landscape was finally protected in 1990, when an area of 41,630 ha (including the Red Hills, the upper Cascade Valley and the Olivine Range) was added to the park, making it today New Zealand's third largest national park (355,543 ha). Then, in 1990, the park acquired international recognition as one of the world's places of 'outstanding universal value' when UNESCO listed it as part of Te Wahipounamu – South West New Zealand World Heritage Area. Finally, in 1996, after a 40-year campaign, the Olivine Wilderness Area became a reality, encompassing 83,000 ha of the wildest parts of the park, including the 5 km long Olivine Ice Plateau, most of the Olivine Range, and the glaciers, peaks, waterfalls and gorges in the remote upper Waiatoto, Waipara, Arawhata, Cascade and Pyke catchments.

Mount Aspiring National Park has a wonderful diversity of landscapes:

- vegetation varying from the wet west to the drier east;
- soils derived from contrasting schist and ultramafic rocks;
- landforms ranging in altitude from 100 m to 3000 m.

Most of its forests consist of three species of beech – red, silver and mountain. The lower Dart, Rees, Routeburn and West Matukituki valleys contain magnificent examples of 30–35 m tall red beech. Mountain beech is a much smaller tree and is often associated with red beech in the south and east, especially in the colder sites closer to treeline. In the wetter north and west, silver beech trees hold sway, their trunks and branches festooned with lichens, especially around Haast Pass/Tioripatea and the section of SH 6 alongside the Haast River above the Gates of Haast. The subalpine shrublands are a colourful, impenetrable band, 60–80 m wide, consisting of shrubby species of *Dracophyllum*, *Coprosma*, *Brachyglottis*, *Olearia*, *Hebe*, *Pseudopanax* and *Hoheria*, along with *Aciphylla* (speargrass), and many small podocarps like snow totara and celery pine (*Phyllocladus*). Snowgrass tussocks (up to six different *Chionochloa* species) become more common as the alpine zone is approached.

The real floristic glory of the park is the many flowering herbs that make summer travel into the alpine parts of the park such a delight. The most spectacular is *Ranunculus*

The red beech trees (*Nothofagus fusca*) of the lower Dart Valley, and tributaries like the Routeburn, in Mount Aspiring National Park are of very impressive stature, and the forests are a delight to tramp through. They are an important habitat for yellowhead, robin, and rifleman.

lyallii, the great mountain buttercup; it is often found in groves in damp areas, the plants up to 1.5 m high, and carrying showy white flowers on long stalks above huge, glossy green, umbrella-shaped leaves. The daisy family is well represented, with different *Celmisia,* two attractive snow marguerites (*Dolichoglottis*), delicate *Helichrysum,* showy *Leptinella* and, at higher altitudes, mats of the South Island edelweiss (*Leucogenes grandiceps*) sprawling over schist debris slopes or tucked into rock crevices. Alpine plants growing as cushion mats abound. On the debris slopes there are sprawling mats of *Haastia sinclairii* and species of *Raoulia* – all also members of the daisy family. Around water seepages different cushion plants feature, with mats of *Phyllachne,* *Oreostylidium,* and *Donatia* in association with the attractive, long-stemmed, white-flowered *Forstera,* or varieties of eyebrights (*Euphrasia*) and *Ourisia* that prefer shady habitats within the splash-zone of waterfalls and streams.

THREATS AND CONSERVATION PRIORITIES

Retirement of Otago's High Country

The high-country tussocklands of inland Otago have been the theatre for one of New Zealand's longest-playing conservation dramas – the co-existence of pastoralism and nature conservation. The Land Act 1948 retained over a million hectares of Otago high country in public ownership and required runholder lessees to practise 'good husbandry' through extensive pastoral grazing. Although the 33-year leases were essentially leases in perpetuity, farmers who desired to intensify or diversify land use through more capital-intensive development became increasingly frustrated at their inability to freehold the land (which had often been farmed by their family for generations) to provide security for development loans. From a modern resource conservation perspective, the Land Act was highly deficient legislation: while it gave lessees rights only to the pasturage, it lacked the teeth to achieve universal soil and water conservation in the high country. It failed to control stock damage, soil nutrient depletion, burning and wilding conifer invasion; and importantly, it completely lacked any provisions for nature conservation or public access rights.

Tension increased over the years as pressure grew for the preservation of representative natural ecosystems in the Otago high country. Despite the powerful legislative requirements of the new Reserves Act of 1977, the culture of the Department of Lands and Survey and the Land Settlement Board was still very much pro-farm development – highlighted by their failure to protect the Nardoo catch-

ment block, Otago's best remaining area of mid-altitude tussock grassland, after the department re-purchased the Waipori run in 1978. The scientific survey of the Otago high country was a priority when the department belatedly instituted the Protected Natural Area Programme (PNAP), and these mid-1980s surveys of the Old Man, Umbrella, and Nokomai ecological districts recommended that large areas with high conservation values be retired from pastoral leases. As the Crown's high-country landlord, the department was in an invidious position; racked by internal policy and administrative conflicts, and lacking funds to purchase back the recommended areas for protection stemming from the PNAP, it largely failed to satisfy either runholder or conservationist aspirations.

The administrative paralysis of government in the pastoral high country was another factor determining the environmental reorganisations of the mid-1980s and the establishment of a powerful departmental advocate for conservation. Gradually, during the 1990s, runholders opted to freely renegotiate their leases, restoring to full Crown ownership (and subsequent management by DOC) those areas with 'significant inherent value' (usually the upper slopes and crests of the block mountains, alpine wetlands, and a few altitudinal sequences from valley floors to the summits of the ranges). In return, runholders have been able to freehold those areas capable of 'ecologically sustainable' economic use (though this has extended to some areas of dubious sustainability). Interestingly, this wholesale rationalisation of Otago's land use has not been achieved by local and regional government using the highly trumpeted Resource Management Act 1991; instead a process generally called 'tenure review' was developed by the interested parties – the lessees and the Commissioner of Crown Lands (but with DOC only able to make recommendations) – and consolidated in the Crown Pastoral Land Act 1998. Tenure review does have serious limitations (see discussion in Ch.16, p.309) but there have been impressive conservation and recreation gains in the Otago high country during the past decade.

Creation of Conservation Parks in Otago's High Country

One of the first proposals for a large protected area in the Otago high country was suggested by Federated Mountain Clubs of NZ in 1981 – a Garvie Mountains–Old Man Range–Old Woman Range 'winter wilderness area' – in recognition of its value as the largest contiguous area of winter snow cover in the southern South Island. PNAP surveys during the 1980s also recognised the outstanding biodiversity values of the same uplands, with over 23,000

The Nokomai alpine patterned wetlands at the head of the Roaring Lion Creek and Dome Burn tributaries of the Nevis River, on the western side of the Garvie Mountains, are unique in New Zealand and of international conservation significance.

ha being recommended for protection. Otago's Conservation Management Strategy (1998–2008) subsequently recognised tenure review as critically important in achieving protection of conservation values in at least 20 of the 41 'Special Places' in the region. Various Otago high-country conservation park proposals advanced from time to time by Federated Mountain Clubs and Forest & Bird have been endorsed as medium-term conservation goals by the Minister of Conservation. The first of these, the 21,000 ha Te Papanui Tussocklands Conservation Park, was created in 2003: it covers the easternmost of the schist block mountains, the Lammerlaw and Lammermoor ranges, including the extensive wetlands in the head of the Taieri, Teviot, Beaumont and Waipori rivers (albeit too late to save the Great Moss Swamp in the Taieri headwaters, inundated 15 years earlier by the Loganburn Reservoir).

Five other Otago high-country conservation parks have been proposed and should progressively become a reality during the next decade: Hawkdun/Oteake (including the Hawkdun, Ida, St Marys and St Bathans ranges); Pisa Range (and the adjacent Criffel Range); Rock and Pillar Range; Garvies/Kopuwai (including the Old Man and Old Woman ranges); The Remarkables (including the Hector Mountains).

A major step towards achieving the Hawkdun/Oteake Conservation Park was government's outright purchase of Michael Peak Station in June 2007. This brought the tussock-covered higher altitude portion (7000 ha) of the St Bathans Range into the public domain and was acclaimed by a range of conservationists, artists and wilderness recreation groups. A number of very important wetlands should be key parts of the other conservation parks, especially the Nokomai alpine patterned wetlands in the proposed Garvies/Kopuwai park and the Taieri Scroll Plain wetlands managed as a protected area associated with a Rock and Pillar Conservation Park.

CHAPTER THIRTEEN

SOUTHLAND AND STEWART ISLAND/RAKIURA

'Southland' is a rather boring name for the southernmost part of the equally boringly named South Island. For Southland contains some of our most impressive natural wild landscapes and deserves a much less prosaic name for the land which Maori call 'Murihiku' (the tail end of the land). This more appealing name graces the Murihiku Escarpment, the landform which marks the real geological boundary (the so-called Southland Syncline) between Otago and Southland. Indeed, like the notched tail of some ancient giant dinosaur now petrified to stone, the escarpment curves down from the Eyre Mountains near Mossburn, through the Hokonui Hills, to the south-eastern coastline at Nugget Point. The Aparima, Oreti and Mataura rivers rise in the mountains of northern Southland, then carve their way through the Murihiku Escarpment before spreading out across the Southland Plains. Beyond the western end of the escarpment lie the great mountain ranges of Southland – the Eyre, Takitimu and Livingstone mountains, and the vast wilderness that is Fiordland.

The Southland coastline running from Te Waewae Bay to Nugget Point retains a high degree of naturalness and wild character. There are many long gravel beaches with relatively intact dune systems, and sizeable coastal wetlands and estuaries around the mouths of all the main rivers: a notable example of the latter is the internationally important wading-bird habitat of Awarua Bay–Waituna Lagoon near Invercargill. Only 30 km off this part of the Southland coast lies New Zealand's third largest island, Stewart Island/Rakiura. Until sea levels rose after the Last Glaciation ended around 14,000 years ago, the island was linked to the Southland mainland by dry land. Now, it might as well be a thousand kilometres away across the wild waters of Foveaux Strait/Te Ara a Kiwa – another world where impenetrable rainforest overhangs a coastline dotted with thousands of coves and rocky islets, so different from the manicured order of the agricultural landscapes of the Southland and Waimea Plains.

FIORDLAND NATIONAL PARK

Fiordland National Park – the remote and uninhabited south-west of the South Island – is New Zealand's outstanding wilderness. Its large size (1,260,708 ha) is nearly 5 per cent of the area of the country and nearly three times the size of our next largest national park, Kahurangi. Although most visitors touch only the periphery of the park, its network of access roads, tracks and launch routes gives richly rewarding glimpses of the mountainous interior of Fiordland, a wilderness of fiords and forest, lakes, cliffs and sheer peaks that is difficult to penetrate on foot.

Why is the Fiordland landscape so different? Maori creation mythology tells of the skillful labours of their ancestor Tu-te-Rakiwhanoa in carving out the fiords in the upturned hull of the waka of Aoraki, perfecting his sculpting technique as he moved from south to north until he was skillful enough to chisel out the magnificent, clean walls of the last fiord, Piopiotahi (Milford Sound). In the east, Rakaihautu used his digging stick (ko) to fashion the basin which now contains Lakes Te Anau and Manapouri. The scientific explanation for Fiordland's sheer mountains is less colourful, a combination of geology and past cold climates. For Fiordland is New Zealand's largest area of very hard, crystalline igneous rock: some plutonic (mainly granite, gabbro and diorite), some metamorphised (mainly to gneiss). It is the

Mackay Falls beside the Milford Track in the Arthur Valley, Fiordland National Park.

FRANKLIN MOUNTAINS ●1

STUART MOUNTAINS

EARL MOUNTAINS

LIVINGSTONE MOUNTAINS

MURCHISON MOUNTAINS

KEPLER MOUNTAINS

Lake Te Anau

Te Anau

Lake Manapouri

L. Monowai

L. Hauroko

Mavora Lakes

TAKITIMU MOUNTAINS ●4

Mararoa River

Mossburn

Lumsden

Oreti River

Apatima River

LONGWOOD RANGE

Tuatapere

Winton

Te Waewae Bay

Riverton

Waiau River

SOUTHLAND PLAINS

Invercargill

Oreti River

Awarua Bay - Waituna Lagoon

Bluff

Foveaux Strait / Te Ara a Kiwa

Queenstown

Lake Wakatipu

THE REMARKABLES

Lake Alta Double Cone

Wye Ck

Von River

HECTOR MOUNTAINS

Jane Peak Eyre Peak

EYRE MOUNTAINS ●2

Mataura River

Garston

GARVIE MOUNTAINS

Nokomai Wetlands

Gorge Creek

Dome Burn

Blue Lake Lake Gow

Waikaia River

WAIMEA PLAINS

HOKONUI HILLS

Mataura River

Gore

PISA RANGE

Kawarau River

Rastus Burn

Nevis

CARRICK RANGE

Doolans Ck

Nevis River

OLD WOMAN RANGE

OBELISK RANGE

UMBRELLA RANGE

OLD MAN RANGE

Roxburgh

Lake Dunstan

Cromwell

DUNSTAN MOUNTAINS

Clyde Dam

Alexandra

KNOBBY RANGE

Cluth a / Mata-au River

Teviot River

Lake Onslow

MANUHERIKIA VALLEY

Lauder

Ophir

IDA VALLEY

RAGGEDY RANGE

ROUGH RIDGE

MANIOTOTO PLAIN

Ranfurly

Naseby

UPPER TAIERI SCROLL PLAIN

STYX BASIN

Loganburn Reservoir (Great Moss Swamp)

LAMMERMOOR RANGE

ROCK AND PILLAR RANGE

LAMMERLAW RANGE ●3

Nardoo Strm

Beaumont R.

Raes Junction

Beaumont

Waipori R.

BLUE MOUNTAINS

Murihiku Escarpment

Balclutha

Clutha / Mata-au River

Nugget Point

The `Catlins' ●5

Mokoreta Valley

Mt Pye

Ajax Hill ●5

BERESFORD RANGE

MACLENNAN RANGE

Tahakopa Valley

Maclennan R.

Tautuku R.

Waikawa Valley ●5

●5

●5

Papatowai

Purakaunui Falls
Matai Falls
Tahakopa Bay
Lake Wilkie
Tautuku Bay
Tautuku Peninsula
Waipati Beach (Cathedral Caves)
McLean Falls
Chaslands Mistake

Curio Bay

Kattothyrst Sibena Hill
`Hector's Plateau'

KAKANUI MOUNTAINS

Waianakarua

Hampden
Moeraki Boulde

Trotters Gorge

Macraes Flat

Waihemo (Shag) River

Palmerston

TAIERI RIDGE

Taieri River

Middlemarch

STRATH TAIERI PLAIN

Outram

Mosgiel

DUNEDIN

Blueskin Bay

Port Chalmers

Portobello

Taiar

Pe

Maori Head
Otago Harbour
Hoopers Inlet
Papanui Inlet

Blackhead

TAIERI PLAIN

Taieri River

West Ruggedy Beach
RUGGEDY MOUNTAINS

Mt Anglem / Hananui

Codfish Is. / Whenua Hou ●6

Mason Bay

Doughboy Bay

FRASER PEAKS
Magog
Gog

Titi Islands

Taukihepa / Big South Cape Is.

Mt Rakeahua

TIN RANGE

DECEIT PEAKS

Pearl Island
Port Pegasus / Pikihatiti

Robertson River

Granite Knob

●7

Stewart Island / Rakiura

Ruapuke Is.

Titi Islands

Halfmoon Bay
Bench Island

Paterson Inlet / Whaka a te Wera

Ulva Island / Te Wharawhara Marine Reserve

Port Adventure

Lords River / Tutaekawetoweto

● 1 Fiordland National Park
● 2 Eyre Mountains / Taka Ra Haka Conservation P
● 3 Te Papanui Tussocklands Conservation Park
● 4 Takitimu Conservation Area
● 5 Catlins Coastal Park
● 6 Whenua Hou Nature Reserve
● 7 Rakiura National Park

0   25   50   75

OTAGO, EASTERN SOUTHLAND, STEWART ISLAN

hardness of these rocks that accounts for the stability of the sheer walls of the Darran Mountains and the dramatic landscape traversed by the Milford Road. Everywhere the telltale U shape of the valleys speaks of the imprint of long-gone glaciers, tongues of ice that carved their way deeply into these hard rocks and extended far beyond the present coastline. With the waning of the Last Glaciation, the glaciers melted back into the interior, the sea level rose and the troughs were gradually filled with water. In the east and south, this left the chain of beautiful, deep, fresh-water glacial lakes – Te Anau, Manapouri, Monowai, Hauroko, Poteriteri and Hakapoua. In the west, the sea occupied most of the glacial troughs, creating 15 fiords which now deeply indent Fiordland's 230 km of outer coastline between Milford Sound and Puysegur Point. In Doubtful, Breaksea and Long sounds the sea has penetrated as far as 35 km inland from the outer coastline.

Today, only small remnants of these great Ice Age glaciers remain, most of them hanging glaciers on the peaks of the Darran and Wick mountains. The climate, however, is still very wet, with annual precipitation (combined rain and snow) in some years as high as 9000 mm at sea level in Milford Sound. Fiordland averages more than 200 rain days each year and rainfall of more than 250 mm in one day is not uncommon. The precipitous landscape is capable of shedding this phenomenal amount of water very quickly, the rivers and waterfalls rising (and falling) at rapid rates. The vegetation, too, has adapted well to this extremely wet climate. The mountain soils are thin and, after prolonged periods of rainfall, entire slopes can collapse in debris avalanches – a soggy mass of rock, soil and vegetation.

Beech forests tend to dominate the park's landscape – silver beech seemingly everywhere from sea level to treeline in the wetter west; mountain beech on colder, higher sites; and even groves of large red beech trees on a few warmer and more fertile sites in the drier east (e.g. alongside the Milford Road as it passes through the Eglinton Valley). Yet

taller podocarp trees (especially rimu, kahikatea, Hall's totara and miro) are part of the forest canopy (or emerge above it) in many sheltered, lower-altitude parts of the park, especially the river flats at the head of most fiords, and the shores and islands of Lake Manapouri. The Waitutu coastal terraces, however, are the park's prime location for podocarp forest. East and west of the Waitutu River the mountains of Fiordland are replaced by the South Coast marine terraces, an internationally significant set of 11 ancient beaches progressively uplifted from sea level up to 1000 m altitude and across a band 10–15 km wide. Here competition between beech and podocarp species has produced one of the park's most fascinating botanical

Mt Pembroke (2015 m, left) and Mills Peak (1825 m, centre) stand above superb examples of U-shaped glaciated valleys, on the north side of Milford Sound/Piopiotahi.

mosaics. Dense rimu forests occupy the lower, coastal terraces; however, the higher terraces, which are the oldest and carry soils now heavily leached and degraded, are covered in a tangle of podocarp 'shrub trees' which are tolerant of low soil fertility and poor drainage – yellow-silver pine, silver pine and pink pine. Silver and mountain beech continue to re-invade these podocarp forests along the margins of rivers like the Wairaurahiri, which flows out from the mountainous interior (still a beech stronghold).

The alpine flora of Fiordland is especially rewarding to the visitor prepared to climb to the alpine parts of the park in late spring and early summer. The snow tussocks are a striking sight when in seed, and 14 of New Zealand's 33 species and subspecies of *Chionochloa* snow tussock are found in the park. Often the snow tussocks are interspersed with the sharp-leaved speargrasses (*Aciphylla* species), themselves one of the most diverse features of our alpine flora – Fiordland contains 12 of our 38 species of speargrass. Sustained helicopter hunting over the past decades has severely reduced the number of red deer and chamois, and flowers have returned as a spectacular summer feature of

Lake Manapouri, studded with forested islands, lies on the eastern margin of Fiordland National Park. Like the fiords to the west, the depression in which the lake lies was scoured out by ancient glaciers. Manapouri is the deepest (444 m) of the southern glacial lakes, with its lowest point 266 m below sea level.

the park's alpine herbfields. Some are very showy, like the great mountain buttercup (*Ranunculus lyallii*), the many mountain daisies (*Celmisia* and *Dolichoglottis*), the South Island edelweiss (*Leucogenes grandiceps*) and a wide variety of *Ourisia* species (several, like *O. macrocarpa*, with striking glossy leaves and purple stems). However, the recent

RIGHT A male yellow-crowned parakeet or kakariki (*Cyanoramphus auriceps*) in the red beech forest of Eglinton Valley, Fiordland National Park. Kakariki prefer to nest in holes in old trees, but they are vulnerable to predation by cats, stoats, and ship rats because they sometimes feed on the forest floor (ROD MORRIS). BELOW The endangered takahe or notornis (*Porphyrio mantelli*) is a large endemic rail weighing up to 3 kg. It was considered extinct until 1948 when Dr G. B. Orbell found them in the Murchison Mountains (and then in the Kepler and Stuart mountains) of Fiordland National Park. Their numbers in Fiordland declined so much during the 1960s and 1970s that a number of birds were transferred to establish small populations on Maud, Kapiti, Mana, and Tiritiri Matangi islands. Their total number throughout New Zealand is around 200.

ABOVE Looking into the fiord of Breaksea Sound, with the Gilbert Islands in the foreground. Close by, Breaksea Island and a number of small islands have been designated a 'special area' within Fiordland National Park as a result of a landmark conservation achievement – the eradication of Norway rats. Since 1992, a number of threatened species, such as South Island saddlebacks, yellowheads, and two rare weevil species, have been transferred successfully to the islands. LEFT The Fiordland crested penguin or tawaki (*Eudyptes pachyrhynchus*) is another endangered endemic inhabitant of the remote coastlines and islands of South Westland and Fiordland. They are one of the rarest penguins in the world, numbering only around 2000 pairs.

collapse of the helicopter deer hunting industry illustrates that the market can only be relied on for conservation gains in the short term; in the long term, Fiordland's alpine biota is under serious risk as deer numbers begin to build again.

Fiordland once had a full complement of forest and alpine birds, lizards and insects but its vast size and remoteness has conferred only limited protection to this biodiversity. Wildlife has steadily diminished over the past 200 years for a number of reasons. Early European explorers, sealers and miners introduced rats and mice. Stoats, deliberately introduced into rural New Zealand, stealthily colonised Fiordland from the east and north. And, since the 1970s, the Australian brush-tailed possum, which was introduced to New Zealand in the 19th century to establish a fur industry, has steadily penetrated Fiordland, assisted by bridges for tramper access. Because of its ability to selectively browse and kill off the vegetation, and eat insects, eggs and chicks, the possum has become a major pest. The poignant story of New Zealand's first conservation ranger, Richard Henry of Dusky Sound, who laboured tirelessly but in vain to protect flightless birds like kakapo and brown kiwi from stoats by ferrying them to a last-ditch sanctuary on Resolution Island, is now firmly entrenched as part of Fiordland's folklore.

However, the forests of Fiordland are still a rich habitat for many birds such as tui, bellbird, fantail, South Island robin, New Zealand pigeon, kakariki, blue duck/whio and South Island rifleman, but some of the most interesting birds are struggling for survival. DOC carefully manages the 200 remaining takahe, a rare, large, flightless rail now restricted to the Murchison and Stuart mountains west of Lake Te Anau. The kakapo is probably now extinct in mainland Fiordland, the last stragglers being captured and removed from the Esperance, Gulliver and Sinbad valleys in the Milford Sound catchment in the 1970s and transferred to safer island havens like Codfish Island/Whenua Hou off Stewart Island/Rakiura. Some kakapo were subsequently re-introduced to Chalky Island/Te Kakahu in Chalky Inlet in the hope that this will result in kakapo breeding again in Fiordland.

The marine environment of Fiordland is quite different from the rest of New Zealand. The deeply indented coastline has given rise to two contrasting environments:
• the exposed outer coastline, which is the preferred breeding habitat for fur seals and a wide range of ocean birds like petrels, prions, shearwaters and penguins;
• the sheltered, steep-walled fiords, which have a total shoreline length of nearly 1000 km, depths of up to 420 m, and a unique inversion of the usual pattern of coastal marine life.

Because of the large discharge of freshwater into a relatively calm fiord, the fresh water tends to float on the surface. This results in a distinct lack of shoreline seaweeds and shellfish but, on the other hand, there is a profusion of marine life below 5 m depth. The low-salinity water and the shadows cast by the steep walls of the fiords stop light penetrating far into the water. As a consequence, a fascinating variety of sea animals usually associated with darker water below 30 m depth can thrive at shallow levels. Colourful sponges, black corals, tubeworms, sea pens and sea stars line the walls of the fiords. The waters of the fiords are now known to support the world's largest population of black coral trees (about seven million colonies), some more than 5 m tall and estimated to be up to 300 years old.

Over 940,000 ha of Fiordland were protected as the Sounds Reserve as early as 1904, but it was not until the passing of the National Parks Act in 1952 that more than 1.2 million ha was finally designated as Fiordland National Park. But an overt threat to the integrity of the park – indeed, a threat to the whole concept of a national park being 'preserved in perpetuity' – soon emerged. Government intended raising the levels of Lakes Manapouri and Te Anau as part of a hydroelectricity scheme designed to provide power for Comalco's aluminium smelter at Bluff. The Manapouri controversy of 1965–1975 united a wide section of the New Zealand public in opposition to the raising of the lakes. The government and industry eventually capitulated; the Manapouri power scheme was built to accommodate natural lake levels, which were controlled within strict environmental guidelines determined by a watchdog group of Lake Guardians set up under special legislation. The wisdom of averting this environmental disaster is widely recognised today, for Fiordland National Park steadily increases in popularity, and sustainable tourism contributes significantly to the Southland economy.

However, the longest running conservation controversy was adjacent to the park's southern boundary, over the threat of the logging of the former Waitutu State Forest and the dense coastal terrace rimu forests owned by the Waitutu Incorporation (see above). The intrusion of logging roads would also have threatened the long-standing proposal for a Poteriteri–Waitutu Wilderness Area (see below). For decades the Waitutu Incorporation (consisting of around 800 individual Maori members) sought to achieve an income from these remote forests by selling the cutting rights to a succession of timber companies. Forest & Bird led a sustained campaign to convince government to purchase the cutting rights and negotiate a covenant (kawenata) with the owners which would link this internationally important landscape with the mountainous park interior. Resolution of this complex land issue was finally achieved in the late 1990s, in a way which recognised the need for the Maori owners and the Crown to work together in conserving such a priceless natural heritage. In October 1999, the 48,520 ha Waitutu stewardship land became the largest addition to the park in many years, and the Waitutu Incorporation's 2170 ha area of magnificent coastal podocarp forest (a 1.5 km wide strip of terraceland between the Wairaurahiri and Waitutu rivers) was retained in Maori title, but is now managed as if it were part of Fiordland National Park. Subsequently, the wider public were encouraged to gain an insight into the remarkable ecological and historical values of the Waitutu area by walking the newly-formed Hump Ridge Track, the enterprise of people in the local town of Tuatapere.

STEWART ISLAND/RAKIURA

Stewart Island/Rakiura (172,200 ha) remains the most accessible remnant of wild, pre-human New Zealand that most of us are able to experience. Tilting of the land has resulted in many deep, sheltered inlets along the eastern coastline – Paterson Inlet/Whaka a te Wera, Port Adventure, Lords River/Tutaekawetoweto and Port Pegasus/Pikihatiti. In contrast, on the north-western coastline exposed to the near-constant westerly winds, the aptly named Ruggedy Mountains sweep up to jagged crests 500 m above a coastline only a kilometre distant. The interior of the island is very rugged but not mountainous in the normal sense. The Mt Anglem/Hananui massif, the highest upland on the island, reaches an altitude of only 981 m. Other highlands around Mt Rakeahua and the Tin Range, Deceit Peaks and Fraser Peaks consist of granite rock, some of which has been weathered by a physical process called 'exfoliation' to produce a spectacular landscape of bare rock cones and domes. The best-known are Gog and Magog in the remote Fraser Peaks, and the Granite Knobs ranged along the south-eastern side of the Tin Range in the headwaters of the Robertson River.

The intact nature of its indigenous vegetation is the island's ecological glory, providing an unbroken green mantle from subalpine shrublands down to thick coastal forest.

A fascinating variety of sea animals, usually found at depths greater than 30 m, can be found in much shallower waters in the fiords. Examples are the black coral (top) and a sea anemone (above) found in Milford Sound/Piopiotahi.

ABOVE West Ruggedy Beach, Rakiura National Park. This wild coastline is traversed by the 125 km long North West Circuit Track; the entire trip around the northern part of Stewart Island taking most experienced parties 8–10 days. Inland lies the largely untracked wilderness of the Ruggedy Mountains and the Mt Anglem/Hananui massif. RIGHT The southern tokoeka (*Apteryx australis*) foraging for sand hoppers at Mason Bay, Stewart Island/Rakiura. This interesting bird was formerly known as the 'Stewart Island brown kiwi' but recent genetic research has shown that it is the same species as the Fiordland brown kiwi. A related subspecies, the Haast tokoeka (*A. australis* 'Haast'), occurs in South Westland. With all of mainland New Zealand's kiwi population suffering a steady decline, the southern tokoeka population of around 25,000 birds is probably diminishing at a slower rate (ROD MORRIS).

Rimu is the most common tree (although hardwood trees like kamahi and southern rata are also present), along with plentiful miro and totara, in what are the southernmost podocarp forests in New Zealand. Around Port Pegasus/ Pikihatiti and Doughboy Bay, the forest is lower in stature but very dense, with rimu still common but now joined by the smaller podocarp trees such as yellow-silver pine, pink pine, bog pine and pygmy pine. On exposed coasts with sandy, well-drained soils, the low forest is dominated by mutton-bird scrub, particularly puheretaiko (*Brachyglottis rotundifolia*) and other tough tree daisies and leatherwoods like tete-a-weka (*Olearia oporina*). The Mason Bay duneland, 15 km long in one magnificent sweep, is of national conservation importance because of its range of threatened plants, including the sand tussock *Austrofestuca littoralis*, a rare creeping herb *Gunnera hamiltonii*, and the shore spurge *Euphorbia glauca*.

The forests of Stewart Island/Rakiura are unusual in that a number of New Zealand's common tree species are absent. The most puzzling to ecologists is the lack of any species of beech (*Nothofagus*), even though the cool, moist conditions would seem to have favoured its survival during the Last Glaciation. The celery pines (*Phyllocladus*), and other members of the podocarp family, would usually thrive in the island's humid climate and peaty soils, but they too are absent, as are lemonwood/tarata, kanuka, mahoe and kowhai. The absence of beech accounts for the lack of a sharp treeline, usually such a common feature in most of the mountains of New Zealand. Instead, topography, soil depth and exposure to wind seem to be more important factors than altitude – for taller forest can survive in the sheltered gullies but an impenetrable low forest and shrubland of manuka, mountain leatherwood (*Olearia colensoi*), pink pine, mountain flax, pineapple scrub (*Dracophyllum menziesii*) and inaka (*D. longifolium*) covers the surrounding exposed ridges.

Stewart Island/Rakiura's significance as a habitat for certain terrestrial endangered species was dramatically confirmed in 1977 with the rediscovery of the country's only remaining viable population of the nocturnal ground parrot, kakapo. Because of serious predation by feral cats, all of the kakapo remaining in the low forest/shrublands around the head of the Robertson River, Deceit Peaks and Mt Rakeahua localities were relocated to Codfish Island/ Whenua Hou and other predator-free islands over the following 15 years. Stewart Island/Rakiura is also notable for the southern tokoeka, its own variety of the Fiordland brown kiwi. The tokoeka exhibits some unusual behaviour

The kakapo (*Strigops habroptilus*) is New Zealand's evolutionary oddity of the parrot family, and is the world's largest and rarest parrot. Its unusual features are its flightlessness, owl-like eye discs, solitary and nocturnal habits, lek breeding behaviour, and a strong musk-like smell similar to many mammals. Its main stronghold is on Codfish Island/ Whenua Hou off the north-west coast of Stewart Island/Rakiura.

compared with other kiwi on New Zealand's two main islands: both males and females are thought to forage in daylight, and the young birds do not disperse soon after hatching but tend to stay around for several months within a family grouping. Observing and listening to tokoeka is a delightful feature of any trip through the tussocklands and dunelands around Mason Bay. The island is fortunately still free of certain introduced animal pests such as stoats, ferrets, weasels, mice, goats and pigs, which have caused so much ecological damage elsewhere in the country. However, possums, rats, cats and white-tailed (Virginian) deer are present on the main island and have a detrimental effect on the wildlife and vegetation.

The Cathedral Caves, at the northern end of Waipati Beach, are among the many scenic and recreational attractions of the Catlins coastline.

The cold waters around Stewart Island/Rakiura have a remarkable density and diversity of seaweeds and some interesting species of shellfish. Paterson Inlet/Whaka a te Wera is probably the largest and most pristine sheltered, shallow-water harbour in New Zealand. The combination of hard rocks, peaty soils, relatively gentle topography and intact native vegetation has led to a lack of sediment in its waters. This has allowed a wide variety of seafloor life to flourish – sea cucumbers, sea urchins/kina, starfish and brachiopods – sometimes at depths of only 15–20 m. Around 270 species of seaweed (70 per cent of the seaweeds found around the entire island) are found in the inlet. The inlet is also notable as one of the richest and most accessible brachiopod habitats in the world. Brachiopods, or lamp shells, are a very ancient type of filter-feeding shellfish, 'living fossils' long extinct in most of the world's seas, supplanted in evolution by more modern bivalve molluscs like oysters and mussels.

The special character and conservation values of Stewart Island/Rakiura were recognised early by the strict protection of over 50 per cent of the island as nature reserves, with the huge southern wilderness of Pegasus Nature Reserve (67,400 ha) much larger than national parks like Abel Tasman, Egmont and Paparoa. Unified management and a strategic approach to the protection of the island's natural and historic heritage were compromised for decades because of acute fragmentation of the public land responsibilities among often competing government agencies (the then NZ Forest Service, Department of Lands and Survey, and NZ Wildlife Service). Only with the formation of the Department of Conservation in 1987 was the public land (95 per cent of the island) unequivocally protected for conservation. Interest re-awakened in the concept of a national park during the 1990s, so DOC and the NZ Conservation Authority consulted widely on the boundaries of such a Rakiura National Park. Eventually Rakiura became New Zealand's fourteenth national park, with an area of just under 140,000 ha (or 83 per cent of the island's area), in March 2002. However, protection of the outstanding marine life of Paterson Inlet/Whaka a Te Wera has been more difficult to achieve. The compromise Ulva Island/Te Wharawhara Marine Reserve (1075 ha) has been criticised as being too small in size and fragmented, so effective marine conservation is likely to depend on how well the surrounding Paterson Inlet/Whaka a Te Wera Mataitai Reserve is managed by tangata whenua and the Stewart Island community.

CATLINS COASTAL PARK

The Catlins is the colloquial name for the coastline and forested hills lying between the mouths of the Clutha/Mata-au and Mataura rivers. In landform terms, the Catlins is the coastal part of the South Otago uplands extending south-east of Gore and south-west of the Murihiku Escarpment (see above); a large block of NW–SE trending ridge and valley uplands with a pronounced trellis drainage pattern, so evident in topographic maps of this less-visited corner of the South Island. The attractiveness of the Catlins coastline is largely due to the alternating hard and soft rock bands: the former resisting the eroding onslaught of the sea and remaining as headlands like Nugget Point, Tautuku Peninsula and Chaslands Mistake; the latter eroding to the larger sandy bays like Tahakopa Bay, Tautuku Bay and Waipati Beach. Just about every imaginable small-scale coastal landform can be found along the rocky sections of this Catlins coast: 200 m high cliffs; caves, arches and blowholes; stacks, reefs and islets; and some interesting fossil beds.

Catlins Coastal Park is the term now used to describe about 55,000 ha of discontinuous blocks of conservation land throughout the Catlins. The two largest forest blocks are the Beresford Range (including Mt Pye, the highest point in the park at 720 m) enclosing the upper Maclennan River, and the Maclennan Range around the Tautuku River. Sadly, a century of forest clearance for farming in the Tahakopa, Waikawa and Mokoreta valleys, as well as controversial wood-chipping of private forests, has left the park a fragmented entity. However, it does protect the largest remaining area of lowland indigenous rainforest on the east coast of the South Island and the forest fragments fortunately contain a full altitudinal sequence of vegetation. For example, on the older dunes at Tautuku and Tahakopa bays the forest contains mature rimu, miro, totara and matai; there is pure silver beech forest in the Maclennan and Catlins valleys (marginally the southernmost beech forest in New Zealand); and a subalpine shrub/woodland of stunted kaikawaka, pink pine and *Dracophyllum longifolium* gives way to the red tussock and cushion plants of Ajax Bog at around 660 m altitude below Ajax Hill (700 m). The Catlins beech forests are the habitat of one of New Zealand's largest remaining population of yellowhead/mohua, a bird which is very susceptible to rat predation. As part of Operation Ark, an intensive network of 1080 poison bait stations on the ground (800 stations in 800 ha of forest) has proved very effective at killing off the rats in the lead-up to the birds' summer breeding season in 2006 (see Ch.16, p.308).

Compared to the largely untracked interior forests, the Catlins coastline is much more accessible and contains many scenic gems. These include:

- spectacular Nugget Point, with its prolific wildlife (seabirds including yellow-eyed penguins, New Zealand fur seals and New Zealand (Hooker's) sea lions;
- Lake Wilkie, a forest-fringed dune hollow lakelet just 400 m from Tautuku Beach;
- the coastal forest walks around Papatowai and Tautuku Beach, and Cathedral Caves at Waipati Beach;
- forest waterfalls, like Purakaunui, Matai and McLean falls;
- Curio Bay, with its 160-million-year-old fossil conifer forest exposed by wave action;
- the only place on the entire eastern coast of New Zealand (outside of Bushy Point in the New River Estuary of Invercargill) where the coastal vegetation sequence, from dune/estuary to forest, is intact.

EYRE–TAKITIMU MOUNTAINS

The Eyre Mountains lie between the Mavora Lakes and the southern arm of Lake Wakatipu, where they occupy an interesting ecological transition zone between the wet granite mountains of Fiordland National Park and the drier, schist block mountains of Central Otago. Although Jane Peak (2022 m) and Eyre Peak (1969 m) are the highest peaks in Southland outside Fiordland, the Eyre Mountains could be described as Southland's 'forgotten mountains',

The Eyre Mountains are the 'forgotten mountains' of Southland. They lie south and west of Lake Wakatipu (pictured) and have recently been protected as the Eyre Mountains/Taka Ra Haka Conservation Park.

for they did not attract much scientific or recreational interest until the past decade. The mountains are now considered of high conservation significance because they have been found to harbour quite a number of alpine plants lying at their geographic distribution limits or endemic to the area. These include species of *Hebe, Pimelea,* mountain daisy (*Celmisia*), mountain buttercup (*Ranunculus*), forget-me-not (*Myosotis*) and speargrass (*Aciphylla*). The Eyre Mountains also contain an important population of New Zealand falcon/karearea and the only rock wrens outside the Southern Alps/Ka Tiritiri o te Moana. Overall, the mountains still retain their remote character, despite their proximity to the tourist route between Queenstown and Te Anau. Southlanders have fortunately opposed any plans to open up their beech forests, free-flowing rivers and mountain crests to the increasing numbers of tourists

flocking to the southern lakes region. Their value for facility-free alpine and valley back-country tramping, fishing and hunting was secured in June 2005 when the four large blocks of conservation land in the southern Eyre Mountains (including much of the headwaters of the Oreti and Mataura rivers) were combined to form the 65,160 ha Eyre Mountains/Taka Ra Haka Conservation Park.

The Takitimu Mountains are a group of rugged peaks (up to 1600 m high), separated from Fiordland National Park by the wide Waiau Valley. Perhaps even more so than the Eyre Mountains, the Takitimus are 'transition mountains', for they harbour an assemblage of northern, southern, eastern and western alpine species. It was in the Takitimu Mountains in 1996 that climbers found the Takitimu gecko, *Hoplodactylus cryptozoicus*, a new species of alpine gecko. This discovery created a great deal of interest, and over the past decade there have been several other gecko discoveries in alpine habitats of the South Island. That geckos can be found in such harsh environments may be yet another example of relict species hanging on in isolated alpine localities after pests eradicated most of their population from more favourable but accessible lowland habitats.

Most of the Takitimu mountain range is protected within the 45,510 ha Takitimu Conservation Area. The range is of special cultural, historic and spiritual significance to Ngai Tahu iwi, and this importance is recognised by a topuni (a mantle signifying their mana) placed over the range. The name of the mountains is derived from the great migration waka, *Takitimu*, to commemorate its foundering at the mouth of the Waiau River in nearby Te Waewae Bay. Like the Eyre Mountains, the Takitimu Mountains retain a wild and isolated character, with only limited tracking and modest 2–6 bunk back-country huts. Their mosaic of scattered remnants of beech forest, tussock grassland, shrubland and rock scree provides plenty of scope for tramping, rock-climbing, hunting and trout fishing.

THREATS AND FUTURE CONSERVATION PRIORITIES

Southland's Islands: a Haven for Survival of Threatened Wildlife

A number of islands lying off Fiordland and the Stewart Island/Rakiura coastline are crucial sanctuaries for some of our most endangered fauna. The progressive eradication of pests like rats, possums and stoats from these islands over the past 20 years has entailed enormous effort on the part of DOC staff and volunteers. The landmark poisoning campaign during 1988–1991 to clear Norway rats from the rugged 170 ha Breaksea Island in Fiordland National Park was heralded as an outstanding conservation success; it recreated a refuge for a wide range of endangered animals – saddlebacks, yellowheads/mohua, Fiordland skinks and insects like rare weevils. Experience gained on Breaksea gave DOC confidence to undertake a very ambitious and complex operation during 1998 – the removal of Pacific rats/ kiore from the much larger (1400 ha) Codfish Island/ Whenua Hou off Stewart Island/Rakiura. (The NZ Wildlife Service had already eradicated possums from the island by 1987.) The poisoning operation, however, involved the prior removal of all resident kakapo and most fernbirds

to other rat-free islands. But the intensive Codfish Island/ Whenua Hou project paid major conservation dividends in the summer of 2002 when the best breeding year in the 20 years of the kakapo recovery programme resulted in the hatching of an unprecedented 24 kakapo chicks. Now, after the mixed results of a couple of decades of experimenting with northerly islands like Maud and Little Barrier, DOC has settled on Codfish/Whenua Hou and another island – Chalky/Te Kakahu at the entrance to Chalky Inlet in Fiordland – as key habitats for the survival and recovery of this most endearing and curious of parrots.

The removal of rats from Ulva Island in Paterson Inlet/ Whaka a Te Wera has allowed it to be designated as an 'open sanctuary', where the re-introduction of saddleback, yellowhead, rifleman and robin has made this island gem a popular destination for visitors. DOC's rat eradication programme around Stewart Island/Rakiura is continuing, currently with Bench and Pearl islands, the latter being the first island where the elimination of all three rat species (Norway, ship and Pacific) has been attempted. A healthy partnership between Ngai Tahu iwi and DOC has also led to kiore being removed from many of the Titi Islands, and planning is well advanced for eradicating ship rats from Taukihepa/Big South Cape Island. This large privately-owned island was the site of one of New Zealand's worst ecological calamities when ship rats were accidentally introduced in the early 1960s. They rapidly increased to plague proportions, completely wiping out the last remnants of three endemic species — the greater short-tailed bat, Stead's bush wren and the Stewart Island snipe.

In recent years animal ecologists have also developed greater awareness of the devastating predatory impact of stoats on our endangered wildlife. By careful management (and some incredibly good fortune) Stewart Island/Rakiura has remained mustelid free, but this is far from the case for the islands around the Fiordland coastline. DOC has initiated stoat control on 29 of the smaller Fiordland islands and, since 1998, has eliminated them from three of the largest – Anchor (1280 ha), Chalky/Te Kakahu (511 ha) and Bauza (480 ha). The extra resources supplied by government through the adoption of the New Zealand Biodiversity Strategy has meant that from late 2004 DOC has been able to undertake the ecological restoration of Secretary Island, the second largest island in Fiordland at 8140 ha. This island has probably the most diverse range of habitats of all of Fiordland's islands because its 1196 m summit is well above the bushline; it is also free of rats and mice, with stoats and deer the two pests targeted for eradication. Because of its proximity to the mainland, it will have to be continually monitored to guard against any deer and stoats which may swim back to the island. DOC's successes have now inspired the first privately-funded island restoration project in Fiordland: the clearing of stoats and deer from Coal Island at the entrance to Preservation Inlet through the efforts of the SWNZ Endangered Species Trust. Perhaps in a few more years we may be able to witness the eradication of rats, stoats and deer from the largest of Fiordland's hundreds of islands, 20,870 ha Resolution Island. A pest-free Resolution Island is a very important conservation goal because of its large size as a wildlife sanctuary, its diversity of forest habitats and its excellent stream habitat for blue duck/whio.

Threats to the Wilderness Areas in Fiordland and Rakiura National Parks

Southland shares with the West Coast the outstanding wilderness landscapes of New Zealand. There are two designated wilderness areas within Fiordland National Park – Pembroke (18,000 ha, centred on Mt Pembroke in the northern Darran Mountains) and Glaisnock (125,000 ha of the Franklin and Stuart mountains). A long-standing proposal for a third large wilderness area in the south-west sector of the park, between Preservation Inlet and Lake Poteriteri, was refined by Federated Mountain Clubs of NZ and the Wilderness Advisory Group in the early 1980s. For many years the Waitutu Forest controversy stopped a final resolution of such a Southern Fiordland (Poteriteri-Waitutu) Wilderness Area. After 25 years of procrastination, vested tourist and hunting interests have become well established, and the wilderness area proposal has been gutted in the 2006 Fiordland National Park management plan by eliminating Lakes Poteriteri and Hakapoua from the proposal and moving the boundaries further to the west to give a much shrunken South-West Wilderness Area.

Pembroke Wilderness Area in the northern Darran Mountains suffers from the increasing noise pollution of tourist overflights en route to Milford airstrip. Milford airstrip has averaged 17,000 air movements per annum over the past 10 years, and on fine days this results in an incessant drone intruding upon the natural quiet of the wilderness area. Because regular bad weather restricts flights to 200–250 relatively fine days each year, the landings and take-offs can be as high as 200 per day – a level of air traffic which is about half of that at Christchurch International Airport! In addition, DOC and the Southland Conservation Board have further compromised the wilderness area by allowing up to 500 aircraft landings per year on the Ngapunatoru Plateau in the shadow of Mt Tutoko, the snowfield on the boundary of the wilderness area. And even more unfathomable, the park management plan will now allow helicopter landings for nine months of the year at Turners Bivvy on the upper slopes of Mt Tutoko – an action which shows a hypocritical disdain for the spirit of the topuni over Mt Tutoko, agreed to with Ngai Tahu.

A Pegasus Wilderness Area of around 63,000 ha was also proposed for the southern sector of Stewart Island/Rakiura by Federated Mountain Clubs of NZ in the early 1980s (and subsequently endorsed by the Wilderness Advisory Group), to protect the wild, remote landscape south of the Rakeahua River and inland from Port Pegasus/Pikihatiti. Since then, these highlands around the Tin Range and Deceit and Fraser peaks have been managed by DOC as a wilderness zone (or *de facto* wilderness area). With the formation of Rakiura National Park in March 2002, there seems to be no remaining reason to delay the Pegasus Wilderness Area becoming a *de jure* reality.

Limiting the Impact of Tourism around Milford Sound

In 2006 Fiordland National Park received more than half a million visitors, most of them day visitors attracted to the scenic grandeur of Milford and Manapouri. Increasingly the environs of Milford Sound are under environmental stress, primarily from the congestion, aircraft noise and pollution associated with tourism, which is growing too fast. In 1992 the number of visitors to Milford Sound was 247,000 annually; by 2004 this had almost doubled to 470,000. The World Heritage values of this iconic site are being insidiously eroded, diminishing not only the scenic experiences on the Sound itself, but also the naturalness of the long drive along the Milford Road and the enjoyment of walkers on the Milford Track. The management authorities, DOC and the Southland Conservation Board may have put up a brave fight but have shied away from the radical step of simply limiting the number of visitors. Instead, the 2006 Fiordland National Park management plan displays a naively optimistic faith that this type of exponential growth can be maintained at the same time as preserving the World Heritage values and the quality of the visitor's experience. Certainly, some of the mitigating actions suggested – better impact research, spreading the timing of peak visitor flows to reduce congestion, encouraging less noisy/higher-capacity aircraft – will help. But the overwhelming impression for most New Zealanders who have witnessed this growth phenomenon elsewhere is that Milford is going to be another casualty of the New Zealand

tourism economic boom, an icon which is rapidly becoming tarnished and will end up a tawdry commercial tourism *entrepot* like Rotorua, Queenstown and Franz Josef village.

Gog (foreground) and Magog, two of the most spectacular granite domes in the remote and untracked Fraser Peaks in southern Stewart Island/Rakiura. This wild landscape is the heart of the proposed Pegasus Wilderness Area.

Incorporating the Fiord Marine Life within Te Wahipounamu WHA

The fiords are an integral part of the Fiordland landscape and ecosystem. Yet, incredibly, they were excised from Fiordland National Park in the early 1960s and were not included when Fiordland National Park was listed as a natural World Heritage site in 1986. When the World Heritage Committee listed the park, it recommended the New Zealand government 'note the importance of the waters of the fiords as an integral part of the area and welcome any initiatives to bring them under the control of the park authorities'.

But, formal protection of the natural heritage of the Fiordland marine zone has been lamentably slow. In June 2003, the 'Fiordland Marine Conservation Strategy' was published by the Guardians of Fiordland's Fisheries and Marine Environment, a widely representative stakeholder group of commercial and recreational fishers, Ngai Tahu whanui, boat charter operators, government agencies, and community, environment and marine science interests. The strategy was given legal standing in the Fiordland Marine Management Bill in 2005 which, *inter alia,* created eight new marine reserves in: Sutherland Sound, Bligh Sound, Gold Arm of Charles Sound, Gaer Arm of Bradshaw

Sound, Malaspina Reach of Doubtful Sound, Wet Jacket Arm, Dusky Sound (between Five Fingers Peninsula and Resolution Island), and Long Sound of Preservation Inlet. These marine reserves, however, seem to have been chosen to avoid areas of high biodiversity, especially the outer fiords and open coast – presumably to avoid conflict with commercial fishing.

With these legal measures adopted to increase the protection of the Fiordland marine environment, the entire marine area within the fiords should be added to New Zealand's tentative list of potential World Heritage sites – an addition which would greatly enhance the ecological integrity of Te Wahipounamu (South West New Zealand) World Heritage Area.

The Threat of Didymo to the South Island's Rivers

In October 2004 a very serious biosecurity risk to the health of New Zealand's wild rivers was first recognised in Southland's Mararoa and upper Waiau rivers. The didymo alga (*Didymosphenia geminata*) is a highly invasive organism native to Europe, from where it spread to North America. New Zealand is the only Southern Hemisphere country in which it has been recorded. By November 2005 it had spread to, or was already present in, the Oreti, the Von, Hawea and upper Clutha/Mata-au in Otago, and the Buller in North Westland; by late 2006 it had reached the Takaka River in Golden Bay, thus posing a real threat to one of New Zealand's iconic freshwater features – Waiko-ropupu Springs.

Didymo poses an extremely serious threat to 70 per cent of the rivers in the South Island and to the rivers of the North Island's central volcanic plateau and axial ranges. There are currently no known methods for control or eradication of didymo in the river environment, and its natural pathways for spreading cannot be controlled. Transfer by humans engaged in recreational or commercial activity in these infected rivers is probably the biggest problem. In Southland, DOC and Fish and Game moved quickly to establish special fishing controls for the rivers of Fiordland National Park, and Biosecurity New Zealand belatedly undertook an awareness campaign to contain it. But there is no way of getting the didymo genie back in the bottle – it is here forever: another environmental cost New Zealand has to suffer as the inevitable downside of burgeoning tourist arrivals.

Mitre Peak (1683 m) reflected in the waters of Milford Sound/Piopiota-hi. The tranquility of this iconic landscape is being seriously threatened by congestion on the Milford Road and the incessant noise of tourist sightseeing aircraft.

CHAPTER FOURTEEN

CHATHAM ISLANDS AND SUBANTARCTIC ISLANDS

Far to the east and south of the New Zealand mainland lie the Chatham, Auckland, Campbell and Antipodes island groups, seeming mere specks of land in the South Pacific Ocean. In reality they are part of a vast underwater plateau of Triassic-age rocks which underlie New Zealand. This continent-sized landmass, often called 'Zealandia' by geologists, broke away from the super-continent of Gondwana more than 80 million years ago. Today, the islands are far-flung castles of land standing boldly above turbulent seas, remote sentinels marking the outer south-eastern limits of New Zealand's territory and its biogeographic domain. They are generally treated as two distinct groupings: the Chatham Islands and the New Zealand subantarctic islands.[1] An important distinction between the two is human habitation: the Chatham Islands have been settled for more than 500 years, whereas all attempts to settle the subantarctic islands have failed, and their paramount importance for biodiversity conservation has been recognised by their protection as both nature and national reserves.

CHATHAM ISLANDS

The remote Chatham Islands are quite unlike the rest of New Zealand. The archipelago lies 850 km east of Christchurch and consists of:

- two main islands (Chatham/Rekohu, 90,650 ha; and Pitt/Rangiauria, 6,326 ha);

- two smaller islands (Southeast/Rangatira, 218 ha; and Mangere, 113 ha);
- numerous islets and stacks, many of which are important habitats for seabirds.

The islands are unlikely to have been connected to New Zealand in the last few million years, but their plants and animals have a biogeographic affinity with the mainland (although their long isolation has resulted in very pronounced changes). Indeed, of all New Zealand's outlying islands, the Chathams show the greatest degree of endemism in their flora and fauna. The oceanic location of the islands accounts for their depressing climate: constant winds, squalls, sea mists, and sunshine levels so low that they are little more than half the average of the New Zealand mainland. But it is these same environmental forces – the ubiquitous presence of water, and winds driving the ever-changing light – which contribute to the visual charm of the Chathams' landscape and seascape.

Chatham Island/Rekohu has an interesting topography, nowhere higher than 300 m above sea level and everywhere studded with lakes strung like a necklace around the island's main feature, Te Whanga Lagoon. The lagoon is an old embayment, cut off from the surrounding Pacific Ocean as sand spits accumulated, forming one of New Zealand's largest (18,000 ha) and least-modified saltwater lagoons, a haven for fish and migratory wading birds. A line of small volcanic cones stands out across the northern end of the island; far to the south, the undulating southern tablelands are likewise of volcanic origin but are now deeply covered with peat. These southern tablelands are the wildest part of the island, terminating in an impressive bank

[1] Strictly speaking, the environment of these islands is cool–temperate because they lie well north of the Antarctic Convergence and have a mean annual air temperature above 5°C, which is sufficient to allow the growth of some trees and other woody plants. Nevertheless, they are commonly referred to as New Zealand's 'subantarctic' islands.

Shy mollymawks (*Diomedea cauta*) nesting on the cliffs near South West Cape, Auckland Island.

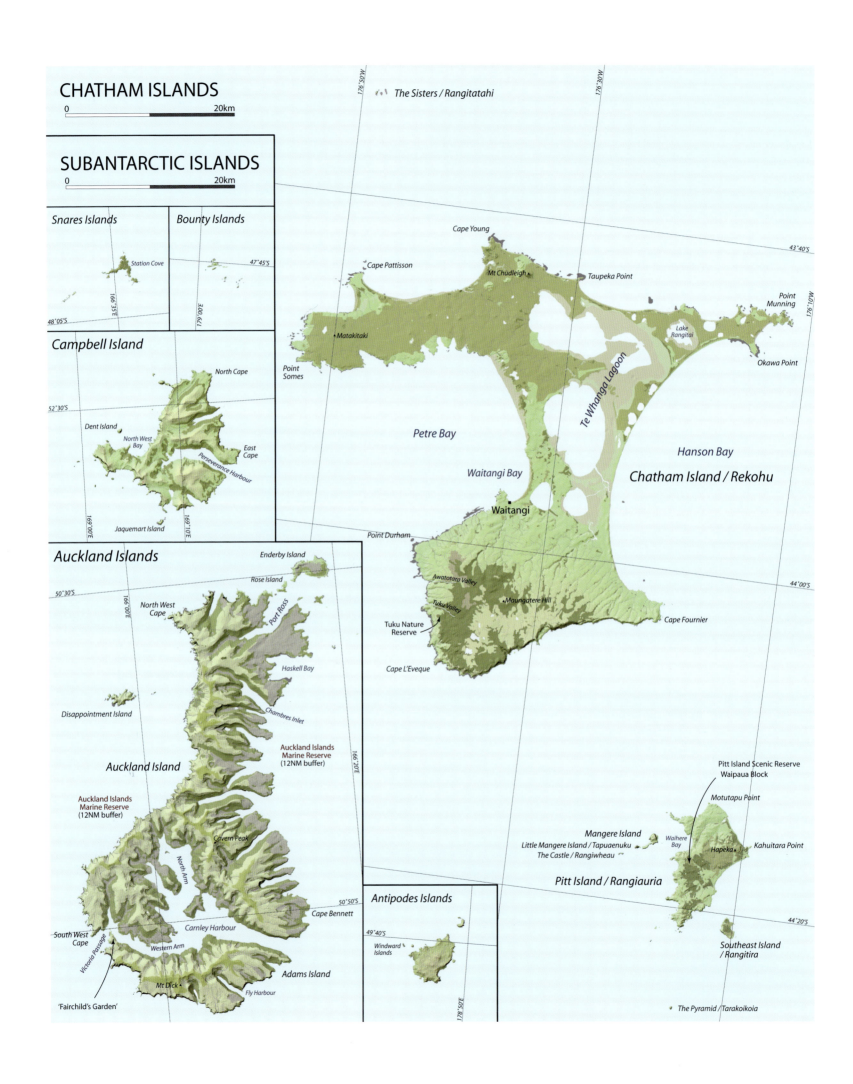

CHATHAM ISLANDS

0 |———————————| 20km

SUBANTARCTIC ISLANDS

0 |———————————| 20km

Snares Islands

Station Cove

47°45'S

166°35'E

Bounty Islands

179°00'E

48°05'S

Campbell Island

North Cape

52°30'S

Dent Island

North West Bay

Perseverance Harbour

East Cape

Jaquemart Island

169°00'E · 169°10'E

Auckland Islands

Enderby Island

Rose Island

50°30'S

North West Cape

Port Ross

Haskell Bay

Chambres Inlet

Disappointment Island

Auckland Island

Auckland Islands Marine Reserve (12NM buffer)

Auckland Islands Marine Reserve (12NM buffer)

Cavern Peak

North Arm

166°00'E · 166°20'E

South West Cape

Victoria Passage

Western Arm

Carnley Harbour

Cape Bennett

50°50'S

Mt Dick

'Fairchild's Garden'

Fly Harbour

Adams Island

Antipodes Islands

49°40'S

Windward Islands

178°50'E

176°50'W · 176°30'W

The Sisters / Rangitatahi

Cape Young

43°40'S

176°10'W

Cape Pattisson

Mt Chudleigh

Taupeka Point

Point Munning

Matakitaki

Lake Rangitai

Okawa Point

Point Somes

Te Whanga Lagoon

Petre Bay

Hanson Bay

Waitangi Bay

Chatham Island / Rekohu

Waitangi

Point Durham

Awatotara Valley

44°00'S

Tuku Valley

Maungatere Hill

Tuku Nature Reserve

Cape Fournier

Cape L'Eveque

Pitt Island Scenic Reserve Waipaua Block

Motutapu Point

Mangere Island

Little Mangere Island / Tapuaenuku

The Castle / Rangiwheau

Waihere Bay

Hapeka

Kahuitara Point

Pitt Island / Rangiauria

44°20'S

Southeast Island / Rangitira

The Pyramid / Tarakoikoia

of 200 m high cliffs extending for 30 km. The southern tablelands carry the most extensive remaining forests on the islands, especially in the Tuku and Awatotara catchments. These forests are a habitat of critical importance for two of the world's most endangered birds: the Chatham Islands pigeon/parea and the magenta petrel/taiko.

Pitt Island/Rangiauria has the Chathams' last areas of original rocky coast vegetation, as well as some of the group's best mature broadleaved forest. Pitt is free of rats and possums and is the second largest (after Fiordland's Secretary Island) rat-free temperate-zone island in the world. If the remaining pests are removed from a network of fenced protected areas in the central and southern parts, Pitt Island has the potential to be the key site for the long-term survival of most Chatham Island threatened species. Nearby, Mangere and Southeast Island/Rangatira are inaccessible islands ringed with sheer cliffs. Both are nature reserves, free from mammalian predators, and consequently support dense breeding colonies of seabirds. Mangere Island is the main habitat for the endangered Chatham Island yellow-crowned parakeet (also known as Forbes' parakeet) and the rare Dieffenbach's spaniard, *Aciphylla dieffenbachii*, and it played a key part in saving one of New Zealand's iconic birds, the endemic Chatham Islands black robin. Incredibly, a tiny population of 20–30 black robins had managed to survive in about 6 ha of scrub forest on the summit of tiny, sheer-cliffed Little Mangere Island/Tapuaenuku for nearly a century after predators eliminated the birds from the rest of the Chathams. Rangatira Island is one of New Zealand's most important island sanctuaries, for it is the main habitat for the Chatham Island subspecies of snipe, tomtit, tui and red-crowned parakeet, and is the only breeding site for the rare Chatham Islands petrel. Four small outlying island groups – Star Keys/Motuhope, The Pyramid/Tarakoikoia, The Sisters/Rangitatahi and the Forty Fours/Motuhara – are breeding grounds for albatross, mollymawks and giant petrels.

The native vegetation of the Chatham Islands is vaguely reminiscent of New Zealand but it is particularly interesting because of the absence of the usual forest trees (like the familiar beech and podocarp species, as well as common coastal trees like rata, kohekohe and tawa). Consequently, the limited number of hardy, woody shrubs that managed to migrate across this oceanic barrier tended to evolve into gigantic forms. For instance, akeake (*Olearia traversii*) grows to 15 m tall, and is the largest of New Zealand's many tree daisies – indeed, it is probably the largest tree daisy in the world. Likewise, common New Zealand

The sanctuary islands of The Castle (left), Little Mangere (centre, partly obscured) and Mangere (right) from above Waihere Bay, Pitt Island.

shrub genera such as hebe and coprosma have evolved tree forms like *Hebe barkeri* and *Coprosma chathamica* on the islands. Another example is tarahinau (*Dracophyllum arboreum*), its Latin descriptor denoting the treelike form (up to 12 m high) of this Chatham-endemic member of a genus which otherwise occurs as shrubs in the montane environment of mainland New Zealand. In all, 42 species and subspecies of the higher plants (or 11 per cent of the Chatham Islands' total) are endemic. This number includes two very attractive megaherbs – the blue-flowered Chatham Islands forget-me-not (*Myosotidium hortensia*) and the purple Chatham Island sow thistle (*Embergeria grandifolia*), each the only species known in these genera.

The Chathams' marine environment is distinctive and of great economic significance, although it was plundered during the crayfish boom of the late 1960s. The islands lie on the Subtropical Convergence, where the mixing of the warm subtropical and cold subantarctic currents over the Chatham Rise produces a highly productive marine food chain. The waters around the islands are nutrient-rich and clear (because of the lack of any significant sediment run-off from the land); this accounts for the abundant fish stocks and numerous coastal or open-sea birds. The marine fauna is not yet fully known but is considered to be a diverse and unique assemblage, quite different from central New Zealand's but with similar elements to those of

TOP The Chatham Island pipit (*Anthus novaesee-landiae chathamensis*) is one of four subspecies of the New Zealand pipit, two being on the New Zealand mainland and the Antipodes Islands, with the fourth subspecies on both the Auckland and Campbell islands. They are common throughout the Chatham Islands where the large expanse of open country seems to suit them. MIDDLE The white-faced storm petrel (*Pelagodroma marina maoriana*) breeds in the Chatham Islands, especially on Southeast Island/Rangatira where the largest colony (around one million breeding pairs) in the New Zealand region occurs. BOTTOM This immature New Zealand shore plover (*Thinornis no-vaeseelandiae*) is one of a small colony of 100–140 birds on Southeast Island/Rangatira. This endemic bird is endangered because it is very vulnerable to predators like cats, and efforts to try and establish other island colonies from birds raised in captivity have had mixed success.

LEFT The saving of the black robin (*Petroica traversi*) by the NZ Wildlife Service (and subsequently DOC) is one of the world's outstanding avian conservation success stories, now part of New Zealand's biodiversity conservation folklore. In 1976, the entire remaining population of seven birds was transferred from inaccessible Little Mangere Island to a better habitat on Mangere Island. Since that time intensive management and further transfers to Southeast Island/Rangitira have boosted the population to around 250, although their status is still endangered (ROD MORRIS).

BELOW The Pitt Island shag (*Stictocarbo featherstoni*) is widespread, with around 600 pairs on Chatham/Rekohu and Pitt/Rangiauria islands and other small islands in the group. They mostly feed in coastal waters up to 20 m deep but are also found feeding in the brackish waters of Te Whanga Lagoon.

CLOCKWISE FROM TOP LEFT Forest interior, Southeast Island/Rangitira. The endemic Chatham Island snipe (*Coenocorypha pusilla*) on Southeast Island/Rangitira. The Chatham Island tree daisy or keketerehe (*Olearia chathamica*) is a spectacular shrubby tree, which has been reduced to remnants on inaccessible cliffs by farming and feral animals. The buff weka (*Gallirallus australis hectori*) was introduced to the Chatham Islands in 1905 before it became extinct in Canterbury and the eastern South Island. The Chatham Island forget-me-not (*Myosotidium hortensia*) is the most impressive of the island's megaherbs, so much so that it is now widely grown in gardens throughout mainland New Zealand (ROD MORRIS).

northern and southern New Zealand. Notable Chatham marine features include:

- seven seaweeds endemic to the islands;
- giant kelp 'forests', including an endemic bull kelp, *Durvillaea chathamensis*;
- numerous paua and kina and more than 90 species of starfish, sea cucumbers and sea urchins;
- more than 300 species of fish.

Fur seals probably number more than 2000, and other marine mammals, such as sea leopards and sea elephants, are infrequent visitors. One puzzling marine mammal phenomenon is the regular stranding of pilot whales (known locally as blackfish) on the beaches around Waitangi Bay on the western side of Chatham Island.

NEW ZEALAND'S SUBANTARCTIC ISLANDS

The subantarctic islands are the remotest and wildest fragments of New Zealand (see Overview map and p.268). Five separate island groups are included:

- the Auckland Islands (62,560 ha) are by far the largest;
- the Campbell Island group (11,331 ha) and the Antipodes Islands (2,097 ha) are quite significant in size;
- the Snares are much smaller (328 ha) and are the closest to the mainland of New Zealand (209 km from Bluff);
- the remote Bounty Islands, just 135 ha in total area, are mere wave-washed rocky specks in the vast Southern Ocean.

All are true oceanic islands, none having been connected to the New Zealand mainland during the Ice Ages. What they lack in size, however, they more than make up for in biological importance, for along with Australia's Macquarie Island they are the only land in the Pacific sector of the Southern Ocean. Consequently they are of international conservation significance as breeding grounds and haul-out havens for the millions of seabirds and thousands of marine mammals that inhabit the cold waters around Antarctica.

The subantarctic islands have a colourful history – an epic saga of seal slaughter, failed settlements and farming, shipwrecks and whaling. In particular, the Auckland Islands were (and still are) a major obstacle for mariners, and more than 100 lives have been lost from at least eight shipwrecks on their rocky, cliffed coastline. The bravery and resilience of shipwreck castaways forced to survive in such a hostile and lonely environment until they could be rescued is a celebrated aspect of the islands' dramatic human history. Today, the subantarctic islands do not support any permanent human settlements, although DOC maintains seasonal field stations on all except the Bounty Islands.

All five island groups lie on the Campbell Plateau, a wide submarine platform with relatively shallow waters up to 1000 m deep. Their geological make-up varies, however. The Snares and Bounties are composed of granite, reflecting the underlying continental nature of the Campbell Plateau (and the wider Zealandia underwater continent – see Ch.1, p.11). The Auckland Islands, Antipodes Islands and Campbell Island have their basement rocks overlaid with very old volcanic landforms. These are recognisable in the caldera of Carnley Harbour, the spectacular cliffs of Adams Island and Campbell Island, and the many erosion-resistant volcanic plugs like the stacks of the Windward Islands off the western coast of the Antipodes. These three volcanic island groups are quite high islands compared with the Chatham Islands, with the main ridge-crests of Campbell Island and the Auckland Islands lying between 400 m and 650 m above sea level. Indeed, Campbell and the Auckland islands are high enough to retain an impressive range of glacial landforms dating from the Ice Ages: cirques, U-shaped valleys, fiords, moraines, and periglacial topography where sediments are exposed (such as raised beach gravels).

The climate of the subantarctic islands is indescribably bleak – even bleaker, in fact, than the Chathams'. The islands lie in latitudes known to mariners as the Roaring Forties and Furious Fifties, and are swept incessantly by strong wet westerly winds; over the entire year the winds scouring Campbell Island have a mean hourly speed of more than 30 km/h. Nineteenth-century sailing ships sought out these winds as they plied these latitudes from west to east, and today's round-the-world yacht racers likewise strike far into southern waters to capitalise on the winds' constancy and speed.

While the islands' annual rainfall, at 1200–1800 mm, is not high compared with much of mainland New Zealand, it is remarkably constant, with precipitation on more than 300 days of the year. Consequently, sunshine is very limited; Campbell Island, for example, has only 660 hours of sunshine annually, a mere third of that in Christchurch. Over thousands of years, the cool, moist climate has induced a mantle of peat, blanketing all the islands (except the soil-less Bounty group) to a thickness of 1–5 m.

The vegetation of the islands is montane in character,

RIGHT Enderby Island in the Auckland Islands group is one of the four main breeding sites for the New Zealand (or Hooker's) sea lion (*Phocarctos hookeri*). Their total population in the Auckland Islands is around 15,000. This harem of females, some of them with pups, is under the watchful eye of a 'beachmaster' bull sea lion. BELOW An adult Antipodean wandering albatross (*Diomedea exulans antipodensis*) flying at sea. This magnificent bird breeds mainly on the Antipodes Islands (with a few nests on Campbell Island), where 10,000 pairs breed (5000 each alternate year). Their main food is squid, so their numbers have been severely reduced due to entanglement in long lines baited with squid by boats fishing for tuna (ROD MORRIS).

LEFT A sooty shearwater or titi (*Puffinus griseus*) off the Snares Islands. Sooty shearwaters are circumpolar and are estimated to number more than 20 million. They have breeding colonies on islands off Stewart Island/Rakiura, the Chatham Islands, and the New Zealand subantarctic islands. The largest colony in the New Zealand region is around 3 million on the Snares (ROD MORRIS). BELOW Thousands of Snares crested penguins (*Eudyptes robustus*) navigate the 'Penguin Slope' near their Station Cove landing place. This endemic penguin only breeds at the Snares Islands where there are around 25,000 pairs in more than 100 colonies.

and the flora has developed in deep, peaty soils which are acidic and of low fertility, except where burrowing seabirds have aerated and enriched the soil. Both climate and soils have suited the development of a moorland of tussocks across the islands' rolling summits. On Campbell and the Auckland Islands the tussocklands consist of *Chionochloa antarctica*, a species from the same genus as the New Zealand mainland snow tussocks; on the Snares and Antipodes the tussocklands are a mixture of *Poa* species. Within the grasslands there are many large megaherbs which bring so much colour and character to the island landscapes. Most belong to familiar genera, like *Anisotome* (carrot family), *Celmisia* (daisy family), *Gentiana* (gentian family) and *Myosotis* (forget-me-not family), but here they are often endemic species with large and/or brightly coloured leaves and flowers. In late spring these herbfields are an amazing

Carnley Harbour, which separates Auckland Island (foreground) from Adams Island, is the sea-breached caldera of the southernmost of two ancient volcanoes that formed the Auckland Islands.

sight, even to people familiar with the flowering profusion of the mainland's alpine fellfields. In the Southern Alps/ Ka Tiritiri o te Moana and Fiordland the alpine flowers are generally white, or pale mauve or yellow, and many of the most palatable plants are now restricted to inaccessible ledges where they cannot be reached by introduced deer, chamois, hares and thar. But here in the mist-drenched herbfields, like the remarkable Fairchild's Garden on Adams Island (Auckland group), the colours are more vibrant. There are the blue-flowered *Myosotis antarctica* and *Hebe benthamii*; a delightful range of pink, mauve, red, deep brown and purple abounds in the spectacular species of

Pleurophyllum (an endemic genus of megaherb in the daisy family), and in other plants like *Anisotome antipoda, Gentianella concinna* and *Damnamenia vernicosa*. Some of the megaherbs – the several species of *Stilbocarpa*, for example – are as attractive for their large glossy leaves as for their flowers.

Campbell Island and the Auckland Islands have some of the southernmost forests in the world, but there are none of the tall conifers and beech trees of the mainland. Dwarf forests of southern rata and *Dracophyllum* are enfolded in sheltered coastal gullies of the Auckland Islands. This distinctive forest has a tight canopy because of the constant winds, while the tree trunks are gnarled into a fantastic variety of forms, and the peaty ground surface is largely free of shrubs. On Campbell Island the 5 m high dwarf montane forest consists mainly of hardy *Dracophyllum* and

Fly Harbour, on the exposed south-eastern side of Adams Island, is a perfect little fiord where the retreating glacier has left a cirqued head-wall (immediately below the photographer) and the sea has invaded the U-shaped trough left by the glacier.

Coprosma species. Overall, the diversity of higher plants on the different subantarctic islands is roughly proportional to their size. For instance, the Auckland group has nearly 200 native taxa; Campbell Island 128; the Antipodes group 68; and the much smaller Snares group only 20. The tiny Bounty Islands, although of significance for breeding seals and seabirds, are botanically little more than a group of lichen-covered rocks. Although significant, the degree of plant endemism in the New Zealand subantarctic islands (as well as Macquarie Island) is not as great as that of the Chatham Islands.

The herbfields of 'Fairchild's Garden' at the north-western tip of Adams Island are a botanical wonderland. Adams Island is one of only a handful of New Zealand's islands to have remained free from the destructive impact of introduced grazing herbivores which have so modified our flora. RIGHT The yellow flower heads of the megaherb *Bulbinella rossii*. BELOW Two of the most spectacular of the subantarctic islands' megaherbs – (left) *Anisotome latifolia*, a giant herb member of the carrot family, and (right) *Stilbocarpa polaris*, which can grow up to 2 metres across.

LEFT The impressive volcanic cliffs around South West Cape of Auckland Island. BELOW The twisted trunks of stunted southern rata trees on Enderby Island, the understorey trampled regularly by the large numbers of Hooker's sea lions resident on the island.

Seabirds and marine mammals are the outstanding coastal wildlife feature throughout the subantarctic islands, although the limited land bird fauna is interesting because of its high level of endemism. In all, 14 endemic land birds are known within the islands; however, all except one of them (the Antipodes Island parakeet) are considered sub-species derived from land birds blown to the islands from Stewart Island/Rakiura or Australia. Campbell Island is an outstanding habitat for albatrosses (five species), especially the southern royal albatross. Penguins are a highly visible feature of the coastal wildlife. Four species – the yellow-eyed, Snares crested, erect-crested and rockhopper penguins – breed in the islands, and another seven species are occasional visitors.

The extraordinary density of seabirds on the small Snares Islands group is graphic proof of the birds' ability to thrive on the richness of the Southern Ocean's marine environment – provided they have breeding sites free of predatory land mammals. The most populous of the 23 different species of breeding seabirds on the Snares are sooty shearwater/titi: nearly three million pairs of them have honeycombed the peaty soils with their burrows. Along with the endemic Snares crested penguin, they are so numerous that the dwarf forest and tussockland habitats have become a teeming, noisy and rather malodorous 'petropolis', where the colonies undermine or kill whole groves of trees and tussocks before moving on to another choice piece of island real estate, leaving the natural cycle of regeneration, growth and subsequent collapse to start all over again. At dawn the shearwaters take off like a black swarm of giant feathered locusts from any vantage point; the excitement of their mass return at dusk is considered, by those privileged enough to have witnessed it, as one of the most enthralling of all wildlife experiences. The Snares are indeed one of the world's priceless wildlife habitats, to be protected at all costs from invasion by rats and other alien mammals. Their biodiversity significance is often illustrated by a simple (and perhaps over-simplified) comparison: the number of seabirds living on the tiny area of the Snares is roughly equal to the entire seabird population of Great Britain and Ireland.

Some of the other subantarctic islands are also fortunate enough to be free of introduced mammals. Although sealers devastated the seal population of the Bounty Islands

The southern royal albatross (*Diomedea epomophora epomophora*) breeds throughout the New Zealand subantarctic islands, but most – around 14,000 pairs – on Campbell Island. Only half that number breed each year because of their biennial breeding pattern.

RIGHT The northern giant petrel or nelly (*Macronectes halli*) ranges widely throughout the subantarctic region and breeds on the Antipodes, Auckland and Campbell islands. BELOW The Antipodes Island parakeet (*Cyanoramphus unicolor*) is endemic to the Antipodes Islands, where its main habitat is the tall, dense tussocks and sedges which cover much of the main island. It is the largest of New Zealand's three parakeet species and its numbers are around 3000 (ROD MORRIS).

TOP The eastern rockhopper penguin (*Eudyptes chrysocome filholi*) is the most comical-looking of the penguins inhabiting the New Zealand subantarctic islands. They breed in equal numbers at the Antipodes and Campbell islands, with around 50,000 pairs at each. However, their numbers at Campbell Island were as high as around 800,000 pairs in 1942, and the reasons for this sharp decline are still a mystery. LEFT A bull southern elephant seal (*Mirounga leonina*) at North West Bay, Campbell Island – a haven for both sea lions and elephant seals. Mature male southern elephant seals can grow to nearly 6 m in length and are estimated to weigh almost 4 tonnes, making them the largest flippered marine mammal.

A pair of New Zealand black-browed mollymawks (*Diomedea melano-phrys impavida*). They breed on Campbell Island and range widely through the Southern Ocean and Tasman Sea.

during the early 19th century, they fortunately did not introduce any land mammals (or, for that matter, higher plants) into the teeming mass of mollymawks, shags and several million erect-crested penguins that still occupy every rock surface on these very inaccessible islands. Within the large Auckland Islands group, Disappointment Island (566 ha) and the much larger Adams Island (10,119 ha) are outstanding pristine islands; indeed, Adams Island is one of the largest pristine islands in the world. On the other hand, the main Auckland Island (50,990 ha) has pigs, cats and mice but, fortunately, no rats. Despite these mammalian predators, the Auckland Islands group has the most diverse bird fauna of the New Zealand subantarctic islands: 17 different breeding species of albatross and petrel, plus four endemic land birds (a rail, a tomtit, a pipit and a snipe) and the endemic Auckland Island teal. The Campbell Island group, too, has an endemic teal (the Campbell Island teal) which had been eliminated from the main island and survived locally only on tiny Dent Island offshore. It is probably the rarest teal in the world, but a small population has been saved through successful captive breeding on the New Zealand mainland and was reintroduced to Campbell Island during 2004–05. The Antipodes group has one mammalian invader, the house mouse, which has little effect on the islands' extremely large seabird populations (although undoubtedly a serious impact on their invertebrates).

The marine environments of the islands differ in their range of seaweeds and fish but have not yet been well studied. What does stand out, however, is the very low diversity of marine plants and fish compared with coastal Otago, Southland and Stewart Island/Rakiura. On the other hand, while marine species may be limited in variety, those found are present in great abundance. This is an enigma which scientists find intriguing but difficult to explain. Most of the common red, brown and green seaweeds are missing, but the islands share fields of the massive bull kelp (*Durvillaea antarctica*) with all the other coasts of southern New Zealand.

Common shellfoods like paua, crayfish and scallops, and edible fish like tarakihi and blue cod, are also absent.

No account of New Zealand's subantarctic islands would be complete without acknowledging their importance for the conservation of marine mammals. Four species of seal breed on, or regularly visit the islands: the New Zealand fur seal, the New Zealand sea lion, leopard seal and southern elephant seal. The New Zealand sea lion is the rarest of the world's five sea lion species. The islands also lie on the north–south migratory routes of many South Pacific Ocean whales. The sheltered inlets and harbours of the Auckland Islands and Campbell Island are very important for the survival of one of the baleen whales, the southern right whale. The whales bear their calves and suckle them in these locations – restoring, painfully slowly, the population of a species that was all but exterminated by whalers in the mid-19th century. Two centuries ago there were some 60,000 of them in the Southern Ocean; today there are probably fewer than 1000. Other baleen whales (humpback, blue, fin and sei) are sometimes seen in the waters around the subantarctic islands, as well as toothed whales (sperm and orca) and dolphins (southern bottlenose and dusky).

THREATS AND CONSERVATION PRIORITIES

Chatham Islands: Conserving with the Community

The Chathams' environmental canvas is a mixed one: some outstanding conservation triumphs brightening an otherwise dark historical picture of appalling loss of habitat and biota. Sadly, the Chathams represent probably the worst example of human impact causing loss of indigenous biota on New Zealand's outlying islands. A total of 26 native birds have become extinct on the islands in around 500 years of human settlement. Today, the Chathams contain around 14 per cent of New Zealand's threatened indigenous plants, 9 per cent of our threatened freshwater fish, and 20 per cent of our threatened forest and seabirds. The major continuing threats to the islands' flora are feral pigs, wandering stock (many of the forest pockets and wetlands are unfenced), possums and the ever-present wind which carries salt that can, once the protecting shrub layer is broken, desiccate a forest.

Only 7 per cent – a little over 7000 ha – of the area of the islands is protected as conservation land. The most important of these protected areas are:
- the 1238 ha Tuku Nature Reserve on the southern table-lands of Chatham Island/Rekohu;
- the 1348 ha Pitt Island Scenic Reserve and the adjacent Waipaua Conservation Area;
- the two small island nature reserves of Southeast Island/Rangatira and Mangere.

The key to future conservation of the islands' outstanding remaining biodiversity lies, therefore, in the attitudes and actions of the Chatham islanders themselves, especially landowners and land managers. The large number of pockets of private land gifted as reserve areas, or protected by covenants or kawenata, is evidence of the islanders' desire to conserve their natural and cultural heritage. To support this, DOC has worked hard to develop partnerships and productive working relationships with the community on both Chatham and Pitt islands. The fact that the Chatham Islands have their own conservation board indicates the importance DOC places on achieving a high degree of involvement of this small community of only 760 permanent residents in the conservation and sustainable management of their natural resources. The Pitt Island Reserves Committee, too, has been established to involve the 50 Pitt Islanders in the island's conservation management, including the drive to remove cats and relocate feral sheep. Indeed, the vision of a Pitt Island Sanctuary involving this most isolated of New Zealand's human communities is one of the most exciting conservation possibilities for the entire island group.

Restoration of the Subantarctic Islands following Elimination of Animal Pests

In recognition of their outstanding landforms and biota, and the vulnerability of their ecosystems, the five New Zealand subantarctic island groups have been given the highest level of protection possible in New Zealand law – both nature reserve and national reserve status under the Reserves Act 1977. Furthermore, in 1998, UNESCO recognised their international biodiversity significance by listing them as the New Zealand Subantarctic Islands World Heritage site.

However, the historical presence of a number of animals, both stock and pests which can prey on indigenous wildlife, has always threatened the biological integrity of the islands. Fortunately the islands are free of three of the main pests decimating mainland New Zealand's biodiversity: possums, stoats and deer. Cattle were eliminated from Campbell Island by 1984, and the pace of alien animal destruction (or removal) on the islands quickened after the advent of the Department of Conservation in 1987. Many

the rugged 11,268 ha Campbell Island. This remarkable achievement gained wide praise in international conservation circles, and has already allowed the re-introduction of the Campbell Island teal (see above) and natural re-colonisation by the Campbell Island snipe, which had survived in very small numbers on nearby Jaquemart Island (only 19 ha in area). The Campbell Island snipe story is a good example of how our indigenous fauna can naturally re-establish themselves once the pressure of predation by pests is removed. Interestingly, it also seems that cats have died out naturally on Campbell Island, either through the marked increase in vegetation density with the removal of grazing animals, or through disease or loss of easy prey.

The pigs and cats of Auckland Island remain the greatest pest challenge; both have had a serious impact on burrowing petrel populations. Their eradication (as well as the eradication of mice in the long term) will not be easy because of the large size of the island (almost 60,000 ha, nearly twice the size of Egmont National Park), its rugged terrain, the difficult weather, and the sheer inaccessibility of many parts. When it is achieved it will eclipse the many other outstanding island animal pest-eradication campaigns throughout New Zealand, from the Kermadec Islands to Kapiti Island.

Protecting the Marine Biodiversity of the Subantarctic Islands

The seas around the Auckland Islands became a major trawl fishery for squid in 1979–80, and this led to the annual loss (euphemistically termed 'bycatch' in fishing jargon) of around 100 sea lions, as well as significant numbers of fur seals, through drowning in the fishing nets. The international outcry pressured the New Zealand government to designate in 1993 a marine mammal sanctuary over and around the Auckland Islands (including the surrounding seas out to 12 nautical miles from shore) in order to protect these endangered animals. Then, the following year, the International Whaling Commission declared the Southern Ocean Whale Sanctuary (covering the waters south of latitude 40˚S) – a fine concept which was impossible to police, added little protection within New Zealand's territorial waters in addition to the Marine Mammals Protection Act, and was ignored by the Japanese whaling industry. In 2003, the marine mammal sanctuary became the Auckland Islands Marine Reserve. At 484,000 ha, the marine reserve is New Zealand's second largest (after the Kermadecs), protecting deep-sea ecosystems at up to 3000 m depth, as well as the main breeding habitats of the New Zealand sea lion and southern right whale.

Turbulent seas sweep through Victoria Passage, the narrow western entrance to Carnley Harbour in the Auckland Islands.

of the animals, like goats and rabbits, which had been introduced as a food supply for shipwrecked sailors had become genetically isolated and were consequently of considerable scientific and animal-breeding interest – hence opposition to their eradication without first removing some animals for breeding purposes. Progressively, however, goats were eliminated from Auckland Island by 1990, sheep from Campbell Island by 1991, and rabbits from Enderby and Rose islands by 1993, as well as cattle from Enderby the same year. This then left only three of the largest islands with any significant pest animal populations: pigs, cats and mice on Auckland Island; Norway rats and cats on Campbell Island; and mice on Antipodes Island.

During 2001, DOC began the most ambitious rodent eradication attempt on a large oceanic island anywhere in the world – and successfully removed Norway rats from

A group of female Hooker's sea lions resting on Enderby Island. The large Auckland Islands Marine Reserve is meant to protect these marine mammals, as well as albatrosses, mollymawks and petrels, from death through longline fishing bycatch.

Despite the marine protected areas, the problem of fishing bycatch remains – not only of marine mammals but also a variety of seabirds, such as albatrosses, mollymawks and petrels. The need for an effective code of practice to minimise bycatch, particularly for longline fishing, has become an urgent and politically charged management issue. During 2003–04, a code of practice was introduced jointly by the Ministers of Fisheries and Conservation, but it was only voluntary because the industry claimed that it would co-operate in reducing the needless death of seabirds. However, in an unprecedented statement of conservation concern, the Minister of Fisheries ordered most of the squid fishing fleet back to port in May 2005 because of the failure of most operators to implement the voluntary seabird protection code. Forest & Bird are campaigning to have the marine mammal sanctuary extended beyond the 12 mile boundary but allowing squid fishing within the extension by methods (such as jigging, rather than trawling) which result in a much lower bycatch of seabirds and sea lions. A compulsory code for all fishing vessels over 28 m length working around the Chatham Islands and subantarctic islands now requires a variety of bird-scaring devices and the prevention of offal discharge while fishing. Additional measures, such as government observers on boats with a poor record of compliance and increased fines for offenders, will be tried. Whether these measures will have any significant effect is a major conservation question, challenging the government and the good will and commitment of all other stakeholders in sustaining the biodiversity of the Southern Ocean.

The likely geological exploration for oil reserves in the Great South Basin is another major potential threat to the health of the Southern Ocean. Oil or gas rigs, and their service vessels, pose a serious potential for pollution (especially from oil spills), as well as increased pressure for access to the subantarctic islands themselves for the building of shore-based infrastructure.

CHAPTER FIFTEEN

ANTARCTICA BY DEBS MARTIN

Antarctica, the fifth largest continent, is the planet's focal point of climatic extremism. Encircled by the world's most expansive ocean current moving 120 million cubic metres of water per second, the Antarctic is the driest, windiest and coldest place on Earth. With the lowest recorded temperature of -89.6° C, regular winter katabatic winds of over 28 metres per second (51 knots), and annual precipitation as little as 50 mm in the vast hinterlands, the thick ice sheets of the Antarctic have always aroused a sense of elemental wonder. In 1909, British explorer Ernest Shackleton wrote: 'It was as though we were truly at the world's end, and were bursting in on the birthplace of the clouds and the nesting home of the four winds, and one has a feeling that we mortals are being watched with a jealous eye by the forces of nature.'[1]

Both New Zealand and Antarctica were part of East Gondwana until their separation 82 million years ago. Extensive rifting over the next 40 million years carried the expansive Antarctic plate southwards until it blanketed the South Pole. Now covered in ice up to 4 km thick, the presence of *Nothofagus* sp. fragments in the Transantarctic Mountains has caused ongoing debate about the possibility that Antarctica may have been covered in extensive forests as recently as three million years ago.

Although the great white shroud of ice cloaks a single landmass, the politics of territorial claims in the 20th century sliced Antarctica into wedges of varying sizes, with a number of hotly disputed – and overlapping – borders. New Zealand's territorial interests are restricted to the

Ross Dependency. This pie-shaped slice of Antarctica was annexed in 1923 during intense geographical exploration to embed British interests across a growing Empire. Sovereignty issues proved fraught amidst the tense geopolitical manoeuvring of World War Two and the Cold War, including a drop of 4700 US troops on to the continent for ice training. Following international scientific collaboration during International Geophysical Year (1957–58), seven nations, including New Zealand, decided to set aside sovereignty interests and agree to the joint management of the Antarctic under an international regime known as the Antarctic Treaty (1959). Yet New Zealand's interests in the Antarctic remain enshrined in statute and although sovereignty claims are neither denied nor recognised, New Zealand reserves the right to assert sovereignty should the political situation alter.

Now more commonly known as the Ross Sea Region, it is arguably one of the most diverse regions in the Antarctic, with a complex tapestry of volcanism, ice formations, extensive mountain-building, and the southernmost ocean, all of which contribute to its varied and remarkable marine and terrestrial life.

ROSS SEA, THE BALLENY ISLANDS AND MARINE LIFE

Formed around 45 million years ago due to downfaulting in Eastern Antarctica, the Ross Sea is nearly 1000 km wide and is the most southerly oceanic water body in the world – reaching to within 500 km of the South Pole. Extending out to 60°S latitude, it covers an area of 960,000 km². In 2004, the International Union for the Conservation of Nature (IUCN) noted it as the 'largest largely intact marine

[1] Shackleton (1909) cited in Simpson-Housley, P. (1992). *Antarctica: Exploration, Perception and Metaphor*. Routledge: London & New York. pp. 119–120.

Pack ice at the edge of the Ross Sea.

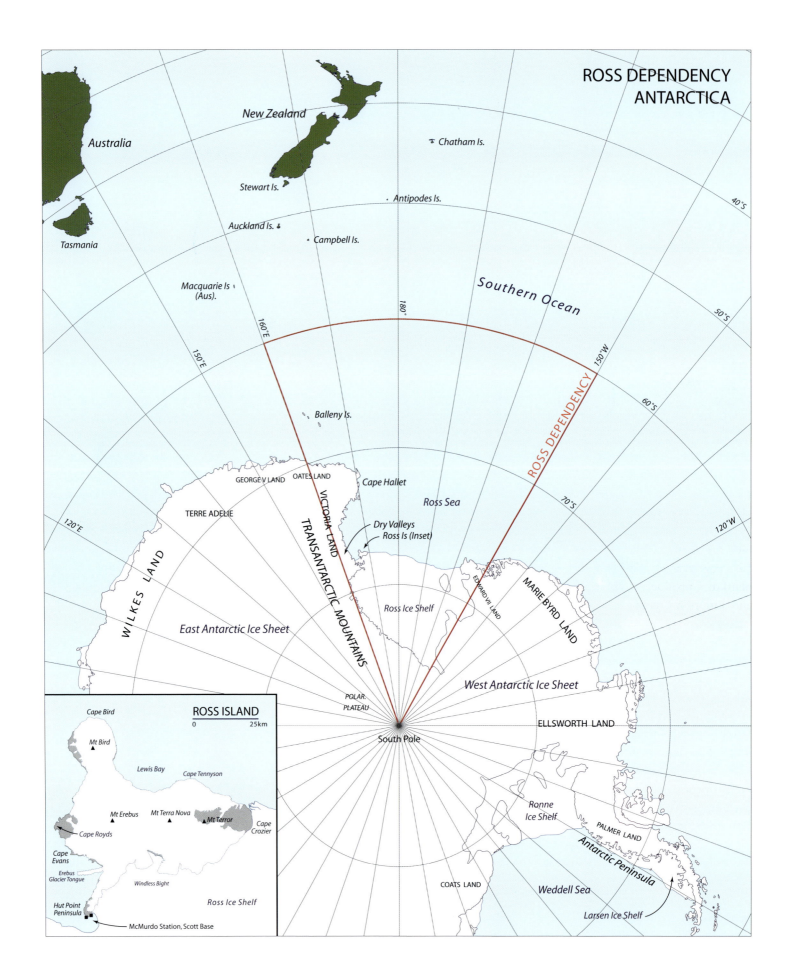

ROSS DEPENDENCY
ANTARCTICA

Australia

New Zealand

Chatham Is.

Stewart Is.

Antipodes Is.

Tasmania

Auckland Is.

Campbell Is.

Macquarie Is
(Aus).

Southern Ocean

40°S

50°S

180°

160°E

150°W

ROSS DEPENDENCY

60°S

150°E

Balleny Is.

70°S

120°E

GEORGE V LAND   OATES LAND   Cape Hallet

Ross Sea

TERRE ADELIE

VICTORIA LAND

Dry Valleys
Ross Is (Inset)

120°W

WILKES LAND

TRANSANTARCTIC MOUNTAINS

MARIE BYRD LAND

EDWARD VII LAND

East Antarctic Ice Sheet

Ross Ice Shelf

West Antarctic Ice Sheet

POLAR
PLATEAU

ELLSWORTH LAND

South Pole

Ronne
Ice Shelf

PALMER LAND

Antarctic Peninsula

COATS LAND

Weddell Sea

Larsen Ice Shelf

ROSS ISLAND

0   25km

Cape Bird

Mt Bird

Lewis Bay   Cape Tennyson

Mt Erebus   Mt Terra Nova   Mt Terror

Cape Royds

Cape
Evans   Cape
Crozier

Erebus
Glacier Tongue   Windless Bight

Hut Point
Peninsula   Ross Ice Shelf

McMurdo Station, Scott Base

Smaller than other baleen whales, minke whales (*Balaenoptera acutorostrata*) are also the most common. After avoiding the plunder of the early 1900s, they are now the target of Japanese whaling (KIM WESTERSKOV/NATURAL IMAGES).

ecosystem remaining on earth'. The huge upwelling of nutrients associated with the cycling of colder deep water meeting rapidly warming water from the temperate zones, has created a sumptuous marine feeding ground. Phytoplankton, produced in massive algal blooms during spring and summer, provide the main source of primary production for an intricate food web that ultimately sustains the largest of our top-end mammalian feeders, the whales of the Southern Ocean.

Both toothed and baleen whales visit the Ross Sea. Killer whales, or orca, and sperm whales are the most common toothed whales found south of the Antarctic Convergence. However, it is only the adult male sperm whales that venture into Antarctic waters to hunt squid. In contrast, orca travel in family units and are high-order co-operative predators, taking seals, penguins and other cetaceans, including large blue whales, in feats of agility that belie their size. Generally larger, the baleen group comprises blue, fin, sei, humpback, minke and southern right whales, that feed on the dense numbers of zooplankton (mainly krill) at the base of the food chain.

Baleen whales were the target for early whaling expeditions from the 1920s. Humpbacks now number

around only 5 per cent of their early 1900 populations, and overall whale numbers have declined by 80 per cent. Except for the smaller minke whales, the decimation wrought by whaling means these mammals are rarely seen in the Ross Sea. Commercial whaling is now regarded as abhorrent by most New Zealanders, and successive governments have maintained a strong stance against it. However efforts initiated by environmental NGOs to establish a Southern Whale Sanctuary in the Ross Sea and Southern Ocean have met with stubborn resistance from whaling nations like Japan and Norway. An initial ban on whaling through the International Whaling Commission stopped commercial activity, but whales continue to be slaughtered every year under the guise of science. Attempts to curb the loophole of 'scientific' whaling have proved fruitless over the years, despite growing international aversion. Environmental NGOs continue to mount pressure on the countries involved in whaling, and Greenpeace, and more recently,

A slivered crack in the disintegrating sea ice is wide enough for Adélie penguins (*Pygoscelis adeliae*) to launch out of the sea and start their onshore pilgrimage. With their characteristic outstretched flippers and determined waddle, Adélie penguins will travel up to 100 km over ice seeking out their inshore breeding sites. Hundreds of thousands of breeding pairs congregate at Cape Adare on the northern tip of Victoria Land. Shrieks, squawks and other chatter from a high-spirited colony can be heard up to 50 km away.

Sea Shepherd, have pursued the whaling boats in the Ross Sea and throughout the Southern Ocean, to blockade and disrupt any whaling.

Amidst the veritable marine jungle of the Ross Sea are the southernmost colonies of emperor (*Aptenodytes forsteri*) and Adélie (*Pygoscelis adeliae*) penguins. Emperor penguins are the lords – and ladies – of the Antarctic penguin manor. Standing at one metre tall, and with burnished orange adorning sleek black and white heads, emperor penguins are endemic to the Antarctic. Powerful divers, they feed on squid, krill and other small fish. Incubating their chicks through the long Antarctic winter, colonies of penguins range high into the Antarctic latitudes, including on pack ice at the base of the Ross Sea. With less than 200,000 breeding pairs, their evolution into true Antarctic birds means they, like most niche species, are highly susceptible to any differences in the voluminous ice mass. In contrast, Adélie penguins, dubbed the 'dinner suit' birds for their jet black and white plumage, are the most abundant and widely distributed penguin population throughout the Antarctic, with around 2.5 million breeding pairs. The 'Bluebird chip' penguin of the Antarctic, Adélies frequently come into contact with humans, making them one of the most studied species in the Ross Sea region.

Hidden deep in the waters throughout the Ross Sea is a fish pushed to the highest latitudes by intense fishing practices. The toothfish, also known as Chilean sea bass (or 'white gold' by the fishing industry), comprises two distinct but very similar species. Patagonian toothfish (*Dissostichus eleginoides*) is the better known of the two, but its relative, the Antarctic toothfish (*Dissostichus mawsoni)* lives closer to the South Pole and dominates toothfish populations in the Ross Sea. Toothfish can live for up to 50 years and grow up to 2.2 m, although the Antarctic toothfish is slightly smaller and shorter-lived than its more temperate-dwelling cousin. Fishing in the Ross Sea is controlled by the Convention for the Conservation of Antarctic Marine Living Resources (CCAMLR), a 'wise-use' approach to fishing management adopted in 1980 by the Antarctic Treaty parties as a means to control a possible boom in krill fishing. Although the boom didn't eventuate, a number of nations, including New Zealand, are now heavily involved in toothfish fishing. Interest in krill fishing has since resurfaced as an option for feeding a burgeoning fish-farming industry. Fishing remains one of the most contentious conservation issues in the Ross Sea.

But the nutrient-rich feeding grounds of the Antarctic are not restricted to animals at home in the water. Swooping with wingspans of between 2 m and 3.6 m, seven species of albatrosses, including mollymawks, are well adapted to life above the southerly ocean swells. The blustery winds gracing these seas supply the birds with the wind speeds needed for them to stay comfortably airborne for long

periods at sea. As they do around the subantarctic and Kermadec islands, albatrosses surround the fishing fleets and can become hooked on the long-lines used to catch toothfish. Although CCAMLR has adopted measures to control fishing practices, not all vessels adhere to the strict conditions and any illegal fishing, of course, flagrantly disregards rules and best practice.

Nineteen hundred kilometres south of New Zealand towards the Antarctic continent, a chain of volcanic mountains rises 3 km from the ocean floor of the Ross Sea. Five mountain tips break the surface and comprise the Balleny Islands, an exposed and harsh haven for a multitude of wildlife, including chinstrap and Adélie

Stretching like a white desert, the Ross Ice Shelf is the largest in the world, equivalent in size to France. Fed by ice streams and glaciers flowing off the Antarctic continent, it is a floating mass of frozen fresh-water.

penguins, Weddell seals (the most southerly living seal) and many of the southern albatrosses. The abundant marine life around these far-flung extinct volcanoes is due to an unparalleled diversity of marine algae, possibly greater than the entire Ross Sea. Surrounded by pack ice for 11 months of the year, research on these white-capped islands has been limited, but a 2006 expedition found a thriving population of over 300 chinstrap penguins, previously

ABOVE Seals and penguins come ashore on sea ice and coastal shorelines to rest and breed. Slow and reluctant movers on ice, with endearing whiskery faces, Weddell seals (*Leptonychotes weddelli*) are the southernmost naturally occurring mammals on Earth. Using their canine and incisor teeth, Weddell seals maintain their breathing holes in the sea ice throughout the winter. RIGHT A chinstrap penguin (*Pygoscelis antarctica*) with a pair of chicks. Females lay two eggs in pebble nests, frequently alongside colonies of Adélie and gentoo penguins. They nest around the Antarctic Peninsula and the subantarctic islands. An outlier population thrives on Sabrina Island in the Balleny archipelago. They are aptly named for the thin black line under their throat, reaching to their black-capped head (ROD MORRIS).

LEFT As white as the surrounding snow, a greater snow petrel (*Pagodroma nivea nivea*) shows its tenacity by nesting in snow at Commonwealth Bay, East Antarctica. Snow petrels open their fan-like tails in flight, with swift wing-beats and abrupt zig-zag movements, enabling them to ride low over the Southern Ocean in search of squid, fish and krill (ROD MORRIS). BOTTOM Courtship rituals by emperor penguins (*Aptenodytes forsteri*) display a gentleness and intimacy in contrast to the harsh conditions of their breeding cycle. True Antarctic birds, emperor penguins incubate their eggs throughout the winter. Colonies of up to 5000 males hold the eggs at 35° C in an abdominal pouch between their feet and belly for an amazing 60–70 days, while the female returns to the ocean to feed. During this time they may lose up to half of their body weight. The females return as the eggs are due to hatch, and in a celebration of shared parenting, the parents take turns to nurse the chicks and seek food. At just under 200,000 breeding pairs, emperor penguins are less common than other smaller, and more widely distributed penguin species.

thought to number only a few dozen birds. The islands' isolated location makes it a potential hotspot of Antarctic marine life, and scientists believe it may be critical to the health of the entire Ross Sea ecosystem. Sabrina Island, one of the Balleny archipelago, is protected under the Antarctic Treaty, but more comprehensive protection for the entire archipelago and surrounding waters is urgently required.

ROSS ISLAND AND THE ICE SHELVES

Sitting astride 80°S latitude, the Ross Ice Shelf covers the southern portion of the Ross Sea. This floating mass of freshwater ice, the size of France, is around 200 m thick and formed by ice streams flowing off both the East and

Mt Erebus from Cape Royds. Dominating Ross Island, Mt Erebus is the thermo-centre of the 'young' volcanic island. Blocks of icebergs, calved from the ice shelves, become trapped in the surrounding sea ice until freed by the brief summer thaw in December.

West Antarctic Ice Sheets. The East Antarctic Ice Sheet sits high on the polar plateau and is partly constrained by the Transantarctic Mountains. At around 750,000 years old it is regarded as the more stable of the two, with the West Antarctic Ice Sheet being younger (about 90,000 years old) and more susceptible to the vagaries of changing temperatures.

Ross Island is located at the north-west corner of the Ross Ice Shelf and is the southernmost land accessible by ship. Ice is the essential ingredient to the plethora of natural features of the island. The strident Erebus Glacier rolls off the volcano and stretches out across the winter sea ice. Barne Glacier is a monolithic fortress of deeply crevassed ice, its snout terminating in a formidable symmetrical wall where land meets sea. Ice sculptures shaped by the wind curl round the entrance to caves of silent blue-white cathedrals, with ice stalactites shafting down from the ceilings. Crevasses are cleaved through the ice, the layers defining age like tree rings. Features carved and frozen by the katabatic winds and shifting ice streams give the island an artistic intimacy. But perhaps one of the more interesting formations are the frozen pressure waves, where the giant ice shelf abuts the peninsula, buckling and folding as it ends its journey.

Ross Island was originally formed by volcanism in the Pliocene and early Pleistocene, and a further intense period of activity in the last million years produced Mt Erebus, the island's largest volcano towering at 3795 m. A true hot spot amidst the frozen tundra, Mt Erebus remains active, erupting up to 10 times daily from a permanent lava lake. This giant heater supports the Antarctic's only 'warm', thermophilic algae, thriving at 45° C. The wisps of steam stretching across the top of Mt Erebus mark its presence wherever you are around Ross Island. This towering cone is a reminder of the tragic Air New Zealand flight TE 901, when a DC10 crashed on 28 November 1979 killing 257 people.

New Zealand, the United States and Italy all have bases in the Ross Sea region – the only permanent human footprints. New Zealand's sole base is Scott Base on Hut Point Peninsula at the edge of Ross Island. Built for the Trans-Antarctic Expedition commemorating New Zealand's involvement in the 1957–58 International Geophysical Year, Scott Base was the starting point for Sir Edmund Hillary's trip to the South Pole. Nearby is the US McMurdo Station, the Antarctic's largest base which holds up to 1200 summer personnel (ten times the number of Scott Base) and supplies a smaller US base at the South Pole.

TRANSANTARCTIC MOUNTAINS AND THE DRY VALLEYS

Emerging above the thick ice along the western side of the East Antarctic landmass are the Transantarctic Mountains. The downfaulting and tilting that created the Ross Sea gave rise to this extensive chain of peaks beginning at Northern Victoria Land, the northernmost landmass adjoining the Ross Sea. With limestone rocks of Cambrian age (c. 500 million years), the mountains define the coastal margin

With a distinctive white circle around their eyes, Adélie penguins are adept ice floe riders. Spending the winter at sea, Adélies forage in small groups dining on krill – a huge biomass of open-ocean crustaceans.

before stretching off across the continent towards the South Pole (See map p.290). Sedimentary rocks of Devonian age (c. 370 million years) in Northern Victoria Land display identical features to rocks in the Nelson region of the South Island, confirming the close geological links between New Zealand and Antarctica.

On a continent renowned for its thick blanket of ice sheets, ice-free areas are a surprising feature. Covering only 2 per cent of the landmass, these oases of bare rock are densely packed with biodiversity – at least in Antarctic terms. Nestled at 78°S amongst the Transantarctic Mountains, the Dry Valleys are the largest ice-free area in the Antarctic. Extending around 2500 km² the three valleys of rock, gravel and ice became 'dry' when the glaciers that carved them were unable to keep pace with the rate of uplift. Left isolated, these huge glaciers rolling off the polar plateau have retreated, leaving a lunar landscape that more closely resembles Mars than Earth. The Dry Valleys are blasted by intense katabatic winds that sculpt rocks into monolithic statues (called 'ventifacts') and evaporate any moisture; the precipitation is less than in the Sahara Desert. The presence of a number of frozen saline lakes and Antarctica's longest non-glacial river provide an intricate, interesting and ancient ecosystem. Hidden on and within rocks and the freshwaters in the valleys are some of the oldest life forms on Earth. Lichens provide tenuous shelter for the less hardy mosses – both of which grow extremely slowly. A small nematode survives being freeze-

dried through the harsh winters, and minute organisms live inside rocks for warmth. Bird life is restricted to the ever-opportunistic skua, sometimes finding carcasses of crab-eater seals and penguins that have strayed off their normal migratory routes.

Since the 1950s, the Dry Valleys has become an area of intense scientific interest – and from once being a pristine landscape shaped by extreme environmental events, is showing signs of overcrowding. Near-permanent summer campsites are frequently set up, and in an environment where a footprint can last a lifetime, some scientists and environmentalists are querying if the cumulative impacts may be too great, resulting in permanent damage.

THREATS AND CONSERVATION PRIORITIES

Shielded by the extremes of an inhospitable climate, the Antarctic has escaped the huge changes in landscape and biodiversity, species extinction, and introduction of pests and weeds wrought upon New Zealand. But the life that has evolved in this last frontier of wilderness, sheltered amongst the rocks and ice, and hidden in the depths of a chilling blue ocean, increasingly faces major human-induced threats.

LEFT Upper Wright Valley, Dry Valleys. Blasted by katabatic winds, these glacial valleys were carved from rocks up to two million years old. High in the valley, the icefalls of the Upper Wright Glacier plunge spectacularly from the Polar Plateau. ABOVE The saline Lake Vanda in the Wright Valley has 12 stratified layers, each saltier than the one above.

Commercialising the Antarctic

The Antarctic continent and surrounding seas have become the focus of rapidly increasing commercial attention. The Antarctic has long been a 'must tick' destination for world travellers, with the historic huts in the Ross Sea making the region the second most visited place in the Antarctic.[2] Over 25,000 visitors set foot on the ice in the 2005/06 season, double that of four years earlier. Larger cruise ships are heading south, like the 109,000 tonne *Golden Princess* that visited in January 2007 with a total of 3000 passengers and crew. In the same month, the MS *Nordkapp* ran aground manoeuvring near one of the Antarctic islands. Although there was no environmental damage, the incident highlights the danger of fuel spills. The type of tourism is also changing, with a recent surge in adventure seekers – the Antarctic providing an expansive playground for climbers, kayakers, and even paragliders. Attempts to control tourism by the Antarctic Treaty System have failed to provide consensus on any regulatory measures, although the International Association for Antarctic Tour Operators (IAATO) has voluntary codes of conduct. Land-based hotels have been proposed along the Antarctic Peninsula, and small land-bases throughout the Ross Sea region.

The greatest threat to the environment is mining, with extractive industries also eyeing the Antarctic for profitable ventures. Geologically known to contain large amounts of fossil fuels, the Antarctic came under intense scrutiny in the 1980s for a potential mineral 'grab'. Negotiations were tense as New Zealand officials headed the development of the Convention on the Regulation of Antarctic Mineral Resource Activities (CRAMRA), a regime to control the environmental impact and promote the benefits of sharing mining activity. In a campaign fought in Wellington, Paris, Canberra and throughout the Antarctic Treaty nations, the New Zealand branch of the Antarctic and Southern Ocean Coalition (the official Antarctic environmental NGO) worked with the international community and successfully managed to engineer the abandonment of CRAMRA. Soon afterwards a 50-year ban on any prospecting, exploration or mining below 60°S was imposed. In a major victory for conservation, then Prime Minister Geoffrey Palmer stated, 'risks had to be taken to keep the policy growth up to the speed of world opinion'. Although the negotiated strength

of the 50-year ban should not be underestimated, it does not guarantee mining will never occur. The ban can be overturned by Antarctic Treaty nations – or simply by the actions of other nations who perceive the risks as less than any pecuniary gain. One of the most destabilising aspects of these threats may be a military build-up in the Ross Sea region, undermining the current management regime.

Marine Protection for the Ross Sea

The task of maintaining the pristine state of the vast Ross Sea demands attention. Until 1995, the extreme isolation and dense icepacks kept it off the fishing charts. However, since then fishing activity, both legal and illegal, has risen dramatically, with New Zealand fishing fleets pioneering toothfishing at the highest latitudes – deep into the Ross Sea. Arguably, with stronger protection measures than on vessels in New Zealand Exclusive Economic Zone waters, the fishing industry has fine-tuned its operations to target toothfish, a species that scientists are still seeking to understand.

Early in 2001 Forest & Bird and ECO (Environment and Conservation Organisations of New Zealand) called for a moratorium on New Zealand fishing in the Ross Sea. In a 2002 review of fishing, the Department of Conservation took a similar stance, asking Cabinet to advocate for a global moratorium on trade in toothfish. The department's recommendations were ignored by Cabinet and fishing continued virtually unchallenged while marine protection languished in a back room. In 2005 a revised Ross Sea Strategy saw NGOs calling once again for a moratorium on fishing – supported by a resolution by the IUCN urging all Antarctic Treaty parties to 'provide comprehensive protection of the whole of the Ross Sea'. Cabinet's response was to pronounce the moratorium unworkable. Yet in stepping up their commitment to improving marine protection, they rejected the industry's demands to open up the fishery and moved debate about marine protection in the Ross Sea on to the international agenda.

Some early weak proposals by the New Zealand government to secure marine protection around the Balleny Islands were construed as territorial assertions within the Antarctic Treaty system and given little support. Recent scientific trips by a New Zealand research team on board the yacht *Tiama* have given greater depth to the Balleny Islands proposal, and more subtle political manoeuvring has moved it forward. Broader comprehensive protection for the Ross Sea is now the subject of international discussions within the Treaty system. Yet much of New Zealand's

---

[2] The Ross Sea Region receives about 500 tourist visits a year, many of whom come ashore to see the historic huts of Robert F. Scott and Ernest Shackleton. The most visited place is the Antarctic Peninsula with a growing visitor population of over 10,000 tourists annually. Nearly all tourist visits are by boat.

marine research is funded by the Ministry of Fisheries, and although CCAMLR demands an ecosystem approach, the resistance to no-take marine reserves is readily apparent. The path to comprehensive marine protection will no doubt be a long journey, while fishing continues. The call for a moratorium while marine protection is put in place is imperative if we are to protect the largest largely intact marine ecosystem left on earth.

Scientific Footprint

Bases and associated scientific fieldwork have the greatest localised impact through the construction of roads and airstrips, the disposal of waste, and the concentration of human activity. Dust from roads increases glacial and snow melt in the immediate vicinity of the bases as the dark basaltic rock, exposed by earthworks and dispersed by vehicles, acts as a suntrap rapidly melting the surrounding ice. And in a practice that seems unthinkable today, waste from the bases was unceremoniously dumped in the Ross Sea in a process known as 'ice-staging'. Oil drums, vehicles – even old huts – were towed out onto the winter sea ice to sink when the summer thaw came.

Emperor penguins, Ross Sea. With inquisitive sideways glances, emperor penguins survey their icy surrounds. At one metre tall, they dwarf the smaller Adélie penguin in their midst.

The sites chosen for bases also create problems for any resident life. The Adélies' chosen breeding grounds on ice-free shores frequently coincide with sites favoured for human bases. The now-dismantled New Zealand-United States base at Cape Hallett was built in the middle of a colony, disrupting the breeding site of 6000 birds in the 1950s.

A growing awareness engendered by environmental NGOs in the 1980s resulted in the adoption of environmental protection measures into a protocol within the Antarctic Treaty System. Now any proposals for activity in the Antarctic require an environmental evaluation, which in the case of any new bases, is subject to international scrutiny. Although the political pressure invokes better standards, the lack of a consistent monitoring mechanism means these standards differ according to individual nations' commitment to protecting the Antarctic environment.

Climate Change

Carrying 90 per cent of the world's fresh water, the ice sheets covering the Antarctic are the focus of obvious attention as the world grapples to understand the implications of climate change. With a surface area of 12.1 million km² (over 40 times the size of New Zealand's land mass), and a total ice volume of 29 million km³, the melting of the Antarctic ice sheets would cause sea levels to rise by 60–90 m. Thankfully, the relative stability of the East Antarctic Ice Sheet and current climate change predictions do not anticipate such a dramatic rise – but change is certainly evident.

The impacts of climate change on the ice sheets and shelves of the Antarctic is the focus of concerted research by scientific programmes, including New Zealand's. As ice cores reveal the historical state of the ice, there is a growing understanding of the dynamic interplay between the ice sheets feeding ice shelves, and the eventual breaking off or 'calving' of large chunks of ice. A 25 x 70 km long 'iceberg' calved off the Larsen Ice Shelf in the Weddell Sea in 1995, and the numerous icebergs seen riding an oceanic conveyor belt up the east coast of New Zealand in the 2006/07 summer were the result of the normal activity of ice-calving. But it is the rate and the cumulative size of the resultant calved icebergs that will change with increased temperatures. Recent research reveals that the Ross Ice Sheet has melted at only slightly higher temperatures in the past. This could rapidly increase the drainage of the West Antarctic Ice Sheet, hastening its demise and possibly adding around 6 m to current sea levels.

Calving icebergs not only contribute to climate change, but also cause angst to land-based penguin colonies. Another large iceberg collapsed in 2002, becoming wedged against the Ross Sea in successive summers, stopping the summer break-up of sea ice and landlocking a large penguin colony. The extra ice traversed by the penguins in their feeding forages resulted in high chick mortality and the failure of one colony to fledge.

Climate change throws up other threats to this frozen land, so long without vigorous vegetation growth. Warming temperatures can raise the summer average above freezing level, and coupled with any lax biosecurity, could culminate in an invasion of non-native species to the ice-free areas. Recently the international Antarctic Committee for Environmental Protection recognised non-native species as one of the biggest threats to biodiversity in the region.

World Park Antarctica

In the 1980s, during the later-abandoned minerals regime negotiations, ECO, Greenpeace and Forest & Bird all argued for the establishment of a World Park Antarctica. Greenpeace operated a year-round World Park Base alongside Scott's Terra Nova hut at Cape Evans on Ross Island from 1987 to 1992. The intense scrutiny on bases was instrumental in highlighting the pollution caused by slack management practices across the continent. Their own base was deconstructed leaving no sign of inhabitation, and the legacy has become part of the Environmental Protocol that now regulates scientific and logistic activity throughout Antarctica. Hastily constructed after the collapse of CRAMRA, the Antarctic Environmental Protocol set guidelines for best environmental practice, and established the 50-year ban on mineral prospecting, exploration and mining. At the signing and eventual ratification of the Environmental Protocol in 1991, much of the environmental campaigning in the Antarctic went quiet.

However, the Environmental Protocol may have become a 'green' smokescreen, a compromise deflecting any designation of a World Park for the Antarctic. Scientific activity has continued to increase over the past few decades, and although the impacts are ameliorated through some of the protocols, science still has the biggest localised impact. The construction of a 'road' route (by blasting and infilling crevasses) from the US base at Ross Island through to the South Pole has been widely criticised as an unnecessary destruction of wilderness. But science and its supporting logistics are not the only problem. Tourism continues to grow with increased pressure for land-based adventure tourism, giant cruise ships, and visits to the historic huts in the Ross Sea region. Fishing, absent until just over a decade ago, has grown incrementally, changing the once pristine ecosystem of the Ross Sea. Whaling continues under the guise of science and in a world ever-hungry for minerals, the agreed ban on prospecting, exploration and mining, is already being challenged. Alongside comprehensive marine protection for the Ross Sea, which must include no-take marine reserves, the vision of a World Park Antarctica to protect the wilderness and pristine places of the Ross Sea region – our last frontier – should not be lost.

The peaks of the Transantarctic Mountains emerge from kilometres-thick ice sheets. Funnelling down valleys, glaciers flow out to the Ross Sea.

CHAPTER SIXTEEN

FUTURE PROSPECTS

In contemplating the future of New Zealand's wilderness heritage, there is so much that could be written about how it can best be conserved. It is now 20 years since the Conservation Act was enacted; over this period the Department of Conservation (DOC) has matured into an agency whose wide-ranging activities are no longer considered a cost to our society but rather a crucial investment in our nation's future ecological, economic, social and spiritual well-being. 'Wilderness heritage' and 'biodiversity' may not yet be household terms, but news items about saving kiwi, kakapo, whales or blue duck/whio are a daily occurrence. It is no exaggeration to say that there has been an extraordinary change in community attitudes and awareness of conservation in recent decades. We are probably still too smug about the 'clean, green' and '100 per cent pure' image that our Tourism Board loves to project internationally. Yet the political environment for nurturing our wilderness heritage today is light years ahead of that which confronted those of us who lived through (or were an active part of) the bitter and protracted conservation battles of the 1960s and '70s – protesting against the ill-conceived exploitation of our wilderness, whether through the damming of wild rivers, forest clearance, wetland drainage, mining, tourist roads, foreign ownership of high country and coastlands, or unsustainable commercial fishing.

The leadership of DOC, the persuasive skills of a number of Ministers of Conservation, the resolve of a rejuvenated array of conservation and outdoor recreation NGOs, a more critical investigative media highlighting the environmental plight of the over-developed world, and thousands of volunteers, many of them school children, doing their bit to restore the 'tattered cloak of Tane' – all have contributed to the monumental effort of protecting much of our wilderness heritage and stemming the inexorable loss of our indigenous biodiversity. And appreciation of the importance of our mountain, forest and tussockland wilderness in providing pure water and acting as a sink for carbon dioxide is going to grow rapidly in the coming years.

So what lessons have been learned for the future? Chapter 1 charted the origins of our wilderness, the distinctive character of our indigenous geodiversity and biodiversity, the values of wilderness and our impact on it both individually and collectively. Chapters 2–15 were a journey through the many wild places remaining in our islands and the Ross Dependency of Antarctica, indicating some threats to these special places and a number of conservation priorities for each region. Much of what needs to be done nationally is also stated in these regional chapters.

Five wilderness conservation issues, however, stand out as future priorities for action. They have been singled out because of their widespread nature or the degree of threat which they pose, or because they urgently need political commitment and wisdom for their solution. They are:

- halting the steady decline in New Zealand's indigenous biodiversity by making our system of protected areas more representative of our diverse habitats, and by more effective control of weed and animal pest threats;
- achieving greater protection of our marine ecosystems;
- protecting the wilderness values of the eastern South Island high country;
- ensuring reasonable access to the back country throughout New Zealand;
- regulating the impact of tourism and the increasing numbers of visitors on our wilderness.

The beech forests of the Eglinton Valley in Fiordland National Park are the habitat of the yellowhead or mohua, one of more than 50 endangered plants or animals benefitting from species recovery plans.

TURNING THE TIDE: HALTING THE LOSS OF OUR BIODIVERSITY

To address the inexorable decline in our indigenous biodiversity, DOC has developed a strategic approach to making the best use of money, staff and volunteer skills, technology and new research findings. Particularly impressive efficiency gains have been made through:

- species recovery plans, not only for iconic species like kakapo, kiwi, and tuatara but at least another 50 threatened plants and animals;

- a NZ Threat Classification System, developed to classify around 2400 threatened species according to the level of threat of extinction that they face;

- the progressive elimination of serious animal pests from islands, both offshore and outlying, rendering them safe havens for the conservation (including re-introduction) of threatened biodiversity;

- the combination of GPS technology with helicopters to accurately and rapidly target pest control operations over thousands of hectares of wildlands;

- the launching of the Weedbusters programme, a joint effort between DOC, regional authorities and district councils to fight established weeds, and new ones (from the pool of more than 24,000 introduced higher plant species) which each year invade our native vegetation;

- the development of a Natural Heritage Management System (NHMS), an inventory and monitoring programme which should build up vital trend information on the health of key ecosystems.

A fresh look is being taken at traditional programmes to protect biological diversity. In particular, the relationship between high ecosystem diversity and high landform diversity and/or stability is being considered as a quicker way to identify key biological communities needing conservation. Areas of high landform stability and certain rock types in New Zealand are, in general, much richer in endemic species. Consequently, regions of low tectonic activity, like Northland, and those where a high proportion of landforms escaped the ice-sheets of the Pleistocene glaciations (north-west Nelson, Marlborough, Central Otago) or which contain particular rock types such as limestone or serpentine, are likely to be priority areas for protection.

There are two main approaches in trying to halt the loss of indigenous biodiversity: to increase the area and diversity of land, freshwater and marine ecosystems protected for conservation; or to control more effectively the weed and animal pest threats in areas already under legal protection. With respect to the first approach, both the Queen Eliza-

beth II National Trust (QEII) and the Nga Whenua Rahui Fund have proved effective at protecting key indigenous ecosystems in private and Maori trust ownership. Since its formation in 1977, QEII has achieved over 3000 covenants covering around 100,000 ha of private land – many of these are priceless fragments of endangered ecosystems, especially lowland forest and wetland. The Nature Heritage Fund (NHF), and its independent committee, can be singled out and commended for an unswerving commitment to filling the gaps that the Protected Natural Areas Programme (PNAP) identified in New Zealand's protected area system. Since it was established by government in 1990, the NHF committee has developed a sophisticated strategic approach to ranking the importance of potential acquisitions by emphasising concepts like ecosystem representativeness, size, shape, buffering from surrounding land uses, linkages to other protected areas, and landscape integrity. This has allowed the NHF to rank ecosystems currently poorly represented in our protected area system – lowland podocarp forests, coastal forest, estuarine wetlands and dunelands, freshwater wetlands and riparian forests, braided rivers, and tussock grasslands. The NHF has proved a highly successful mechanism for achieving the protection of nature on private land, either through direct purchase or through protective covenants. To date, around 718 approved projects have protected more than 256,000 ha of indigenous ecosystems, at an average cost to the taxpayer of around only $388 per hectare. Many of these are wild areas highlighted in the preceding regional chapters – ranging from magnificent Waikawau Bay on the Coromandel Peninsula to isolated Greville Harbour on D'Urville Island; and from entire large pastoral runs like Birchwood Station in the Ahuriri valley and Mount Michael around the St Bathans Range, to the small, spectacular and strategically-important Stonewall block linking Cape Palliser with Aorangi Forest Park.

The second approach is probably the biggest biodiversity challenge facing DOC (and indeed the New Zealand government and people), for the gravity of the pest problem is graphically outlined in the NZ Biodiversity Strategy. Most of these alien plants and animals are well established, having been here for a century or more (see Ch.1, p.21); others like wasps, sea squirt and didymo are more recent; and the biosecurity threat of the potential entry of myriads of alien organisms (such as fire ants or avian diseases) is the inevitable and unfortunate consequence of globalisation in trade, tourism and immigration. New Zealand is no longer an isolated island wilderness. However, DOC has largely

won the battle to secure biodiversity havens on more than 80 offshore and outlying islands – though at enormous cost. Nevertheless, although priceless, these islands (and the six mainland islands) are less than 3 per cent of New Zealand's total area of conservation land. Another 32 per cent of conservation land benefits from less intensive pest management, but that leaves around 65 per cent with little or none. The review of the first five years of the NZ Biodiversity Strategy lauds the gains (albeit costly) for some iconic bird species like kiwi, kakapo and stitchbird, but laments that: '77 per cent of the acutely or chronically threatened species still lack targeted recovery work and are most likely in decline. The inability to deal with these "priority" species appears to be due to a lack of resources.'[1]

Indeed, the inexorable march towards extinction for many of our plant and animal species is illustrated in DOC's 2007 Threatened Species List, which classifies another 416 taxa as more threatened than when the list was first published in 2002.[2] During this period 40 native birds are considered to have worsened in status, but only four birds are considered to have improved their long-term

A mature male orange-fronted parakeet or kakariki (*Cyanoramphus malherbi*) on mountain beech in Hope Valley, Lake Sumner Forest Park. The bird's conservation status is 'nationally critical', with a high risk of extinction as there are only 100–200 left in the wild (ROD MORRIS).

chances of survival. Almost half of the nearly 6000 native plant and animal species evaluated fall into one of the seven threatened categories; and another 3000 are likely to be threatened but there is not enough information to assign them to a specific category.

So can the war on pests be won? The problem is that DOC has to wield a sword at the existing pests with one hand while, with the other, it has to beg for increased resources to try and develop more effective and efficient control techniques. So the question becomes whether DOC should commission more pest research at the expense of maintaining the current level of pest control operations. Clearly this is a situation fraught with 'opportunity costs', and the dilemma facing DOC is well summed up by the Director-General of Conservation in his 2006 Annual Report to Parliament:

The more we learn, the more we understand the size of the challenge and the limits we face – the job of conservation is complex and huge. Our knowledge of New Zealand's extraordinary natural heritage, while ever growing, is still limited, and the resources to manage it are finite. This means setting priorities is vital and we will always have to make choices about what we do to give the best results for the fewest resources. There are, and always will be, areas and species that will receive little or no specific management.[3]

A most encouraging trend is the growing army of volunteers dedicating their leisure time to pest eradication. A notable feature of this huge volunteer effort is that it is in no way confined to DOC-sponsored programmes on conservation lands. Rather, hundreds of projects are complementing DOC's work by targeting pests in natural

Chalky Island/Te Kakahu, at the entrance to Chalky Inlet in Fiordland, is one of around 80 islands which are now havens for threatened biodiversity because predators have been eliminated.

habitats on the urban fringe – through groups as various as Forest & Bird's *Ark in the Park* at Cascade Kauri Park in the Waitakere Ranges, or MIRO (Mainland Island Restoration Organisation) in the Eastbourne hills of East Harbour Regional Park. There is also the hope that efficiency gains will be made with the shift in focus from individual pest species to an integrated site-led approach, where all pests and environmental factors at specific places are first evaluated so that the control measures chosen can deal with them as a whole.

No aspect of pest eradication has been more controversial than the aerial distribution of 1080 (sodium monofluroacetate) poison by DOC and the Animal Health

Board (AHB). After decades of criticism from deer and pig hunters and citizen groups fearful of the possible impact of 1080 on non-target animals, as well as the accidental contamination of human water supply, DOC and the AHB in 2007 submitted 1080 for re-assessment by ERMA (the Environmental Risk Management Authority). Their intent is to use the weight of scientific evidence to force their critics to 'put up or shut up', so confident are they in the safety of 1080 and its unique importance in targeting possums in large tracts of wilderness that cannot be covered economically with hand-laid poison bait stations. The devastating impact of possums in our lifetime has been truly appalling. Blue duck/whio have disappeared from the rivers of most North Island ranges (such as Kaimanawa and Tararua); kaka and kiwi, once widespread, are now confined to isolated pockets of habitat; mistletoe, with its lovely red flowers draped on beech trees in early summer, has gone from most mountain valleys, along with rata, fuchsia and other palatable plants. To stop aerial 1080 operations against possums is not really an option if we want to reverse this loss of wilderness biodiversity. DOC and the AHB claim that there is no practical alternative to 1080 for large-scale aerial poison drops; if ERMA bans aerial use, it would cost the taxpayer an extra $40 million a year by 2025 to control the expected upsurge of TB-infected possums (thereby placing at risk billions of dollars of agricultural exports), as well as placing several native bird species at risk of extinction.

However, public fears must be addressed more effectively, especially concern at poisoning operations in forests on the urban fringe and in water supply catchments.

ACHIEVING MORE MARINE PROTECTED AREAS

New Zealand's marine zone is probably our last great 'commons', inexorably losing its biodiversity through over-fishing and pollution. This is indeed a marine 'Tragedy of the Commons', akin to that postulated by Garrett Hardin for the grazing of a terrestrial commons, where each individual herdsman sought to maximise his gain at the expense of the rest of the herding community – and the pastoral ecosystem itself.[4] There is also a potential tragedy for the 'commons' of New Zealand's lowland rivers, as the threat of water abstraction and pollution from dairying escalates sharply.

To address our unsatisfactory marine environment protection situation (see Ch.1, p.35), the New Zealand government carried out wide consultation with all marine stakeholder groups and, in January 2006, released a policy and implementation plan for developing a network of marine protected areas.[5] Proposed new legislation will place greater emphasis on the role of marine reserves in conserving biodiversity. The policy stresses a science-based approach to marine habitat and ecosystem classification, and the involvement of regional councils, tangata whenua, commercial and recreational fishers, and conservation groups in achieving the Biodiversity Strategy goal of conserving 10 per cent of New Zealand's marine environment in some form of protected area by 2010.

The West Coast coastal and marine environment, which currently has no marine protected areas, has been chosen to trial this radical but sensible approach to determining the practicalities of marine protection. A West Coast Marine Protection Forum, established as a broad-based citizen and sectoral interest group, is working with DOC and the Ministry of Fisheries to see if it can achieve community 'buy-in' from the earliest stage. The Forum has begun by publishing in April 2007 a detailed compilation of existing information on the region's coastal and marine environment, and then seeking additional information and comment from the community.[6] Since then the Ministers of Conservation and Fisheries have jointly released draft papers suggesting a framework to be used for achieving sufficient protection for marine biodiversity that is based around (a) a classification of our marine environments and (b) a protection standard to be used to help decide which marine protection areas and tools (such as marine reserves, mataitai, taiapure, seasonal closures to fishing, or area closures to certain fishing measures) should be used.

There are high hopes that this policy and a more inclusive process will allow significant progress to be made in marine protection, while seeking to minimise impacts on existing recreational, customary and commercial users of the marine environment.

IMPROVING SOUTH ISLAND HIGH COUNTRY LAND TENURE REFORM

How to best conserve the wild high-country tussocklands of Marlborough, Canterbury, Otago and northern Southland is a conundrum that has frustrated generations of Crown administrators, hunters, fishers, trampers and conservationists – as well as the pastoral runholders. Some of the background to this vexatious high-country pastoral lease issue is given in the Canterbury (see p.221) and Otago (see p.242) chapters. The area in question is enormous – 2.2 million hectares, or 8 per cent of New Zealand's land area – and includes the iconic tussock grassland landscapes fringing the glacial lakes of the Mackenzie Basin, Central Otago's flat-topped block mountains, and dozens of mountain ranges extending from the Inland Kaikoura Range in Marlborough to the Garvie Mountains in northern Southland. The first pastoral leases were granted by the Crown in 1856, in the earliest phase of European settlement of the grassland interior of the eastern South Island. But the Crown as landlord had little knowledge at that time of ecological integrity or the need for protected areas to safeguard biodiversity. So this outstanding grassland landscape – our small version of the great steppes of Eurasia, the prairies of North America, and the pampas of Patagonia – was carved up into more than 300 pastoral runs, with scant concern for geography. What did matter was a balance of summer and winter grazing and access to water; consequently, many of the larger runs extended from valley floors with their streams and wetlands to mountain crests. When this historical situation was consolidated under the Land Act 1948 it perpetuated all the anachronisms inherent in the 19th century surveys, such as the inclusion in runs of glaciated peaks like Mt Earnslaw/Pikirakatahi (2830 m) and Mt Sibbald (2804 m), whose upper slopes were of no pastoral use but of high recreational appeal and conservation value. Resumption to full Crown control of pastoral leasehold land, for water and soil conservation or wilderness protection, was hardly ever contemplated; when it rarely occurred (like the 1973 addition to Mount Aspiring National Park of 9250 ha of Earnslaw Station, including the mountain itself and much of the Forbes Range) it provoked a storm of outrage from the influential high-country pastoral community.

Despite the public lands conservation fervour of the 1970s and 1980s, there was initially no widespread questioning of this form of high-country tenure, even though the land was the public's natural heritage (albeit considerably compromised in terms of its perpetually-renewable leases). The most contentious property right which the Crown had conferred on the pastoral lessee was that of trespass. While this was invoked to stop hunters from crossing pastoral runs (even to reach the parks beyond), most trampers, fishers and mountaineers were usually granted access if it was sought, and many also experienced the generous hospitality of the isolated runholders and their families. It was perhaps a time of commercial innocence, of respect for each other's pursuits and livelihoods, and a mutual love of the mountains by both runholder and recreator. But times began to change. Some runholders were frustrated at their in-

ability to freehold the land and carry out more intensified farming or subdivide into lifestyle blocks; others were open about their desire to exclude the public and start up tourist enterprises such as resorts, skifields, and safari parks. Public concern began to grow when leases began to be snapped up by rich foreigners, and was particularly fuelled by the appalling lapse of the Crown in allowing Lilybank Station in the upper Godley (adjacent to Aoraki/Mount Cook National Park) to fall into the hands of the criminal son of a corrupt and disgraced Indonesian dictator.

Government's response, in the Crown Pastoral Land Act 1998, was to allow runholders to voluntarily enter into tenure review, whereby they could gain freehold title to the productive portion of the run while areas of high conservation value would pass to DOC unfettered (usually the high altitude slopes and peaks of no value for grazing but also, more contestably, the wetlands and river margins). At first it seemed a political 'win-win'; deals could be done without compulsion or public scrutiny, allowing each party to retire to its own high-country heaven. In 2003, government agreed on 10 high-country objectives to achieve desirable economic, social and conservation outcomes. They included all the laudable buzz words of 'ecologically sustainable', protecting 'significant inherent values', and observing the 'principles of the Treaty of Waitangi'. But there were three objectives of paramount interest to wilderness advocates:

- to secure public access to and enjoyment of high-country land;
- to ensure the conservation outcomes for the high country were consistent with the NZ Biodiversity Strategy;
- to progressively establish a network of high-country parks and reserves.

In addition, Landcare Research was commissioned to analyse the vegetative cover of the reviewable land to give a first approximation of its biodiversity value. They found that more than one million hectares (or 45 per cent of the total pastoral high country) were snow tussock grassland, snow tussock/herbfield, bare ground, and perennial ice and snow; another 750,000 ha were short tussock grassland, and there were 300,000 ha of indigenous shrubland and forest, mostly the former.[7]

It is very difficult to ascertain the conservation and wilderness recreation value of the reviews completed, or accepted by the lessee, to date (59 out of a total of 304 runs). Between 1992 and 2005, the land allocation split has been estimated at 58 per cent to the farmers (165,000 ha) and 42 per cent to DOC.[8] But this is only the area split and

Looking eastwards across Lake Heron in winter, towards the Mt Somers Range. This iconic Canterbury high-country landscape is a typical scene in Hakatere Conservation Park – one of many tussockland conservation parks proposed for the eastern South Island high country (DON GEDDES).

there is no published summation of the qualitative value of the land – although it is highly likely that the more productive and economically-valuable land has been freeholded.

Two events in 2006 generated enough controversy to finally get the national media to focus on tenure review, and what indeed taxpayers were getting (or giving away) for their money. First, a young American Fulbright political science scholar, Ann Brower, brought an international objectivity to the debate with her highly controversial and damning research conclusions, particularly:

- that there is no effective advocate for the public interest during tenure review;
- that the Crown is failing to advance the wider interests of the New Zealand people and instead taking a neutral stance in the face of powerful special interests;
- that farmers were also being paid handsomely to take possession of what till then was public land.[9]

During the period of her research, farmers were getting on average 3000 ha of freehold land – as well as an average $300,000 in payment from the taxpayer!

The second event was the shock outcome of the review of Richmond Station on the eastern shores of Lake Tekapo in the Mackenzie Country. Incredibly, here the lessee was given the freehold to 60 per cent of the 9567 ha farm, which included 9 km of Lake Tekapo lakefront, as well as $325,000. The Richmond decision places at risk one of New Zealand's best known scenic views, the alpine vista across Lake Tekapo from the Church of the Good Shepherd. It prompted an outcry from a wide cross-section of public opinion – regional government (Environment Canterbury), Forest & Bird, the Canterbury/Aoraki Conservation Board, and others – and demands for a government moratorium on tenure review. Government responded to the growing concern in late June 2007, when the Ministers of Lands and Conservation acknowledged that there was a major problem by jointly announcing the future exclusion of any pastoral lease land with 'highly significant lakeside, landscape, biodiversity or other values that are unlikely to be protected satisfactorily by tenure review'.

There is clear evidence that so many parties have lost faith in the process (if not the principle) that the whole high-country review should itself be reviewed. Even 37 per cent of pastoral lessees (as of April 2007) have already opted to stay out of tenure review. Many of these runholders consider themselves to be passionate conservationists and believe that they can do a better job by getting freehold title to their entire property and then covenanting the parts of conservation value. This way they can remain on site to control weeds, animal pests and fires, or shut out visitors' 4WD vehicles or jetskis from fragile areas – all day-to-day management actions unlikely to be carried out by increasingly desk-bound absentee DOC conservation officers. Furthermore, the scientific community is critical of the outcomes to date; Landcare Research scientists have concluded that too much of the higher biodiversity land (such as valley floors and wetlands) was ending up in the farmers' freehold and that there was clear evidence that these indigenous habitats and species were more likely to disappear once the land was privatised – all in contravention of one of the government's own high-country objectives.[10] Professional landscape architects likewise are critical of the lack of covenants (stemming from a review decision), or district planning scheme provisions, to protect the integrity of iconic high-country landscapes, especially around lake margins.[11]

What is DOC's place in all of this? While DOC has a conservation advocacy role under the Conservation Act 1987, its failure to take an overt advocacy stance during something so important to the future conservation of New Zealand's wilderness heritage as tenure review is inexplicable. To an interested citizen, it is not really clear what DOC's aspirations are for each run being reviewed. Do other government agencies besides DOC make an input to the process; and who indeed conveys the Crown's wider interests in the deliberations? The whole flawed tenure review process requires, instead, an independent expert tribunal making truly balanced review recommendations to the Minister

of Lands – just as the Waitangi Tribunal recommends on Treaty claims. After all, there are inherent similarities in the need to right historical wrongs or inappropriate land uses: on the one hand confiscations or illegal purchases of tribal (or private) lands; on the other, the need to reallocate Crown-held property rights to competing private and public claimants.

PUBLIC ACCESS TO THE BACK COUNTRY

An associated issue, the free and enduring right of public access to the back country in public ownership, has still not been resolved after years of wrangling. The high-country conundrum has indicated the fragility of access across back country where there is no legal right of way and the risk of trespass. After years of procrastination, in early 2005 the government proposed to legislate for 5 m wide public access strips along all significant waterways. Farmer and private property interest groups made it a heated issue for the 2005 election, and the government backed down. A new Walking Access Advisory Panel was set up and asked to look at the issue again (and the 1400 submissions, indicating the level of interest by all parties in the issue). Their February 2007 report goes a long way towards finally unravelling this Gordian knot of access.[12] It clarifies the rights of the public to traverse legal unformed roads through private property; and it recommends the setting up of a NZ Access Commission, which would negotiate public access to the back country, compile a public access map database, create and administer walkways, develop an agreed back-country behaviour code, and refer legal access disputes to 'an appropriate authority' for resolution. Government would be wise to act quickly on the panel's sound recommendations, for access opportunities to wild nature are steadily disappearing, particularly through foreign ownership and/or subdivision of our coastlines.

HOLDING THE TAIL OF THE TOURISM TIGER

The number of international visitors to New Zealand doubled between 1993 and 2006, to reach 2.42 million in 2006. The NZ Tourism Strategy 2015 estimates that this number will grow by around 4 per cent per annum and result in 3.5 million arrivals in 2015.[13] Tourism depending on the attractions of conservation lands can generate substantial economic benefits to local communities, but the strategy hardly recognises that there may be any undesirable on-site environmental consequences to encouraging such burgeoning

Looking south-west from Key Summit towards Mt Ngatimamoe and other peaks of Fiordland National Park. Key Summit is a fragile alpine wetland and herbfield, which DOC has protected with boardwalks to avoid trampling by tourists walking the Routeburn Track.

rates of international visitor growth. For every historic town like Hokitika that has clearly benefited from tourism and retained much of its gold rush character, there are other tourist towns on the edge of the wilderness, like Franz Josef and Queenstown, that have lost their charm through bad planning, degenerating into ugly, over-crowded eyesores, pulsating to the noise of helicopters and night-long revelry. Unfortunately, the worldwide hallmark of commercial tourism is its inability to recognise when too much of a good thing is well on the way to becoming a bad thing. We all want to travel to exotic places; yet we all contribute to the crush of humanity clambering to see the great sights of the world – Yosemite, the moai of Easter Island/Rapanui, the Great Wall of China, the extraordinary wildlife of the Galapagos Islands, Angkor Wat, and so many others. Every one of these globally outstanding sites (and the cultures of their indigenous peoples) has suffered acutely from the im-

pacts of mass tourism. Site management authorities, if they exist at all, are simply overwhelmed, such is the exponential growth of tourism. Is New Zealand really any smarter? Can we really expect that we can somehow tame the tourism tiger and stop it destroying our wilderness heritage?

Those of us who learned how to travel safely through our wilderness in our youth 30–40 years ago rarely encountered visitors from overseas. Now the network of around 1000 huts and 12,000 km of tracks, and the vast backdrop of unspoilt wilderness on our conservation land, is an irresistible magnet for hundreds of thousands of foreign backpackers who appreciate only too well that the world's

wilderness is shrinking everywhere except in New Zealand … at least for now. So today in the huts on DOC's Great Walks, Kiwis are very much a minority. Does this really matter? Perhaps not to DOC or the NZ Tourism Board, but ask most local trampers why they no longer frequent the Tongariro Crossing or the Abel Tasman Coastal Walk and they are likely to say it is because of the loss of solitude and the crowds of overseas visitors who make them feel like strangers in their own country. Ironically, tourism was invoked by the conservation movement as the universal panacea throughout the natural resource conflicts of the 1970s and 1980s; instead of employment from unsustainable timber, mineral, or water exploitation, communities were encouraged to switch to eco-tourism, and young people to re-train for the hospitality industry. But the tourism tiger is no longer content to pace its package tour cage; it is indeed out, stalking the back country.

Nature-based tourism is very dependent on preserving the quality of New Zealand's natural environment and the NZ Tourism Strategy 2015 rightly recognises that 'values important to tourism such as vistas, water quality and coastal access should be identified, and mechanisms established to protect them.' Most of these natural values lie within conservation lands. DOC is required to *foster* recreation on conservation lands (provided that this is not inconsistent with their conservation), but only to *allow* tourism (defined as paying for facilities and services provided by a private sector concessionaire). Any such concessionaire activities must not 'compromise the intrinsic natural … values of areas managed by the department', have to be 'actively managed to avoid compromising the experiences of other visitors', and must safeguard the 'qualities of solitude, peace and natural quiet'.[14] Yet these fine policies are being steadily eroded and compromised by sectors of the tourist industry and DOC's inability (or unwillingness) to stem the pressures – from the over-crowding of Milford Sound and the Milford Road (see p.262) and the foot approaches to the terminal of the Franz Josef Glacier; to unscrupulous tour bus drivers disgorging ill-prepared tourists onto the Tongariro Crossing, or the granting of helicopter landings at Bevan Col adjacent to Mt Aspiring/Tititea or Turner's Bivvy on the slopes of Mt Tutoko (see p.262) – all to make the mountain climb quicker and easier for tourists on tight time schedules.

Untracked lowland rainforest on the Haast coastal plain, South Westland. The nearby Ship Creek rainforest walk is a good example of how biodiversity interpretation facilities can be sensitively constructed beside major highways through the wilderness – without tourist infrastructure intruding far into the hinterland.

At the same time, a subtle undermining of the Conservation Act has begun with the erasure of the word 'tourism' from the Conservation General Policy (2005), and attempts by the tourism bureaucracy to imply that indigenous visitors to conservation lands have no more rights than foreign visitors – all are deemed by them to be tourists. The fallacy of this type of thinking has been forcefully pointed out by David Round: 'When we visit our own places we cannot be tourists. Tourists are strangers; we are not.'[15] This position is not one of reactionary xenophobia; rather, it is akin to what tangata whenua feel as 'people of the land'; a special nurturing bond, born of a long association with New Zealand's wilderness places and a deep knowledge of their character. Just as tangata whenua are accorded a privileged position as the first people of Aotearoa, so too should all New Zealand citizens expect that their recreational needs in the back country will take precedence over those of overseas tourists. But there are many claims that DOC's building of front-country facilities and back-country 'comfort seeker' lodges over the past decade is a massive subsidy for tourism from Vote Conservation.

The nature of back-country recreation has also changed. Time is now one of society's most precious commodities and a younger generation with more money and less available time is impacting on the wilderness in very different ways from earlier generations. Helicopters carry rafters and kayakers to the headwaters of the Karamea, Hokitika, Landsborough and a multitude of other wilderness rivers; mountain-bikers to the heart of the Kaimanawa Mountains or Pureora Forest Park; and hunters virtually anywhere. There is probably no mountain wilderness in New Zealand any longer free from the noise of planes and helicopters, and DOC is powerless to control overflights of these aircraft (and their noise), and hard-pressed to even prosecute unauthorised landings or poaching. The offensive noise, and damage to sensitive wildlife, from jetboats and jetskis in our wilderness rivers and lakes is also increasing.

This type of adventure tourism in the back country is heavily marketed as a hallmark of the 'New Zealand Tourist Experience'. But as David Round, again, aptly points out: 'adventure tourism is a contradiction in terms. Adventure involves being unsure what will happen; tourism requires a predictable, saleable experience. Tourism therefore inevitably involves a commercial element, and tourists are consumers of experiences. Their purpose is not so much to re-create and refresh themselves as to collect experience trophies.'[16]

Essentially then, there needs to be much better planning to accommodate both wilderness recreation and adventure tourism, but separated to avoid conflict as much as possible. One way is to channel visitors through well-planned tourist highways through the wilderness. A good example is SH 6 through South Westland and the Otago lake country, part of Te Wahipounamu (South West New Zealand) World Heritage Area. Here DOC has provided short walks and interpretation of natural heritage, both on-site and in visitor centres[17]; and concessionaires have developed quality wilderness lodges and eco-tourism enterprises, as well as DOC-authorised adventure tourism which takes the visitor some way into the back country flanking the highway (by plane, jetboat and helicopter) – but not into the real wilderness beyond.

WHO WILL LOOK AFTER THE WILDERNESS?

Finally, who can best protect our wilderness for future generations to enter and enjoy – on its terms? The best long-term proposition for keeping the number of visitors to the carrying capacity of any wilderness area in New Zealand is still physical difficulty – as advanced by Garrett Hardin, who argues that other management approaches like merit, a ballot, or 'first come, first served' are unacceptable in an egalitarian society.[18] Physical difficulty is the intent of DOC's Wilderness Policy (see p.29); not to deny access in the hope of protecting it, but instead to leave the wilderness open for those with enough physical and mental toughness to travel there, enjoyably, safely, and without the need for 'mountains with handrails'. Nor can DOC, as the New Zealand government's natural heritage kaitiaki, be expected to single-handedly defend our wilderness – especially given the widening gulf in wilderness knowledge and experience between DOC's field staff and a senior management increasingly recruited from a management class who have to operate in a much more politicised public service. Rather, we all have to take responsibility – and part of that involves trying to change our society's dominant paradigm of growth and consumption; learning to restrain our own acquisitiveness and desire to manage everything, and experience every outdoor recreational thrill and every wild place. Only then will we feel the immense satisfaction of leaving some of New Zealand's wilderness for future generations to discover – or even some that no one will ever visit; places that should be left to just exist in their state of wildness. For, ultimately:

Wilderness preservation is a conscious attack upon our idolatrous commitment to material growth, an opting for the type of restraint and moral growth preached by Edmund Burke and latter-day economic prophets like Georgescu-Roegen, Daly, and Schumaker. It is in sympathy with the spirit and wisdom of Te Heu Heu when he gifted the volcanic peaks of Tongariro National Park to the nation to avoid their exploitation. It is the spirit which motivated the Nepalese Government to refuse permission for climbers to set foot on one superb peak, Machapuchare – 'forever virgin, a symbol of the untouchable and the inviolate'.[19]

ENDNOTES

1 Wren Green & Bruce Clarkson, 'Turning the Tide? A Review of the First Five Years of the New Zealand Biodiversity Strategy', Conference paper prepared for the Department of Conservation, 2005.

2 R. Hitchmough, L. Bull & P. Cromarty (Comps.), *New Zealand Threat Classification System Lists 2005*, Department of Conservation, Wellington, 2007.

3 Department of Conservation, *Annual Report for the Year Ended 30 June 2006*, DOC, Wellington, p. 21.

4 Garrett Hardin, 'The Tragedy of the Commons', *Science* 162, 1968, pp. 1243-1248.

5 Department of Conservation and Ministry of Fisheries, *Marine Protected Areas: Policy and Implementation Plan*, Wellington, 2005.

6 D.M. Neale, *The West Coast Marine and Coastal Environment*, (L. F. Molloy Ed), West Coast Marine Protection Forum, Hokitika, 2007.

7 Peter Newsome, Janice Willoughby & Grant Hunter, *South Island Pastoral Lease Tenure Review: an Interim Vegetation Cover Map*, Landcare Research, Palmerston North, 2003.

8 Ann Brower, *Interest Groups, Vested Interests, and the Myth of Apolitical Administration – the Politics of Land Tenure Reform on the South Island of New Zealand*, Fulbright Thesis, University of California, Berkeley and Lincoln University, Canterbury, 2006.

9 Ibid.

10 Susan Walker, Bill Lee, Janice Willoughby & Peter Newsome, *Representativeness of Protected Areas for Biodiversity in the South Island High Country*, Landcare Research, Dunedin, 2004.

11 Mike White, 'High Country Hijack', *North & South*, November 2006, pp. 40–52.

12 Walking Access Consultation Panel, *Outdoor Walking Access: Report to the Minister for Rural Affairs*, Ministry of Agriculture and Forestry, Wellington, 2007.

13 Ministry of Tourism, NZ Tourism Industry Association & Tourism NZ, *Draft New Zealand Tourism Strategy 2015*, Wellington, 2007.

14 Department of Conservation *Visitor Strategy 1996*, DOC, Wellington, 1996.

15 David Round, 'Not Good Enough! Tourism and Recreation', *FMC Bulletin*, November 2006, Federated Mountain Clubs of NZ, Wellington, pp. 14–15.

16 Ibid.

17 Leslie F. Molloy, 'Te Wahipounamu – an Approach to the Interpretation of World Heritage Wilderness', *Proceedings of the Heritage Interpretation International Third Global Congress*, Nov. 1991, Honolulu, Hawaii. University of Hawaii.

18 Garrett Hardin, 'The Economics of Wilderness', *Natural History*, June–July, 1969.

19 Les Molloy, 'Wilderness Recreation – the New Zealand Experience', in *Wilderness Recreation in New Zealand: Proceedings of the FMC 50th Jubilee Conference on Wilderness, August 1981*, Federated Mountain Clubs of NZ, Wellington, 1983, pp. 4–19.

RECOMMENDED READING

Australia's Wilderness Heritage, Vol. 1, 'World Heritage Areas', Leo Meier, Penelope Figgis, Geoff Mosley; Vol. 2, 'Flora & Fauna', Leo Meier, Tim Flannery, Tony Rodd, 1988, Weldon Publishing, Sydney.

Bellamy, David, Brian Springett & Peter Hayden, *Moa's Ark: the Voyage of New Zealand*, 1990, Penguin Books, Auckland.

Brown, Rob, *Rakiura: the Wilderness of Stewart Island*, 2006, Craig Potton Publishing, Nelson.

Cameron, Ewen, Bruce Hayward & Graeme Murdoch, *A Field Guide to Auckland: Exploring the Region's Natural and Historic Heritage*, 1997, Godwit, Auckland.

Coates, Glen, *The Rise and Fall of the Southern Alps*, 2002, Canterbury University Press, Christchurch.

Cox, Geoffrey, *Slumbering Giants: the Volcanoes and Thermal Regions of the Central North Island*, 1989, Collins, Auckland.

Cox, Geoffrey & Bruce Hayward, *The Restless Country: Volcanoes and Earthquakes of New Zealand*, 1999, Harper Collins, Auckland.

Darby, John, R. Ewan Fordyce, Alan Mark, Keith Probert & Colin Townsend (Eds), *The Natural History of Southern New Zealand*, 2003, University of Otago Press, Dunedin.

Dawson, John, *Forest Vines to Snow Tussocks*, 1988, Victoria University Press, Wellington.

Dawson, John & Rob Lucas, *Nature Guide to the New Zealand Forest*, 2000, Godwit, Auckland.

Dennis, Andy, *South West New Zealand World Heritage Highway Guide*, 2007, Poutini Press, Westport.

Dennis, Andy & Craig Potton, *Images from a Limestone Landscape*, 1987, Craig Potton Publishing, Nelson.

Dennis, Andy & Craig Potton, *The Alpine World of Mount Cook National Park*, 1984, Department of Lands & Survey/Cobb Horwood Publications, Auckland.

Enting, Brian & Les Molloy, *The Ancient Islands*, 1982, Port Nicholson Press, Wellington.

Gibbs, George, *Ghosts of Gondwana*, 2006, Craig Potton Publishing, Nelson.

Hayden, Peter & Rod Morris, *Living Treasures of New Zealand*, 1995, Harper Collins, Auckland.

Homer, Lloyd & Les Molloy, *Fold of the Land*, 1988, Allen & Unwin, Wellington.

Leopold, Aldo, *A Sand County Almanac*, 1949, Oxford University Press, London.

Maclean, Chris, *Tararua: the Story of a Mountain Range*, 1994, Whitcombe Press, Wellington.

Mark, Alan, 'Indigenous Grasslands of New Zealand', in R. T. Coupland (Ed.), *Natural Grasslands – Eastern Hemisphere: Ecosystems of the World 8B*, pp. 361–410, 1992, Elsevier, Amsterdam.

Molloy, Les & Gerald Cubitt, *Wild New Zealand*, 1994, New Holland, London.

Molloy, Les & Roger Smith, *Landforms: the Shaping of New Zealand*, 2002, Craig Potton Publishing, Nelson.

Molloy, Les & Jim Wilson, 'Why Preserve Wilderness?', in J. Howell (Ed.), *Environment and Ethics: a New Zealand Contribution*, pp. 7–22, 1986, NZ Environmental Council, Wellington.

Morton, John, John Ogden, Tony Hughes & Ian Macdonald, *To Save a Forest: Whirinaki*, 1984, David Bateman, Auckland.

Nash, Roderick, *Wilderness and the American Mind*, 1982 (3rd edition), Yale University Press, Connecticut.

Peat, Neville & Brian Patrick, *Wild Dunedin*, 1995, Otago University Press, Dunedin.

Peat, Neville & Brian Patrick, *Wild Fiordland*, 1996, Otago University Press, Dunedin.

Peat, Neville, *Land Aspiring: the Story of Mount Aspiring National Park*, 1994, Craig Potton Publishing, Nelson.

Peat, Neville & Brian Patrick, *Wild Central*, 1999, Otago University Press, Dunedin.

Peat, Neville, *Subantarctic New Zealand: a Rare Heritage*, 2003, Department of Conservation, Invercargill.

Potton, Craig, *Moment and Memory – Photography in the New Zealand Landscape*, 1998, Craig Potton Publishing, Nelson.

Potton, Craig, *The Southern Alps*, 2005, Craig Potton Publishing, Nelson.

Potton, Craig, *Tongariro: a Sacred Gift*, 1987, Craig Potton Publishing, Nelson.

Potton, Craig & Bill Green, *Improbable Eden: the Dry Valleys of Antarctica*, 2003, Craig Potton Publishing, Nelson.

Rundle, John, *The Tararua Book*, 1981, Millwood Press, Wellington.

Rundle, John & John Gordon, *Mountains of the South*, 1993, Random House, Auckland.

The Chatham Islands: Heritage and Conservation, (various contributors), 1996, Department of Conservation, Wellington.

Wakelin, Dave & Rob Greenaway, *The Restless Land*, 1998, Department of Conservation & Tongariro Natural History Society, Turangi.

Young, David, *Our Islands, Our Selves: a History of Conservation in New Zealand*, 2004, University of Otago Press, Dunedin.

GLOSSARY OF TECHNICAL TERMS

alluvium—material such as sand, silt or gravel, that has been deposited by rivers, streams and other running waters.

amphibians—animals (such as frogs) that are adapted to live either on land or in water.

andesite—a dark-coloured volcanic rock, intermediate in composition between rhyolite and basalt. Andesitic eruptions usually feature both lava flows and tephra.

axial ranges—a series of mountain ranges forming the axis or 'backbone' of the land—in this context, of the North Island.

basalt—a type of volcanic rock that is rich in iron and magnesium but poor in silica. Molten basalt flows easily and usually gives rise to oozy volcanic eruptions with little ash being formed.

biodiversity—the variety of all biological life, including plants, animals, fungi and micro-organisms.

biogeographical—the geographical distribution of plants and animals over the surface of the land.

biota—plant and animal life.

block mountains—mountains bounded on most sides by faults, so that they have a characteristic rectangular shape.

brachiopod—a bivalve mollusc with, on each side of the mouth, a long spiral arm used for procuring food.

braided river—a river with a network of interconnecting convergent and divergent channels (resembling the strands of a braid of hair).

breccia—a coarse-grained rock composed of angular rock fragments held together by a cement of fine-grained material.

butte—a conspicuous flat-topped hill with steep sides.

caldera—a large, basin-shaped volcanic depression. May be formed by explosive decapitation of, subsidence of, or erosion of the central part of a volcano.

cirque—a deep, steep-walled, amphitheatre-like ending to a valley; commonly caused by glaciation.

coal measures—any strata containing beds of coal.

conglomerate—a coarse sedimentary rock consisting of pebbles and boulders set in sand or silt and commonly cemented by iron oxide or other minerals.

Cretaceous—the period of geological time extending from 135 to 65 million years ago; sometimes termed the 'Age of the Dinosaurs'.

cuesta—a hill or ridge with a steep slope on one side and a gentle slope on the other.

Devonian—the period of geological time extending from 395 to 345 million years ago.

doline—a circular depression or hollow on the surface of a karst landscape, caused initially by dissolution of the limestone.

dolomite—a calcium magnesium carbonate mineral.

down-faulted—that part of the land that has moved downwards with respect to the other side of the fault (which can remain relatively unaffected).

drowned valley—a former river valley that has been inundated through a rise in sea level.

dune lake—a small lake lying within sand-dunes.

dunite—an ultramafic rock containing a very high proportion of the mineral olivine; exposed rocks weather to a dun-coloured outer surface.

ecosystem—a functioning biological, chemical and physical system where organisms interact with their environment.

endemic—organisms unique to a certain region (or country) and not found elsewhere.

escarpment—a long cliff or steep slope separating two more-or-less level surfaces.

estuary—that part of the coastline where saline and fresh water are mixed by the ebb and flow of tides; usually at the broad mouth of a river.

exfoliation—the breaking off of scale-like pieces from a large mass of rock.

fan—a gently sloping, fan-shaped mass of material (detritus) formed at the base of a steep slope, often by the action of a stream.

fault—a fracture in rock strata due to strain, resulting in displacement which is observable. Most faults occur in groups, termed a **fault zone**.

fauna—the animal population of a given area.

fellfield—the upper part of the alpine zone, generally consisting of scattered herbs and cushion plants.

fiord—a long, narrow arm of sea between steep slopes, resulting from the flooding of a former glacial trough.

floodplain—the relatively smooth land adjacent to a river channel and built of alluvium deposited by the river. Valley terraces are abandoned floodplains.

flora—the plant population of a given area.

fluvioglacial—relating to meltwater streams flowing from glaciers.

foraminifera—microscopic planktonic organisms with shells of calcium carbonate.

foredune—the line of sand-dunes closest to the coastline.

fumarole—a small vent in a volcanic area, usually giving rise to steam or gases under pressure.

gabbro—a black, coarse-grained igneous rock.

geodiversity—the variety of geological phenomena, including rock types, landforms and fossils.

geothermal—relating to hot water or steam emitted at the surface, after being heated deep in the Earth's crust.

geyser—a hot spring that at regular or irregular intervals throws a jet of hot water into the air.

glacier—an extensive body of land ice that flows downslope.
    cirque glacier—a small glacier occupying a cirque basin.
    piedmont glacier—a broad glacier at the base of a mountain range, formed through a number of valley glaciers coalescing.
    valley glacier—a glacier that occupies a pre-glacial valley.

gneiss—a hard metamorphic rock often similar in appearance and composition to granite; usually has some banding.

Gondwana—often called 'Gondwanaland', the ancient super-continent that existed in the Southern Hemisphere up to Triassic–Jurassic times.

It contained precursors of modern South America, Africa, Madagascar, India, Australia, Antarctica and New Zealand.

granite—a hard igneous rock that has crystallised deep below the Earth's surface. It is rich in quartz crystals, feldspars and shiny black and white micas.

greywacke—a dark grey sandstone, flecked with dark angular fragments of finer rock and formed by the hardening of deposits in ancient ocean basins. The major rock type of central New Zealand.

habitat—the environment in which a particular plant or animal lives.

hanging valley—a higher, side branch of a mountainous river system usually connected to the main valley by a waterfall or series of rapids. The origin of a hanging valley is generally glacial (a smaller, feeder glacier).

hogback—a ridge with a sharp summit and similar steep slopes on both sides.

igneous rocks—rocks that were once molten. If they crystallise deep below the Earth's surface they are termed 'plutonic' (e.g., granite); if they are erupted they are termed 'volcanic' (e.g., rhyolite).

ignimbrite—thick sheets of rock formed by the welding together of extremely hot particles of rhyolitic ash during volcanic eruptions; the name means 'fire-rock'.

interglacial—the period between two periods of glaciation.

inter-montane basin—a basin situated between, or surrounded by, mountains or mountain ranges.

invertebrates—animals without backbones (e.g., insects, worms, snails).

isthmus—a narrow piece of land separating two bodies of water, and connecting two larger pieces of land.

Kaikoura orogeny—the most recent of New Zealand's three main recognised orogenies, beginning in the Miocene Epoch 10–15 million years ago and extending to the present day. An orogeny is a major period of mountain building, during which sediments are deformed (by folding, faulting and thrusting) and compressed into linear mountain chains, often as a result of plate tectonic forces.

karrenfield—blocks of limestone covered with narrow grooves caused by the dissolving action of water on the rock surface.

karst—a type of landscape characterised by sinkholes, caves and underground drainage; often formed in limestone by the dissolving action of water.

kettlehole lakes—a water-filled hollow in a recently glaciated area, formed through the melting of buried glacial ice underneath.

lahar—a flow of volcanic material, both ash and coarser products, mixed with water; often caused by the spilling over of a crater lake. Also used to describe the mound formed on the ringplain where the lahar stops.

landform—any feature of the Earth's surface having a characteristic shape and produced by natural causes.

Last Glaciation—the last of the Pleistocene glacial advances which began about 80,000 years ago, reached a peak 25–20,000 years ago, and receded 14,000–10,000 years ago. Often termed the 'Otiran Glaciation' after the Otira valley.

lava—the molten rock that exudes from a volcano. Also the solid rock formed from cooling the molten material.

lek display—a courtship behaviour in which male birds try to attract potential female mates to their courtship areas by a combination of calls and displays.

limestone—a rock composed predominantly of calcium carbonate.

loess—a blanket deposit of silt-sized material, usually carried by wind from dry river beds or outwash plains like those in Canterbury.

longshore drift—the movement of sand and gravels along a shoreline through the effect of waves breaking obliquely on the beach.

magma—molten rock from the Earth's mantle (the region beneath the crust); highly gaseous and mobile in nature and capable of escaping to the Earth's surface regions either through volcanism as a flow of lava or by being intruded into crustal rocks.

mantle rocks—dense, ultramafic rocks which lie between the Earth's crust and core.

marble—a hard, metamorphic rock consisting predominantly of the calcium carbonate mineral calcite.

marine terrace—a platform formed by coastal sea waves, that has been exposed by uplift or by lowering of the sea level.

massif—a mountainous mass with fairly uniform rock type and geological structure.

mesa—an isolated flat-topped hill, bounded by cliffs.

Mesozoic Era—the 'middle' era of geological time, about 225 – 65 million years ago.

metamorphic rocks—rocks that have been altered by heat and pressure deep below the Earth's surface.

Miocene—one of the epochs of the Tertiary period of geological time, from 24 to 5 million years ago.

mollusc—a soft-bodied animal that may or may not have an external or internal shell; includes most shellfish (such as oysters, limpets, and snails).

montane—the middle altitudinal belt, lying above the lowlands but below the subalpine zone.

moraine—a mound or ridge of debris (till) carried down and deposited by a glacier.
    lateral moraine—is deposited at the sides of a glacier.
    medial moraine—is deposited between two tongues of ice.
    terminal moraine—is deposited at the front end of a glacier.

mudstone—a soft sedimentary rock formed from material that contains a large proportion of clay.

mustelid—a member of the Carnivora family, Mustelidae. In the New Zealand context, the term usually refers to stoats, weasels, and ferrets.

névé—an area of freshly deposited snow in the accumulation zone (upper part) of a glacier.

Oligocene—one of the epochs in the Tertiary period of geological time, from 37 to 24 million years ago.

olivine—a greenish or brownish rock-forming silicate mineral; a magnesium iron silicate. Common in ultramafic rocks.

ophiolite belt—an assemblage of mantle rocks previously intruded as sea floor, and later scraped off as the 'sea floor' plate descended beneath a 'continental' plate through subduction. Ophiolite rocks are generally ultramafic in their mineral composition and they are often found in mountainous situations close to plate margins.

orogeny—a major period of mountain building, during which sediments are deformed (by folding, faulting and thrusting) and compressed into linear mountain chains, often as a result of plate tectonic forces. In New Zealand, three main orogenies are recognised – Tuhua, Rangitata and Kaikoura – the last beginning in the Miocene period 10–15 million years ago and extending to the present day.

outwash—mainly sand and gravel washed out from a glacier by meltwater streams, and usually deposited near the moraine.

ox-bow lake—an almost cut-off loop of a stream; also termed a 'horseshoe bend'. When the loop is cut off an ox-bow lake is formed.

pakihi—a particular type of wetland found on the West Coast of the South Island. Pakihi land is generally flat or gently sloping, with underlying wet infertile soils, and carries the sedge/fern/restiad/rush/moss (and sometimes manuka) vegetation that occurs with a mean annual rainfall of more than 2200 mm.

parabolic dunes—long scoop-shaped hollows of sand with points tapering to windward.

patterned ground—a general term for the type of geometric forms (such as soil stripes, nets, polygons, circles and stone pavements) found on ground surfaces subject to intensive frost action. The phenomena are best-developed where there is frequent freeze-thaw action, usually in a periglacial environment.

patterned mire—a type of bog formed in a periglacial environment, consisting of levees of peat and cushion plants interspersed with depressions that are often filled with water to form shallow tarns (sometimes called **'string bogs'**).

peneplain—a landform of low relief formed by prolonged erosion.

periglacial—relating to the processes, areas or climate adjacent to glaciers or ice sheets.

piedmont landscape—the landscape containing landforms 'at the foot of the mountain', that were formed by past glaciers extending beyond the present-day margin of the mountains.

pillow lava—the rounded, pillow-like, smooth-skinned masses of lava extruded under water.

plate boundary—the margin of tectonic plates, the large slabs of the Earth's crust (and upper mantle) that move in relation to each other through large-scale thermal convection currents in the Earth's core. Earthquakes and volcanoes are usually located close to plate boundaries.

Pleistocene—the first epoch of the Quaternary period of geological time, extending from around 2 million to 10,000 years ago; marked by the most recent of the Earth's ice ages.

podocarps—a group of conifers, predominantly in the Southern Hemisphere, that includes the genera *Podocarpus*, *Dacrydium* and *Dacrycarpus*. The Latin name means 'seed with a foot', referring to the coloured, fleshy 'fruit-like' stalk on the end of the seed.

precipitation—the deposition of water in a solid or liquid form on the Earth's surface. It includes water from dew, hail, rain and snow.

pumice—a soft, light-coloured, frothy, glassy rock with the appearance of a sponge; usually formed by the trapping of bubbles of volcanic gases in molten rhyolite.

pyroclastic flow—an adjective (literally 'broken by fire') describing the material ejected in various forms during a volcanic eruption. Sometimes referred to as 'tephra', it includes volcanic ash, scoria, pumice, lapilli, lava, ignimbrite, etc.

quartz—crystalline silica, a hard glassy-looking mineral.

rain-shadow environment—an area with a relatively low annual precipitation because it is sheltered by a mountain range from the prevailing rain-bearing winds.

ratites—a group of large, flightless birds with strong legs, reduced wings and flat breastbones; besides kiwi and the extinct moa, the group includes ostrich, emu and cassowary.

resurgence—the reappearance at the ground surface of a stream that disappeared underground (usually on reaching calcareous strata).

rhyolite—a type of volcanic rock that is rich in silica, but poor in iron and magnesium. Molten rhyolite is very still and usually gives rise to explosive volcanic eruptions with the emission of large quantities of ash. Granite is the plutonic equivalent of rhyolite.

rift valley—a linear depression or trough formed by the sinking of the crust between two parallel strike-slip faults.

ringplain—the lower and flatter part of the cone of a typical basaltic or andesitic volcano. The upper limit is usually where the lava flows have stopped.

roche moutonnée—a small protruding knob of erosion-resistant rock that has been sculptured by the moving ice of a glacier. Sometimes called a 'sheepback' or 'whaleback'.

sandspit—a narrow, elongated accumulation of sand projecting into a body of water (usually the sea).

sandstones—sedimentary rock consisting of compressed or cemented sand-sized particles.

scarp—a steep slope terminating in a plateau.

schist—a metamorphic rock that has developed distinct layering; can be split into slabs or flakes. Mica appears as characteristic flecks in the rock.

scoria—a volcanic rock, usually formed by the trapping of bubbles of volcanic gases in andesitic or basaltic lava; denser and darker than pumice.

scree—a steep slope of loose rock fragments; sometimes called a 'talus slope'.

scroll plain—that part of a river floodplain that is characterised by a density of meanders, ox-bow lakes, and low curving bars (scrolls) running parallel with the meander. From the air, the whole riverine pattern can look like a series of rolled-up scrolls.

sedimentary rocks—rock resulting from the consolidation of loose material that has accumulated in layers, usually on the bed of the sea, in lakes, or in rivers.

shield volcano—a broad volcanic cone, with very gentle slopes and a wide circumference (owing to the fluid nature of the lava, generally basalt, that built up the cone).

silica sinter—the deposit of siliceous minerals around the mouth of a geyser or hot spring.

siltstone—a fine-grained rock consolidated from silt.

soil stripe—see **'patterned ground'**.

solifluction terrace—the very slow movement of waterlogged soil down a slope. Often the presence of underlying frozen ground, which acts as a barrier to the drainage of the water, is an important factor.

speleothem—a calcium-containing mineral deposit formed in caves (includes both stalagmites and stalactites).

stack—an isolated rock pillar rising steeply from the sea.

stone net—see **'patterned ground'**.

strata—a number of layers of sedimentary or volcanic (pyroclastic) material (singular, **stratum**).

string bog—a type of bog formed in a periglacial environment, consisting of levees of peat and cushion plants interspersed with depressions filled with water (forming shallow tarns).

stripes—a type of **patterned ground** with parallel lines of stones and intervening strips of soil fines, the latter often covered in cushion vegetation.

subduction zone—a zone where a crustal plate is overridden by another plate, and forced down into the underlying **mantle**.

syncline—a large fold in rocks in which the strata dip downwards from both sides, often giving rise to a large depression in the landscape.

tableland—an undulating area of high relief.

tarn—a small lake, usually in a mountainous area.

taxa—a named group of organisms, including all, regardless of subspecies, species, genus, family or higher order.

tectonic—pertaining to the internal forces that deform the Earth's crust (causing fracturing and warping).

tephra—a general term for all solid (rather than molten) materials ejected from a volcano during an eruption (e.g., boulders and ash).

terminal lake—a lake left impounded behind a **terminal moraine** by the melting of ice at a glacier's terminal end.

terrace—a nearly level, narrow plain bordering a river, lake, or sea. Rivers are often bordered by a number of terraces at different levels.

Tertiary—the period of geological time from 65 to 2 million years ago; marked by the rise of the mammals and flowering plants.

tombolo—a sandy or shingly spit linking an island to the mainland. May be produced by longshore drift of beach materials.

tor—an isolated pinnacle of bedrock exposed on a hilltop (or slope) by the erosion of overlying unconsolidated material.

tuff—a general term for consolidated volcanic tephras.

ultramafic rocks—igneous rocks with very high contents of dark-coloured minerals containing iron and magnesium.

watershed—a divide, usually a ridge, separating one river catchment from another.

wave-cut platform—a smooth platform, generally only exposed at low tide, being cut by ocean waves in a coastline.

LIST OF ACRONYMS AND ABBREVIATIONS

AHB—Animal Health Board

BOP—Bay of Plenty

CMS—Conservation Management Strategy

DOC—New Zealand Department of Conservation/Te Papa Atawhai

EA—Ecological Area

Forest & Bird—Royal Forest and Bird Protection Society of New Zealand Inc.

FMC—Federated Mountain Clubs of New Zealand Inc.

GPS—global positioning system

g—gram

ha—hectare

IUCN—The World Conservation Union (International Union for the Conservation of Nature and Natural Resources)

kg—kilogram

km—kilometer

m—metre

mm—millimeter

NHF—Nature Heritage Fund

NWCO—National Water Conservation Order

PNAP—Protected Natural Areas Programme

RHA—Recreational Hunting Area

UNESCO—United Nations Educational, Scientific and Cultural Organisation

WAG—Wilderness Advisory Group

INDEX

ABOUT THE AUTHORS

Dr Les Molloy is the author of a number of books on New Zealand natural history, notably *The Ancient Islands* (with photographer Brian Enting), *The Fold of the Land* (with photographer Lloyd Homer), *The Living Mantle: Soils in the New Zealand Landscape,* and *Landforms: the Shaping of New Zealand,* with Roger Smith. He has a long-standing involvement in protected areas and the conservation of mountain wilderness, both within New Zealand and internationally. Originally a soil scientist by profession, Les worked for 10 years at the Department of Conservation's head office where he had planning oversight of the department's natural history interpretation. Now a private natural heritage consultant, he is an advisor to the department on potential natural world heritage sites. He also travels widely internationally evaluating natural World Heritage proposals for the World Conservation Union (IUCN) and UNESCO.

Craig Potton is now established as one of New Zealand's leading landscape photographers and is a noted conservationist. Born in Nelson, he gained degrees in Eastern Religion and English, then, after a brief teaching career, began working full-time for the conservation movement. He remains actively involved in conservation work more than thirty years later.

In pursuit of his photography, Craig has tramped and climbed extensively in New Zealand, its subantarctic islands, the Dry Valleys and Ross Sea areas of Antarctica and the Nepal Himalaya. More recently, he has worked as Location/Stills Photographer on *The Lord of the Rings, Peter Pan* and *The Lion, The Witch and The Wardrobe* motion pictures, and has had a major retrospective exhibition at North Carolina's Rowe Gallery in the United States.

Craig is the founder of Craig Potton Publishing, based in Nelson. His photographic publications include *Images of a Limestone Landscape*; *Above New Zealand*; *Offerings from Nepal*; *Wearable Art*; *Classic Walks of New Zealand*; *Wild and Scenic New Zealand*; *Moment and Memory*; *Improbable Eden*; *The Southern Alps*; the bestselling pictorial book, *New Zealand – Aotearoa*.

ACKNOWLEDGEMENTS

It is impossible to write a book with such a wide geographic horizon without calling on many colleagues to provide specialist knowledge of places or issues. We both value our independence as wilderness heritage advocates who have spent our adult lives working for conservation (in Les's case that included 10 years in the Department of Conservation). However, while we both knew what we wanted to say and illustrate, it was clear that we couldn't do it effectively without having access to key people in DOC, and to places that they manage. We are both grateful to Bill Mansfield and Hugh Logan, previous Director-Generals of DOC, and Wren Green, for support from DOC's technical staff for information or comment on the draft text and help in photographing sensitive conservation areas. They advised their staff accordingly and below we gratefully acknowledge several of them who subsequently helped us. But the opinions expressed are always our own, not theirs. In places the book is complimentary of DOC, in other places critical; but overall we believe it is a balanced account of our wilderness heritage and their management of it.

We are grateful to the following who helped with local information for the regional chapters, permission to quote, or commented on a draft text: Dave Towns, Greg Martin, Jason Roxburgh, Ken Catt, Colin Ogle, Keith Broome, Simon Smale, Bruce Hayward, Chris Ward, Jill Hudson, Paul Dale, Bronwyn Hunt, Ken Hunt, Dave Lumley, Ross Jackson, Chris Richmond, Wayne Devine, Allan McKenzie, John Morton, Nigel Parrott, Kevin Hackwell, Nadine Gibbs, Ian Millar, Martin Heine, Neil Clifton, Mike Johnstone, Murray Reedy, David Round, Gerry McSweeney, Jeff Connell, Neville Peat, Alan Mark, Carol West and Kevin O'Connor.

To supplement Craig's photography, Rod Morris has, as ever, come through with extraordinary flora and fauna images.

Once again it was a pleasure to work with Roger Smith of Geographx on his maps and the book has benefitted enormously from his aesthetic judgment and cartographic skills. Thanks also to Stuart Waring and Chris Edkins of the Department of Conservation, who supplied Roger with the spatial boundary information for the public conservation lands administered by DOC.

We are also grateful to Debs Martin for so cheerfully coming to our assistance and writing the Antarctica chapter when Les was reluctant to do so because of his lack of field knowledge of the frozen continent's wilderness.

Finally, we both acknowledge a heartfelt thanks to Robbie Burton, Tina Delceg and Arnott Potter at Craig Potton Publishing for expertly shepherding the book through editing and production.

Les Molloy and Craig Potton

First published in 2007 by Craig Potton Publishing
98 Vickerman Street, PO Box 555, Nelson, New Zealand
www.craigpotton.co.nz

Photography © Craig Potton and individual photographers
Text © Les Molloy and Debs Martin

Maps by Geographx

Design by Robbie Burton

ISBN 978-1-877333-63-7

Printed in China by Midas Printing International Ltd